EC-Council
E-Business Certification Series

®

Knowledge Management (KM)

Student Courseware

Course: Certified E-business Associate - Exam 212-69

Knowledge Management

Developer

Thomas Mathew

Publisher

OSB Publisher

ISBN No

0-9729362-0-3

Trademarks

EC-Council and EC-Council logo is a trademark of International Council of E-Commerce Consultants. All product names and services identified throughout this book are trademarks or registered trademarks of their respective companies. They are used throughout this book in editorial fashion only. No such use or the use of any trade name is, intended to convey endorsement or other affiliation with the book. Copyrights of any screen captures in this book are the property of the software's manufacturer.

Disclaimer

EC-Council makes a genuine attempt to ensure the accuracy and quality of the content described herein: however EC-Council, makes no warranty, express or implied, with respect to the quality, reliability, accuracy, or freedom from error of this document or the products it describes. EC-Council makes no representation or warranty with request to the contents hereof and specifically disclaims any implied warranties of fitness for any particular purpose. EC-Council disclaims all liability for any direct, indirect, incidental or consequential, special or exemplary damages resulting from the use of the information in this document. Mention of any product or organization does not constitute an endorsement by EC-Council of that product or corporation. Data is used in examples and exercises are intended to be financial even if actual data is used or accessed. Any resemblance to, or use of real persons or organization should be treated an entirely coincidental.

Copyright Information

International Council of E-Commerce Consultants
67 Wall Street, 22nd Floor
New York, NY 10005-3198

http://www.eccouncil.org

Phone: 212.709.8253
Fax: 212.943.2300

TABLE OF CONTENTS

Module III: Organizational Learning and Learning Organizations..................104

Module IV: Organizational Culture, Change Management and Communities of Practice 161

Module VIII: Knowledge Management Assessment and Planning 398

Icons Legend

Various icons have been used through out this courseware to draw the reader's attention. The icon legend is as given below:

Icon	Description
	Module objective
	Key Concept
	Exam Tip
	Reference
	Exercises
	Multiple Choice Questions

Knowledge Management (KM)

Module I: Introduction to Knowledge Management

Exam 212-69 Certified e-Business Associate

Module Objectives

⊙ Introducing Knowledge Management

⊙ Understanding Key Terminology

⊙ Discussing the principles of Knowledge Management

⊙ Understanding the Significance of KM

⊙ Tracing the Evolution of Knowledge Management

⊙ Knowledge Management - Management Challenges

⊙ Critical Success Factors for Knowledge Management

EC-Council

Objectives

☞ **Module Objectives**

On completion of this module, you will have gained a brief overview of the subject that Knowledge Management deals with. This module engages in discussing the following key areas:

➢ Introducing Knowledge Management

➢ Understanding Key Terminology

➢ Discussing the principles of Knowledge Management

➢ Understanding the Significance of KM

➢ Tracing the Evolution of Knowledge Management

➢ Knowledge Management - Management Challenges

➢ Critical Success Factors for Knowledge Management

You will be able to appreciate the significance of knowledge management strategy in the current global scenario, and leverage that insight to perceive the value that can be derived by adopting a knowledge management strategy. The module discusses the various phases through the evolution of knowledge management as a subject and a management practice. It also highlights a few implementation challenges that organizations come across while adopting a knowledge management strategy. This module is to be considered as a foundation module for further modules and serves the purpose of introducing the subject to the reader from a business perspective.

"The only sustainable advantage a firm has comes from what it collectively knows, how efficiently it uses what it knows, and how readily it acquires and uses new knowledge."
Source: Davenport & Prusak (1998)

EC-Council

Classical economics identified three primary *factors of production*: (1) land, (2) labor, and (3) capital. These factors were priced in the marketplace as:

(1) *Rents* for land and other resources,

(2) *Wages* for various kinds of labor, and

(3) *Interest* rates for capital assets.

However, the past 50 years have witnessed the emergence of a fourth element -- *knowledge* -- as the frequently dominant factor of production.

Ranging from the formerly-mundane know-how for the management, collection, processing and disposal of wastes to the complexities of designing, producing, distributing and supporting advanced computer operating systems, knowledge is increasingly the critical resource in an enterprise, obscuring the traditional factors of production.

It is in this context that the quote from Thomas. H. Davenport and Lawrence Prusak become thought provoking.

"The only sustainable advantage a firm has comes from what it collectively knows, how efficiently it uses what it knows, and how readily it acquires and uses new knowledge.

Clearly, these knowledge-creating activities take place within and between humans. But since it is axiomatic that a firm's greatest asset is its knowledge, then the firm that fails to generate new knowledge will probably cease to exist."

Defining Knowledge Management

Thomas H. Davenport and Laurence Prusak, are considered as pioneers in the field of knowledge management and give the following definition in their book 'Working Knowledge: How organizations manage what they know.'

"Knowledge is a fluid mix of framed experience, values, contextual information, and expert insight that provides a framework for evaluating and incorporating new experiences and information. It originates and is applied in the minds of knowers. In organizations, it often becomes embedded not only in documents or repositories but also in organizational routines, processes, practices and norms."

The Delphi Group defines knowledge management as:

"The leveraging of collective wisdom to increase responsiveness and innovation."

The Applied Knowledge Resource Institute states:

"Knowledge Management is intended to allow organizations to protect and develop their knowledge resource."

Michael Bookbinder, author of 'Enterprise Knowledge Management: Convergence at the Desktop' states:

"Knowledge management is not a technology, nor a system, although it uses technology. KM is an environment, a culture and a business ethic enabled by the application of technology, people and business processes. Technology is the Knowledge Enabler."

"Knowledge is not a "thing", or a system, but an ephemeral, active process of relating. If one takes this view then no one, let alone a corporation, can own knowledge. Knowledge itself cannot be stored, nor can intellectual capital be measured, and certainly neither of them can be managed." (Stacy 2001).

Other popular definitions are also discussed below:

➤ An emerging academic discipline and management process that addresses how people, workgroups, and organizations use knowledge principles, processes, technologies, and training to leverage intellectual capital by increasing knowledge flow, organizational learning, innovation, and performance.

➤ "Knowledge Management is the systematic, explicit, and deliberate building, renewal, and application of knowledge to maximize an enterprise's knowledge-related effectiveness and returns from its knowledge assets." Karl Wiig

➤ "Knowledge management (KM) enables organizations to capture, formalize, organize, store, access, apply, and share knowledge, experience, and expertise to enable superior performance. Additional benefits from managing knowledge include better business solutions and decisions, better collaboration and knowledge sharing, and improved workforce proficiency and knowledge." Tom Beckman, IRS

➤ "At its core KM is the process through which an enterprise uses its collective intelligence to accomplish strategic objectives." Ramon C. Barquin. Barquin and Associates, Inc.

➤ "The systematic process of creating, maintaining and nurturing an organization to make the best use of knowledge to achieve:
        - sustainable competitive advantage or
        - sustainable high performance."
    David and Alex Bennet, Mountain Quest Institute

➤ "Knowledge management is a systematic approach (with a background in information technology, human resources, strategy, and organizational behavior) that views implicit and explicit knowledge as a key strategic resource and aims at improving the handling of knowledge at the individual, team, organization, and inter-organizational level in order to improve innovation, quality, cost-effectiveness and time-to-market." Dr. Martin Eppler, MCM institute, University of St. Gallen

> "Knowledge management is…
>
> - o getting the right knowledge to the right people at the right time
> - o helping people share and put information into action in ways that strive to improve operational performance.
>
> Carla O Dell and C. Jackson Drayson Jr

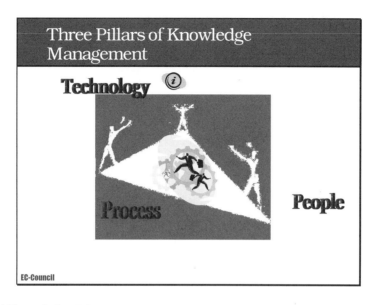

Three pillars of Knowledge Management

Peter F. Drucker, in his book "The Coming of the New Organization" cited a scenario. In an orchestra, there are probably few orchestra conductors who could coax even one note out of French horn, let alone show the horn player how to do it. But the conductor can focus the horn player's skill and knowledge on the musicians' joint performance. And this focus is what the leaders of an information-based business must be able to achieve. As soon as a company takes the first tentative steps from the "data" to "information", its decision processes, management structure, and even the way its work gets done begin to be transformed.

The foundation of knowledge management rests on three critical elements – People, Processes and Technology.

Knowledge management solutions and strategies encompass:

> ➤ People aspects: training, development, recruitment, motivation, retention, organization, job design, cultural change and encouraging thinking and participation.

> ➤ Process aspects: process innovation, re-engineering; both for radical and continuous improvement.

> ➤ Technology aspects: information and decision support systems, knowledge-based systems

Any approach to knowledge management has to factor these three critical elements to ensure that it meets its objectives and obtains the results it strives for.

Objectives of
Knowledge Management

⊙ Davenport et al. (1998) describe four broad
objectives of knowledge management systems
in practice:

- Create knowledge repositories.
- Improve knowledge access.
- Enhance the knowledge environment.
- Manage knowledge as an asset.

EC-Council

Objectives of knowledge management

The primary role of KM is to connect to "knowledge nodes" both the knowledge providers and the knowledge seekers.

The knowledge of the mind of one provider may thus be ultimately transferred to the mind of someone who seeks that knowledge, so that a new decision can be made or situation handled. KM provides a means of capturing and storing knowledge and brokering it to the appropriate individual.

Based on a study of thirty-one KM projects in twenty-four companies, Davenport, De Long and Beers identified four business objectives that fulfill this primary role:

These objectives of knowledge management can be broadly stated as:

➢ Create knowledge repositories.

This focuses on taking documents with knowledge embedded in them, store them in a repository, and retrieve easily. Examples are Memos, reports, presentations, articles / discussion database.

Basic types of repositories include the following:

o   External knowledge: competitive intelligence

▪   Filtering, Synthesis, Add context to information

- o Structured internal knowledge: research reports, marketing reports, methods, and techniques

  - Add value of information and knowledge through categorization & pruning

- o Informal internal knowledge: discussion database

  - To transfer tacit knowledge from individuals to a repository

  - Community-based electronic discussion

➤ Improve knowledge access.

The objective here is to facilitate the processes of knowledge transfer between individuals and between organizations.

➤ Enhance the knowledge environment.

Proactively facilitating and rewarding knowledge creation, transfer and its use achieve this.

➤ Manage knowledge as an asset.

Some companies include their intellectual capital in the balance sheet; while others are leveraging their knowledge assets to generate new income from or to reduce costs with their patent base.

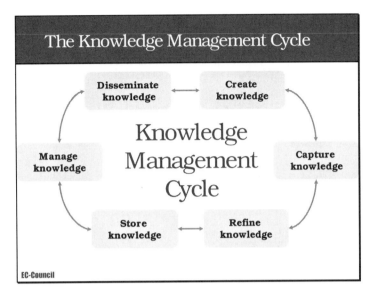

For humans the process of transforming data and information into knowledge and then back into value-added information is a cycle that is natural and on going. The above figure depicts this knowledge management cycle as consisting of six fundamental steps that involves the creation, capture, refinement, storage, management and dissemination of knowledge.

Small organizations of 2 to 20 persons are able to emulate the knowledge management cycle of an individual with some degree of success. Information and requests received from customers, partners, and the government is stored within individual memories, in documents and in simple database systems. Information processing takes place in individual brains as well as at productive meetings where the strengths and weakness of the individuals are well understood, accepted and utilized. Communication is primarily via ad-hoc meetings augmented by telephone, fax and email messages when a person is traveling or at home.

Knowledge consolidation by each individual is facilitated by a collective effort to ensure that failure does not recur for the same reasons and that success can be repeated as often as possible. Consequently, small organizations are said to be smooth, creative and able to move quickly to meet a changing environment with a high degree of synergy where the value derived from a project can often be greater than the sum of the individual efforts.

Larger organizations have a difficult time emulating the knowledge management. Large companies and institutions receive proposals, queries and other forms of information from a multitude of customers, channels, partners, government and regulatory bodies. Information is stored in various formats and locations that include policy documents, filing cabinets, internal process and product databases as well as external customer and distribution databases, tapes and CD.

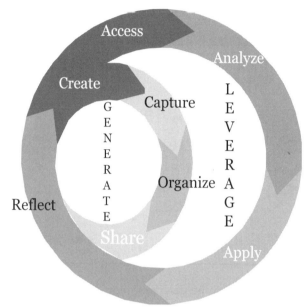

As seen in the above figure, this cycle of creation, capture, refinement, storage and dissemination is a closed loop with several processes being iterated as the organization evolves.

The intelligent organization is therefore a learning organization that is skilled at creating, acquiring, organizing, and sharing knowledge, and at applying this knowledge to design its behavior. Organizational learning depends critically upon information management -- the capacity to harness the organization's information resources and information capabilities to energize organizational growth.

An organization behaves as an open system that takes in information, material and energy from the external environment, transforms these resources into knowledge, processes, and structures that produce goods or services, which are then consumed in the environment.

The relationship between organizations and environment is thus both circular and critical: organizations depend on the environment for resources and for the justification of their continued existence. Because the environment is growing in complexity and volatility, continuing to be viable requires organizations to learn enough about the current and likely future conditions of the environment, and to use this knowledge to change their own behavior in a timely way.

An intelligent organization pursues its goals in a changing external environment by adapting its behavior according to knowledge about its external and internal settings. In other words, an intelligent organization is a learning organization that is skilled at creating, acquiring and transferring knowledge, and at modifying its behavior to reflect the new knowledge and insights.

Learning thus begins with new knowledge and ideas, which may be created in-house, or may come from external sources, but must be applied to change the organization's goals and behaviors in order for learning to be complete.

Organizational learning necessarily includes unlearning about the past - the organization should not restrict learning and exploration to its existing markets, products or practices, but should rediscover new goals and responses by stepping out of habitual frames of reference and reexamining norms and assumptions.

Similarly, adapting to an environment necessarily includes creating an environment that is advantageous to the organization. After all, the external environment consists of other organizations, and every organization is in fact part of larger ecological systems whose members are bound together by common interests and interlocking activities.

In creating the environment, an organization, either by itself or with its partners, develops foresight about future benefits that it can deliver, grows capabilities to provide these benefits, and so ensure a future for itself.

Creating the environment is more than reactively enacting or interpreting the environment, and more than finding a matching fit with the environment. In effect, the intelligent organization can engineer such a fit through its deep understanding of the forces and dynamics that give shape to the future.

The organizational intelligence/learning process is a continuous cycle of activities that include sensing the environment, developing perceptions and generating meaning through interpretation, using memory about past experience to help perception, and taking action based on the interpretations developed.

Knowledge Management Perspectives

⊙ KM as a <u>Technology</u> - Systems, Methods, Practices

⊙ KM as a <u>Discipline</u> - Multidisciplinary, Integrative

⊙ KM as a <u>Management Practice and Philosophy</u> - Focus on Effectiveness, Culture, and Stakeholders

⊙ KM as a <u>Societal and Enterprise Movement</u> - Focus on Broad Societal, Enterprise, and Personal Basic Values

⊙ Also: KM as a <u>Profession</u> – as a Business – as a Belief System .... ??

EC-Council

Knowledge management perspectives

There are several ways in which the topic of knowledge management could be addressed.

➤ KM as a <u>Technology</u> - Systems, Methods, Practices

Knowledge management can be considered as a technology involving systems, methods and practices to help organizations manage their intellectual capital

➤ KM as a <u>Discipline</u> - Multidisciplinary, Integrative

It can also be addressed as a discipline that involves several knowledges or knowledge bases that are integrative in nature and multidisciplinary

➤ KM as a <u>Management Practice and Philosophy</u> - Focus on Effectiveness, Culture, and Stakeholders

This perspective of knowledge management can be considered to be part of the corporate strategy, and focuses on invisible value such as greater effectiveness, changed organization culture and participative stakeholders.

➤ KM as a <u>Societal and Enterprise Movement</u> - Focus on Broad Societal, Enterprise, and Personal Basic Values

Knowledge management also has an economic and social perspective. Here, the focus is on achieving economic and social development and also inculcating personal value systems at an individual level.

➢ KM as a <u>Profession</u> – as a Business – as a Belief System

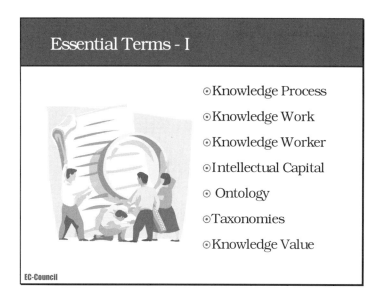

Essential Terms

Knowledge Process: A process in which knowledge is used to achieve a desired goal. Knowledge processes explicitly define the points at which knowledge is added to the process and the points at which knowledge is produced by the process. In defining a knowledge process it is possible to identify valuable knowledge that needs to be part of the process, i.e., if a certain piece of knowledge is not available the process will be seriously inhibited.

Knowledge work is generally characterized as having many variables, elements of choice based in human judgment, and involvement of learning. As the world advances, knowledge work domains tend to become more complex and require increasing levels of augmentation from computer and communication technologies.

Knowledge Workers: Professionals who perform work that requires complex reasoning, significant decision-making, and sophisticated action based on a myriad of discreet inputs related to a specialized domain of knowledge.

Intellectual Capital: Includes all of the knowledge resources of an organization, including human capital, social capital, customer capital, and organizational capital (explicit enterprise knowledge codified, for examples, in regulations, codes, processes, copyrights and patents).

> **Human Capital**: The individual and collective capabilities of the employees of the organization, including their knowledge, skills, abilities, competencies, education, and experience.

(1) Increasingly, employees' capacity for learning and their abilities to be creative and innovative are highly valued assets.

(2) While previously the predominant view was to consider employees as costs, today employees are more frequently viewed as assets. The newer trend is to view employees as investors.

Social Capital: The informal networks, relationships, trust, and shared understanding between individuals in organizations. Social capital is manifested in the structure of relationships between employees as they interact in the organization. In addition to interactions across the networks built on relationships, social capital also takes into account all the aspects of language (culture, context, etc.) and patterning (sequence, amount, timing, etc.) of exchange.

Structural/Enterprise Capital: Everything that is left when the employees go home. Includes property, patents, copyrights, business processes, systems, codified policies and procedures, etc. Also includes relationships with stakeholders. Often, organizations have highly developed structural capital that uniquely enhances their efficiencies and effectiveness.

Customer Capital: The quality of the interaction and the relationship between the organization and the customers that enables the organization to effectively serve the customers.

(1) External capital is measured by criteria such as the efficiency of product or service delivery and the satisfaction and loyalty of the customer.

(2) Interaction with customers is increasingly virtual and is evolving to enable self-service and a collaborative relationship.

Ontologies: Attempt to describe all the parts of a field or subject. Ontologies usually include taxonomies, but they also include all terms related to the subjects, the meaning of terms, and their interrelationships. Ontologies show relationships between subparts that cannot be seen in taxonomies, because usually in taxonomies the subparts are under separate branches. Ontologies may also include axiomatic inference rules about interrelationships of items.

Taxonomies: Classification schemes, which attempt to describe all the parts of a field or subject. A taxonomy is generally viewed as a tree with branches like the taxonomy of plants and animals, where a subspecies is a branch under a larger branch of species. Unlike ontologies, taxonomies do not usually show interrelationships. To build a taxonomy, it is helpful to have an ontology that includes terms and definitions.

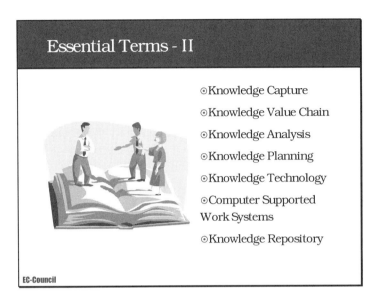

Knowledge Capture: The acquisition of knowledge from individual, group, or organization. Once knowledge is captured it can be codified and stored to promote reuse.

Knowledge Value Chain: Assuming that knowledge is a commodity of value, how it is created, how it is prepared for market, how it is marketed, how it is priced, and how it is purchased are all elements of the knowledge value chain. In the value chain there are knowledge providers, knowledge marketers, and knowledge users. Each of these roles play a part in a process and within the process knowledge value is created.

Knowledge Analysis (KA): In Knowledge Analysis we model a knowledge source in such a way that we can analyze its usefulness, its weaknesses and its appropriateness within the organization. Knowledge Analysis is a necessary step for the ability to manage knowledge. Within Knowledge Analysis we can use knowledge modeling and knowledge acquisition techniques.

Knowledge Planning (KP): When an organization has a grip on its knowledge (i.e. has performed Knowledge Analysis), it will be able to plan for the future. An organization will now be able to develop a multi-year knowledge plan that defines how the organization will develop its knowledge resources, either by training its human agents, or by developing knowledge-based systems to support the human agents, or by other means that allow the organization to stay competitive.

Knowledge Technology (KT): This is, as the word already implies, the (application of) techniques and methods from the field of AI, or to be more specific, the field of knowledge-based systems. KT has been around for quite some time, and most people know about the application of KT in the form of expert systems, and decision support systems. Techniques and methods to design these kinds of systems are well known; the best-known methodology for building knowledge-based systems is CommonKADS (formerly known as KADS).

Computer Supported Work Systems (CSWS): This is a formal and informal (human) activity system, within an organization where the (human) agents are supported by computer systems. The application of Knowledge Technology is very helpful in such work systems, although definitely not the only important factor in the analysis and design, nor in the effectiveness of the activity system.

Knowledge Repository: A place to store knowledge. An individual, group, or organization can all have knowledge repositories. Basic requirements for a repository are the ability to store various types of knowledge and the ability to retrieve that knowledge. A low-tech knowledge repository could be a set of file folders. A high-tech knowledge repository might be based on a database platform.

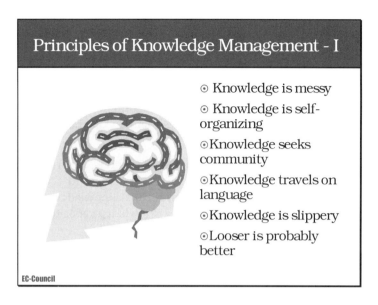

Principles of Knowledge

➤ **Knowledge is "messy."**

In organizations every aspect of knowledge is connected to everything else. You cannot neatly isolate the "knowledge" component of anything. Organizational knowledge relates to culture, structures, technology and the unique configuration of individuals that make up the organization. Knowledge also sits in the larger social context of national and global "knowledge environment." So, any attempt to identify knowledge factors faces an inherent messiness. In the knowledge universe you cannot pay attention to just one thing. No matter how you try to isolate knowledge, you find something else clinging to it.

➤ **Knowledge is self-organizing.**

Every day, knowledge is created, sustained, killed off and renewed in an organization. Knowledge has a life of its own; it is a self-organizing entity. The "self" that knowledge organizes around is organizational or group identity and purpose.

➤ **Knowledge seeks community.**

Knowledge wants to happen, just as life wants to happen and both want to happen as community. Nothing illustrates this principle more than the explosive growth of the Internet. Communities of knowledge are so powerful that they now involve people in conversation with each other all over the globe.

➤ **Knowledge travels on language.**

Language is the verbal blueprint of our experience. Without a word or a language to describe our experience we cannot communicate what we know. Every mode of knowledge travels on a different language. Language initiates us into a particular world of experience. For example, traditional management uses the language of statistical control, inspection, and balance sheets. One is not "initiated" into management ranks without learning this language. Expanding organizational knowledge means we must expand the languages we use to describe our work experience.

➢ **Knowledge is slippery**.

The more you try to pin knowledge down, the more it slips away. It is tempting to try to tie up knowledge as codified knowledge, documents, patents, intellectual property, libraries, and databases. Yet, too much rigidity and formality lead to the unwanted side effect of stifling creativity and new knowledge development. This principle brings to mind the tragedy of King Midas whose daughter turned to solid gold at his touch. He gained a golden statue but lost the living, breathing vibrancy of the daughter he loved.

➢ **Looser is probably better**.

Highly adaptable systems look sloppy. But the survival rate of diverse, decentralized systems is higher. This means we can waste resources and energy trying to control knowledge processes too tightly.

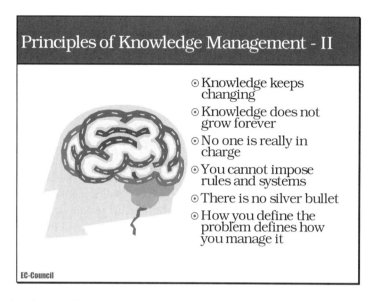

> **Knowledge keeps changing**.

There is no final solution in knowledge management. The patterns of knowledge are always changing. Knowledge is always changing. In an organization, knowledge changes around products, services, processes, technology, structures, roles and relationships. No sooner do we think we have identified a pattern of knowledge than a new one seems to appear.

The best approach or solution for the moment is one that keeps things moving along while keeping options open. Flexibility in approach and in thinking is a must. There are always different approaches to try. In fact, the on-going conversation about knowledge is much more important than coming up with the right answer.

> **Knowledge does not grow forever--something eventually dies or is lost**.

A number of people in knowledge management hold an unchallenged assumption that knowledge continuously grows. Yet, think how exhausting it would be to only have continual growth. Constant growth does not hold true in nature and it does not hold true for knowledge. There is a big difference between advancing knowledge and simply building knowledge. Unlearning and letting go of old ways of thinking, even retiring whole blocks of knowledge and expertise, contributes to the vitality and evolution of knowledge.

> **No one is really in charge**.

At the core, knowledge is a social process. Only people *together* make knowledge happen. No one individual makes knowledge happen. What this means is no one person can take responsibility for collective knowledge. Knowledge managers cannot really manage knowledge itself. However, they can and do help devise and manage processes for acquiring, creating, sharing and applying knowledge. A knowledge manager can also attend to strategies for removing barriers and creating a supporting culture for those processes.

➤ **You cannot impose rules and systems.**

If knowledge is truly self-organizing, then the most important way you can advance it is to remove the barriers to self-organization. Knowledge will take care of itself in the right supporting environment. It is a waste of effort to create guidelines, rules or technology systems that no one cares about or supports. It is more valuable to see what is working well and devise ways to support and enhance the natural processes.

➤ **There is no silver bullet.**

Knowledge management is not a technology. Companies who deploy "silver bullet" solutions that depend on technology alone often see disappointing results. Often companies who find roadblocks on their way to KM success have a solution that relies solely on technology. There is no one magical leverage point or best practice to advance knowledge and expand organizational intelligence. Knowledge must be supported at multiple levels and in a variety of ways if it is truly valued. Genuine solutions require a systems approach, careful thought, reflection, experimentation and constant adjustment.

➤ **How you define the knowledge "problem" determines what and how you try to manage.**

The knowledge question can present itself in many ways. If an organization is concerned with ownership, then energy focuses on acquiring codified knowledge that can be protected with copyrights and patents. If people are concerned with knowledge sharing, then they emphasize communication flow and documentation. Concern with key knowledge competencies for the future leads to seeking more effective ways to create, adapt and apply knowledge. Attending to all of these areas would reflect an extremely high value for knowledge and requires a great deal of commitment.

Given all that, there are still a number of ways that we can advance knowledge. It is possible to identify processes, structures, and organizational enablers that support the creating, sustaining, sharing and renewing of knowledge.

(Excerpt from Verna Allee's management book, The Knowledge Evolution: Expanding Organizational Intelligence, published by Butterworth-Heinemann, 1997.)

Business Environment

- Increasing Work Complexity
- Achieving sustainable growth is rare
- Growing Need for Knowledge and Learning
- Global slowdown increases pressure on corporates
- Declining trend seen in company profitability
- Increasing trend seen with regard to market growth expectations
- The bearing of management decisions is considered the most critical driver in realizing company growth or decline

EC-Council

Business Environment

The e-business scenario is changing the way in which goods and services are traded. The emergence of widely accessible electronic market places provides new opportunities to sell knowledge assets and knowledge-intensive products. Exploiting these to their full potential requires new approaches and thinking organizations that can seize opportunities as they emerge.

A 10 Year study of 1,900 public G-7 companies with over $500M sales showed that achieving sustainable growth is becoming increasingly difficult. Twenty seven percent of the companies studied were able to show a revenue growth of over 5.5%, sixteen percent could achieve a profit growth of over 5.5% and a mere thirteen percent showed earned cost of capital during the period of study. The figure below shows the increasing pressure being faced by corporates globally.

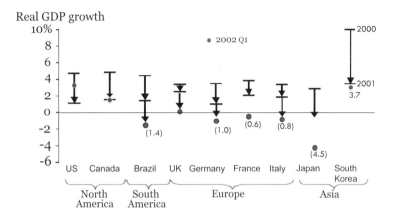

Source: Dresdner
Kleinwort
Wasserstein; CIBC

Apart from the global slowdown, there has been a declining trend in company profitability as indicated by the return on assets - shown in the graph below.

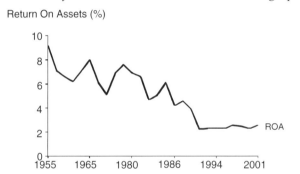

Source: InvesTech Research

Despite this, market expectations have not declined as depicted in the figure above.

It becomes increasingly clear that management decisions are having a greater impact in the resulting growth or decline of organizations worldwide. The figure below emphasizes the need for management to take better-informed decisions and this is where knowledge management can add value.

This is depicted in the figures below.

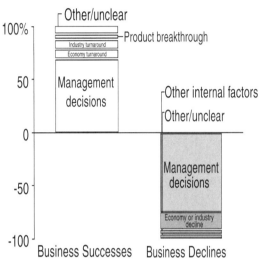

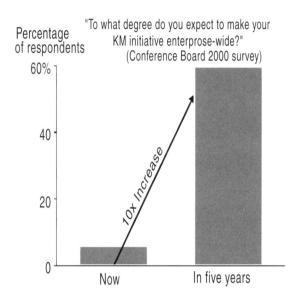

The slide discussed here highlights the need to adopt an effective knowledge management strategy given the current business environment.

New ways of thinking and doing business is being required by corporates to survive and succeed in the ebusiness environment. The key external forces that are transforming the enterprise are rapid nature of change in business environment and competition that has become more demanding in terms of organizational resources.

These external forces have fostered new ways of thinking, resulting in new approaches being adopted by the management and the creation of a collaborative environment where everyone participates.

On part of the workers, traditional and conventional forms of education are proving to be inadequate, as more knowledgeable counterparts who can essay multiple roles are being increasingly preferred.

This has led to workers demanding a greater say and involvement in the operations of the organization and taking the role of participative stakeholders. All the above has resulted in the work area transforming into a more complex one.

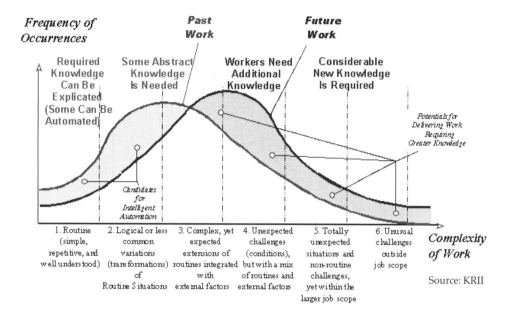

Source: KRII

Hence the organization has to reinvent itself in order to survive, succeed and gain competitive advantage.

The figure above shows the various phases that evolve as complexity of work increases. What was routine work characterized by simple, repetitive and well understood work specifications, evolve into situations where logical input is required of the worker and this is a little more abstract work specifications. These two phases are where automation can be utilized to a certain extent.

As the work or role progresses, there is an increased integration with external factors that increase the complexity of the work further. With time, workers are expected to face unexpected challenges that arise in the course of routine work and external interactions. Workers need additional knowledge to meet the demands of their work now.

Totally unexpected situations and non-routine challenges are to be tackled by the workers as part of their larger job scope. The last phase shown here is where challenges of unusual nature are to be addressed even if they are outside the scope of the job specifications. It can be seen that as the complexity of work increases, the need for knowledge increases with each new phase.

Thus, it is not just the organization that reinvents itself, but the employees also have to mature in terms of knowledge assets to fulfill their responsibilities. The key to achieving the required synergy lies in adopting a sound knowledge management strategy.

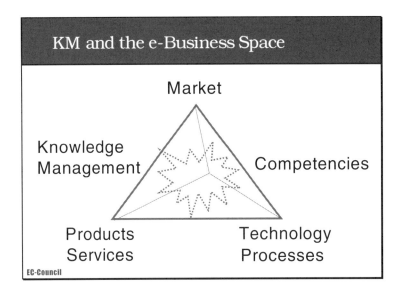

KM and the e-Business Space

Where does knowledge management fit in the e-business space? Today knowledge management integrates the market space, products and services, as well as technology and processes by harnessing competencies required to excel in the business space.

The knowledge management movement has steadily progressed into the e-space--the e-business space, the business-to-business space and the portal space--allowing us to experience its real potential. KM has united business, IT and economic interests into a large community.

B2B creates value chains with higher velocity. Businesses have always worked together to create value chains based on "lock-in," intended to stop the suppliers from supplying the competition by not having the value chain easily replicated.

However today, competitive advantage is gained by being able to swap in and out of value chains and to syndicate parts of what the organization knows, parts of the organization process, with other value chains. Value chains are no longer linear and serial. Form a business by creating a demand chain, and the supply chain will create itself.

KM is about creating communities, reducing time to communities, whether two people, 200 or two million. The Web is the single most important milestone. It allows the formation of instantaneous communities across expanses of both time and distance, allowing those who know to connect with those who need to know.

Delphi terms these business spaces as "vortals"--the market communities that allow access to all the supplies and buyers in a particular market. When a request is submitted for a new business to the B2B interface, it is submitted to myriad industry vortals and getting from those vortals suppliers and other capabilities that meet the requirements.

Significance of Knowledge Management - I

⊙ KM improves business performance through better management of intellectual capital and knowledge resources

- Knowledge is available and leveraged amongst different parts of the organization
- Employees in distant locations are able to collaborate
- Activity or process times are positively impacted through the instant availability of knowledge

EC-Council

Significance of Knowledge Management

Knowledge management is about harnessing insight and constant innovation.

There is a fundamental shift in management approach. Traditional organizations are giving way to knowledge-based businesses.

Key differentiators in the knowledge-based economy are intangible assets such as databases, customer loyalty, alliances, personal know-how, workplace collaboration, technical understanding, market knowledge, sophisticated distribution capabilities and organizational flexibility.

The emergence and convergence of powerful technologies for capturing, storing, retrieving and sharing information are the building blocks for this innovation.

➤ At the strategic level the organization needs to be able to analyze and plan its business in terms of the knowledge it currently has and the knowledge it needs for future business processes.

➤ At the tactical level the organization is concerned with identifying and formalizing existing knowledge, acquiring new knowledge for future use, archiving it in organizational memories and creating systems that enable effective and efficient application of the knowledge within the organization.

At the operational level knowledge is used in everyday practice by professional personnel who need access to the right knowledge, at the right time, in the right location.

Despite all of the hype over Knowledge Management, there is often confusion about what it can really do for a business, how it can be put to use, and what benefits can be seen. The question arises as to how can one translate knowledge management strategy to achieve competitive intelligence?

KM improves business performance through better management of intellectual capital and knowledge resources

This is more so because knowledge is available and leveraged amongst different parts of the organization by employees in distant locations, who are now able to collaborate. Therefore, activity or process times are positively impacted through the instant availability of knowledge.

Improved business decisions result in achieving greater customer satisfaction and expands market share. There is scope for enhancing learning within the organization and maximizing the potential for re-usability (rather than wheel re-invention approach). It helps in developing a better organization culture, enabling knowledge and experiences to be retained in-house. This improves information and knowledge flows within the organization and makes better use of (and adding value to) internal systems and resources, offering a new/enhanced market proposition encouraging growth of knowledge sharing and working.

Knowledge management also helps in improving the leverage of tangible and intangible assets, and thus enabling their valuation.

How can an intangible asset such as knowledge be managed in a business context? Every organization needs to adopt a knowledge framework that can address its strategic goals and form the basis for the corporate knowledge strategy.

However, it has been often seen that organizations give prominence to acquiring technological knowledge without understanding the finer conceptual details. This is compounded sometimes with the ever-changing technology scenario leading organizations to focus on the next generation of tools than utilize the available resources.

Often, the creation and capture of knowledge is sidetracked in the interest of condensing knowledge for executive consumption. This leads us to the question "Can we predict critical knowledge areas?"

It is possible to a large extent for organizations to predict critical areas of knowledge. This is dealt in detail in the module on knowledge framework and strategies.

At a superficial level, there are a few guiding ideas for managers to handle knowledge in a better manner. The focus at any level should be to transform both raw materials and raw ideas within the organization into productive assets. The organization management should strategize to leverage both capital and knowledge assets. There should be real collaboration and cooperation within and between companies. There is also the basic need to disseminate knowledge through teaming and re-teaming structures within the organization.

Significance of Knowledge Management - II

⊙ Knowledge Management is information put to work
- Human Interaction is the focal point surrounding the collection, distribution and reuse of information
- Decision-making is facilitated by the almost immediate availability of information and the tools to analyze it

EC-Council

KM is information put to work. Here, human interaction is the focal point surrounding the collection, distribution and reuse of information. This results in better and informed decision making. Decision-making is facilitated by the almost immediate availability of information and the tools to analyze it.

Capturing individual knowledge so that it can be understood and applied by an entire organization is a key objective of most knowledge management (KM) initiatives. One approach that has proved effective in many companies is to set up communities of practice, which allow workers to share knowledge on a particular topic.

Information technology can provide the infrastructure to help the groups communicate. But the main goal is to enable person-to-person communication.

KM solutions bind enabling technologies together and provide an entry point to the knowledge that exists within an organization. KM solutions take the document management and search solutions one step further by organizing the information by subject in taxonomy and also by linking the experts within a company to the subject matter topics -- the "expertise." Employees can then put the information available into context by collaborating with the subject matter experts within their organizations

In general, KM solutions provide value for companies because they:

➢ Help organizations to gain competitive advantage by allowing information to be easily accessible and readily available to employees

➢ Allow outside vendors, customers and business partners to work more efficiently together

➢ Eliminate employee "rework" thereby saving time

Collaborative technologies, such as instant messaging, e-meetings and presence awareness make it easier for workers to find, contact and confer with the subject matter experts within their companies, enabling workers to do their jobs better and faster.

Presenting the technology to workers along with a change management strategy can help realize competitive advantage. Managers can work with internal teams to educate workers on the benefits of sharing knowledge as well as provide them with "how-to" tutorials on how to best use KM technologies. In addition, companies can alter the ways in which employees access other technologies and make the KM solution a greater part of the average workday.

Though the short-term returns on investment are significant, it is the long-term benefits that provide an even larger return to companies, giving them a sound and efficient way to preserve existing intellectual capital and manage future corporate knowledge.

An example of mapping technology at various levels of understanding is shown below.

Level of Understanding	Technology
Data	Online transaction processing (OLTP) systems
Information	Ad hoc query and reporting applications
Analytic	Online analytical processing (OLAP) applications
Knowledge	Data mining applications
Wisdom	The human mind

Significance of Knowledge Management - III

⊙ Helps maintain an organization's intellectual capital

- An employee's knowledge about a customer, solution or process is available to the entire organization
- Attrition has less of an impact on the organization since an individual's knowledge is already captured

EC-Council

When companies undergo a major organizational change, relationships between teams and between managers and employees are altered and new collaborative relationships are formed, rendering confusion about who holds what subject matter knowledge and affecting an organization's ability to respond quickly and effectively to customer and market demands.

Among other factors, there are three major catalysts that can institute organizational changes today and in the future: a batch of old generation employees is retiring, the economic downturn is continuing to cause layoffs and an increased amount of mergers, acquisitions and divestitures are creating organizational confusion. With mass exoduses of employees, organizations are at risk of losing the competitive advantage furnished by their knowledge workers' expertise.

When companies such as Yahoo, Amazon, and eBay leap virtually overnight to market capitalization in the billions of US dollars--surpassing the valuations of some 100-year-old, blue chip marketing companies--it has become clear that an organization's real market value cannot be computed by measuring its physical assets alone. Intellectual Assets Age companies do not necessarily own substantial physical assets; it is their knowledge assets that define their market value. It becomes paramount for these organizations to nurture, capture, mine, and preserve the intellectual capital their employees hold in their minds, since it represents the true wealth of the organization.

Throughout the various major organizational changes taking place worldwide, IT is critical as a strategic differentiator in enabling enterprises to operate efficiently. It is important for organizations to begin planning now for the retirement of the older generation of employees and for future losses of intellectual capital. For example, the old generation technology professionals built many of the federal government's applications on COBOL. The younger government workers are trained on newer programming languages, such as Java or .Net. Without maintaining the knowledge of COBOL after those experts leave, the government will have a difficult time maintaining these applications. Setting up Knowledge Management (KM) tools to preserve institutional expertise and to make it more broadly available within the organization will help organizations better plan for and cope with any impending losses.

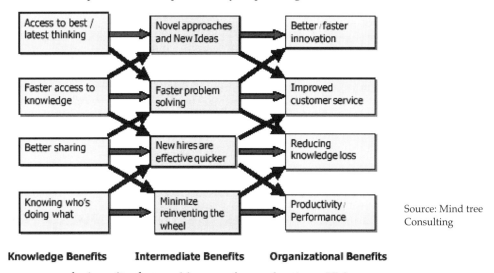

Source: Mind tree Consulting

Knowledge Benefits   Intermediate Benefits   Organizational Benefits

The above figure presents the benefits that could accrue from adopting a KM strategy.

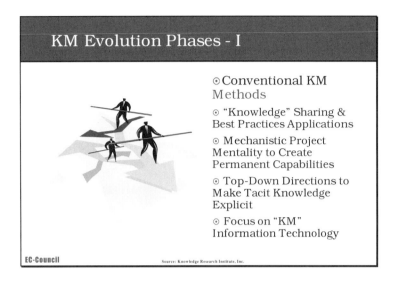

KM Evolution Phases - I

⊙ Conventional KM Methods

⊙ "Knowledge" Sharing & Best Practices Applications

⊙ Mechanistic Project Mentality to Create Permanent Capabilities

⊙ Top-Down Directions to Make Tacit Knowledge Explicit

⊙ Focus on "KM" Information Technology

EC-Council

Source: Knowledge Research Institute, Inc.

Evolution of Knowledge Management - Methods

No discourse on knowledge management is complete without a discussion on its evolution. Here, we discuss the first phase of its popular existence, where methods dominated the KM scenario.

The first age, prior to 1995 saw knowledge being managed, and the focus was on the appropriate structuring and flow of information to decision makers and the computerization of major business applications leading to a technology enabled revolution dominated by the perceived efficiencies of process reengineering.

However, an excessive focus on methods resulted in achieving efficiencies at the cost of effectiveness. This also resulted in downsizing, and most organizations had laid off people with experience or natural talents, vital to their operation, of which they had been unaware.

This is aptly summarized by a quote from Hammer and Champy, the evangelists of reengineering: "How people and companies did things yesterday doesn't matter to the business reengineer" (1993). The failure to recognize the value of knowledge gained through experience, through traditional forms of knowledge transfer such as apprentice schemes and the collective nature of much knowledge, was such that the word knowledge became problematic.

➢ Conventional KM - Methods

　　o "Knowledge" Sharing and Best Practices Applications

　　o Mechanistic Project Mentality to Create Permanent Capabilities

　　o Top-Down Directions to Make Tacit Knowledge Explicit

o   Focus on "KM" Information Technology

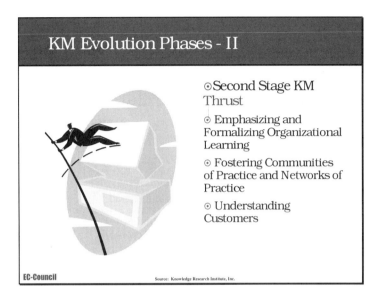

Evolution of Knowledge Management - Thrust

By 1995 collaborative computing, increasing access to e-mail and the growth in intra and extranets were becoming commonplace. Introduction of collaborative technologies, especially Intranets or groupware, for rapid information access were highly popular.

The next stage in the evolution saw the approach of 'Thrust' being adopted by organizations. Customers began getting more attention and were being addressed through the corporate strategy. Customer satisfaction and service standards were considered important to the firm. This saw the reuse of knowledge at customer support centers e.g. via case-based reasoning.

Portals and communities of practice began to emerge and 'sharing' was no longer just a concept. This gained more prominence with the advent of Internet and with organizations going multinational. This led to the creation of Knowledge webs - networks of experts who collaborate across and beyond an organization's functional and geographic boundaries.

More emphasis was being placed on formalized organizational learning. The second major thrust of knowledge-focused strategies was that of innovation, the creation of new knowledge and its conversion into valuable products and services. This is referred to as knowledge innovation (Amidon 1997).

This required an environment where creativity and learning flourished and knowledge was encapsulated in a form from where it could be applied. Hence organizations undertook development of knowledge centers - focal points for knowledge skills and facilitating knowledge flow. This phase also saw the augmentation of decision support processes, such as through expert systems or group decision support systems.

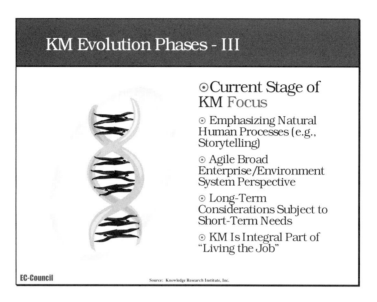

Evolution of Knowledge Management - Focus

The current state of knowledge management is oriented towards achieving effective Performance and is people-centric. Organizations now pursue business goals through knowledge management practices. This improves competitiveness and functional effectiveness by broadening the perspective of knowledge governance, and leverages intellectual capital assets.

Here, the focus is on innovation, knowledge renewal and deployment. The organization fosters a knowledge-supportive infrastructure and has a reduced focus on KM-IT linkage. The organization culture is one of leveraging knowledge everywhere.

The human element is given more prominence and knowledge management themes such as story telling are more pronounced.

There is more focus towards transforming into an agile broad enterprise, that is more sensitive to its environment – both external and internal.

The long-term considerations of the knowledge management strategy are subject to meeting short-term needs. This is marked departure from earlier approaches to the KM strategy.

Knowledge Management is no longer considered to be an additional job requirement; rather it is seen as an integral part of the job specifications. Readers are encouraged to revisit the figure on increasing complexity of work and the notes given therein.

Refer the next figure to see the evolution of KM through the years.

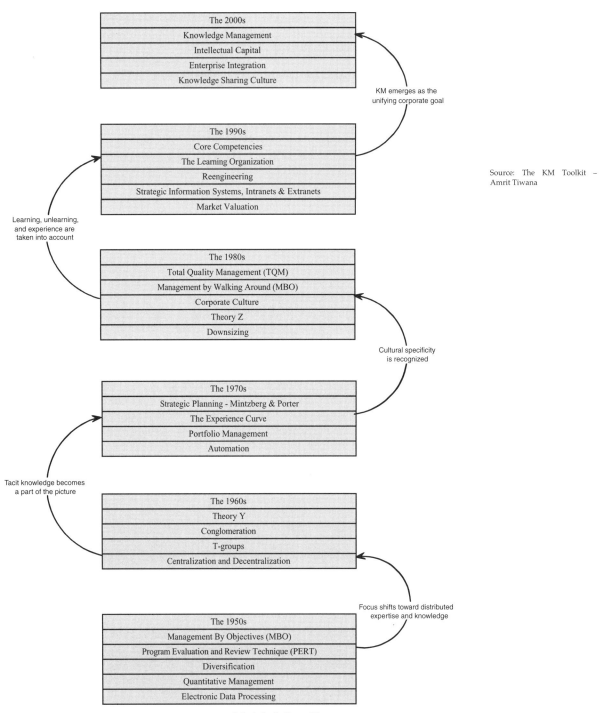

Source: The KM Toolkit – Amrit Tiwana

Knowledge Management Technology Scene

⊙**Knowware** are technology tools that support KM.

⊙**Collaboration tools**, or groupware, were the first used to enhance collaboration for tacit knowledge transfer within an organization.

⊙**KM suites** are complete KM solutions out-of-the-box.

⊙**Knowledge Servers** contain the main KM software, including the knowledge repository.

⊙**Electronic document management systems** focus on the document in electronic form as the collaborative focus of work.

⊙**KM Tools** capture knowledge unobtrusively (with minimal effort and impact).

- E.g. Tacit Knowledge Systems' KnowledgeMail

⊙**Enterprise knowledge portals** are the doorway into many KM systems.

⊙**XML** provides standardized representations of data structures so data can be processed without case-by-case programming.

⊙**Application Software Providers** have evolved as a form of KMS outsourcing on the Web.

EC-Council

Knowledge Management Technology Scene

Effective KM technology and systems must be:

➢ Scalable — must be able to support a large number of users and a robust, industrial strength database;

➢ Extensible — capable of expanding as needed by the organization;

➢ Compliant with industry standards, allowing companies to leverage existing resources;

➢ Secure;

➢ Relevant and Timely;

➢ Collaborative — although many efforts start with a single department of group, the best KM programs grow to encompass input from across the organization;

➢ Powerful off-line analysis;

➢ Allow for complex queries;

➢ Fast and easy to administer and deploy;

➢ Flexible - The technology should be able to handle knowledge of any form, including different subjects, structures and media. It should be able to handle forms which do not as yet have been defined;

> Heuristic - The systems should learn about both its users and the knowledge it possesses as it is used. Over time, its ability to provide users with knowledge should improve. For example, if the solution deals with many requests on a particular subject, it should learn how to assist users in more depth on that subject;

> Suggestive - The solution should be able to deduce what a user's knowledge needs are and suggest knowledge associations that he is not able to do himself;

Some of the enabling technologies are highlighted here:

> <u>Knowware</u> are technology tools that support KM.

> <u>Collaboration tools</u>, or groupware, were the first used to enhance collaboration for tacit knowledge transfer within an organization.

> <u>KM suites</u> are complete KM solutions out-of-the-box.

> <u>Knowledge Servers</u> contain the main KM software, including the knowledge repository.

> <u>Electronic document management systems</u> focus on the document in electronic form as the collaborative focus of work.

> <u>KM Tools</u> capture knowledge unobtrusively (with minimal effort and impact).

   o E.g. Tacit Knowledge Systems' KnowledgeMail

> <u>Enterprise knowledge portals</u> are the doorways into many KM systems.

> XML provides standardized representations of data structures so data can be processed without case-by-case programming.

Application Software Providers have evolved as a form of KMS outsourcing on the Web.

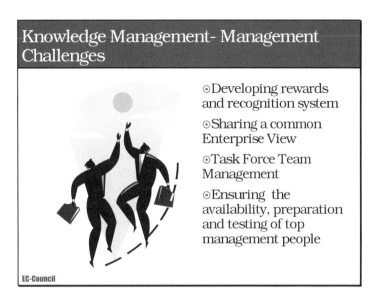

Knowledge Management- Management Challenges

- ⊙ Developing rewards and recognition system
- ⊙ Sharing a common Enterprise View
- ⊙ Task Force Team Management
- ⊙ Ensuring the availability, preparation and testing of top management people

EC-Council

Management Challenges

The information-based organization also poses its own special management problems and these are:

Developing rewards and recognition system: The first challenge that faces an information-based company is developing rewards and recognition. Opportunities for specialists in an information-based business organization should be more plentiful within that specialty. Advancement into management will be exceptionally low because of the fewer or no middle-management positions to move into an information-based business. Also, creating parallel opportunities for individual professional contributors can be considered as rewarding. Whatever scheme will be developed it will work if the values and compensation structure of business are drastically changed.

Sharing a common enterprise vision: The second challenge that management faces is giving its organization of specialists a common vision, a view of the whole. A business simply cannot function without communicating to the whole organization its vision, objectives, expectations etc. It needs a view of the whole and a focus on the whole to be shared among a great professional specialist.

Task force team management: Thirdly, a problem is relying heavily on task force teams in an information-based organization. One way to foster professionalism is through assignments to task forces. And the information-based organization will use more and more small self-governing units. The role and function of the task-force leaders are risky and controversial, because the assigned leader will act as supervisor or manager. Conflicts arise on this scenario, whether it carries a rank or whether the assignment is considered a task or a position? So there is a need to have a clear trend and understanding as to what it entails in handling a specific task force.

Ensuring the availability, preparation and testing of top management: Finally, the toughest problem will probably be to ensure the supply, preparation and testing of top management people. This is an old and central dilemma for the general acceptance of decentralization in large businesses. Peter Drucker proposes a framework similar to the "German Gruppe" in which the decentralized units are set up as separate companies with their own top management. The Germans use this model to promote people in their specialties, especially research and engineering; if they did not have available commands in near independent subsidiaries to put people in, they would have little opportunity to train and test their most promising professionals. The entire top management process – preparation, testing, and succession – will become problematic. There will be a growing need for experienced business people to go back to school. And business schools will surely need to work out what successful professional specialists must know to prepare themselves for high-level positions as business executives and business leaders.

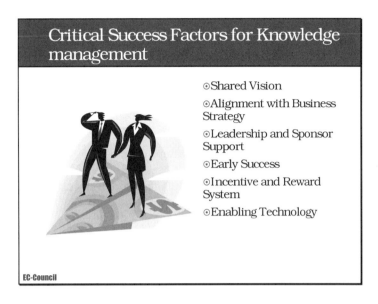

Critical Success Factors

Shared Vision

The organization should have a common enterprise view and a shared vision regarding their knowledge management initiative. This should be communicated across the organization and ensure enterprise wide participation. Sharing must be inspired by a common vision. The people affected by the new process or technology must all buy in to this vision and believe it will work.

Alignment with Business Strategy

Clear business benefits should be demonstrated through the KM vision. KM programs are more likely to succeed if they are part of the organizational business strategy. This should involve tracking success and developing new measures

Incentive and Reward System

A knowledge sharing culture (teams that work across boundaries) is vital to KM success. Organizations have to maintain a balance between intrinsic and explicit rewards in order to encourage employee behavior. The most effective use of explicit rewards has been to encourage sharing at the onset of a KM initiative.

Leadership and Sponsorship

Leadership plays a key role in ensuring success in almost any initiative within an organization. Its impact on KM is even more pronounced because this is a relatively new discipline. Nothing makes greater impact on an organization than when leaders model the behavior they are trying to promote among employees.

Early Success

Nothing succeeds like the sign of success. If the organization can demonstrate benefits that can be felt by the organization, it will be easier to steer the knowledge initiative to its desired goal.

Enabling Technology

Without a solid IT infrastructure, an organization cannot enable its employees to share information on a large scale. Yet the trap that most organizations fall into is not a lack of IT, but rather too much focus on IT. A KM initiative is not a software application; having a platform to share information and to communicate is only part of a KM initiative.

Summary

- Knowledge is reckoned to be the last competitive advantage
- Knowledge management is necessary to survive in the knowledge based economy
- There are twelve basic principles about knowledge
- KM evolved from methods to thrust and then into process based focus
- People, Processes and Technology are the three pillars of knowledge management

EC-Council

Summary

 Recap

➢ Knowledge is reckoned to be the last competitive advantage

➢ Knowledge management is necessary to survive in the knowledge-based economy

➢ There are twelve basic principles about knowledge

➢ KM evolved from methods to thrust and then into process based focus

➢ People, Processes and Technology are the three pillars of knowledge management

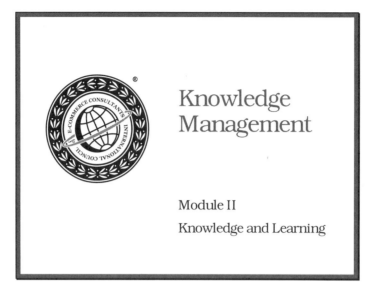

Knowledge
Management

Module II
Knowledge and Learning

Knowledge Management (KM)

Module II: Knowledge and Learning

Exam 212-69 Certified e-Business Associate

Module Objectives

- ⊙ Distinguishing Knowledge and Learning
- ⊙ Understanding the Knowledge Hierarchy
- ⊙ Perceiving Knowledge as a Resource
- ⊙ Knowledge Types and Classifications
- ⊙ Comprehending Knowledge Transfer Modes
- ⊙ Exploring Individual Learning
- ⊙ Understanding Learning Delivery Types
- ⊙ Introducing the concept of e-learning

EC-Council

Objectives

👉 **Module Objectives**

On completion of this module, you will have gained insight into knowledge classification, modes of transfer and e-learning. This module engages in discussing the following key areas:

- ➢ Distinguishing Knowledge and Learning
- ➢ Understanding the Knowledge Hierarchy
- ➢ Perceiving Knowledge as a Resource
- ➢ Knowledge Types and Classifications
- ➢ Comprehending Knowledge Transfer Modes
- ➢ Exploring Individual Learning
- ➢ Understanding Learning Delivery Types
- ➢ Introducing the concept of e-learning

Defining Knowledge

- ⊙ Knowledge is created by people and reflects their know-how and involves their education, experience, thinking, decision-making, and all other capacities for creating choices and taking action.
- ⊙ Corporate knowledge is derived from individuals and may be documented and embedded in organizational resources. Knowledge is more than data and information.
- ⊙ "Knowledge is about reasoning about information and data to enable performance, problem solving, decision making and learning" Tom Beckman, IRS
- ⊙ "Knowledge is the human capacity (potential and actual ability) to take effective action." David Bennet

EC-Council

Defining Knowledge

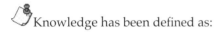Knowledge has been defined as:

1. The act or state of knowing; clear perception of fact, truth, or duty; certain apprehension; familiar cognizance; cognition. "**Knowledge**, which is the highest degree of the speculative faculties, consists in the perception of the truth of affirmative or negative propositions." *Locke.*

2. That which is or may be known; the object of an act of knowing; cognition; -- chiefly used in the plural.

Knowledge is different from data and information and this can be seen in the knowledge hierarchy discussed later in this module. It is important that readers learnt o distinguish knowledge from related terms such as information and wisdom.

Knowledge is created by people and reflects their know-how and involves their:

(1) education, (2) experience, (3) thinking, (4) decision-making, and all other capacities for creating choices and taking action.

Corporate knowledge is derived from individuals and may be documented and embedded in organizational resources. "Knowledge is about reasoning about information and data to enable performance, problem solving, decision making and learning" Tom Beckman, IRS

"Knowledge is the human capacity (potential and actual ability) to take effective action." David Bennet

> ## Defining Learning
>
> ⊙ Learning – The acquisition and integration of knowledge so that it may be used and applied.
> ⊙ Levels of learning:
>   - Knowledge: memorization of facts or terms
>   - Comprehension: translating or paraphrasing information or rules
>   - Application: using information in new situations, applying rules
>   - Analysis: breaking information down into discrete parts
>   - Synthesis: constructing a new idea from parts of others
>   - Evaluation: placing a value judgment on data
>
> EC-Council

Defining Learning

Learning is different from knowledge and has been defined as "The acquisition and integration of knowledge so that it may be used and applied." Learning uses knowledge and harnesses its application value.

Bloom's Taxonomy identifies different learning levels, which are discussed below. According to Blooms taxonomy of learning there are six levels that represent the strengths of learning: knowledge, comprehension, application, analysis synthesis and evaluation. The skills demonstrated at each level of competence are highlighted along with examples.

Knowledge - observation and recall of information such as knowledge of processes, knowledge of major ideas, mastery of subject matter

Associated Vocabulary: list, define, tell, describe, identify, show, label, collect, examine, tabulate, quote, name, who, when, where, etc.

Comprehension – ability to understand information, grasp meaning, translate knowledge into new context, interpret facts, compare, contrast order, group, infer causes and predict consequences

Associated Vocabulary: summarize, describe, interpret, contrast, predict, associate, distinguish, estimate, differentiate, discuss, extend

Application – capability to use information, use methods, concepts, theories in new situations; solve problems using required skills or knowledge

Associated Vocabulary: apply, demonstrate, calculate, complete, illustrate, show, solve, examine, modify, relate, change, classify, experiment, discover

Analysis - seeing patterns, organization of parts, recognition of hidden meanings, identification of components

Associated Vocabulary: analyze, separate, order, explain, connect, classify, arrange, divide, compare, select, explain, infer

Synthesis - use old ideas to create new ones, generalize from given facts, relate knowledge from several areas, predict, and draw conclusions

Associated Vocabulary: combine, integrate, modify, rearrange, substitute, plan, create, design, invent, what if?, compose, formulate, prepare, generalize, rewrite

Evaluations - compare and discriminate between ideas, assess value of theories, presentations, make choices based on reasoned argument, verify value of evidence, recognize subjectivity

Associated Vocabulary: assess, decide, rank, grade, test, measure, recommend, convince, select, judge, explain, discriminate, support, conclude, compare, summarize

The significance of discussing learning and blooms levels of learning here is with regard to corporate internal training, without which knowledge management becomes an uphill task that is more likely to be abandoned.

It has to be emphasized that learning is a critical success factor in every phase of a knowledge initiative.

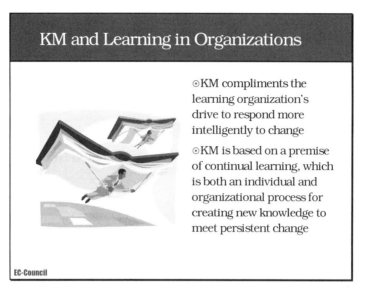

KM and Learning in Organizations

Organizational learning is an integral part of any knowledge management initiative. KM compliments the learning organization's drive to respond more intelligently to change. KM is based on a premise of continual learning, which is both an individual and organizational process for creating new knowledge to meet persistent change.

The drivers behind 'learning' within organizations are:

- The need to adapt to fast changing environment, make quicker and informed decisions

- Improve effectiveness, meeting customer product and service expectations – both internal and external to the organization

- Innovate: the emergence of knowledge as a key focus of policy and strategy

- Improve or perish: lose funding or jobs contracted out, obtain and improve upon a new capability

- Collaboration: the ability to work and trade over large geographic distances.

- The power of technology and especially the acceptance of the Internet as a key business enabler. Thus organizations with operations and employees around the world are now able to mobilize their expertise from whatever origin to apply rapidly to new situations. As a result, clients are coming to expect from global organizations, not merely the know-how of the particular team that has been assigned to the task, but the very best that the organization as a whole has to offer.

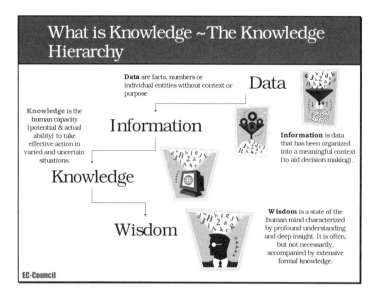

The Knowledge Hierarchy

Before we can address knowledge management, we need to understand the knowledge hierarchy. This means we need to differentiate between data, information, knowledge and wisdom. Most often, information management and data management are misinterpreted as knowledge management.

At a basic level, Data are facts, numbers or individual entities without context or purpose.

Since the invention of the database management system and advances in data storage technology, organizations have been collecting, processing, storing and accumulating vast amounts of data about people, locations, transactions, concepts and events that can be easily analyzed. A great deal of this data is associated with the functional processes of the organization. Data are discrete, unorganized, scattered statements about reality

For example, a grocery store collects data about the items an individual purchases at the time of checkout. The grocery clerk scans the products into the system, and the system identifies the price of the item and calculates the total sales price. Through this transaction, the system has collected the following data elements: item, quantity, price, date, which cash register, the grocery clerk and, in certain cases, who conducted the purchase.

Information is data that has been organized into a meaningful context (to aid decision making).

On an individual basis, data elements such as "item" do not provide meaning unless they are presented in conjunction with other data elements. The accumulation of data into a meaningful context provides information.

For example, the accumulation of item, quantity and price provides information about the items that are purchased, the quantity and the price. By calculating the extended sales amount for each item, one can then rank and determine the item that generated the greatest and least sales by dollar amount.

Data are statements about reality or about other data. They are representations about the world – be it physical, social, psychological, organizational, or any other form of reality.

Data become information when they are organized according to certain preferences and placed in a context, which defines their meaning and relevance. Information is meaningful, contextual data, but not yet knowledge.

Knowledge is the human capacity (potential & actual ability) to take effective action in varied and uncertain situations.

The next level of elevated understanding is knowledge. Knowledge is different from data, information or analytics in that it can be created from any one of those layers, or it can be created from existing knowledge using logical inferences.

It is clear that as compared to information, which is an objectification, knowledge involves subjectivization.

Information can become knowledge when a human being interacts with it, appropriates it and makes it her/his own, contextualizes it by placing it in relation to other knowledges that are already her/his own, and internalizes it by making it a part of his belief system.

Knowledge involves a human interaction with reality (or with information about reality, or information about other knowledge or information), where the human is the subject and acts as the active, creative element, and modifies the latter by way of reconstructing it. Knowledge involves attribution of meaning and significance by the knower as a person. In fact, every reconstruction is a reinterpretation as well.

Knowledge involves a judgment, a sub-assumption of the particular under the universal. It involves a certain amount of synthesis and integration of discreet information under a category, a construction or an attribution of a causality or justifiability, relative to the knower's frame of reference.

Wisdom is a state of the human mind characterized by profound understanding and deep insight. It is often, but not necessarily, accompanied by extensive formal knowledge. Wisdom is the utilization of accumulated knowledge. By utilizing knowledge, a higher level of understanding of the data is created.

Organizations that have been collecting data from their transactional systems have the opportunity to realize potential of the data as an asset to the organization and leverage that asset in a manner that provides greater understanding of the subject matter.

The Data – Information – Knowledge Wisdom hierarchy can understood as portrayed below.

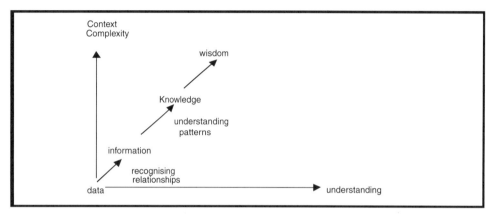

Figure 1: Data - information - knowledge - wisdow continuum. (Developed after Bellinger, 2001)

Knowledge is acquired through experience and/or study. Knowledge is "...richer and more meaningful information put into productive use... Because it is intuitive, it is difficult to structure, can be hard to capture on machines, and is a challenge to transfer. Since knowledge is derived from information, people must work to transform information into knowledge." Knowledge can be placed in two fundamental categories, explicit knowledge and tacit knowledge.

In the context of KM the following distinctions can be made:

> Data: data may be totally described through structural, formal representations, are quantified or quantifiable and thus are purely *syntactic*.

> Information: Information is organized data that can be communicated. A fundamental distinction between data and information is that the former is purely syntactical, and the latter necessarily contains *semantics* (implied by the word "meaning").

> Knowledge: information (i.e. organized data) that can be used to achieve some or other result. We associated information to semantics. Knowledge is associated to *pragmatics*, that is, it is related to something existing in the "real world" of which we have a direct experience.

> Wisdom: selection of appropriate knowledge for a specific task. Wisdom is the ability to know what to do with and how, when and where to apply knowledge.

Data are purely *objective* – they do not depend on their user. Information is *objective-subjective*, in the sense that it is described in an objective way (texts, pictures, etc.) but its meaning is subjective, depending on its user. Knowledge is purely *subjective* – each person experiences something in a different way. Competency is *subjective-objective*, in the sense that it is a purely personal characteristic, but everybody may examine its outcome.

A further example to reinforce the concept is given below: Data: 20; Information: 20 degree Celsius; Knowledge: 20-degree Celsius is a comfortable office temperature for most people; Wisdom: People work better in comfortable office temperatures.

Knowledge as a Resource

⊙<u>Know-how</u>: skills base of an organization that was developed over time, includes trade secrets, engineering standards and the expertise of the enterprise

⊙<u>Know-who</u>: identifies people with information, internally and externally, the informal network that gets things done

⊙<u>Know-when</u>: sense of timing and rhythm in developing new products, managing lead times, closing out old product and pacing the market

⊙<u>Know-what</u>: mastery of a consistent set of meanings, includes data elements in a database, applications, group technology, classification and coding, test specifications or standards, consistency in meaning makes it possible to see significant patterns move easily, predict trends and develop customized solutions

⊙<u>Know-where</u>: ability to identify appropriate market niches

⊙<u>Know-why</u>: knowledge of context and how it relates to particular efforts

EC-Council

Knowledge as a Strategic Resource

➢ <u>Know-how</u>: skills base of an organization that was developed over time, includes trade secrets, engineering standards and the expertise of the enterprise. A learning organization leverages this knowledge asset to gain primary competitive edge. Document mapping, internal knowledge sharing programs, are used to achieve this.

➢ <u>Know-who</u>: identifies people with information, internally and externally, the informal network that gets things done. This is where the value chains can be extended and knowledge sharing gains importance. This is dealt in detail in the following pages.

➢ <u>Know-when</u>: sense of timing and rhythm in developing new products, managing lead times, closing out old product and pacing the market. Product innovation, market intelligence developed as a result of having extended value chains comes into play here. There is an analytical component to the knowledge resident in the organization.

➢ <u>Know-what</u>: mastery of a consistent set of meanings, includes data elements in a database, applications, group technology, classification and coding, test specifications or standards, consistency in meaning makes it possible to see significant patterns move easily, predict trends and develop customized solutions

➢ <u>Know-where</u>: ability to identify appropriate market niches. As mentioned above, product innovations combined with customer intimacy and market intelligence makes it possible for the organization to identify market niches and leverage the same for success.

> ➤ <u>Know-why</u>: knowledge of context and how it relates to particular efforts. A frequently asked question: "why things worked the way they did?"

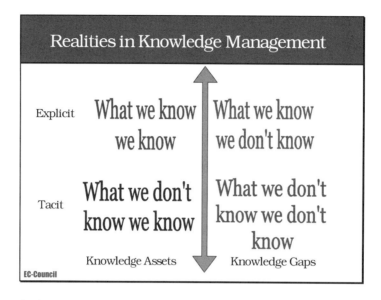

Realities in Knowledge Management

All the knowledge in the world divides into the following four categories:

> **What we know we know**

There's the set of things we know that we know. We hope that this is a constantly changing set of things. And not because things we used to know are dropping out of this category into things we used to know but have forgotten, a subset of things we don't know we don't know (or, alternatively, a subset of the set of things we don't know we know if they're things we would remember if someone just reminded).

> **What we don't know we know**

This is a relatively smaller category of knowledge – 'we don't know we know'. Some of these things hop back and forth between the category of things we don't know we know to the category of things we know we know when, for instance, something happens to dredge up that particular bit of information (like remembering all the components of a biochemical cycle whenever I see the chemical formulae) or when someone points out something that they see in you but that you've never particularly noticed, like "Do you know you always interrupt me when I'm talking to you?"

> **What we know we don't know**

The second big category is the one that contains things we know we don't know. For instance, I know I don't know Japanese or Russian (though it was once learnt in the form of the alphabet from a book). However, I know Japanese or Russian language exists. And I don't know anything about it. And because I know, I could, if I needed to for some reason, learn it. This is not possible for the next category.

➢ **What we don't know we don't know**

The biggest and the most dangerous category by far is the one that contains things that we don't even know we don't know. We can't discuss them. We can't ask questions about them. We can't develop a plan for gaining knowledge with a comprehensive set of classes; outside reading and helpful discussion because we don't know these things are out there. We don't know these things even Exist. We don't know. And if we don't know, we can't take any of these things into account when we make decisions, we can't adjust your worldview. These things are simply missing, like black holes in the overall picture of life.

Everything we learn, everyday, gets moved from one of the other categories into Things we know we know. Everyone's set of things is unique too. And one of the ways we contribute to the world is passing on the things we know we know to other people.

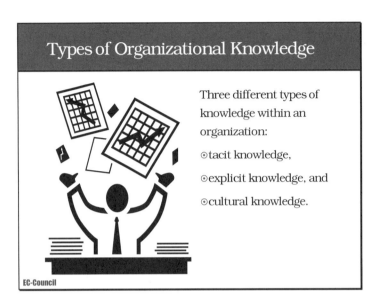

Types of Organizational Knowledge

Within an organization, Knowledge can be categorized into three broad classes.

➤ **Tacit knowledge**

This is represented by individual or group experience and expertise, is implicit: used for sense making, problem solving & gaining of perspective, and is personal: held within us and rarely documented.

➤ **Explicit knowledge**

This is based on policies, procedures, instructions, standards and results, readily communicated, often through written documentation, and provides a record of "organizational or institutional memory"

   o   Examples include the knowledge in business processes, written standard operating procedures, expert systems (programs that emulate human thought processes in well-defined problem domains), rules, regulations, and copyrights/patents.

   o   Some KM authors discuss implicit knowledge, which is more than tacit, but not yet explicit. If you ask a person a question, and they can easily give you an answer that is not written or codified anywhere yet, they are transmitting implicit knowledge. It is accessible through query or discussion.

> ## Cultural knowledge

   This forms the basis for what we deem to be fair and trustworthy, an underlying comprehension of how we treat new truths and situations, and is often tied to an organization's vision, mission and overall philosophy.

Common to many organizations across all industry sectors, there exists islands of knowledge and data that are not connected nor linked and therefore, not usable where and when required. Corporate memory, information and records include: policies, procedures, manuals, records, sales information, technical manuals etc. (explicit knowledge).

Some practitioners also classify knowledge into additional segments such as:

> **Social Knowledge** is shared informally between individuals, and within groups, communities, and networks. It may be either explicit or tacit. As tacit knowledge, it is sustained through interaction and is especially demonstrated by the synergy in high performance teams. It is related to capacity for cooperation, and shared norms, values and objective.

> **Customer Knowledge** is both knowledge the customer holds and knowledge about the customer. Ideally, this knowledge is beneficial to both the organization and to the customer.

Knowledge management must go beyond these collections of written information and include the experiences and perspectives of employees and the organization as a whole and access what is maintained in their heads (tacit knowledge).

One of the principle objectives of a KM program is to capture and record to the extent possible available tacit knowledge and convert it to explicit knowledge, which is more easily shared. Of the two categories of knowledge, tacit knowledge is the most fragile; it is more likely to go out the door when an employee leaves or retires. The challenge for all organizations in securing tacit knowledge for future use is to gain the active and cooperative participation of its employees. To guarantee such cooperation, the organizational culture must actively nourish the sharing of relevant knowledge and individual participation in such sharing.

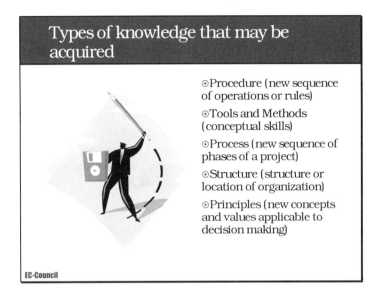

Types of Knowledge Acquired

> A **procedure** is a sequence of steps.

Procedural Knowledge allows people to perform actions step by step. The focus of learning is to ensure that learners don't think/act in wrong sequence. Procedural knowledge units or procedures define <u>how</u> the employee will achieve each task in the learning organization. These may range from requirement analysis, designing a product strategy etc.

> A **concept** is an identity of a group of objects, events that share some common characteristics. Most of the words in a language are concepts. A concept consists of two parts: (1) an identity and (2) the meaning (description or definition) associated with the identity, which is often expressed by a group of other concepts.

Whether you have knowledge of a concept is whether you have the ability of assigning an appropriate identity or label to given scenarios or phenomenon. With the correct or proper identification of a situation, we are able to retrieve and apply other knowledge related to that concept to solve problems or guide our actions. The challenge of understanding a concept is that one concept may look similar to other concepts from some aspects or perspectives.

A concept is the basic building block of more complex knowledge structures. It's best understood in the context. Conceptual knowledge units are seen as *tools and methods* in a business context and are used to describe <u>what</u> the employee must use to complete his job requirement. These may include analysis of results, knowledge units, product design, service delivery, etc.

➢ **Processes** are those that encourage interaction across boundaries. These are infrastructure, development and management processes, as opposed to business operational processes. These may be strategic and scenario planning, competitor analysis, capacity planning etc

➢ **Structure** refers to organizational structure or location. An organizational system is a group of components interacting together to achieve common goals. The components, behaviors (interaction) and goals are often described by concepts. The organizational structure captures both structural and behavioral aspects. Upon identifying a phenomenon as a particular structure of the organization, we have the opportunity to use a set of well-structured knowledge at our disposal for analysis and decision-making.

➢ **Principles** are explanations or predictions of why things happened in the world. Principles involve relationships between concepts. A principle consists of preconditions and consequences. If preconditions meet, then consequences occur. Strategic knowledge units or principles (strategies, rules, heuristics) enable the employee to decide <u>when or why</u> certain choices should be made while using a procedure or a concept: principles to group knowledge into learning units, principles to adjust learning goals to learning needs, principles to choose corporate strategies or decision making, etc.

Knowledge Transfer Modes

	Tacit	Explicit
Tacit	Tacit to Tacit Socialization	Explicit to Tacit Internalization
Explicit	Tacit to Explicit Externalization	Explicit to Explicit Combination

Source: Nonaka & Takeuchi

EC-Council

Knowledge Transfer Modes

Four basic patterns for knowledge-creation in any organization:

> - Socialization (tacit knowledge formation and communication)

> - Externalization (formation of explicit knowledge from tacit knowledge)

> - Combination (use of explicit knowledge)

> - Internalization (formation of new tacit knowledge from explicit knowledge)

Tacit knowledge is what the knower knows, which is derived from experience and embodies beliefs and values. Tacit knowledge is actionable knowledge, and therefore the most valuable.

Furthermore, tacit knowledge is the most important basis for the generation of new knowledge, that is, according to Nonaka: "the key to knowledge creation lies in the mobilization and conversion of tacit knowledge."

Explicit knowledge is represented by some artifact, such as a document, which has typically been created with the goal of communicating with another person. Both forms of knowledge are important for organizational effectiveness.

These ideas lead us to focus on the processes by which knowledge is transformed between its tacit and explicit forms, as shown in figure above. Organizational learning takes place as individuals participate in these processes, since by doing so knowledge is created, shared, articulated, and made available to others. Creation of new knowledge takes place through the processes of combination and internalization. Thus the knowledge cycle is completed.

- ➢ From Tacit to Tacit (Socialization) – when knowledge is acquired.

    An individual shares tacit knowledge, (non-formal) technical skills and know-how directly with another. The other individual learns tacit skills through observation, imitation and practice until it becomes a part of his tacit knowledge base. But socialization is a limited form of knowledge creation. Knowledge doesn't become explicit and cannot be leveraged by the company as a whole.

    For instance, IBM's Knowledge Socialization project is a research project being conducted at IBM's T.J. Watson Research Center.

    The project's goals in brief are:

    - o To identify how stories can be best included in a knowledge management effort -- how best to collect them, organize them, present them, and provide facilities to search through them and navigate among them.

    - o To identify how technology can be best applied to the use of stories in a knowledge management effort.

    - o To identify how the use of stories as a knowledge management activity can be supported and enhanced at IBM.

    In other words, tacit-to-tacit knowledge transfer when done without capturing knowledge to an explicit form is called socialization. Stories are one form of tacit-to-tacit knowledge transfer. Other means can be sharing experiences through observation, imitation and practice. (E.g., workshops, seminars, internships, etc.)

    Socialization involves sharing information and communication of tacit knowledge between people, e.g., in meetings. Davenport and Prusak states that knowledge sharing is often done without ever producing explicit knowledge and, to be most effective, should take place between people who have a common culture and can work together effectively. Thus tacit knowledge sharing is connected to ideas of communities of practice and collaborative environments. A typical activity in which tacit knowledge sharing can take place is a team meeting during which experiences are described and discussed.

    An oft-quoted example is that of Matsushita. More than a year of studying the kneading technique of a master baker led Matsushita's software developer and project engineers to come up with product specifications for a bread-making machine that set record sales for a kitchen appliance.

The most typical way in which tacit knowledge is built and shared is in face-to-face meetings and shared experiences, often informal, in which information technology (IT) plays a minimal role. However, an increasing proportion of meetings and other interpersonal interactions use on-line tools known as groupware. These tools are used either to supplement conventional meetings, or in some cases to replace them.

➢ From Explicit to Explicit (Combination) – When knowledge is standardized (and formalized).

Acquired (communicable) knowledge is transcribed into standard (formal) knowledge usable within the company. An individual combines discrete pieces of explicit knowledge into a new whole.

Explicit knowledge can be shared in meetings, via documents, e-mails, etc., or through education and training. The use of technology to manage and search collections of explicit knowledge is well established. However, there is a further opportunity to foster knowledge creation, namely to enrich the collected information in some way, such as by reconfiguring it, so that it is more usable. An example is to use text classification to assign documents automatically to a subject schema. A typical activity here might be to put a document into a shared database.

Once tacit knowledge has been conceptualized and articulated, thus converting it to explicit knowledge, capturing it in a persistent form as a report, an e-mail, a presentation, or a Web page makes it available to the rest of the organization.

Technology already contributes to knowledge capture through the ubiquitous use of word processing, which generates electronic documents that are easy to share via the Web, e-mail, or a document management system. Capturing explicit knowledge in this way makes it available to a wider audience, and "improving knowledge use" is a goal of many knowledge management projects. One issue in improving knowledge use is that individuals may not be motivated to use the available tools to use the knowledge. Technology may help by improving their motivation or by reducing the barriers to generating shareable electronic documents.

➢ From Tacit to Explicit (Articulation / Externalization) – when knowledge is translated (and communicated).

This involves the translation and conversion of tacit (non-formal) knowledge into (communicable) explicit knowledge. It involves the transfer of knowledge from the minds of its holders to an external repository in the most efficient way possible. Externalization tools help build Knowledge Maps. They capture and organize incoming bodies of Explicit Knowledge and create clusters of bodies of knowledge.

Converting tacit to explicit knowledge is finding a way to express the inexpressible. Creating new knowledge is not just a matter of mechanistically processing objective information. It depends on tapping the tacit and often highly subjective insights, intuitions and ideals of employees. Making this available for testing and use by the company as a whole.

Examples are slogans, analogies and metaphors playing prominent roles in product development. It's about ideas leading to other ideas which fuel innovation. It is a way for individuals grounded in different contexts and with different experiences to understand something intuitively through the use of imagination and symbols without the need for analysis or generalization. It puts two different ideas in one phrase. Driven by intuition and link images that seem remote from each other at first glance.

The Honda Project Team, after being tasked of creating a new car design came up with the "Theory of Automobile Evolution" and "man maximum, machine minimum" slogans which led to the "Tall Boy" product-concept resulting into the Honda City, the company's distinctive urban car.

It is a more structured process of reconciling contradictions and making distinctions. It seeks to clarify how different ideas are like and alike and harmonizes the contradictions in the metaphor. It can be considered to be the intermediate step between pure imagination and logical thinking.

The Canon Project Team, while discussing design problems of the disposable copier drum for their mini-copier over a couple of drinks, compared of one of the disposable aluminum beer cans with the proposed disposable copier drums. Speculations whether the process for making aluminum beer cans could be applied to the manufacture of an aluminum copier drum enabled the team to come up with the process technology that could manufacture an aluminum copier drum at low cost.

Representative activities in which the conversion takes place are through discourse among team members, in responding to questions, or through the elicitation of stories.

According to Nonaka, the conversion of tacit to explicit knowledge (externalization) involves forming a shared mental model, then articulating through discussion. Collaboration systems and other groupware (for example, specialized brainstorming applications) can support this kind of interaction to some extent.

On-line discussion databases are another potential tool to capture tacit knowledge and to apply it to immediate problems. To be most effective for externalization, the discussion should be such as to allow the formulation and sharing of metaphors and analogies, which probably requires a fairly informal and even unrestrictive style. This style is more likely to be found in chat and other real-time interactions within teams.

Newsgroups and similar forums are open to all, unlike typical team discussions, and share some of the same characteristics in that questions can be posed and answered, but differ in that the participants are typically strangers. However, it is found that many people who participate in newsgroups are willing to offer advice and assistance, seemingly driven by a mixture of motivations including philanthropy, a desire to be considered as an expert, and the appreciation and positive feedback contributed by the people they have helped.

Most open discussion groups are known to contribute knowledge in response to a request for help. Often speed of response and active participation are noted on such forums. The archive of the forum becomes a repository of useful knowledge. It is easier to identify experts and locate them.

The point to be highlighted here is that although the exchange is superficially one of purely explicit knowledge, the expert must first make a judgment as to the nature of the problem and then recommend the most likely solution, both of which bring his or her tacit knowledge into play. Once the knowledge is made explicit, persons with similar problems can find the solution by consulting the archive.

Quantitative studies have shown that the great majority of interchanges are of this question-and- answer genre, and it has also been noted that even though a large fraction of questions were answered by just a few persons, an equal proportion were answered by persons who only answered one or two questions. Thus the conferencing facility has enabled knowledge to be elicited from the broad community as well as from a few experts.

➢ From Explicit to Tacit (Internalization) – when knowledge is shared.

The transfer of Explicit Knowledge from an external repository (temporary or permanent) to an individual, in the most useful and efficient way possible is called internalization. New (formal) knowledge is shared (communicated) through out an organization. Other employees begin to internalize it resulting into the expansion, broadening and re-framing of their own tacit (non-formal) knowledge base.

In order to act on information, individuals have to understand and internalize it, which involves creating their own tacit knowledge. By reading documents, they can to some extent re-experience what others previously learned. By reading documents from many sources, they have the opportunity to create new knowledge by combining their existing tacit knowledge with the knowledge of others. However, this process is becoming more challenging because individuals have to deal with ever-larger amounts of information. A typical activity would be to read and study documents from a number of different databases.

Technology to help users form new tacit knowledge, for example, by better appreciating and understanding explicit knowledge, is a challenge of particular importance in knowledge management, since acquisition of tacit knowledge is a necessary precursor to taking constructive action.

A knowledge management system should, in addition to information retrieval, facilitate the understanding and use of information. For example, the system might, through document analysis and classification, generate meta-data to support rapid browsing and exploration of the available information. It seems likely that the future trend will be for information infrastructures to perform more of this kind of processing in order to facilitate different modes of use of information (e.g., search, exploration, finding associations) and thus to make the information more valuable by making it easier to form new tacit knowledge from it.

Other processing of explicit knowledge can support understanding. For example, putting a document in the context of a subject category or of a step in a business process, by using document categorization, can help a user to understand the applicability or potential value of its information. Discovery of relationships between and among documents and concepts helps users to learn by exploring an information space.

Information overload is a trend that motivates the adoption of new technology to assist in the comprehension of explicit knowledge. The large amounts of (often redundant) information available in modern organizations, and the need to integrate information from many sources in order to make better decisions, cause difficulties for knowledge workers and others. Both of these trends result directly from the large amounts of on-line information available to knowledge workers in modern organizations.

Information overload occurs when the quality of decisions is reduced because the decision maker spends time reviewing more information than is needed, instead of reflecting and making the decision. Various approaches to mitigating information overload are feasible. An agent can filter or prioritize the messages, or compound views can make it easier to review the incoming information. Finally, visualization techniques can be applied in an attempt to help the user understand the available information more easily.

Perhaps a more promising application of visualization is to help a user grasp relationships, such as those between concepts in a set of or the relationships expressed as hyperlinks between documents. This use is more promising because of the difficulty of rendering relationships textually. Furthermore, figuring out the relationships within a set of documents is a task that requires a lot of processing, and computer assistance is of great value.

When tacit and explicit knowledge interact, something powerful happens. Externalization and internalization are critical stages in the spiral of knowledge. It requires active involvement of the self or the individual.

Once the pattern is complete, the spiral knowledge begins all over again but in a higher level. Newly acquired knowledge can then be used to formulate equivalent quality standards. In this way, the organization's knowledge base grows even broader.

KM and Individual Learning

- ⊙ Knowledge begins with the individual.
- ⊙ Motivators for Learning
  - Survive and meet basic needs
  - Growth
  - Professional development and marketability
  - Curiosity and intellectual enjoyment
  - Gain edge over competitors
- ⊙ Knowledge workers must be lifelong learners
  - Skills must be continually renewed or become obsolete
  - New skills must be acquired
  - To respond to change and new technologies people must be enabled to learn how to create, innovate and employ new processes

EC-Council

KM and Individual Learning

Knowledge begins with the individual and individual learning paves the way to creating organizational knowledge.

Among the motivators for individual learning are the need to survive and meet basic individual needs, growth, professional development and increasing marketability. Learning also satiates curiosity and provides intellectual enjoyment. The most cited motivator for learning is to gain a competitive edge over competitors.

The importance of individual learning arises from the need for knowledge workers to be lifelong learners. This is crucial as individual skills must be continually renewed or they must face obsolescence. Moreover, as work complexity increases, there is an increasing need to acquire new skills. Learning, done in an organization environment helps individuals respond to change in a better and informed manner.

Learning also equips individual workers create, innovate and employ new processes to improve their work environment. Learning is a basic requirement to foster a conducive culture for knowledge management. Knowledge transfer modes are effective only if individuals are open and receptive to learning. Workers prefer learning that is experiential, oriented to problem solving, and focused on useful and immediate value. They learn by doing and prefer learning that is self-directed.

The nature of learning can be cognitive such as expertise, skills, experiences, anecdotes, stories, context information, strategic decision-making, and tacit knowledge. Alternatively it can be domains of learning or even subject matter knowledge - technical knowledge, organizational knowledge, and personal knowledge.

Optimal characteristics of learners

⊙ Motivation to try potentially better processes

⊙ New or improved skill or ability desired

⊙ Trust in abilities and validity of those providing knowledge

⊙ Flexibility and agility

⊙ Curiosity

⊙ Safe environment

⊙ Flow State: A sense of highly focused attention, mental enjoyment of the activity for its own sake, a sense of being outside of time, a match between the challenge at hand and one's skill

EC-Council

Optimal Characteristics of Learners

It is important to identify the optimal characteristics of a learner and that of an organization so that organization-learning strategies can be formulated in an effective manner.

Generic characteristics of learners are highlighted in the slide above.

In an organizational context, characteristics of learners are:

➢ Problem-centered; seek educational solutions to where they are compared to where they want to be in life.

➢ Results-oriented; have specific results in mind for education - will drop out if education does not lead to those results because their participation is usually voluntary.

➢ Self-directed; typically not dependent on others for direction.

➢ Often skeptical about new information; prefer to try it out before accepting it.

➢ Seek education that relates or applies directly to their perceived needs, that is timely and appropriate for their current lives.

➢ Accept responsibility for their own learning if learning is perceived as timely and appropriate

The underlying philosophy is that individual workers learn best not only by receiving knowledge but also by interpreting it, learning through discovery while also setting the pace of their own learning. Organizational strategies should be designed to facilitate their learning, designing experiences through which students acquire new knowledge and develop new skills.

Learning Delivery Types

⊙ Blended learning models: combine as many as possible in one learning experience for economy and re-enforcement: classroom, online courseware, virtual classrooms and collaboration tools

⊙ Individual or group, mentoring, classroom

⊙ One time experiences: lectures, seminars, or on-going courses or processes

⊙ Same time and place: classroom training

⊙ Different time and place: learners chooses when to access

⊙ TV Video, online access of text/audio/video modules

⊙ Same time, different place

⊙ Satellite telecast, Internet chat learning experiences, teleconferencing learning modules, web casts

⊙ Long course versus just-in-time learning "bullet"

⊙ 15 minutes e-learning "experiences"

⊙ Push learning bullets to staff in their "off times"

EC-Council

Learning Delivery types

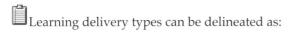Learning delivery types can be delineated as:

➤ Blended learning models: These combine as many as possible in one learning experience for economy and re-enforcement. Examples include classroom, online courseware, virtual classrooms and collaboration tools

➤ Individual or group. Examples include mentoring, classroom

➤ One-time experiences: Examples of one time learning experience include lectures, seminars, or on-going courses or processes

➤ Same time and place: Example of same time and place learning experience is classroom training

➤ Different time and place: Here, learners choose when to access the learning resources. Examples of different time and place learning experience include

o TV Video, online access of text/audio/video modules

➤ Same time, different place: Examples of same time but different place learning experience include

o Satellite telecast, Internet chat learning experiences, teleconferencing learning modules, web casts

➢ Long course versus just-in-time learning "bullet". Examples include 15 minutes e-learning "experiences" and pushing learning bullets to staff in their "off times".

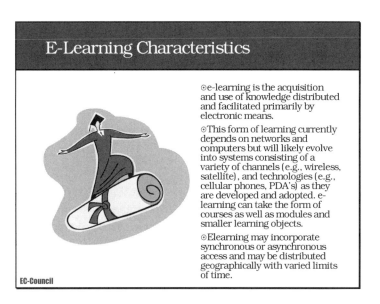

E Learning Characteristics

Today more than ever, businesses need to keep their staff up-to-date to stay ahead. Knowledge and effective training need to be available immediately and effectively. e-learning can provide this facility - training at a time, pace, place and style that suit the modern business environment. In principle, eLearning is a kind of distance learning; learning materials can be accessed from the web or CD via a computer, and tutors and learners can communicate with each other using e-mail or discussion forums.

e-learning is the acquisition and use of knowledge distributed and facilitated primarily by electronic means. This form of learning currently depends on networks and computers but will likely evolve into systems consisting of a variety of channels (e.g., wireless, satellite), and technologies (e.g., cellular phones, PDA's) as they are developed and adopted. e-learning can take the form of courses as well as modules and smaller learning objects. e-learning may incorporate synchronous or asynchronous access and may be distributed geographically with varied limits of time.

e-learning is established and here to stay. It can benefit all sizes of businesses in terms of effectiveness and efficiencies in training. e-learning can be used as the main method of delivery of training or as a combined approach with classroom-based training.

Research by the Institute of Management has shown that consistent training has a marked improvement on turnover. Smaller companies (with less than 100 employees) have increased formal training by 25% in only four years. Of these about 60% are reporting financial benefits.

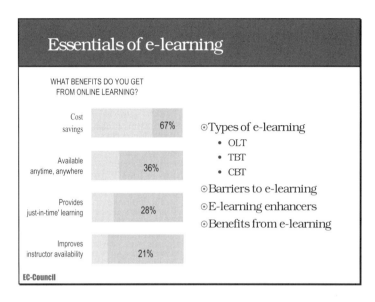

Essentials of E Learning

The climate of learning is changing, putting the learner in control of the experience (learner centered rather than tutor centered). This allows learning to be more involving, faster and effective.

Also eLearning provides flexibility, enabling: Just-in-time training when and where needed integration into the workplace for relevancy, access to experts and collaboration for team working.

It is only very recently that eLearning has become common parlance. Some of the terms that one may come across in this context are (not necessarily eLearning):

> ➤ On Line Training (OLT)

> ➤ Web Based Training (WBT)

> ➤ Technology Based Technology (TBT)

> ➤ Computer Based Technology (CBT)

Also one may come across these types of web sites for eLearning: portals, forums, and online catalogues

As we move toward a knowledge age, we are seeing the term e-learning used to described learning interventions such as Knowledge Management.

Some of the barriers to e-learning are: Easy Boredom outside confines of physical structures such as common classroom; requires self motivation on part of learner and lack of social stimulation of the classroom/ solitary environment.

Factors that can enhance e-learning are: Quality content, short, just in-time segments, organization culture that values e-learning, built in evaluations, holding managers accountable for success of employees and establishing on-line classroom communities.

e-learning brings proven benefits to businesses. Some of them are:

➢ Providing training with savings in both time and cost

➢ Improved effectiveness and efficiency.

➢ Encouraging staff to take responsibility for their own learning

➢ Flexible learning

➢ Staff is more motivated to learn organized learning delivered to suit their own circumstances

➢ With eLearning there are options for training at a place, time, pace and style to meet both business and learner needs.

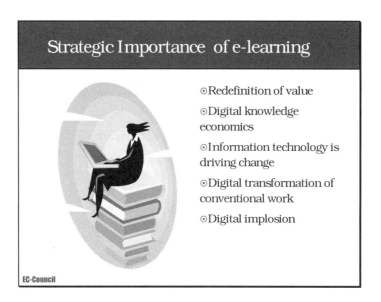

Strategic Importance of E Learning

The concept of the learning organization has grown exponentially with the technological era. Today, corporate learning and the learning organization have ascended to a position of strategic prominence in the context of managing and growing the enterprise. In the knowledge-based economy, there is a paradigm shift in the way education is viewed and delivered, and huge knowledge gaps as significant trends that have given rise to e-learning.

The increase in complexity and velocity of the work environment brought about by technological changes are also major issues that have fueled the demand for e-learning. During the shift from the industrial to the knowledge era, rapid technological change, the ever shortening product developmental cycles, lack of skilled personnel, enterprise resource planning, and migration towards a value chain integration and the extended enterprise have been prominent contributors to the e-learning value chain. The increasingly competitive global business environment has been central to the e-learning movement requiring companies to work together to create online networks of customers, suppliers, and value-added processes – that is, an ebusiness community (EBC).

The trends discussed above have given birth to several business issues that need to be quickly addressed if companies are to retain their competitive edge.

First, the redefinition of value must be addressed because wealth creation, communication, commerce and distribution converge on common digital, networked platforms. Industry boundaries blur, causing providers to rethink the basis of value creation.

Second, digital knowledge economics must be understood well because hoarding knowledge is typically counterproductive and nearly impossible. In the digital economy knowledge must be shared.

Third, information technology is driving change everywhere. Thus, every executive, in every industry, must embrace the pace and dynamics of the information technology industry.

Fourth, jobs, business processes, companies, and even entire industries face elimination or digital transformation. This means that customers will be gaining both tangible (quality and cost) and intangible benefits (information, control, relationships) while they contribute ever more value to the system.

Lastly, the digital implosion drives dis-aggregation and specialization, undermining the economic rationality of the vertically or horizontally integrated firm. Digital knowledge reduces the time and financial costs of information and coordination.

It is now economically feasible for large and diverse sets of people to have the information they need to make safe decisions in near real time. Thus, companies can increase wealth by adding knowledge value to a product through innovation, enhancement, cost reduction, or customization at each step in its life cycle.

The e-business forces discussed above set the stage for e-learning's strategic importance. As companies digitally transform their businesses, knowledge and training become rapidly obsolete, just-in-time training becomes a basic survival need, and identification of cost-effective ways of reaching a diverse global workforce becomes critical. Additionally, new learning models are needed given the skills gap and demographic changes. Flexible access to lifelong learning is highly desired. Managing organizational competency, providing employees with competency roadmaps, distributing latent knowledge within the organization, aligning business objectives and learning outcomes, and extending learning to value chain partners are bottom line e-business issues.

Validating outcomes directly with increased ROI, providing on-demand task related resources, rationalizing duplicative training, and reducing delivery costs and increasing organizational efficiency are also e-business related issues that write out the strategic importance of e-learning

Along with the e-business forces, there are several factors that facilitate the strategic importance of e-learning. Internet access, for example, is becoming a given at home and work.

Second, advances in digital technologies have and continue to enrich the interactivity and media content of the web.

Third, increasing bandwidth and better delivery platforms make e-learning feasible and attractive.

Fourth, a growing selection of high-quality e-learning products and services is now available.

Lastly, technology standards, which facilitate compatibility, and usability of e-learning products, are emerging. The Internet and its distributive architecture will, for the first time, give corporations the power to combine a series of discrete, unlinked and unmeasured activities into an enterprise-wide process of continuous and globally distributed learning that directly links business goals and individual learning outcomes.

<table>
<tr><td>

Effectiveness of e-Learning

- Staff are thoroughly prepared and competent as training is readily available at the right time and performance can be tested
- Learning at workplace/desk top is more relevant
- Each member of staff gets a consistent message
- Learning can be tailored to individual needs
- Tracking systems provide better management of learning
- Can link into human resource planning

EC-Council

</td></tr>
</table>

Effectiveness of E Learning

E-learning is here to stay as the fast changing pace of technology, the shortening product development cycles, lack of skilled personnel, competitive global economy, the shift from the industrial to the knowledge era, the migration towards a value chain integration and the extended enterprise, fuel it's strategic importance and realization. A recent study revealed that e-learning could indeed become the major form of training and development in organizations, as technologies will improve to create a fully interactive and humanized learning environment.

e-learning has enhanced effectiveness as:

➢ Staff is thoroughly prepared and competent as training is readily available at the right time and performance can be tested

➢ Learning at workplace/desk top is more relevant

➢ Each member of staff gets a consistent message

➢ Learning can be tailored to individual needs

➢ Tracking systems provide better management of learning

➢ Can link into human resource planning

A quite different set of technologies applies to the formation of tacit knowledge through learning, especially in the domain of on-line education or distance learning. Within organizations, on-line learning has the advantage of being able to be accomplished without travel and at times that are compatible with other work. A wide variety of tools and applications support distance learning.

Summary

- Knowledge differs from data, information and wisdom
- Organizations gain competitive advantage through continuous learning
- Knowledge can be tacit or explicit and there are four modes of knowledge transfer
- Knowledge is a strategic resource and individual learning must be capitalized in organizations
- E-learning is a popular form of knowledge sharing.

EC-Council

Summary

 Recap

➢ Knowledge differs from data, information and wisdom

➢ Organizations gain competitive advantage through continuous learning

➢ Knowledge can be tacit or explicit and there are four modes of knowledge transfer

➢ Knowledge is a strategic resource and individual learning must be capitalized in organizations

➢ E learning is a popular form of knowledge sharing.

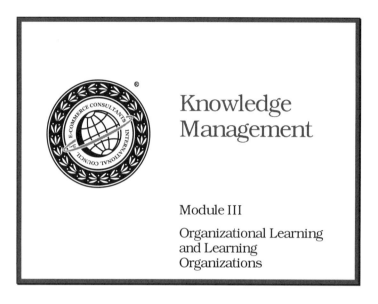

Module III

Organizational Learning
and Learning
Organizations

Knowledge Management (KM)

Module III: Organizational Learning and Learning Organizations

Exam 212-69 Certified e-Business Associate

Module Objectives

- Defining Organization Learning
- Motivation for Organization Learning
- Understanding a Learning Organization
- Five Disciplines of a Learning Organization
- Characteristics of a Organization that Learns
- Learning Strategies
- Related disciplines of Knowledge Management

EC-Council

Objectives

Module Objectives

On completion of this module, you will have gained insight into Organizational Learning and learning organizations. This module engages in discussing the following key areas:

➢ Defining Organization Learning

➢ Motivation for Organization Learning

➢ Understanding a Learning Organization

➢ Five Disciplines of a Learning Organization

➢ Characteristics of a Organization that Learns

➢ Learning Strategies

➢ Related disciplines of Knowledge Management

Defining Organizational Learning

All definitions of organizational learning have the learning process at its core. It has been variously defined as "process of detecting and correcting error", "use of learning processes" or simply "knowledge acquisition".

Knowledge acquisition or generation refers to the learning process as either incorporating knowledge from outside the organization or creating knowledge inside the organization. Nonaka and Takeuchi have dealt with the concept of organizational learning extensively.

For our purpose, we adopt the definition of organizational learning as a process of knowledge acquisition or generation of an organization, performed through individuals, which can be accomplished by teams. This definition is based on organizational memory that is expanded, and which can improve organizational actions.

Individuals are included as the prerequisite of organizational learning as stated in various literatures as "members of the organization act as learning agents for the organization" and "organizational learning ... happens in an interplay of individual and organization". Individuals are a necessary condition for organizational learning to take place; teams are a sufficient but very constructive condition.

Teams are included as a further part of the working definition given here. This is because although individual learning may benefit an organization, organizational learning differs from individual learning which may improve only the individual's knowledge of, and capacity to act either in their personal or work environment. Practically however, such teams are only a sufficient condition for organizational learning.

Organizational knowledge is seen only as a sufficient condition for organizational actions, as it does not necessarily lead to improved actions either because the expanded organizational knowledge is not conducive to improve actions or it is not in the organization's interest to improve its actions. Therefore it is implicit that organizational learning is a collective process dependent on interactions and the learning from inter-relationships, and that it comes from the synergy of healthy interactions between employees.

Organizations with a learning focus and knowledge creating organization are continually improving their capacity for analysis, decision-making, and action. It is a unique approach to understanding people, work and the environment surrounding the organization. Since every organization is a reflection of its efforts and accomplishments, it is essential to understand how people can use their skills to continuously reach their capacities and adapt to both internal and external change. Teams that master the tools of organizational learning find that mutual trust, extraordinary achievement, and synergy are all traits that define their success.

Organizational Learning Types - I

- Organizational learning can be distinguished between sourced externally (i.e. from outside to inside an organization) and internally (i.e. within an organization).
- External organizational learning means that an organization acquires or generates new knowledge in an organizational learning process
  - External organizational learning of implicit knowledge
    - insiders that turn into outsiders,
    - outsiders that become insiders,
  - External organizational learning of explicit knowledge
    - prepared material,
    - unprepared material,

EC-Council

Organizational Learning Types

Organizational learning can be broadly categorized as one that is sourced externally (i.e. from outside to inside an organization) and another sourced internally (i.e. within an organization). The prominent technology solutions that gain relevance here from an interaction perspective are Intranet, Extranets and Portals. However, this does not mean that other solutions are not significant.

External organizational learning is "inter-organizational learning", which involves learning from outside - other organizations. Organizations seeking to extend their value chains and involve their partners and collaborate in the knowledge initiatives have high degree of external organizational learning capabilities.

Inter-organizational learning concentrates on the learning of individuals and especially teams with members from other organizations. These teams can be mixed horizontally across different functional departments (cross-functional) as well as vertically across different hierarchical levels (cross-organizational). Enterprises that have several organizational units can also involve two (or more) organizations for joint product improvement, development or production.

External organizational learning can further take the form of:

  ➤ External organizational learning of implicit knowledge

  External organizational learning of implicit knowledge can normally only easily be transmitted directly through people and have the form of either:

- o Insiders that turn into outsiders, such as employees acquiring information from seminars, conferences, factory visits, social events or joint-development teams of different companies (normally for a short- to medium-term period).

- o Outsiders that become insiders, like information via consultants or coaches from consultancies, academia, customers, suppliers or other organizations; or new employees through hiring, acquisition, merger or joint venture (normally for a medium- to long-term period).

➢ External organizational learning of explicit knowledge.

External organizational learning of explicit knowledge, which is normally independent of people, can be divided into:

➢ Prepared material, from other organizations like technical reports and news, as well as other printed or stored material.

➢ Unprepared material, where further work needs to be completed so that it is useful, such as, e.g., database research or compiling of special studies.

Organizational Learning Types - II

⊙ Internal organizational learning means that an organization acquires or generates new knowledge inside the organization within an organizational learning cycle
- Internal organizational learning of implicit knowledge
  - individual work in an unstructured approach
  - team work in an unstructured approach
- Internal organizational learning of explicit knowledge
  - individual work in a structured approach
  - team work in a structured approach

EC-Council

The other broad category of organizational learning is internal organizational learning. Internal organizational learning represents "intra-organizational learning", which focuses on the learning within an organization. Again, this organizational learning takes place between individuals and/or teams, but within the organization.

Here, team learning is focused on the learning inside an organization, and this can happen not only on the same level within a department, but also in a vertical and/or a horizontal way, i.e. between different hierarchies and/or different departments.

Internal organizational learning can either have the form of:

➢ Internal organizational learning of implicit knowledge (or)

➢ Internal organizational learning of explicit knowledge.

Internal organizational learning of implicit knowledge, can be based on either:

➢ Individual work in an unstructured approach, like architect's ideas or spontaneous ideas, successes or mistakes of any employee's project, informal individual R&D; or

➢ Team work in an unstructured approach, like questioning assumptions, informal team R&D or pilot projects (i.e. project to test how something on a larger scale would work).

Internal organizational learning of explicit knowledge, which can normally be structured and divided into:

> ➢ Individual work in a structured approach, like systematic and formal individual R&D or employee suggestion systems; or

> ➢ Team work in a structured approach, like systematic and formal team R&D, team improvement systems for processes or formal dialogues.

Intranet, Groupware applications, Messaging and collaboration tools facilitate internal organizational learning.

The next section discusses the various levels of learning in an organization. This is essentially different from the types of learning discussed here, as the source and sink of the knowledge flow have been the primary differentiating factor.

In discussing the various levels of learning the primary focus is on the feedback mechanism built within the learning systems in the organization.

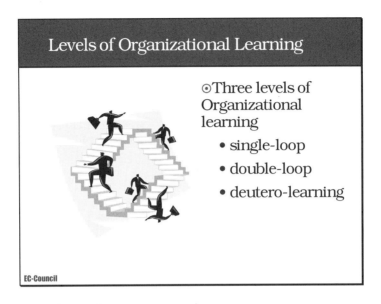

Levels of Organizational Learning

⊙ Three levels of Organizational learning
- single-loop
- double-loop
- deutero-learning

EC-Council

Levels of Organizational Learning

The primary level of organizational learning is the single-loop learning (also known as adjustment learning). Single loop learning occurs when the organization takes corrective action for any deviations registered from its set goal or objective. The scope of any deviation is restricted to a given set of fundamental variables. Therefore, single-loop learning is the adjustment of the consequences of organizational action that were originally not intended or planned.

Single-loop learning can also be described as a regulating loop in that it attempts to correct deviations detected. The significant point is that the fundamental values, are not altered, but only an improvement in effectiveness is attained through adjustment within the given frame, set by the organizational norms. Therefore, effectiveness is a measure for success of single-loop learning.

The second level of organizational learning is the double-loop learning. Here, the learner questions the underlying fundamental values in themselves, in order to attain optimal efficiency.

Double loop learning is also known as change learning. Double loop learning takes place when the fundamental operational values are questioned and changed, because the regulation of the learning process within the single loop learning process does not appear to be sufficient anymore. Thus, the organization's fundamental values, i.e. underlying norms, policies and objectives, are modified, which will lead to a different set of possible action.

The question of which new course of action is adopted, often depends on the stakeholders and the say they possess within the organization. However, the problem-solving capability of the organization is likely to increase every time double-loop learning takes place. Therefore, double-loop learning can also be described as an amplifying loop.

In most organizations, alternative problem solving has a chance to be accepted only if the members of the organization believe that they can more easily attain their targets by choosing the alternative. Probability for a change in the paradigm increase to the same extent as the gap between intended and actual results widens.

That means, if single-loop learning is no longer sufficient to reach the goal, or at least the minimum aim (survival), then the fundamental values are changed within the framework of double-loop learning. Both types of organizational learning can be analyzed through deutero learning, which is discussed next.

The third, and highest, organizational learning level of the organizational learning model is deutero-learning. Deutero learning is predominantly used for reflection about single-loop learning, and not double loop learning. In practice, however, organizational learning is normally limited to single-loop learning, and does not engage in double-loop learning.

A practical application of the three different learning levels would be the case of a typical manufacturing organization that finds too many service calls to attend with regard to its products. Single-loop learning would apply to the increase of scrutiny, which would be learning within the normal fundamental values. Double-loop learning would be a change towards organizational learning systems for employees or teams, and delegating the quality.

Deutero-learning try to learn from the analysis of the performance of learning on both levels and try to improve them, as well as implement the lessons learnt in other areas of the organization.

Single-loop learning, double-loop learning and deutero-learning, are divided by into four phases of an organizational learning cycle, which are discovery of problems, invention of a solution, production and evaluation, and generalization of outcome.

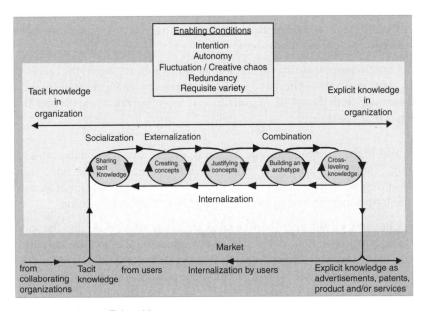

Source: Nonaka and Takeuchi

Motivation for Organization Learning

- The growing digital knowledge-based economy
- Increased demand for efficient, accurate service, to end-users as well as other internal and external clients and business partners
- Declining or constraints on budgets for budgets for capturing, maintaining, distributing and accessing of information
- Increased global competition
- The need for business innovation to achieve market share and differentiation
- Achieving operational efficiency
- The need to maximize human resources

EC-Council

Motivation for Organizational Learning

In the previous module we had discussed some of the reasons, benefits and challenges in Knowledge Management. Some of the business drivers behind knowledge management are discussed here.

> Declining or constraints on budgets for budgets for capturing, maintaining, distributing and accessing of information

> Customer intimacy- Cultivating relationships to gain customer knowledge: Delivering what specific stakeholders want

> Product leadership- this is about delivering the best products and services ---offerings that push performance boundaries. This is more so, due to the demands of the growing digital knowledge-based economy. The need for business innovation to achieve market share and differentiation is heightened due to increased global competition.

> Operational excellence – this involves delivering solid products and services at the best price and with the least inconvenience. This is due to increased demand for efficient, accurate service, to end-users as well as other internal and external clients and business partners.

> Employee capability – This seeks to leverage human intellectual capital in service design and delivery. There is an increased need to maximize human resource productivity, as there is a trend of declining head counts.

These can be further crystallized for specific industries or business segments.

Understanding a Learning Organization

⊙ A "Learning Organization" is one in which people at all levels, individually and collectively, are continually increasing their capacity to produce results they really care about.

⊙ A learning organization is skilled at creating, acquiring, and transferring knowledge, and at modifying its behavior to reflect new knowledge and insights.

⊙ The Learning Organization is an ideal, a vision. Various organizations or parts of organizations achieve this in varying degree.

EC-Council

Understanding a Learning Organization

Like Knowledge Management, the term 'learning organization' has been rendered several definitions. Peter Senge originally introduced it in his book 'The Fifth Discipline'.

Peter Senge in his book 'The Fifth Discipline' states that a learning organization is one that discovers "how to tap people's commitment and capacity to learn at all levels of the organization." The Fifth Discipline Field book defines a learning organization as an organization committed to "the continuous testing of experience and the transformation of that experience into knowledge." Learning organization has also been defined as a group of people continually enhancing their capacity to create what they want to create."

David Garvin, author of 'Building a Learning Organization,' Harvard Business Review defines a learning organization as one that is skilled at creating, acquiring, and transferring knowledge, and at modifying its behavior to reflect new knowledge and insights.

Other popular definitions are also included here for the reader's benefit.

➢ A learning organization is an organization skilled at creating, acquiring, and transferring knowledge, and at modifying its behavior to reflect new knowledge and insights. Organizational learning means the process of improving actions through better knowledge and understanding.

➢ A learning organization is an organization that has woven a continuous and enhanced capacity to learn, adapt and change into its culture. It's value, policies, systems and structures support and accelerate learning for all employees. This learning results in continuous improvement in all areas and successful business.

➢ A learning organization demands self-directed learning from their employees, promotes mentoring, coaching, facilitating, role-modeling and widens the concept of performance support to focus on outputs, not inputs.

➢ An entity learns if, through its processing of information, the range of its potential behaviors is changed. Organizations are seen as learning by encoding inferences from history into routines that guide behavior.

➢ Organizational learning is a process of detecting and correcting error.

➢ Organizational learning occurs through shared insights, knowledge, and mental models… [and] builds on past knowledge and experience – that is, on memory.

"The essence of organizational learning is the organization's ability to use the amazing mental capacity of all its members to create the kind of processes that will improve its own" (Nancy Dixon 1994)

"A Learning Company is an organization that facilitates the learning of all its members and continually transforms itself" (M. Pedler, J. Burgoyne and Tom Boydell, 1991).

Learning Organization

⊙ The term learning organization refers to an organization's capability of learning from its past experience.

⊙ To build a learning organization, it must tackle three critical issues:

(1) Meaning (determining a vision of the learning organization);

(2) Management (determining how the firm is to work); and

(3) Measurement (assessing the rate and level of learning).

EC-Council

Learning Organizations

We have seen the various definitions that have been rendered for a learning organization. A learning organization is an organization skilled at creating, acquiring, and transferring knowledge, and at modifying its behavior to reflect new knowledge and insights.

However, there are three Critical Issues that must be addressed before a company can truly become a learning organization:

For an effective implementation, managers first need to know what a learning organization is exactly. They need a reasonable, well-founded definition, which must be functional and easy to apply.

Next, there is the question of management that provides clear guidelines for practice filled with functional recommendations.

Thirdly, the assessment of appropriate tools to measure an organization's performance and the level of learning will be shown.

Measuring learning is critical. Learning curve is one time-tested measurement technique (i.e., costs expected to decline by some constant percentage each time cumulative production doubles. Half-life curves measure how long it takes to gain a 50% improvement on any metric, e.g., lead-time. While half-life curves can work on any output measure and are not confined to cost or price, they still focus solely on results. However, some types of knowledge take years to reflect visible changes in performance. Any measures focused only on results are unlikely to capture such learning. Hence, a more comprehensive framework is needed.

Organizational learning usually goes through 3 overlapping stages:

> ➤ Cognitive: members are exposed to new ideas, expand their knowledge, and begin to think differently.

> ➤ Behavioral: employees begin to internalize new insights and alter their behavior

> ➤ Performance improvement: changes in behavior leading to measurable improvements in results.

Because cognitive and behavioral changes typically precede improvements in performance, a complete learning audit must include all three.

Surveys, questionnaires, and interviews are useful for this purpose. At the cognitive level, they would focus on depth of understanding: have employees truly understood the concepts, or are the terms still unclear. To assess behavioral changes, surveys must be supplemented by direct observation. Finally, half-life curves or other performance measures are essential for ensuring that cognitive and behavioral changes have actually produced results.

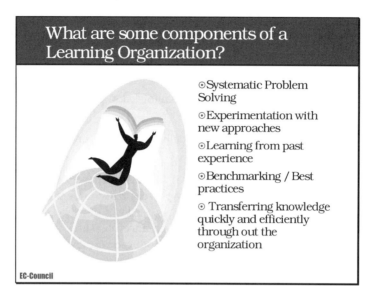

What are some components of a Learning Organization?

⊙ Systematic Problem Solving

⊙ Experimentation with new approaches

⊙ Learning from past experience

⊙ Benchmarking / Best practices

⊙ Transferring knowledge quickly and efficiently through out the organization

EC-Council

Activity Profile of Learning Organizations

 According to Garvin, learning organizations are skilled at five main activities:

➢ **Systematic problem solving**

Reliance on the scientific method for diagnosing problems ("Plan, Check and Act" cycle)

➢ **Experimentation with new approaches**

For example, Xerox's Problem-Solving Process

- o Identify and select problem
- o Analyze problem
- o Generate potential solutions
- o Select and plan the solution
- o Implement the solution
- o Evaluate the solution

➢ **Learning from past experience**

Companies must review their successes and failures, assess them systematically, and record the lessons in a form that employees find open and accessible.

➢ **Learning from the best practices of others**

Of course, not all learning comes from reflection and self-analysis.

According to one expert, "benchmarking is an ongoing investigation and learning experience that ensures that best industry practices are uncovered, analyzed, adopted, and implemented.

➢ **Transferring knowledge quickly and efficiently throughout the organization**.

For learning to be more than a local affair, knowledge must spread quickly and efficiently throughout the organization

Learning organization cultivate that art of open, attentive listening. Managers must be open to criticism

The stages of knowledge seen in learning organizations are (adapted from work by Ramchandran Jaikumar and Roger Bohn)

➢ Recognizing prototypes

➢ Recognizing attributes within prototypes

➢ Discriminating among attributes

➢ Measuring attributes

➢ Locally controlling attributes

➢ Recognizing and discriminating between contingencies

➢ Controlling contingencies

➢ Understanding procedures and controlling contingencies

What does a Learning Organization look like?

⊙ Organizational system learns as a whole,

⊙ People in organization recognize that ongoing, organization-wide learning is critical.

⊙ Learning is a continuous, process that is integrated with work.

EC-Council

Characteristics of a Learning Organization

Learning organizations are those that have in place systems, mechanisms and processes, that are used to continually enhance their capabilities and those who work with it or for it, to achieve sustainable objectives - for themselves and the communities in which they participate. Some of the characteristics of a learning organization are given below:

> ➢ Organizational system learns as a whole. People in the organization recognize that ongoing, organization-wide learning is critical.

> ➢ Learning is a continuous, process that is integrated with work. People in organization are driven by desire for continuous improvement

> ➢ Organization believes systems thinking is fundamental. This concept is detailed below.

> ➢ People in organization have access to important information and data resources.

> ➢ Organizational climate encourages and rewards individual and group learning. Workers are innovative in networking, both inside and outside organization.

> ➢ Organization embraces change and views failures as opportunities to learn and is agile and flexible.

> ➢ Aspiration, reflection, and conceptualization characterize organizational activities.

> ➢ Core competencies serve as launching points for new products/services. Organization continuously adapts and revitalizes in response to changing environments.

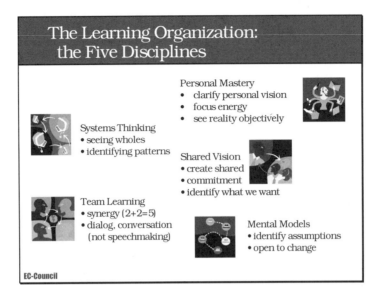

Five Disciplines of Learning Organizations

The five "learning disciplines" are a set of practices for building learning capabilities in organizations. Drawn from the fields of organizational learning, system dynamics, action science, "double-loop learning," process consultation, the creative orientation, dialogue, governance design, scenario planning, quantum physics, and ecology, the five disciplines were first codified by Peter Senge in his book The Fifth Discipline. Each of the disciplines represents a lifelong body of study and practice for individuals and teams in organizations.

> Personal Mastery: This discipline of aspiration involves formulating a coherent picture of the results people most desire to gain as individuals (their personal vision), alongside a realistic assessment of the current state of their lives today (their current reality).

Learning to cultivate the divergence between vision and reality can expand people's capacity to make better choices, and to achieve more of the results that they have chosen. In learning organizations the individual's personal and professional development are viewed as crucial to the organization's success.

Personal mastery means charting a course of development that leads to a special level of proficiency through life-long learning. This learning is not only in the areas related to the product or service of the organization but includes such areas as enhancing interpersonal competence, personal awareness, emotional maturity, and an enlarging understanding of the ethical/moral dimensions of organizational life.

This kind of personal mastery leads people to make a unique contribution because of their deepening understanding of and commitment to their personal vision expressed in concert with others pursuing personal mastery. Personal mastery must be pursued from a systems perspective if it is to be useful to the individual, the team, and the organization.

➤ Mental Models: This discipline of reflection and inquiry skills is focused around developing awareness of the attitudes and perceptions that influence thought and interaction. By continually reflecting upon, talking about, and reconsidering these internal pictures of the world, people can gain more capability in governing their actions and decisions.

One of the more powerful principles of this discipline is the "ladder of inference," which can show how people leap instantly to counterproductive conclusions and assumptions. Our responses to new situations are influenced by our ingrained assumptions and generalizations about how things work in organizations. These mental models enable us to rapidly size up new situations and take action and can be found at the individual, team, and organizational level. However, the problem is that sometimes these mental models are limiting or even dysfunctional and prevent adaptation that would strengthen the person, team, or organization.

In the learning organization mental models are freely shared, rigorously scrutinized, and revised as necessary at the personal, team, and organizational levels. If an organization is to become a learning organization it must overcome the fear or anxiety that prevents its members from challenging established ways of thinking and doing.

Some organizations may also have to overcome a "bias for action" that can prevent a more self-reflective appraisal. The mental models that survive scrutiny and prove most useful will be those that view the individual, the team, the organization, and its environment from a systems perspective.

➤ Shared Vision: This collective discipline establishes a focus on mutual purpose. People learn to nourish a sense of commitment in a group or organization by developing shared images of the future they seek to create, and the principles and guiding practices by which they hope to get there.

Goals, values, and missions will have the most impact on behavior in an organization if they are widely shared and owned by persons throughout the organization. This larger shared picture of the future emerges from the partial visions of individuals and teams.

A shared vision produces a much higher level of sustained commitment than is possible when the vision is imposed from above. Systems thinking is necessary in order for shared vision to translate into coordinated action involving all of the individuals and teams in an organization.

> 📋 <u>Team Learning</u>: This is a discipline of group interaction. Through techniques like dialogue and skillful discussion, teams transform their collective thinking, learning to mobilize their energies and actions to achieve common goals, and drawing forth an intelligence and ability greater than the sum of individual members' talents.

Teams exist in all organizations. They may be called departments, units, divisions, committees, etc. Often a person functions on several teams. For example a person may be part of the A Department, a member of D Committee, and a member of H Taskforce. Each of these team settings will have its own dynamic processes. Team learning has to do with improving the processes in a team to improve its effectiveness. Of particular interest is the phenomenon of defensive routines (activities that help a team avoid knowing) that can undermine learning by preventing a team from accurate appraisal of its processes and the consequences of those processes on the work of the team.

When effective processes are in place the team can engage in its primary task of providing a product/service. Team learning requires a systems perspective so that persons see themselves as interdependent with other team members and their team as interdependent with other teams that make up the larger organization.

> 📋 <u>Systems Thinking</u>: In this discipline, people learn to better understand interdependency and change, and thereby to deal more effectively with the forces that shape the consequences of our actions. Systems thinking is based upon a growing body of theory about the behavior of feedback and complexity - the innate tendencies of a system that lead to growth or stability over time.

Tools and techniques such as system archetypes and various types of learning labs and simulations help people see how to change systems more effectively and how to act more in tune with the larger processes of the natural and economic world. Persons in learning organizations engage in systems thinking as they view their role in their workteam, the role of their workteam in the organization, and the organization's relationship to the larger environment.

At the heart of systems thinking is an awareness of the interconnectedness (and varying levels of interdependency) of persons in teams, of teams in organizations, and organizations in the larger environment. To take a systems perspective also means to function individually and as part of a workteam to optimize the organization as a whole (even if that means that one's workteam subsystem is sub-optimized).

Learning organizations take these five very powerful ideas and pursue them simultaneously. Because the simultaneous pursuit of these is difficult, Peter Senge calls them "disciplines" in the sense that one has to deliberately and studiously attend to them in the course of functioning as a member of an organization.

The exercise of the five disciplines contributes to increased organizational effectiveness in carrying out its primary mission, greater capacity for organizational adaptation to changing internal and external environmental demands, a fuller utilization of the members' abilities and motivation, and higher level of job and personal satisfaction by organizational members.

The five disciplines described in the model focus primarily on the issues of "what is" a learning organization (LO) and not "how to" implement or develop the five disciplines in an organization.

However, on the practical side, questions arise -for example, how will an organization realize that it has attained its objective of being a learning organization. What concrete changes in behavior are required? What policies and programs must be in place?

The widely asked question is about whether Peter Senge's LO model will bring about value-for-money results. The five disciplines are quite clearly individual and team level learning tools and capacities.

However, in organizational science theory, there is always this question of levels of analysis issue —individual (and/or team) learning does not necessarily mean organizational learning nor does individual (and/or team) learning always translate to organizational learning.

For example, an employee can learn a lot during his project assignment but if he does not or cannot transfer the knowledge (especially tacit knowledge) to the incoming colleague who has to take over his responsibilities, the same mistakes can be repeated – at the organizational level, no learning appears to have taken place.

A proper implementation of Peter Senge's LO model can bring about enhanced individual and team learning capacities and to some extent a learning organization. Corporates might have to look at other models of learning organization bring about a more complete framework for organizational learning. For example, systematic problem solving, experimentation with new approaches, learning from their own experience and past history, learning from experiences and past practices of others, and transferring knowledge quickly and efficiently throughout the organization.

The primary difference between individual and organizational learning is that the latter involves an additional phase, dissemination, i.e., the transmission of information and knowledge among different persons and organizational units. LO would therefore need structures and processes to facilitate the quick dissemination of information and knowledge so that they are relevant and effectively used by other organizational members.

Characteristics of Organizations that Learn

- ⊙ Climate of openness and "organizational curiosity
- ⊙ tolerance for complexity and uncertainly
- ⊙ Leadership involved and supporting learning
- ⊙ Perceived performance gap between current and desired performance
- ⊙ Resources committed to quality learning
- ⊙ Organization measures progress
- ⊙ Systems perspective
- ⊙ Processes for maximizing flow of data, information, and people

EC-Council

Some of the common characteristics that mark a learning organization are discussed here.

The organization culture is an important factor that influences learning. Fostering a climate of openness and "organizational curiosity", including a safe environment which permits risk and failures, appreciation of diversity in learners, and tolerance for complexity and uncertainly enhances learning in organizations.

Leadership or champions of knowledge initiatives play a crucial role in nurturing a learning environment.

Organizations that are eager to learn should have an implicit desire to better their efficiency. There is a perceived performance gap between current and desired performance, and learning is sought to bridge this gap, in order to achieve efficiency.

Learning organizations have resources committed to quality learning, both continuously in rich community interactions, e.g. CoP's, CoI's, and episodically in learning events. This is explicitly communicated within the organization.

A learning organization finds it imperative to measure itself periodically to standards it has set within a given set of fundamental operational values. Organizations that measure progress are more inclined to facilitate a learning environment.

Other characteristics include adopting a systems perspective and having processes for maximizing flow of data, information, and people; an interactive rich environment, characterized by fluid movement of people between teams, CoP's, CoI's, and networks.

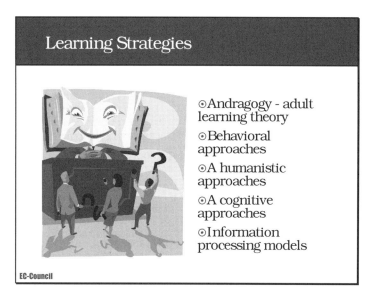

Learning Strategies

> Andragogy - adult learning theory

The andragogic model asserts that five issues be considered and addressed in formal learning. They include:

- o Letting learners know why something is important to learn,

- o Showing learners how to direct themselves through information,

- o Relating the topic to the learners' experiences.

- o People will not learn until they are ready and motivated to learn.

- o Requires helping them overcome inhibitions, behaviors, and beliefs about learning.

In essence adults prefer learning that is experiential, oriented to problem solving, and focused on useful and immediate value. They learn by doing. Also, adults prefer learning that is self-directed

> Behavioral approaches generally involve the following:

- o Breaking down the skills and information to be learned into small units.

o Regular employee work assessment and providing feedback as well as encouragement (reinforcement).

o Teaching "out of context." Employees can learn best when the focus is directly on the content to be taught. Behavioral instruction often takes the material out of the context in which it will be used.

o Direct or "instructor centered" instruction. Conferences, seminars, tutorials, drills, demonstrations, and other forms of controlled teaching tend to dominate behavioral classrooms.

The focus is on facts and learning strategies have specific steps and clear outcomes.

➢ Humanistic approaches to learning are also referred to as 'phenomenological' in approach, as they are almost entirely based on the subjective experience of individuals. Opposed to behavioral approach, which holds that individuals are acted upon by the external environment, humanistic approach believes that each individual acts upon his or her environment, making choices, setting goals, and generally 'self shaping' themselves and their personal worlds.

The focus on experiential learning and de-emphasizes cognitive or rote learning. The approach considers making errors and learning from errors to be beneficial.

➢ Cognitive approaches to learning/teaching with focus on what constitutes authentic learning and on role of the intuitive knowledge base.

The focus is on how learning occurs as well as on content. There is need for context for learning and establishing relationships with existing mental models.

➢ Information processing models approach learning with emphasis placed on memory. It seeks to leverage both short-term memory and long-term memory. The learning strategy is based on eliciting response generation and permitting action based on memory. The learning experiences enable acting on learning in memory.

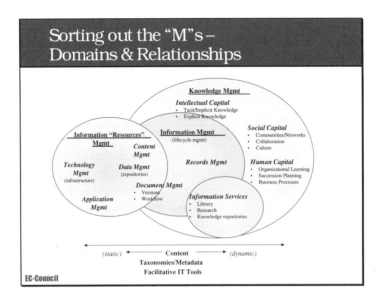

Sorting out Domains and Relationships

It is essential to understand the linkages between the various domains of management such as information management, information resources management, information services and knowledge management.

The above diagram illustrates the overlapping of domains as the nature of content progresses from static to dynamic.

Complimentary disciplines significantly impacting KM are:

> Management Sciences including Business Science, Information Management, Document Records Management, Organizational Development and Change Management

> Social Sciences including Psychology, Sociology, Cognitive Science, Learning, Ethnography and Social Informatics

> Technology and Science including Information Management, Information Technology, Artificial Intelligence, and Complex Adaptive Systems

> Library Science, Archivists

> Financial Management including Economics

Information resources management primarily caters to areas of infrastructure, application management, document management, technology applications such as data repositories and content management. The latter three are the overlapping functionalities between this management domain and that of knowledge management.

Information services can be considered to be a subset of knowledge management as the nature of areas dealt here, are contextual and gleaned from primary sources of knowledge. These include libraries, knowledge repositories and the area of research.

Information Management on the other hand deals with the information lifecycle and forms the intermediate link between information services and information resource management with that of knowledge management. This can also be considered to be a subset of knowledge management as it involves the creation, capture, synthesis, storage and dissemination of information, which forms the basis for the knowledge cycle.

Knowledge management by itself deals with three main areas viz., human capital, intellectual capital and social capital. These are detailed in the next slide.

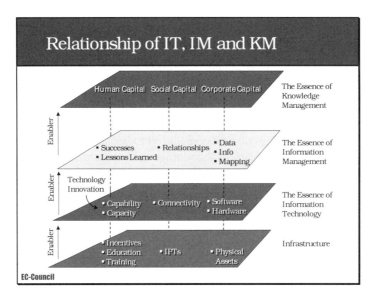

Relationship of IT, IM and KM

We had seen earlier that the three components that sum up the essence of knowledge management are human capital, social capital and intellectual capital. The figure above illustrates the linkages between each of these components as the organization progresses towards being a learning organization.

Human capital can be traced to training, incentives and education at the infrastructure level. These factors act as enablers to leveraging capability and building capacity in the human assets of the organization at the information technology maturity level. This forms the foundation of technology innovation. Enhanced capability and capacity in turn, act as enablers of success and critical lessons are learnt, which are captured as the essence of information management. These successes (or failures) and the lessons learnt during the life of the organization enable the formation of a human capital when perceived from a knowledge management perspective.

Similarly, social capital can be traced back to integrated product teams at the infrastructure level, enabling connectivity at the information technology level, which in turn fosters relationships at the information management level.

Corporate capital can be traced back to physical assets at the infrastructure level that facilitates the use of hardware and software at the information technology level. This in turn makes it possible to capture/ store data, process information and map them resulting in intellectual capital at the knowledge management level. Thus, human capital, social capital and intellectual capital can be influenced by various factors both within and external to the organization.

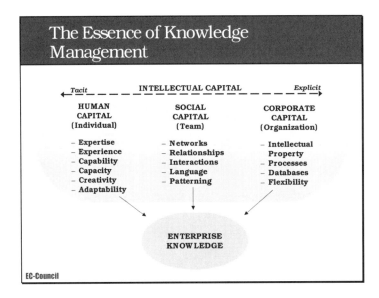

Essence of Knowledge Management

We had discussed the various factors that go into building the three essential components of knowledge management. Here, we shall discuss how these components contribute to the building and sustenance of enterprise knowledge.

Enterprise knowledge is synthesized from interplay of individual, team and organizational memory and knowledge.

o   For instance, expertise gained in individual capacity, based on an individual's unique experience and capability can be transformed into knowledge by harnessing his adaptability and creativity. This will form the human capital of the organization.

o   Similarly teams interactions – be it through networking, relationships or interactions can be captured and patterned to for the social capital of the organization.

o   Likewise, the flexibility of an organization in terms of its culture, it's unique processes, patents (IPR) and organizational memory stored in databases can contribute towards corporate capital.

These very elements discussed above go toward making an organization a learning organization and contribute towards creating the enterprise knowledge.

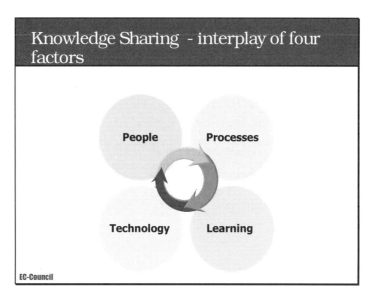

Knowledge Sharing

The success of any knowledge management initiative lies in sharing the knowledge. Knowledge sharing involves the interplay of people, processes, learning and technology. One of the challenges of knowledge management is that of getting people to share their knowledge. Why should people give up their hard-won knowledge, when it is one of their key sources of personal advantage? In some organizations, sharing is natural. In others the old dictum "knowledge is power" reigns.

Culture change is never easy and takes time. But cultures can be changed. Culture is defined in many ways, such as "commonly held beliefs, attitudes and values" (Institute of Personnel Development), "the collective programming of the mind that distinguished one group from another" (Geert Hofstede), and in many other ways that also embrace rituals, artifacts and other trappings of the work environment. These fundamental changes in assets and environment require matching changes in the way we manage. The shift from ownership of knowledge (individual or corporate) to sharing knowledge cannot occur unless cultures are changed at every level of the organization.

Cultures aren't born; they are created. Our cultures are products of the social environment we have been in - in this case, the fragmented professional and work environments of the Industrial Age. These cultures are not in themselves the problem but, rather, the red flags marking the underlying problems. Therefore to change people's actions you have to address the more fundamental underlying layers. This can be done as an organization-wide programme or in small groups or even individually.

People, Places and Things

What makes knowledge transfer so difficult is the fact that most of the valuable knowledge in an organization resides in people's minds. In a true sense, knowledge cannot be managed because it's a dynamic resource, not a passive asset. But the organization can manage an environment in which knowledge can flourish – and that involves interplay of people, places, and things.

Knowledge sharing cannot be achieved without bringing people together in virtual or actual meeting places – so they can form communities that foster knowledge generation. People create knowledge by becoming part of these communities and learning from their peers as they draw upon stores of recorded knowledge. People need places where they can create and act on knowledge. And people need things to help them meet their business goals.

The people can be employees, customers, suppliers, partners, or topic experts. Places represent the virtual workplaces where people come together to brainstorm, learn, and interact. The things are the data, information, and processes that are created, captured, classified, and shared across an organization.

The concept of place is equally important here as a stable notion of place has been fundamental to the way we live our lives; we build mental models of objects in spatial array around us in places; we go to places to do routine things; we put things in places for reasons; different individuals or organizations control what can and cannot be done in a place or put in a place; we all control some limited number of places and expect that things we put in those places will be there for us.

Hence, identifying and creating suitable places where people can share ideas, form communities, learn and find solutions to problems is vital for sharing knowledge.

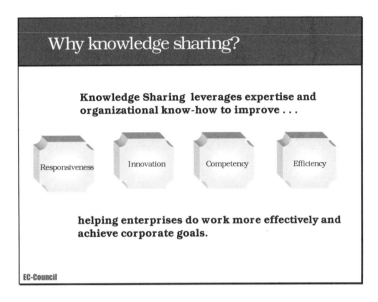

Reasons for Knowledge Sharing

Responsiveness

Knowledge sharing can enable an organization to build a knowledge base that acts as a catalyst for the shaping of and collaboration within and between organizations.

Internal responsiveness considers how quickly competencies can be translated into teams with the skills and tools to bring a product to market. During the first iteration of the Knowledge Chain (the Knowledge Chain is a continuous process) these are almost always small teams of no more than a dozen or so individuals who collaborate closely with a beat-the-clock attitude. These small teams are essential to internal responsiveness. A good knowledge management system allows them to quickly share knowledge and reconfigure themselves as the market demands.

Using enabling technology such as a community knowledge portal, employees can share information and expertise while working together, creating e-business communities. Through collaboration and sharing, employees can turn to internal sources to resolve problems and advance their own skills. Instinct is ultimately about the ability to respond to turbulence outside of the organization by making decisions without having to coordinate and consider all of the factors in a complex business and market environment.

Innovation

The companies that are most successful are the ones that can continue to obsolete their own products before their competitors do. They must assume that competitors will always be able to emulate what they do over time, and the only way that they can stay ahead is to innovate before their competitors, leaving them to play catch-up. These companies have developed a sense about themselves, their competencies, and their intellectual assets that sets them apart.

The timeliness and relevance of an organization's employees' knowledge are major competitive assets to the business in the dynamic new economy. The success of a company is often based on the knowledge that employees share and the innovation that they contribute. Therefore, identifying, organizing and filtering information to reach the proper audience is becoming increasingly important. By facilitating the sharing of knowledge, organizations can evolve into "Knowing Enterprises," due to their ability to "know" when and how to make the right moves in rapidly changing markets, and their vigilance in learning new ways to turn competency into an endless stream of new product.

Competency

Organizations with a rigid functional structure most often define their core competency as their products and services, not their skills. The conventional question has been 'How can we position our products (or product lines) for competitive advantage?' This has changed to, 'What critical skills should we develop to be best in the world from our customers' viewpoint?' The former builds current profits, the latter builds long-term preeminence. Knowledge sharing improves the competency of employees and in turn builds the skills necessary to succeed.

Efficiency

High employee turnover rates and the resulting loss of valuable knowledge, insights and skills can be costly to an organization. Undertaking knowledge sharing activities can help the organization build a repository for team-generated work - including reports, proposals, lessons learned and learning materials.

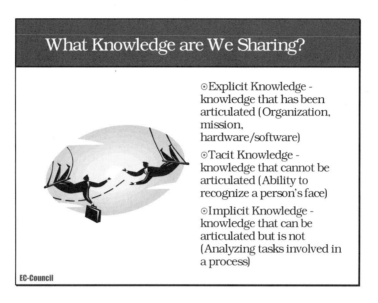

What Knowledge are We Sharing?

⊙Explicit Knowledge - knowledge that has been articulated (Organization, mission, hardware/software)

⊙Tacit Knowledge - knowledge that cannot be articulated (Ability to recognize a person's face)

⊙Implicit Knowledge - knowledge that can be articulated but is not (Analyzing tasks involved in a process)

EC-Council

Types of Knowledge shared

We had discussed the types and categorization of knowledge. How do these knowledge types relate to the concept of knowledge sharing?

All categories of knowledge are crucial to an organization and instances of such knowledge sharing are discussed here.

➤ Tacit knowledge is the hardest one to tap. This is the category of knowledge that cannot be articulated (Ability to recognize a person's face). This is especially important as ideas, processes, information are taking a growing share of global trade from the traditional, tangible goods of the manufacturing economy.

➤ Explicit Knowledge is codified knowledge, such as that in memos and manuals. This is the category of knowledge that has been articulated (Organization, mission, hardware/software)

➤ Implicit Knowledge - knowledge that can be articulated but is not (Analyzing tasks involved in a process)

The challenge before the organization is to create and share new knowledge that moves from tacit to explicit so others can use it.

"Our problem as an organization is that we don't know what we know" is often echoed statement in KM discussions. Large global or even small geographically dispersed organizations do not know what they know. Expertise learnt and applied in one part of the organization is not leveraged in another. The true challenge of knowledge sharing is to 'Know what we know.'

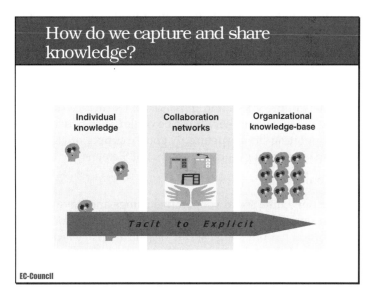

Capturing and sharing knowledge

The context of this discussion is in line with the 'culture' aspect of knowledge management. Here are some activities that might be used to plan and induce change:

A culture audit that involves conducting questionnaires, interviews and team sessions with a cross-section of the organization may be undertaken. This is especially helpful in finding out the difference between what is articulated as the desired culture and what is done (e.g. "we put quality first" but at the same time the organization ships out less than perfect products at the end of a financial quarter to "make the numbers"). It is also common to find several sub-cultures that conflict with overarching goals.

➢ Challenge 'improper' behavior - if you identify people hoarding knowledge unnecessarily: challenge them; though avoid "knowledge rage".

➢ Involvement - some of the best knowledge sharing cultures are where everybody (even novices and newcomers) believes that their knowledge is respected, valued and used to make informed decisions.

➢ Use of role models - identify those people whose behaviors are an example to others. Celebrate and publicize them. Involve them with other groups.

➢ Team-building / organization development sessions - at regular team meetings, allocate time to understand and improve internal processes; too many meetings are task and output focused, but fail to address the means of achieving successful outcomes.

> ➢ Align rewards and recognition to support appropriate behaviors - too many schemes are based on seniority or individual expertise, rather than team effectiveness.

> ➢ Change people - move the knowledge sharers around; get industrial psychologists and behavioral experts on board, it is quality of leadership that will enable all the other culture change techniques to achieve their aims.

📋 Finally, remember that culture goes hand in hand with structure (roles and responsibilities). At every level within the organization, there must be congruence between objectives, structures, processes, people and supporting infrastructure. A good example of changing culture alongside an evolving knowledge management programme is that of Siemens

Challenging Through Co-opetition

Human beings are at the same time social cooperative beings and have a competitive streak. We all like to do better than our peers and excel in something. Yet, in today's complex world, we need help from them to achieve our aims. In an organization, lack of competition - both for individuals and teams - leads to complacency. But competition must be done in a healthy manner. Some things to consider:

> ➢ In early stages of product development, don't simply approve one line of approach. Have several "competing" projects under way but make sure there are mechanisms to exchange knowledge and challenge / encourage each "runner" e.g. through people sharing, peer reviews etc.

> ➢ Continually benchmark internal processes and functions with other organizations and potential suppliers. Encourage them to strive for improvement through learning from each other.

> ➢ Introduce 'competitions', such as the "knowledge champion of the year", the "innovators team award", but invite everybody to the award ceremonies.

> ➢ Compete, not against other people or teams, but set goals vs. challenging targets or external competitors.

> ➢ Above all, let the apparent losers of such competitions share in success, celebrate what they have achieved, and make them feel part of the winning team (the wider organization).

Commitment

Organizations need to create a commitment to culture, to change, to challenge, to compete and cooperate. If, as is often the case, time pressure leads to poor knowledge sharing, then there must be a commitment to allow time for it to happen. Allocate 5 per cent of a project's resources to distilling lessons and sharing. Include time to contribute to knowledge development and sharing in people's job goals (and in the accompanying reward system). Build commitment into team processes.

Commitment to knowledge sharing must be demonstrated throughout the organization. It is apparent through what the leaders of the organization say and do. It is shown by commitment in the organizations' processes, reward systems, and development programmes etc. It is, above all, shown by individuals throughout the organization being committed to share their knowledge with others even if it is not formally part of their job.

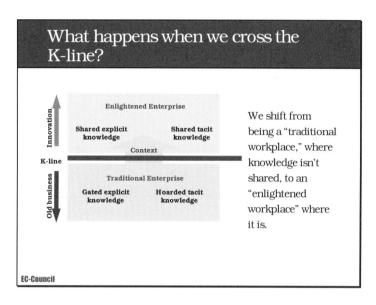

Marvin Minsky, in his work "The Society of Mind," introduced the concept of K-Lines (Knowledge – lines. Minsky's K-lines (knowledge—lines) are the essential construct in his theory of cognition in which knowledge—lines link mental "agents", his term for the simplest of mental processes, into larger agencies and societies, and on up to the society of mind.

From an organization perspective the agents of the organization K-line would be its tacit and explicit knowledge assets. Learning is a process that creates new levels of connections—new "administrative ways" of using already learned societies of mental agencies. This is the "Papert Principle", named for Seymour Papert in the Society of Mind theory.

The Papert Principle suggests that along with developmental changes in cognitive growth, we add levels of connections—new ways of organizing what we already know. These he calls "administrative levels".

As a consequence, we realize that group knowledge is more powerful than individual knowledge. And knowledge sharing brings about organizational learning, transforming a traditional enterprise into an enlightened one.

Both tacit and explicit knowledge has to be shared to achieve a higher level of learning. This brings about a shift from being a "traditional workplace," where knowledge isn't shared, to an "enlightened workplace" where it is.

Why People don't share

"Not invented here" syndrome - this is more common. People have pride in not having to seek advice from others and in wanting to discover new ways for themselves.

Not realizing how useful particular knowledge is to others - an individual may have knowledge used in one situation but be unaware that other people at other times and places might face similar situations. Additionally, knowledge derived for one need may be helpful in totally different contexts; or it may be a trigger for innovation - many innovative developments come from making knowledge connections across different disciplines and organizational boundaries.

"Knowledge is power" - but how true is this really? In today's enterprise, where so much depends on teamwork and collective knowledge, it is only a handful of people who have knowledge for which they can hold their peers and bosses to ransom. It might be the owner-manager of a small company not wanting to lose trade secrets; it may be a particular specialist who has been in the organization many years and built up his or her own unique way of achieving success without perhaps even understanding the deep tacit knowledge of how they do it.

Lack of time - There is pressure on productivity, on deadlines, and it's a general rule that the more knowledgeable an individual is, the more there are people waiting to collar him/her for the next task. How can such an individual possibly find time to add his /her lessons learnt to the knowledge database or have a knowledge sharing session with his/her colleagues?

Other barriers cited by experts include functional silos, individualism, poor means of knowledge capture, inadequate technology, internal competition and top-down decision making. Generally, a mix of structural and infrastructure barriers is exacerbated by the predominance of human ones - social, behavioral and psychological.

Why People share

As there are reasons for people not to share their knowledge, so are there reasons why they do share knowledge. Some of them are discussed below:

➢ They take pride in their expertise. Knowledge is a perishable. Knowledge is increasingly short-lived. If you do not make use of your knowledge then it rapidly loses its value.

➢ They want to contribute to the common good. Even with the low level of knowledge sharing that goes on today – if you do not make your knowledge productive than someone else with that same knowledge will. You can almost guarantee that whatever bright idea you have someone else somewhere in the organization will be thinking along the same lines.

➢ They wish to learn and they expect others to reciprocate. By sharing one's knowledge, one can gain more than one can lose. Sharing knowledge is a synergistic process – one gets more out than one puts in. For instance, if you share a product idea or a way of doing things with another person – then just the act of putting your idea into words or writing will help you shape and improve that idea. If you get into dialogue with the other person then you'll benefit from their knowledge, from their unique insights and improve your ideas further.

➢ They enjoy interacting with peers as their culture encourages sharing. They are loyal to the organization. To get most things done in an organization today requires a collaborative effort. If you try to work alone – you are likely to fail – you need not only the input from other people but their support and buy-in. Being open with them; sharing with them, helps you achieve your objectives.

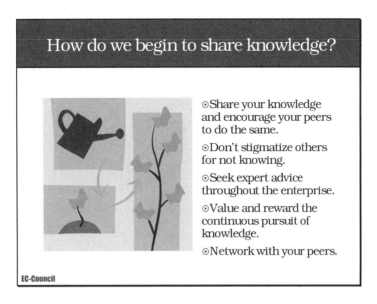

How to share knowledge

What can be done at an individual level to facilitate knowledge sharing and create a learning organization?

People in general feel overwhelmed by the broadness of the topic, do not know how to communicate the value of knowledge management and sharing to their superiors, and do not know where to start. This confusion expresses itself through the following three questions that typically arise at the beginning of any knowledge management/sharing project:

1. Which concrete activities are referred to under the name of knowledge sharing and how do they relate to each other?

2. How can top management be convinced that knowledge-sharing activities are instrumental to reach business goals?

3. How can knowledge sharing be introduced effectively into an organization?

The answer usually lies in walking the talk.

> ➢ Share your knowledge and encourage your peers to do the same.

> ➢ Don't stigmatize others for not knowing.

> ➢ Seek expert advice throughout the enterprise.

> ➢ Value the continuous pursuit of knowledge.

Review and deal with mistakes without assigning blame: Groups won't learn from their mistakes if the same interactions are being used to fix blame, keep score, or humiliate them.

Knowledge Sharing

- ⊙ "Sharing knowledge is not about giving people something, or getting something from them. That is only valid for information sharing. Sharing knowledge occurs when people are genuinely interested in helping one another develop new capacities for action; it is about creating learning processes." (Senge)

- ⊙ Knowledge sharing must be championed and embraced at all levels of an organization

- ⊙ Knowledge sharing is not something "to do" but a way "to be"

EC-Council

'Those of you who have something intelligent to say now have a forum in which to say it. Those of you who will not or cannot contribute also become obvious. If you are not willing to contribute or participate, then you should understand that the many opportunities offered to you in the past will no longer be available'

- Bob Buckman

To summarize the discussion on knowledge sharing,

➢ "Sharing knowledge is not about giving people something, or getting something from them. That is only valid for information sharing. Sharing knowledge occurs when people are genuinely interested in helping one another develop new capacities for action; it is about creating learning processes." (Senge)

There can be several approaches to knowledge sharing. There is no one "right" solution. All knowledge sharing initiatives should begin with a value proposition to get widespread endorsement. Knowledge sharing is about people primarily and this should form the basis for any programs. It is therefore critical to identify human networks

➢ Knowledge sharing must be championed and embraced at all levels of an organization

Organization culture must employ organizational learning and fit technology to people and not vice-versa. The ideal approach would be to start small and gradually expand in alignment with the business strategy

➢ Knowledge sharing is not something "to do" but a way "to be"

Knowledge Sharing Initiatives – Private Sector Sampling

- ⊙ Ford Motor Company
  - COP-driven innovations/process improvements
- ⊙ Charles Schwab
  - Small projects, natural language search tool
- ⊙ Dow
  - Intellectual Asset Model
- ⊙ Xerox
  - Eureka - Technicians knowledge sharing database
- ⊙ 3M
  - Leveraging knowledge bases for innovation

EC-Council

Examples from the Private Sector

Ford: When faced with cutbacks, the company shifted from general knowledge sharing to immediate paybacks and standard setting. They allowed innovations or process discoveries from communities of practice (COP) to become standards. $4.5 million were accrued as benefits in the first 6 months.

Charles Schwab: This corporate adopted metadata standard, and used existing tools to develop taxonomy, and established organizational structure that included a KM forum as support and communication medium. Their natural language search tool reduced volume of calls and email resulting in $125,000/month savings, resulting in a payback in less than one year.

Dow: Took an evolutionary approach to change and started with patents and increased the value of its patents by more than 400% resulting in savings of excess of $50 million related to tax obligations and other costs over ten years. They created an Intellectual Asset Model (IAM) with six phases: strategy, competitive assessment, classification, valuation, investment, and portfolio.

Xerox: The document company created a technicians database creating a savings of $7m.

Knowledge Sharing Initiatives – Public Sector Sampling

⊙ Department of Veterans Affairs
  • Online water cooler for patient advocates
⊙ DoD Electronic College
  • After Action Reviews
⊙ World Bank (Knowledge Sharing vs. KM)
  • Leader in embracing "people" aspects of KM (e.g. story telling)
  • Concept of knowledge as a service commodity
⊙ GAO
  • External audit community (AGNet, Audit Forums, US AuditNet)
  • Eagle (Electronic Assistance Guide for Leading Engagements)
  • National Preparedness "Portal", Virtual Library
  • Knowledge/skills inventory system, Organizational learning initiative

EC-Council

Examples from the Public Sector

<u>VA</u> – The department of Veterans Affairs sought to architect an "Online water cooler" which now has over three hundred national patient advocates. Users maintained best practices database, discussion groups, and experts' teleconferences. This has resulted in better morale and lower turnover.

<u>DoD</u> – The department of defense conceived a electronic College – "gateway model virtual domain dedicated to sharing knowledge". After Action Reviews (AAR) – debriefing sessions - troop experiences are recorded in digitized sound / visual media and "delivered to any soldier who would benefit from access"

<u>World Bank</u> – A well-known knowledge management practitioner, the World Bank has a well-known knowledge and learning Program. Knowledge is considered as a service commodity and there exists active partnering / sharing with clients (e.g., Development Marketplace, Distance Learning Network)

<u>GAO</u> - Examples from the External audit community (AGNet, Audit Forums, US AuditNet), Eagle (Electronic Assistance Guide for Leading Engagements), National Preparedness "Portal", Virtual Library, Knowledge / skills inventory system, Organizational learning initiative.

NPT – Matrixed across GAO, has a Knowledge base for legislative initiatives and analysis, ongoing jobs, agency/Hill contacts, and targeted links to virtual library (daily searches and updates).

(Source: KM.Gov)

Recommendations for sharing knowledge

➢ Integrate into Business strategy and daily work.

For instance, GAO's Strategic Plan states its Strategic objective as "Leverage GAO's Institutional Knowledge and Experience"

The performance goals have been stated as 1) World Wide Web knowledge tool, 2) manage organizational knowledge, 3) strengthen national and international relationships.

➢ Provide a trusting organizational environment

Knowledge sharing / Social Capital / HC are investments and must be ingrained as organizational values. Organizations must be willing to make a long-term resource commitment – and stay with it.

➢ Provide time to engage in knowledge sharing

The importance of "face time" cannot be overemphasized to nurture a knowledge-sharing environment in the organization.

➢ Provide consistent and continual championship.

For instance – Institute a CKO position, brand the company as a knowledge-based organization

➢ Institutionalize learning

Show commitment to human capital values, and make organizational learning as a way of work. Examples of such organizations are:

o   The World Bank spends three percent of its budget to transform itself from a lending to a knowledge bank.

o   GSA uses 'lessons learned' in one area to improve operations throughout the enterprise.

o   US Navy implemented KM because admirals want seamen to be able to make decisions on their own during a crisis.

o   KM saved BP/Amoco millions of dollars, and reduced operational time from hundred days to forty-two days for drilling deep water wells.

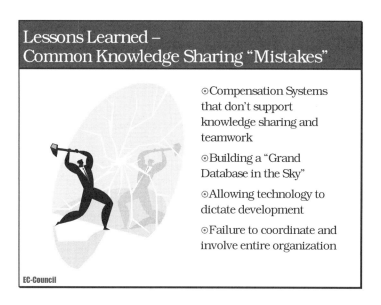

**Lessons Learned –
Common Knowledge Sharing "Mistakes"**

⊙ Compensation Systems that don't support knowledge sharing and teamwork

⊙ Building a "Grand Database in the Sky"

⊙ Allowing technology to dictate development

⊙ Failure to coordinate and involve entire organization

EC-Council

Pitfalls to Avoid

Knowledge management advocates 'learning from other's experience'. In the same spirit we shall discuss some of the fallacies that organizations have committed that has hindered sharing of knowledge.

➢ Compensation systems – When Performance appraisals, bonuses, etc are focused on rewarding the individual rather than the team, it hinders any sharing of knowledge.

➢ Grand database – Often organization mistake technology to be the panacea for knowledge sharing. With no apparent value or incentives for participation, such initiatives are either abandoned midway or end up as inaccessible islands of information.

➢ Technology – This relates to organizations experimenting with new technology or technology that has not matured. Not only does this alienate the users who may be at a loss to use the system, this can also be a case of reinventing the wheel - i.e., the technology component

➢ Failure to coordinate – Knowledge sharing is not personality driven. An example is from the U.S. Postal Service. Both the IT department and HR department had pursued developing a knowledge management process until they discovered each other's efforts by accident. A Corporate (and not singular CKO) Perspective is a critical requirement. Another example is the infamous Ford-Bridgestone fallout that occurred due to failure to share relevant knowledge and resulted not only in monetary loss but also cost a long-standing partnership.

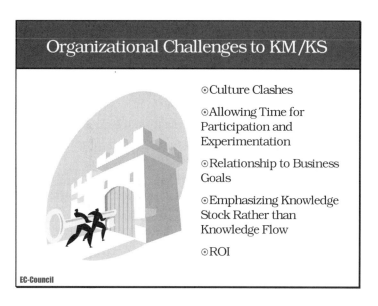

Organizational Challenges

➢ Culture "rules" - Organization has to have clearly defined institutional values. Sharing should be a key institutional value to avoid organizational silos.

➢ Time and commitment are critical to staying on the course with consistency. This means allowing for participation. This can be achieved through story telling, increasing face time and trust building activities.

➢ Business Goals – Any knowledge sharing initiative should be mapped with business goals for easy and widespread adoption.

➢ Often, organizations misplace the focus on the knowledge it has stored, rather than its use or reuse. The emphasis has to be on the flow of knowledge through the organization and not the organizational silos accumulated.

➢ ROI – How can an organization value its knowledge sharing? Most organizations commit the mistake of putting the measurement cart before the knowledge horse.

Often returns can be seen as value-added research time, reuse of data sources (past projects), time to complete engagements and consequences of not doing it.

Summary

- ⊙ Organizational learning is key to survival in the knowledge based economy
- ⊙ Five disciplines of organizational learning exists
- ⊙ Strategies for learning should be adopted according to organization needs
- ⊙ Essence of knowledge management is social capital, human capital and intellectual capital
- ⊙ Knowledge must be shared for increased responsiveness, innovation, efficiency and competency.

EC-Council

Summary

 Recap

➢ Organizational learning is key to survival in the knowledge-based economy

➢ Five disciplines of organizational learning exists

➢ Strategies for learning should be adopted according to organization needs

➢ Essence of knowledge management is social capital, human capital and intellectual capital

➢ Knowledge must be shared for increased responsiveness, innovation, efficiency and competency.

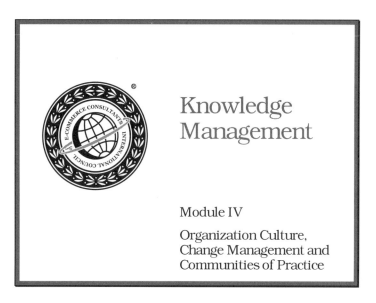

Knowledge
Management

Module IV

Organization Culture,
Change Management and
Communities of Practice

Knowledge Management (KM)

Module IV: Organizational Culture, Change Management and Communities of Practice

Exam 212-69 Certified e-Business Associate

Module Objectives

- Understanding Knowledge Flows
- Significance of Organization Culture
- Culture Aspect of Knowledge Management
- Addressing Change Management in Knowledge Management
- Concepts of Knowledge Sharing and Transfer
- Knowledge Workers – Roles
- Knowledge Collaboration in Groups and Teams
- Communities of practice
- Storytelling as a KM strategic theme.

EC-Council

Objectives

☞ Module Objectives

After completing this module you will be familiar with

➢ Knowledge flows and knowledge networks

➢ Comprehending the significance of organization culture

➢ The culture aspect of knowledge management

➢ Change management in knowledge management

➢ Concepts of knowledge sharing and transfer

➢ Knowledge workers and their roles

➢ Knowledge collaboration in groups and teams as illustrated by communities of practice

➢ Storytelling as a KM strategic theme.

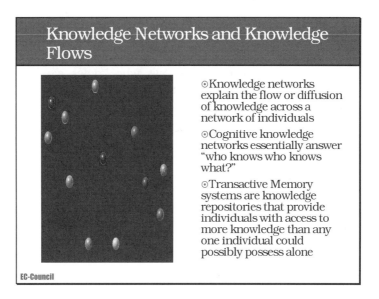

Knowledge Networks and Knowledge Flows

⊙ Knowledge networks explain the flow or diffusion of knowledge across a network of individuals

⊙ Cognitive knowledge networks essentially answer "who knows who knows what?"

⊙ Transactive Memory systems are knowledge repositories that provide individuals with access to more knowledge than any one individual could possibly possess alone

EC-Council

Knowledge Flows and Networks

Knowledge networks (Contractor N.S et.al) explain the flow or diffusion of knowledge across a network of individuals. For instance, in an organization different individuals possess different types of knowledge, and that knowledge may be shared with others.

The fast economy requires flexible, adaptive structures that self-organize internally in response to changes externally. In this knowledge-critical economy we need charts to show us 'who knows what' and as a complement 'who knows who'. In addition to pictures of hierarchy we need visualizations of the massive interconnectivity that occurs in the learning systems that are our organizations. In essence, knowledge networks represent "who knows what" in an organization.

If one illustratively represented the knowledge network it might show spheres (or nodes) that represent individuals in the organization, groups in the organization, or the organization itself. The links that develop, and some times dissolve, represent shared knowledge including interests, skill sets, expertise, workflows, and talents.

Organizational Network Analysis [ONA] is a software-supported methodology that reveals the real workings of an organization. It uses the rigor of systems analysis to reveal the behavior inside and between organizations. Knowledge networks are mapped that uncover interactions within and across the boundaries of the organization. These visualizations are business analogies to x-rays of how things actually get done, which is evidence of adaptation in the organization. ONA exhibits both how knowledge is shared in emergent communities of practice, and how it is utilized in key business processes. It helps uncover the hidden dynamics that support learning and adaptation in the modern organization.

While knowledge networks describe who knows what, each individual in the organization also has his/her own perception of who knows what, or a cognitive knowledge network. Cognitive knowledge networks essentially answer "who knows who knows what?" and vary in their accuracy and completeness. Cognitive knowledge networks are accurate to some extent depending on the degree to which the individuals who are perceived to be knowledgeable say they actually do possess knowledge in the appropriate areas.

Transactive memory systems are a shared cognitive resource for members of a group or team. (Hollingshead, et al)

Essentially, TM systems are knowledge repositories that provide individuals with access to more knowledge than any one individual could possibly possess alone. Transactive Memory Theory examines the process by which individuals determine 'who knows what and who knows who knows what'.

It is an important vehicle for leveraging knowledge networks and gaining access to others' knowledge that may be needed to complete a project one individual cannot complete alone. Additionally, TM systems reduce the time and energy spent learning since they can be accessed to get needed knowledge rather than making every individual learn everything needed to complete a work related project. Furthermore, when individuals work to develop their TM system and can identify who knows what (i.e., identify experts in different knowledge areas) they make better use of knowledge possessed by the group and their groups make decisions more effectively and out perform groups that do not try to develop their TM system.

Transactive Memory systems are developed through four interrelated processes (Wegner & Moreland)

- Expertise recognition - Expertise recognition is the process where each individual determines who the experts are in various knowledge areas.

- Retrieval coordination - Through retrieval coordination, each individual uses his/her perception of who knows what, to contact others in the organization and to retrieve the knowledge needed to complete a task.

- Directory updating - After retrieving the needed knowledge, based on the usefulness and accuracy of the retrieved knowledge, individuals reevaluate the people they perceive to be experts through the process of directory updating.

- Information allocation - Finally, through the process of information allocation, when individuals get incoming information (such as email, news paper articles, listserv addresses) that information will be passed to the individual who is perceived to possess the most expertise in that area. This way, the experts are responsible for storing and maintaining knowledge in specific areas that will be available for others to access if need be.

Social Network Analysis (SNA)

⊙ Social network analysis is focused on uncovering the patterns of people's interconnectedness and interactions.

⊙ The success or failure of organizations and societies may depend on these patterns. Analysis can produce understanding as well as action.

⊙ Applications and current use of SNA is broad and diverse:
  • Knowledge Management
  • Organizational Development
  • Research in economics, social sciences

EC-Council

Social Network Analysis

 Social network analysis [SNA] (Valdis Krebs) is the mapping and measuring of relationships and flows between people, groups, organizations, computers or other information/knowledge processing entities. The nodes in the network are the people and groups while the links show relationships or flows between the nodes. SNA provides both a visual and a mathematical analysis of human relationships.

The metrics used in this context are as detailed below:

➢ Degrees - Degrees denote the number of direct connections a node has and indicates the network activity for a node

➢ Betweenness – Betweenness depicts the transient proximity a node has when considered with a pair of nodes. A node with high betweenness has great influence over what flows in the network.

> Closeness – Closeness marks the proximity of a node to another. They indicate the shortest path between two nodes. They are in an excellent position to monitor the information flow in the network and have the best visibility into what is happening in the network

> Boundary spanners – These are nodes that connect their group to other groups and usually end up with high network metrics. They are well positioned to be innovators, since they have access to ideas and information flowing in other clusters. They are in a position to combine different ideas and knowledge into new products and services.

> Peripheral players – These nodes are often connected to networks that are not currently mapped making them very important resources for fresh information not available inside the company.

> Network Centralization - Individual network centralities provide insight into the individual's location in the network. The relationship between the centralities of all nodes can reveal much about the overall network structure. One or a few very central nodes dominating the network characterize a very centralized network. If these nodes are removed or damaged, the network quickly fragments into unconnected sub-networks.

> Highly central nodes can become critical points of failure. A network centralized around a few well-connected hubs can fail abruptly if those nodes are disabled or removed. Unlike a centralized network, one or a few nodes do not dominate a network with a low centralization score. Such a network has no single points of failure. It is resilient in the face of many intentional attacks or random failures, in that many nodes or links can fail while allowing the remaining nodes to still reach each other over other paths. Networks of low centralization fail gracefully.

 Other metrics include:

> Structural Equivalence - determine which nodes play similar roles in the network

> Cluster Analysis - find cliques and other densely connected clusters

> Structural Holes - find areas of no connection between nodes that could be used for advantage or opportunity

> E/I Ratio - find which groups in the network are open or closed to others

> Small Worlds - find node clustering, and short path lengths, which are common in networks exhibiting highly efficient small-world behavior

The success or failure of organizations and societies may depend on these patterns. Analysis can produce understanding as well as action. Some of the areas of applications and current use of SNA is broad and diverse such as knowledge management, organizational development, and research in economics and social sciences.

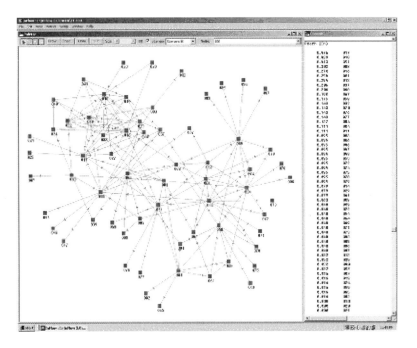

Above: Screenshot of Inflow showing network mapping

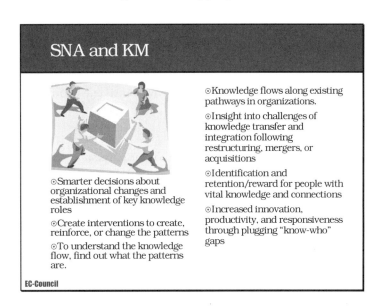

The importance of social network analysis in the context of knowledge management lies in the fact that social networks are at the core of information flow. Most people learn through their social connections, both formal (at work) and informal (family and friends). It has been seen that some people are paid more attention to (called "hubs" or "authorities" in social network analysis) than others. The information age has also made it necessary to constantly scan the literature or question various activities. Therefore, people depend on credible sources to inform them what's important.

For knowledge that is complex and requires judgment (like policy development or counseling), most people learn by asking trusted sources for advice, not by scanning literature. Even when scanned, more attention is paid to the ones published in credible journals or written by authors of subject repute. Hence knowledge flows involve trust, credibility, and limited amount of attention and time.

 The key benefits that SNA renders to knowledge initiatives are:

> Ability to make smarter decisions about organizational changes and establishment of key knowledge roles.

> Aids in creating interventions to create, reinforce, or change the patterns

> Assists in understanding the knowledge flow, and finding out what the patterns are.

> Identify knowledge flows along existing pathways in organizations.

> Gives an insight into challenges of knowledge transfer and integration following restructuring, mergers, or acquisitions

> Identification and retention/reward for people with vital knowledge and connections

> Aids increased innovation, productivity, and responsiveness through plugging "know-who" gaps

> Provides concrete view of flows and relationships

> Helps make concrete how work is happening in comparison to the formal structure.

> Makes visible the aspects of a group that we can work with.

> Qualitative and Quantitative aspects: Graphics are very meaningful to people. Data enable metrics; provide meaningful information when there are very large numbers of people.

> Proven uses in:

>> o Planning for reorganization (or post-reorganization)

>> o Identifying key people prior to mergers or acquisitions

- o Succession planning and retention

- o Knowledge creation and sharing

- o Improving organizational effectiveness

Why Do an Analysis?

⊙ **Six Myths about Informal Networks*:**

- To build better networks, we have to communicate more
- Everybody should be connected to everybody else
- We can't do much to aid informal networks
- How people fit in is a matter of personality (which can't be changed)
- Central people who have become bottlenecks should make themselves more accessible
- I already know what is going on in my network

*Rob Cross, Nitin Nohria, and Andrew Parker, MIT Sloan Management Review, Spring 2002

EC-Council

Need for Analysis

In management, three important developments have aided growth of the social network discipline

- ➢ Primarily, the knowledge and recognition of the coexistence of the informal structure with the formal structure of an organization.

- ➢ Secondarily, the progressive shift towards leaner organizational hierarchy and extended value chains.

- ➢ Lately, the rapid growth outsourcing, joint ventures, alliances, multinational spread and the growth of virtual organizations.

Analysis of social network diagrams helps determine the extent to which certain people are central to the effective functioning of a network, regardless of whether or not divisive subgroups in a network exist or what the overall connection of a given network is.

Things to look for in SNA:

- ➢ Bottlenecks—Central nodes that provide the only connection between different parts of the network.

- ➢ Number of links—Insufficient or excessive links between departments that must coordinate effectively.

➢ Average distance—Degrees of separation connecting all pairs of nodes in the group. Short distances transmit information accurately and in a timely way, while long distances transmit slowly and can distort the information.

➢ Isolation—People that are not integrated well into a group and therefore, represent both untapped skills and a high likelihood of turnover.

➢ Highly expert people—Not being utilized appropriately.

➢ Organizational subgroups or cliques—Can develop their own subcultures and negative attitudes toward other groups.

SNA Applications

- Target knowledge management programs based on opportunities identified in junctures
- Identify and reward individuals for "invisible" work
- Identify key individuals for retention
- As part of team kick-off for cross-functional or cross-organizational projects
- To identify lead users for change management programs

EC-Council

SNA Applications

 The application areas of SNA an the benefits they can accrue to the organization are:

- ➤ Increased retention of people with vital corporate knowledge.

- ➤ Increasing the social capital in the organization. People who are more connected are more likely to be satisfied with their work and more likely to stay.

- ➤ Increased innovation, productivity, and responsiveness within the organization.

- ➤ Capability in closing gaps in people's knowledge of one another's experience and expertise. Decreasing the amount of time it takes for people to locate and access needed knowledge.

- ➤ Increased ability to take smarter decisions about changing the formal organization structure or introducing new processes into organizations.

- ➤ Understanding the structure of the existing social networks. SNA gives insights into how work is really accomplished in an organization, how decisions are made, and the effectiveness of the existing organizational structures.

- ➤ Gaining insight into the challenges of integration following restructuring, mergers, or acquisitions.

- ➤ Identifying specific individuals or groups who are most likely to have the most influence across group borders and boundaries. It may be important to take special steps to retain people who are key to a network.

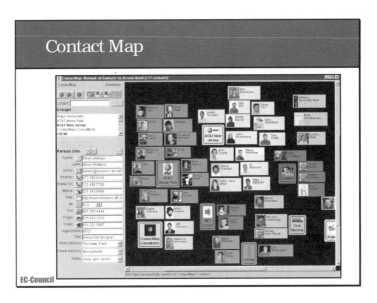

Exhibit - ContactMap

ContactMap is a software tool used to help users with organization tasks by presenting a visual model of their personal social networks.

ContactMap allows users to arrange their individual social networks in a visual map of individual contacts and groups: each node affords a variety of communication functions enabling users to retrieve current and archived information associated with them.

ContactMap tool models users' personal social networks, and show people who are literally central or peripheral to their work and personal lives. Each contact, represented by a picture and a label, is placed in a spatial position reflecting its relationship with both other contacts and the user.

Contacts may be assigned to one or more groups (differentiated by color), resulting in a map resembling a geographic map. The groups themselves are arranged spatially to reflect their relationships with one another. Groups typically constitute social categories, such as friends, family, projects, and organizational affiliations.

For the selected contact in the figure above, the left side of the display shows group affiliations along with contact information, including email address, phone numbers, Web page, fax number, and pager number. Clicking icons associated with communication functions activates the functions to, say, initiate a click-to-dial phone call, address an email message, or show the contact's Web page.

The social network map is also an index of users' information; each node provides access to documents, such as email messages and text files exchanged between user and contact, as well as access to Web pages associated with contacts

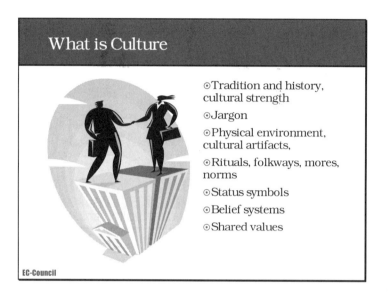

Organization Culture

An organization's culture is the set of norms, values, beliefs, assumptions, and expectations that are deeply held by its members.

Schein (1997) and Schultz (1995) describe three layers of culture that develop over time: artifacts, espoused values, and underlying assumptions. Artifacts are visible aspects of culture such as ceremonies, rituals, pictures, furniture, dress codes, and written and spoken language. Espoused values are articulated statements of an organization's beliefs, as exemplified in vision and mission statements, strategies, codes of conduct, and policies. Underlying assumptions are the implicit, taken for granted outlooks and mindsets that shape perceptions, feelings, and behaviors of individuals and groups.

Bartlett & Ghoshal (2000) use the term "administrative heritage" to describe the values, ingrained norms, and definitions of managerial responsibilities that are passed on from an organization's history. They also refer to the influence wielded by an organization's set of "explicit or implicit corporate values and shared beliefs" as its psychology, complementary to organizational anatomy (structure) and physiology (processes).

Morgan (1997: 151) argues that an organization's culture "rests in distinctive capacities and incapacities that are built into the attitudes and approaches of organizational members." Hofstede

(1997: 182-183) offers a different perspective: organizational cultures differ chiefly with respect to practices, not values.

According to Morgan (1997), it is not uncommon for ritualistic practices associated with espoused values to be undercut by contradictory, deeper norms and agendas. But Morgan (1997) argues that at its deepest level, culture is self-organizing, continually evolving, and beyond ordinary means of managerial control.

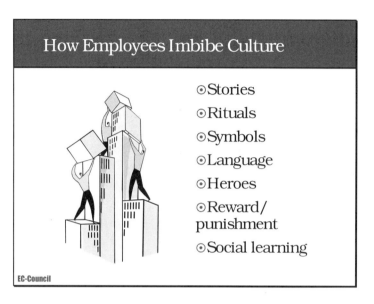

How Employees Imbibe Culture

- ⊙ Stories
- ⊙ Rituals
- ⊙ Symbols
- ⊙ Language
- ⊙ Heroes
- ⊙ Reward / punishment
- ⊙ Social learning

EC-Council

Imbibing Culture

We have seen that organization culture is a result of the values, beliefs, underlying assumptions, attitudes, and behaviors shared by the employees. Culture exists in the organization as language, symbols, stories, legends, and daily work practices.

> Stories are an integral part of organizational culture, as people feel bonded sharing a common experience.

> Rites and Rituals. This may seem trivial, though from an organization culture perspective, nothing is too trivial to dismiss as a ritual. This may be exhibited as play, ceremony, and ritual, with certain outcomes. An example is management rituals such as meetings that have a real purpose and meaning

> Symbols are meant to symbolize the company to outsiders and preserve what makes the organization special

> Language assumes great significance as organizations are getting increasingly multinational and transcend geographical boundaries.

> Heroes make success attainable and human by providing role models

> Reward / Punishment approach sets a standard of performance and motivates employees

Cultural Typologies

- ⊙ Deal & Kennedy - risk and feedback
  - Focus on exec decision making
- ⊙ Reinmann & Wiener - focus of values and source of values
  - focus on values
- ⊙ Schein - every org. is unique
- ⊙ Sonnenfeld - academy, club, baseball team, fortress
  - focus on attraction of personalities

EC-Council

Typologies of Culture

Organization cultures can be categorized into various types depending on the focus they hold. It is apparent that there is no uniform culture for organizations and that there can be variations within an organization – such as dominant culture, subcultures. It may be characterized as weak or strong, formal or informal. However, the broad level classification can be ascertained as detailed below.

 The four types of organizational cultures are:

➢ Networked culture (high sociability; low solidarity)

In the networked culture, members are treated as friends and family. People have close contact with each other and love each other. People are willing to help each other and share information. The disadvantage of this culture is that people are so kind to each other that they are reluctant to point out and criticize the poor performance. Unilever has a typical networked culture.

➢ Mercenary culture (low sociability; high solidarity)

Mercenary culture focuses on strict goals. Members are expected to meet the goals and getting the job done quickly. Since everyone focuses on goals and objectivity, there is little room for political cliques. The negative is that those with poor performance may be treated inhumanely. The Japanese manufacturer Komatsu is an example of classic mercenary culture.

➢ Fragmented culture (low sociability; low solidarity)

In an organization with fragmented culture, the sense of belonging to and identification with the organization is usually very weak. The individualists constitute the organizations, and their commitment is given first to individual members and task work. The downside is that there is a lack in cooperation. Most of the law firms have this kind of culture.

➢ Communal culture (high sociability; high solidarity)

A Communal culture can give its members a sense of belonging, though it also is task-driven. Leaders of this culture are usually very inspirational and charismatic. The major negative is that they often consume a person's whole life. A good example of communal culture is Hewlett-Packard.

Organization Culture

⊙ The ability of an organization to learn, develop memory, and share knowledge is dependent on its culture.
  - Culture is a pattern of shared basic assumptions.

⊙ Over time organizations learn what works and what doesn't work. As the lessons become second nature, they become part of the organizational culture.

⊙ Generally when a technology project fails, it is because the technology does not match the organization's culture.

EC-Council

Characteristics of Organization Culture

A learning organization has a favorable organization culture that facilitates knowledge management.

Most of these organizations have a future, external orientation that helps these organizations develop understanding of their environment. Senior teams take time out to think about the future. There is widespread use of external sources and advisors e.g. customers on planning teams.

➤ There is a free exchange and flow of information - systems are in place to ensure that expertise is available where it is needed; individuals network extensively, crossing organizational boundaries to develop their knowledge and expertise.

➤ There is an implicit commitment to learning, personal development - support from top management, and people at all levels are encouraged to learn regularly. Learning is rewarded. People are encouraged to take the time to think and learn (understanding, exploring, reflecting, developing)

➤ These organizations value people - ideas, creativity and "imaginative capabilities" are stimulated, made use of and developed. Diversity is recognized as strength and there is freedom in the organization to challenge views held by the organization.

➤ The organization climate is one of openness and trust - individuals are encouraged to develop ideas, to speak out, to challenge actions.

> ➢ The organization as a whole learns from experience - learning from mistakes is often more powerful than learning from success. Failure is tolerated, provided lessons are learnt ("learning from past failure" - Peters).

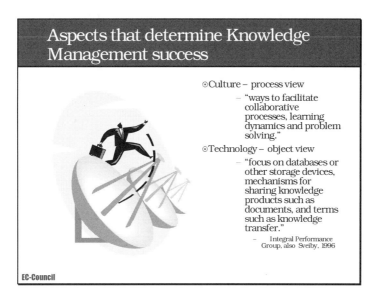

Aspects of Knowledge Management

Knowledge Management is not Technology (e.g., databases) or "Getting the right information to the right person at the right time". It should rather be considered as a process and not as a technology product.

There are two crucial aspects to knowledge management. One is the cultural aspect and the other is the technology aspect. In this module we will discuss the cultural aspect, focusing primarily on knowledge sharing, while the technology aspect will be dealt in detail in later modules.

The cultural aspect of knowledge management seeks to leverage people skills. This involves:

> ➢ capturing expertise,

> ➢ tacit knowledge

> ➢ adoption of cognition

> ➢ and collaboration.

It deals with fostering communication, especially across organizational boundaries and places emphasis on listening and observing as a universal work practice. It encourages mentoring and takes a holistic perspective - seeing the team and organization as a whole, which helps the organization to cope with challenge and uncertainty.

The technology aspect of knowledge management primarily deals with knowledge storage, dissemination and knowledge retrieval. It involves managing formal assets, storing explicit knowledge through the use of Information technology. Use of decision support systems, data storage tools such as databases, disseminating tools such as groupware come under this purview.

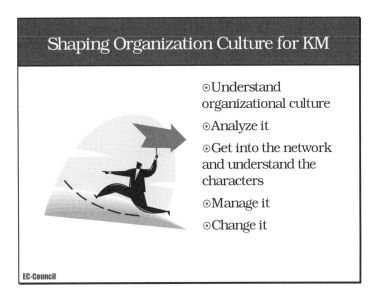

Shaping Organization Culture

From a knowledge management perspective, an organization can streamline and leverage its culture by:

➢ Understanding the organizational culture

Some examples of organization culture objectives are: To perform to highest level of competence always; To take initiative and risks; To adapt to change; To make decisions; To work cooperatively in a team; To be open with info, knowledge, news of impending problems; To trust and be trustworthy; To respect all others and oneself; To answer for our actions, to be accountable; To judge and be judged, to reward and be rewarded, based on performance.

➢ Analyze - Some analysis methods are:

  o Miller - trade winds, temperature, ceiling level

  o Kilmann & Saxton - Culture Gap Survey

  o Schein - 10 step cultural audit

➢ Getting into the network and understanding the characters. This can involve -

  o Tapping into the Cultural Network

- o Treating everyone with the respect shown a CEO till his or her place in the network is determined
- o Asking people to explain the meaning of what is observed
- o Asking each contact for the names of others to contact
- o Reading what the company says about itself
- o Cultivating cultural characters at all levels of the organization and seeking friends
- o Listening to all the stories and antecedents
- o Observing how people spend their time and how they treat customers

- ➤ Strategies for changing the culture
    - o Start at the top
    - o Adopt social learning process
    - o Using group process
    - o Storytelling, rituals, symbols
    - o Get rid of defensive routines/undicussables - retreats
    - o Change people and infrastructure

Change often begins, and begins well, when leaders are convinced of the need for change. The status quo must seem more dangerous than launching into the unknown, top management must be honeslty convinced that business-as-usual is totally unacceptable. The starting point can be bad business results, or higher competition. However transformation is impossible unless hundreds or thousands of people are willing to help. People will accept to support the change process only if they believe that useful change is possible.

People must understand and see the relevance of the change initiative. They must connect 'personally' to the initiative:

- ➤ First, people need to see that there is a focus on business needs
- ➤ Second, they need to understand how they fit in, how they can contribute and how they will benefit.

They must feel capable to reply to the basic question: 'what's in it for me?'.

If this does not happen, people will correctly regard the initiative as just adding more work to their already overfull plates. The change initiative will be considered as a 'management fad'.

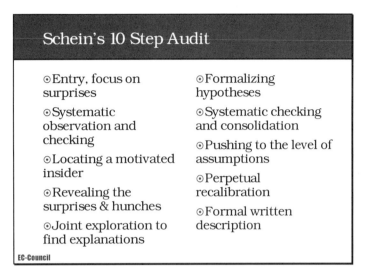

Schein's 10 Step Audit

We have discussed that the corporate culture is the sum total of workplace behaviors — how people do things and how things get done. It includes subcultures such as sales, manufacturing, and information technology.

A Culture Audit is an assessment of the existing culture of the business– its strengths and weaknesses with respect business goals and objectives. Culture Audits measure such attributes as risk tolerance, degree of hierarchy, reward structure, collaboration, values, and innovation vs. adaptation. A Culture Audit can offer valuable insights for social ventures and collaborations as well as in the private sector.

The case for culture audit rests with change management primarily. Whenever the business needs to change directions, the audit will enable it to determine whether the culture is amenable to change, whether two diverse cultures can be merged successfully, and whether new practices can be successful within the existing cultural norms. Highlighted above is the ten-step culture audit as proposed by Schein.

The advantages of undertaking a culture audit are:

➢ Increase in the level of awareness about stated and unstated assumptions.

➢ It facilitates a shared vision – a crucial determinant of KM project success.

➢ It helps the organization design and test new corporate models and systems.

➢ A culture audit can help integrate subcultures.

➢ Helps document and communicate the cultural change process

➢ Energizes and retain key employees

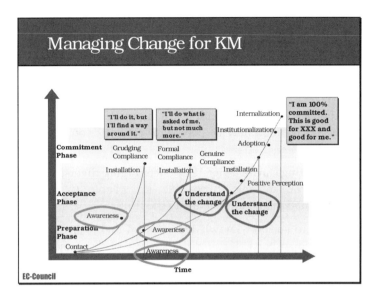

Managing Change

Managing knowledge is essential for the success of any organization. The process of implementing a new knowledge management program, or improvements to an existing program, can be an overwhelming task. However, careful planning, strong leadership, and actions to address needed culture changes can go a long way to ensure success.

Culture can be seen first as an asset to be capitalized upon, managed for synergistic advantage. It can also be seen as posing problems to be solved, obstacles to be overcome. Whether asset or obstacle, the importance of culture needs to be acknowledged, its manifestations and impacts in specific settings assessed, and its role addressed throughout the change management process as companies implement and improve knowledge management systems.

The greatest challenge that culture poses for improving knowledge management may very well lie in the unique combinations of values, mindsets, and practices pertinent to knowledge management that must be taken into account and adapted to in different organizations and national settings. But ultimately, efforts to implement knowledge management-as is true of most organizational changes that occur in a cultural context-must be custom-tailored to fit unique cultural circumstances.

The first step in building a knowledge culture should be to draw up a vision statement for knowledge management. Culture gaps and knowledge gaps are the basis for designing value propositions and actions and programs for change.

A key to making an organization's culture more supportive of knowledge management is to have the active involvement of a broad cross-section of the organization in the KM project. Actions that can reduce culture gaps and support culture change include: participation of employees in developing the project, visible and consistent leadership, proper communication from all levels of management, vivid illustrations of the desired attitudes and behaviors needed, and rewards and recognition that encourage knowledge creation and sharing.

When the project team is composed of culturally diverse members, special steps in team development and team management may be needed to capitalize on diversity and achieve high levels of functioning.

Knowledge creation and sharing can be fostered by encouraging diversity of views, managing the communications environment, making it possible for people to form communities, and enhancing the flow of information and knowledge in the firm.

Norms and values needed to support knowledge creation and sharing include: having a clear vision and objectives, shared responsibility for the success of the project, teamwork, openness, trust, risk taking and empowerment.

In the long term, most organizations will find it most efficacious in overcoming culture-based challenges to transform present organizational cultures into knowledge management cultures sufficiently robust to flourish in a variety of national cultural environments.

As shown in the figure above, the higher the awareness levels and greater the understanding of the knowledge initiative, the commitment towards implementing it is higher. The culture of the organization is reflected in the disposition of the stakeholders.

Organizations which are seeking to 'change the way we are doing things around here' often use large-scale campaigns to get their message across, including training programmes for all staff, etc.

However, many stand-alone cultural efforts do not work and must be carefully prepared and sustained by a high level development strategy.

The graph illustrates the progressive integration of change. However each movement in favor of change can be inhibited as it occurs.

The challenge of fear and anxiety may well be the most frequently faced challenge in sustaining profound change, and the most difficult to overcome. People will express their defensiveness in many ways:

• 'I have no time for this stuff'

• 'Still a new program: it won't succeed, such as the previous ones'

•' I don't believe in the initiative'

• 'It has nothing to do with my business'

or people seem positive, but they do nothing…

The chart also illustrates the different levels of commitment.

✍ As champions of change, one must recognize growing inhibitors as indicators of progress, and deal with them. It is to be noted that cultural change takes twice as long as expected, while serious change, according to Peter Senge, can take eight to ten years to complete, and it require efforts from all sides - individuals cannot do it alone.

Organization Performance Levers

The full value of a KM approach can only be realised if the organisation 'cultivates' attitudes that are open and receptive to new information, to changes and that encourages information sharing.

A pioneer of organizational change, Richard Beckard, once mentioned that: 'People do not resist change; people resist being changed'. Change is intensely personal. For change to occur in an organization, each individual must think, feel or do something differently.

The leaders must win their followers one by one by aligning the organizational levers with the attitudes and behaviors required for driving the KM performance.

If knowledge must be the central component of the company and its strategic process, culture becomes the pre-eminent issue.

Here are some organizational Performance Levers that can be assessed for initiating the change required for sustaining the knowledge sharing culture.

Some of the organization performance levers are performance and pay alignment, leadership effectiveness, education and development, staffing and deployment and communications.

These act at various strategic levers such as organization /enterprise / job level and affect both structure and competencies.

The assessment of the Organizational Performance Levers enables one to evaluate their impact on change success. For example, the figure below relates organization performance levers and change management.

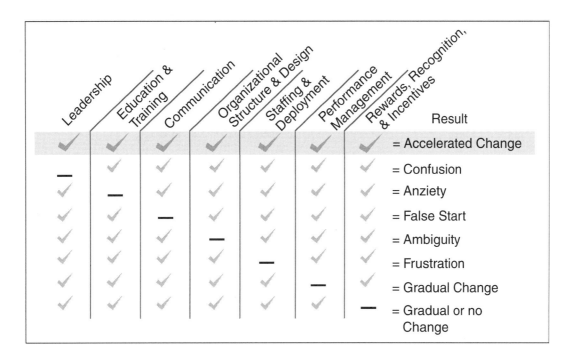

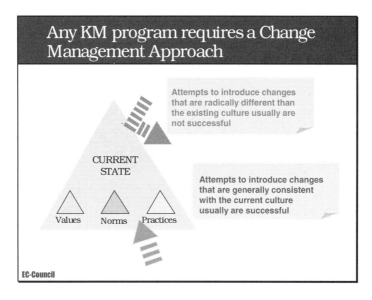

Need for Change Management Approach

The corporate or organizational culture includes three components:

> **Values**: Companies tend to have only a few core values, for example between three or five. Those core values will change seldom, if ever. Example: Sony.

> **Norms**: cultural norms are open to change. It corresponds to business strategies and work habits.

> **Operating practices**, which can be changed at any time!

As values are deeply embedded and very difficult to change, the best way to change behaviors around knowledge use is to change the practices that generate them. The new practices will change the norms over time, providing support for more effective knowledge use.

Japanese organizations are known widely for having an elevated organization culture from the perspective of values, norms and practices. Being a pioneer is looked up at and people are encouraged to try their hand at the impossible.

Individual ability and creativity are encouraged within the organization and appropriately rewarded. It has been noted that attempts to introduce changes that are radically different than the existing culture usually are not successful.

However attempts to introduce changes that are generally consistent with the current culture usually are successful. The importance of having change management addressed within an KM initiative cannot be overemphasized.

Another perspective in approaching change management is necessitating the executive and management commitment as a pre-requisite for any knowledge management initiatives. If the management can practice what they preach, the rest of the organization will find it easier to manage any resulting change.

To initiate this, the management can direct their efforts in the following areas:

> ➢ Identifying KM Values and embedding them into organizational values
> ➢ Developing a corporate KM culture
>> o Embedding knowledge sharing as a way of work in individual and collective objectives
>> o Building trust across borders and companies
>> o Empowering people in relation with KM
>> o Embedding learning and development in the management style
> ➢ Assessing KM culture progress through periodic culture audit
>> o Measure KM initiatives and results
>> o Assessment of KM Pilots through Vitality Indicators
> ➢ Develop Communication Plan (awareness, acceptance & training)
>> o Coaching & mentorship

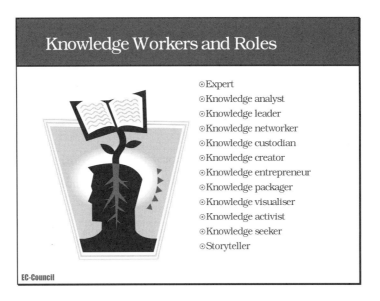

Knowledge Workers and Roles

The expert – This is a person having expertise in a domain of knowledge or a particular skill. Recognized for the expertise and likely to stay with the knowledge domain over many years.

Knowledge analyst – This is a person who assimilates knowledge from many sources. Possess many of the attributes of the expert (but are perhaps not as self-opinionated or self-promotionalist) and also of the packager. Have ability to rationalize knowledge to support their arguments.

Knowledge leader – Possess a broad area of knowledge and build bridges between knowledge (and people) in different domains. He is typically a generalist, and not a specialist. He is able to see the big picture and how knowledge supports organizational objective. Potential CKO or CEO.

Knowledge networker – This person is typically a knowledge broker and connector. He connects people to people and people to knowledge. He is a hybrid of expertise and leadership. Does not have all the right solutions but knows people who have them.

Knowledge custodian – This worker is a knowledge keeper, fond of classifying knowledge and organizing content into taxonomies. Usually takes the role of the knowledge centre manager.

Knowledge creator – He is an innovator. This person is always thinking of new things to do, and never seem to have time to see them through to implementation. His thinking goes off in several directions but he does come up with breakthrough ideas and innovative approaches.

Knowledge entrepreneur – This person may not have the best ideas by himself, but he can recognize those that have potential. He is the bridge between the creator and the packager. A storyteller committed to making a difference.

Knowledge packager – This person is in charge of assembling all the knowledge components to make something worthwhile. Helps knowledge creators realize their dreams.

Knowledge visualizer – A graphics person, excels in communicating visually and contextually. Capable of making his point in images, diagrams and perhaps even cartoons and music.

Knowledge activist – A person committed to a cause and will marshal the knowledge needed to support the case. Can also be a knowledge maverick, often questioning the status quo and raising doubts in others about the efficacy of their hard-won knowledge. Initiates change.

Knowledge seeker – This worker is ever curious, and is seeking new knowledge. The pursuit of knowledge is for personal fulfillment. Always willing to share it enthusiastically.

Storyteller – This person is capable of encapsulating knowledge into highly memorable stories. Possess a strong imagination and look for analogies and metaphors.

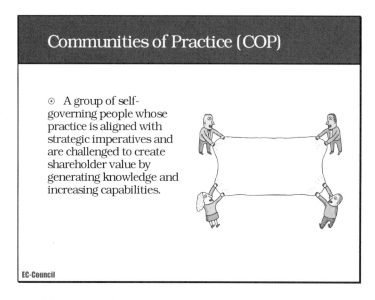

Introducing Communities of Practice

📋 According to Etienne Wenger (1998), a community of practice defines itself along three dimensions:

> ➢ What it is about – its joint enterprise as understood and continually renegotiated by its members.

> ➢ How it functions - mutual engagement that bind members together into a social entity.

> ➢ What capability it has produced – the shared repertoire of communal resources (routines, sensibilities, artifacts, vocabulary, styles, etc.) that members have developed over time.

A community of practice involves much more than the technical knowledge or skill associated with undertaking some task. Members are involved in a set of relationships over time and communities develop around things that matter to people. The fact that they are organizing around some particular area of knowledge and activity gives members a sense of joint enterprise and identity.

For a community of practice to function it needs to generate and appropriate a shared repertoire of ideas, commitments and memories. It also needs to develop various resources such as tools, documents, routines, vocabulary and symbols that in some way carry the accumulated knowledge of the community. In other words, it involves practice: ways of doing and approaching things that are shared to some significant extent among members.

The interactions involved, and the ability to undertake larger or more complex activities and projects though cooperation, bind people together and help to facilitate relationship and trust.

Features of communities

- Self-governance: agreed upon conventions
- Members assume accountability to support one another
- Function through a governance structure, principles and conventions, the shared leadership of members and effective facilitation
- Share knowledge through collaborating and learning
- Knowledge base is created by members
- Use a variety of synchronous and asynchronous collaborative tools, including face-to-face meetings and on-line platform
- Supported by the organization as a valid way to learn and collaborate; adds value to the organization
- Productive inquiry fuels knowledge creation and exchange

EC-Council

Characteristics of Communities

 Characteristic features of communities of practice include:

> Self-governance: Members interact and involve in activities based upon an agreed set of conventions

> Members assume accountability to support one another. Mutual help and availing synergistic benefits form the core value of a COP

> Members create the shared knowledge base. This is drawn from individual expertise and experience.

> Productive inquiry fuels knowledge creation and exchange. Common interactions allow for brainstorming and knowledge conversion from tacit to explicit forms.

> Share knowledge through collaborating and learning. Learning is an implicit quality of COP. Collaboration facilitates learning.

> Use a variety of synchronous and asynchronous collaborative tools, including face-to-face meetings and on-line platform

> Function through a governance structure, principles and conventions, the shared leadership of members and effective facilitation

➢ Supported by the organization as a valid way to learn and collaborate; adds value to the organization

Facilitators

- ⊙ Shared sense of purpose and ownership
- ⊙ Self-initiated view of learning and readiness to learn from each other
- ⊙ Climate of trust and involvement
- ⊙ Partnering mindsets and capabilities
- ⊙ Strong technology platform
- ⊙ Supportive context and leadership endorsement
- ⊙ Realistic expectations for return on investment on the part of management

EC-Council

CoP Facilitators

➢ Communities of practice are fostered in environments where there is a shared sense of purpose and ownership.

➢ The members are open to learning and hold a self-initiated view of learning and exhibit readiness to learn from each other.

➢ A fundamental characteristic of al communities is a climate of trust and involvement exhibited by the participants.

➢ Members find it natural to partner mindsets and capabilities within the community.

➢ Communities of practice can be successful only if collaboration is supported. This requires a strong technology platform and allied tools.

➢ The organization seeking to foster a community of practice should provide a supportive context and the leadership should encourage and endorse the activities of the community.

➢ A COP delivers value to the business and there should be realistic expectations for return on investment on the part of management.

Strategic purpose of communities

- Strategic theme
- Core organizational competency
- Common development need
- Distributed functional expertise
- Cross-generational knowledge exchange
- Create the capabilities needed to link strategy with performance
- Generate meta-capabilities and new knowledge
- Create organizational readiness for change – (e.g.Value Creation Networks)
  - Multiple partners with individual expertise
  - Collaboration and partnership capabilities and mindsets
  - Technology enabled

EC-Council

Strategic Purpose of Communities

A number of categories that illustrate the type of strategic purpose a community of practice might meet in the organization are discussed below.

Strategic theme – a community purpose that is directly aligned with a theme that is articulated in the organization's strategic imperatives.

Core organizational competency – a community purpose that is focused on increasing a core competency through collaboration and learning. For example, due to the cross-functional groups that were being created to meet customer demands for integrated products, there might be the need to establish a standardized approach to project management – an approach that would be used throughout the organization so that as teams came together they would know what is expected, what process would be followed to manage the projects. Under the leadership of project management experts, a community can be formed to help identify the standard as well as to increase the capabilities of individual members in the practice of project management.

Common development needs – a community purpose that supports the development of competencies in a specific area that may be used in a number of areas of an organization. For example, due to the complexity of providing customer service a number of specialized customer call centers may be operational. The customer service representatives have a common set of competencies that are required plus a specialized content area. A community of practice was created for people who train customer service representatives with the purpose of standardizing approaches based on best practice that existed within the separate units.

Distributed functional expertise provides forum for dispersed expertise.

Cross-generational knowledge exchange creates peer-learning space to address demographics.

The COP needs to create the capabilities needed to link strategy with performance. It should be capable of generating meta-capabilities and creating new knowledge.

Ford has been known for fostering productive communities of practice. As of 2002, they have had 10,000+ replications/yr of their best practices. Ford has 2,800+ active high value practices that have resulted in $1.5+ Billion of identified value and $1 Billion of actual value added to the company. Currently they have fifty-three Communities of Practice launched with 2,115 Focal Points.

Communities have an important role to play in readying the organization for chain. An example is the creation of value creation networks. These can have multiple partners with individual expertise. Communities of practice exist in any organization. COP fosters collaboration at various formal levels and enhances partnership capabilities. Because membership is based on participation rather than on official status, these communities are not bound by organizational affiliations, they can span institutional structures and hierarchies.

The value of team-based projects that deliver tangible products is easily recognized, but it is also easy to overlook the potential cost of their short-term focus. The learning that communities of practice share is just as critical, but its longer-term value is subtler to appreciate. Organizations must therefore develop a clear sense of how knowledge is linked to business strategies and use this understanding to help communities of practice articulate their strategic value. This involves a process of negotiation that goes both ways. It includes understanding what knowledge–and therefore what practices–a given strategy requires.

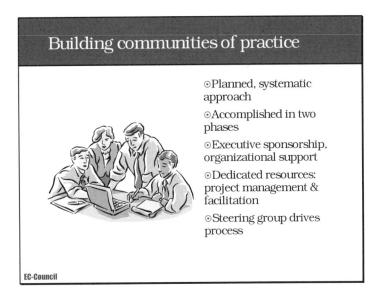

Building CoP

While building a community of practice, it is advised to take a planned and systematic approach. It is crucial to garner executive sponsorship and organizational support. The organization should be able to dedicate resources for proper project management and facilitation. This can be achieved by constituting a steering group to drive the critical process. The figure below illustrates a two-phased methodology to building a COP.

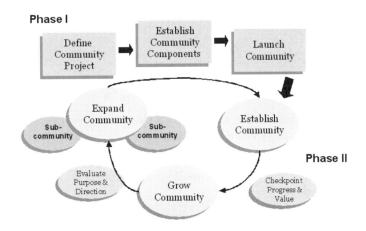

Knowledge Management Copyright © by **EC-Council**

Building communities of practice –
Phase I , II

⊙Define Community
Project
  - Identify community elements
  - Set context
  - Outline project

⊙Establish Community
Components
  - Identify issues and approaches
  - Plan project tasks

⊙Launch Community

⊙Establish Community
  - Develop sense of community

⊙Assess: Progress & Value
  - Solicit feedback on development

⊙Grow Community
  - Increase community value

⊙Evaluate purpose and direction
  - Assess value and goals

⊙Expand Community
  - Membership and scope
  - Sub-communities
  - Network of communities

EC-Council

CoP PhaseI,II

Phase I

> **Define community project**. The community development project is planned – the elements of the community are identified (setting the context) and the project is outlined.

> **Establish community components**. The project tasks are identified (often in the form of issues to be resolved) and completed.

> **Launch community**. The online community is made accessible to the members using a Web-based application.

Phase II

> **Establish the community**. A sense of community is developed through knowledge creation and exchange in member discussions, shared resources, and related activities.

> **Assess progress and value**. The community's value to its members and sponsors as well as the development approach is informally assessed.

> **Grow the community**. Directions are identified for increasing the community's value through community building, knowledge creation and sharing, and knowledge navigation approaches.

> **Evaluate Purpose and Direction.** The values and goals of the community is assessed.

> ➤ **Expand Community.** The membership and scope of the community is decided and well defined. It is communicated to all members. There may be sub communities that arise and link to the community. These are fostered to form a network of communities.

Stages of Development

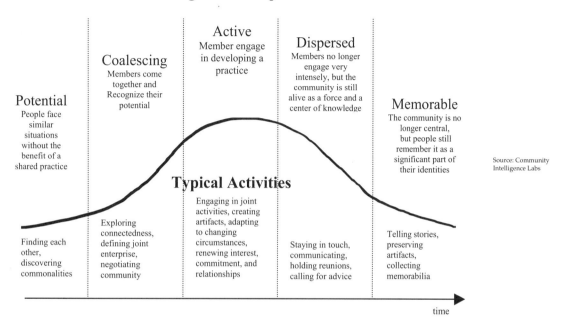

The figure above shows the various stages of development in a COP.

📋 A community of practice is different from a business or functional unit in that it defines itself in the doing, as members develop among themselves their own understanding of what their practice is about. A community of practice is different from a team in that the shared learning and interest of its members are what keep it together. It is defined by knowledge rather than by task, and exists because participation has value to its members.

Components of COP

- Governance – community conventions & norms
- Membership – community participants
- Technology – enabling infrastructure
- User support – maximizing collaborative tools
- Content – community knowledge base
- Learning – capability to participate in community
- Facilitation – moving the community forward; realizing purpose
- Communication plan – establishing credibility, sharing the value proposition

EC-Council

Components of CoP

Components that go into the making of a successful community of practice are discussed below.

➢ **Governance** – the structures needed to guide policy and process development – to make decisions about the community's purpose, directions, and approaches.

➢ **Membership** – the selection criteria and invitation process.

➢ **Technology Infrastructure** – the computer application or software chosen to support community development and knowledge sharing; the collaborative tool used to support the virtual community.

➢ **User Support** – the help desk issues and solutions or approaches needed to ensure access to the community and usability of the application.

➢ **Content** – the personal data for member profiles and seed content that will populate the community at launch and during the initial community development stages.

➢ **Training** – the materials and resources to familiarize community members with accessing and using the computer application.

➢ **Facilitation** – the moderator, guide, cheerleader, and traffic cop who ensures the smooth exchange of ideas, nurtures community building, and provides liaison with stakeholders, the application vendor, and other interested parties.

➤ **Communications** – the public relations activities to promote the use of the community as well as to keep sponsors, senior management, community members, and stakeholders informed of the community's development process.

Benefits from communities

⊙ Accelerates the generation of capabilities

⊙ Improves and enhances meta-capabilities

⊙ Shapes a "boundary-less" culture for greater synergy

⊙ Connects people into a network for greater speed

⊙ Promotes innovation through collaboration and problem-solving situated in work

⊙ Prevents knowledge loss from the organization through exchange of cross-generational expertise

EC-Council

Benefits from communities

Communities of Practice and their networks can help organizations to:

➢ Organize work in ways that makes people grow and be happy

➢ Accelerate business cycles

➢ Learn faster than the competition

Communities of Practice deliver goods by:

➢ Accessing tacit knowledge; making job-critical knowledge persistent. Developing and spreading better practices faster

➢ Combating isolation and creating networks. Connecting "islands of knowledge" into self-organizing, knowledge sharing networks of professional communities

➢ Feeding and being fed by web-based repositories of both proven solutions and new approaches

➢ Fostering cross-functional and cross-divisional collaboration. Readies the organization to participate in external value creation networks.

➢ Increasing members' ability to initiate and contribute to projects across organizational boundaries

➢ Promote innovation through problem-solving, learning, and knowledge creation.

➢ Contributing to a new organizational infrastructure. Contributing to shaping culture and identifying values

Lessons Learned

- Team effort required
- Technology challenges
- Under promise; over deliver
- Time is a factor
- Educate your sponsors
- Liability and security issues
- Duplication of resources
- Facilitation required
- Confidentiality of contributions

EC-Council

Recommendations

Communities of practice are not a new kind of organizational unit; rather, they are a different cut on the organization's structure–one that emphasizes the learning that people have done together rather than the unit they report to, the project they are working on, or the people they know. Communities of practice differ from other kinds of groups found in organizations in the way they define their enterprise, exist over time, and set their boundaries.

Lessons learnt from organizations that have fostered COPs indicate that team effort is crucial to the success of a COP. through a disciplined approach to sharing processes, best practices and lessons learned. Team effort help COP manage knowledge in a constructive manner.

Technology challenges arise in a COP- whether it be web-enabled knowledge solutions; allowing two communities on one site, open and closed discussion boards, direct e-mail interface within the closed communities, customized knowledge share areas, custom designed search features, computer-based learning tools or identifying user metrics to verify functionality and use of tools by the communities of practice.

Under promise; over deliver: For the initial phases, it's better to under promise and over deliver in order to meet skeptical expectations as well as to highlight the inherent potential of COP

Time is a critical factor. A community of practice's life cycle is determined by the value it provides to its members, not by an institutional schedule. It does not appear the minute a project is started and does not disappear with the end of a task. It takes a while to come into being and may live long after a project is completed or an official team has disbanded.

Apart from the above, there is the need to educate the sponsors - as organizations grow in size, geographical scope and complexity, it is increasingly apparent that sponsorship and support of communities of practice can improve organizational performance.

There is also the need to address security concerns of members and ascertain liability for breaches. Duplication of resources must be judged according to strategic needs of the community and the organization at large.

Confidentiality of contributors may need to be assured in communities to promote innovation and more informal knowledge flows. The factors that facilitate communities of practice also need to be considered as discussed within this module.

Story Telling

📋 Stephen Denning describes story as "…anything told or recounted; more narrowly, something told or recounted in the form of a causally-linked set of events; account; tale; the telling of a happening or connected series of happenings, whether true or fictitious.'

There are many different types* of stories, with different labels. The most generally used terms include:

> Story: This is the telling of a happening or connected series of happenings, whether true or fictitious; a descriptive account or narration

> Narrative: In the broadest sense it is anything told or recounted and more narrowly, something told or recounted in the form of a story / account / tale.

> Springboard story: A springboard story is a story that enables a leap in understanding by the audience so as to grasp how an organization or community or complex system may change. A springboard story has an impact not so much through transferring large amounts of information, but through catalyzing understanding. It enables listeners to visualize from a story in one context what is involved in a large-scale transformation in an analogous context.

> Anti-story: An anti-story is a story that arises in opposition to another. Any story that has a significant impact in a group or organization will give rise to similar stories as well as anti-stories. Anti-stories aim at undermining the original story.

As pointed out by Dave Snowden, an anti-story can arise as a negative or cynical counter to stories of official goodness. But it's not limited to the situation of stories of official goodness. It also arises in response to negative or cynical stories where again the intent is to undermine the original story.

The phenomenon of anti-story is something that one needs to be aware of when telling stories in an organization. The phenomenon will occur spontaneously and naturally, no matter how powerful the story one tells. The scene then becomes a battle between competing stories. The competing stories may co-exist for an extended period, or one story may "overcome" the other, and become the accepted account of what is going on.

*(Source Stephen Denning, *The Springboard: How Storytelling Ignites Action in Knowledge-Era Organizations*. Boston, London, Butter worth Heinemann, October 2000)

 Potential benefits of storytelling include the following:

➢ Quick Communication: Storytelling communicates ideas holistically. As a result, listeners can get complicated ideas not laboriously, dimension by dimension, but all at once.

➢ Natural Communication: Storytelling is our native language, which is learnt as toddlers. Abstract language by contrast is something learnt as schoolers.

➢ Clear Communication: Storytelling helps make sense of the seemingly chaotic by connecting us with time and space and human purpose of a sequence of events so as to make sense.

➢ Truthful Communication: Stories can communicate deep holistic truths, while abstract language tends to slice off fragments.

➢ Collaborative Communication: In abstract discussions, ideas are bounced. Narrative by contrast comes collaboratively.

➢ Persuasive Communication: It is easy to persuade the listener as he can relate to the story.

➢ Accurate Communication: Storytelling provides the context in which knowledge arises, and hence becomes the normal vehicle for accurate knowledge transfer.

➢ Intuitive Communication: The role of tacit knowledge has become a major preoccupation because it is often the tacit knowledge that is most valuable. Storytelling provides an answer since by telling a story with feeling; we are able to communicate more than we explicitly know.

➢ Entertaining Communication: Abstract communications are dull and dry because they are not populated with people but with things. Stories enliven and entertain by involving people.

➢ Moving Communication so as to get action: Storytelling eliminates the gap by stimulating the listener to co-create the idea. In the process of co-creation, the listener starts the process of implementation in such a way that there is no gap.

➢ Communication alive with feeling: Storytelling enables discussion of emotions in culturally acceptable and elegant way.

➢ Interactive Communication: Storytelling is inherently interactive. The storyteller sparks the story that the listeners co-create in their own minds.

(Reference: Katalina Groh)

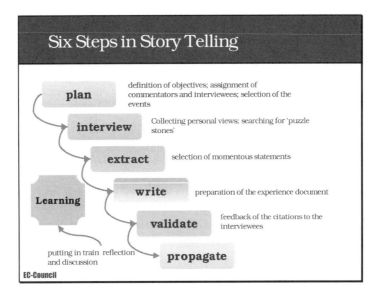

Six steps in Story Telling

There are six stages in effective story telling. As highlighted in the slide above, these are:

> Planning: This involves definition of objectives, assignment of commentators and interviewees and selection of the events to be includes in the exercise.

> Interviewing: Collecting personal views within the parameters of the story. Also searching for 'puzzle stones' – these are parts that make the whole of the story.

> Extracting: This involves selection of momentous statements that contain the lessons to be learnt from the story.

> Writing: The story has to be captured in explicit form and stored in order to collaborate and corroborate with similar contexts. This is achieved by the preparation of the experience document.

> Validating: The story needs to be validated for accuracy and relevance. Validation involves getting feedback of the citations to the interviewees.

> Propagating: The story needs to be shared to elicit its value. This is achieved by putting in the story train to enable reflection and discussion on the various aspects of the story.

Learning is the effect from the above steps. The learning can facilitate knowledge sharing, intellectual capital management, best practice management, aid a learning organization, and is effected by the process of communicating complex change ideas and getting rapid action towards implementation.

Successful Stories

- ⊙ Are understandable to the audience
- ⊙ Are told from the perspective of a single protagonist:
- ⊙ Have a protagonist who is prototypical of the organization's business.
- ⊙ Have a degree of strangeness or incongruity
- ⊙ Are eerily familiar.
- ⊙ Should embody the change idea as fully as possible
- ⊙ Should be recent, and true.
- ⊙ Should be told as simply as possible.
- ⊙ Often have a happy ending

EC-Council

Characteristics of Stories

 Successful stories have certain common characteristics. These are:

➤ Successful stories are understandable to the audience and the listeners can relate to them. They need to have elements that are known to the listener.

➤ Are told from the perspective of a single protagonist and have a protagonist who is prototypical of the organization's business. Storytelling enables the individuals in an organization to see themselves and the organization in a different light, and, through storytelling take decisions and change their behavior in accordance with these new perceptions, insights and identities

➤ Stories need to capture and retain attention therefore, they have a degree of strangeness or incongruity

➤ Stories should have a contextual familiarity to elicit any learning value.

➤ Should embody the change idea as fully as possible.

➤ Should be recent, and true. The truth of the story is a key part of getting the springboard effect. It's the truth of the story that gives it a sense of urgency.

> ➤ Should be told as simply as possible. It should not have distracting elements and should be minimalist, exploring only the learning objective in focus.

> ➤ Often have a happy ending. This helps put in the perfect frame of mind to be thinking about a new future, a new identity for the listener or the organization.

Summary

- ⊙ Corporate culture is a critical determinant of knowledge management project success
- ⊙ Any KM initiative should address change management before embarking on the same.
- ⊙ Communities of Practice is a KM strategic theme that facilitates knowledge sharing.
- ⊙ Story telling can be leveraged as an effective way of capturing tacit knowledge and nurturing knowledge sharing
- ⊙ Knowledge flows can be mapped using SNA.

EC-Council

Summary

 Recap

- ➢ Corporate culture is a critical determinant of knowledge management project success
- ➢ Any KM initiative should address change management before embarking on the same.
- ➢ Communities of Practice are a KM strategic theme that facilitates knowledge sharing.
- ➢ Story telling can be leveraged as an effective way of capturing tacit knowledge and nurturing knowledge sharing
- ➢ Knowledge flows can be mapped using SNA.

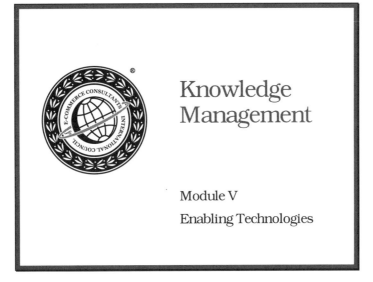

Knowledge Management (KM)

Module V: Enabling Technologies

Exam 212-69 Certified e-Business Associate

Module Objectives

⊙ Technology Aspect of Knowledge Management

⊙ Addressing KM related Technology Issues

⊙ Discussing Internet, Intranets and Portals

⊙ Discussing Collaboration Tools and Content Management

⊙ Discussing Decision Support Systems in KM

⊙ Discussing Groupware, Document Management and Workflow Applications

⊙ Overview of other supporting KM Technologies

EC-Council

Objectives

Module Objectives

The role of technology in knowledge management is an integral one. The prominent tools on the technology map include:

➢ Intranets

➢ Groupware and

➢ Collaborative solutions.

Even before the availability of solutions such as Lotus Notes on which many contemporary knowledge management solutions are based, companies were deploying intranets, such as EPRINET, based on early generations of networking and computer technology that improved access to knowledge. However, this access was not on an online basis.

Collaboration and knowledge sharing solutions subsequently arose from the development of on-line conferencing and forums. The role of technology is often to overcome barriers of time or space that otherwise would be the limiting factors.

For example, a research organization divided among several laboratories in different countries needs a system that scientists with common interests can use to exchange information with each other without commuting, whereas a document management system can ensure that valuable explicit knowledge is preserved so that it can be consulted in the future.

However, there are limitations to adopting technology. It has been noted that in many respects the state of the art is such that many of the social aspects of work important in knowledge management cannot currently be addressed by technology. Ackerman has referred to this aspect as a "social technical gap". Also, the interaction of behavior and technology is one that change in one aspect is reflected in the other. This is particularly important as technology continues to evolve at unprecedented speed.

The introduction of technology may influence the way individuals work. People can and do adapt their way of working to take advantage of new tools as they become available, and this adaptation can produce new and more effective communication within teams.

On completion of this module you will be familiar with different aspects that deals with technologies that enable knowledge management solutions. This module engages in discussing the following key areas:

> Technology Aspect of Knowledge Management

> Addressing KM related Technology Issues

> Discussing Internet, Intranets and Portals

> Discussing Collaboration Tools and Content Management

> Discussing Decision Support Systems in KM

> Discussing Groupware, Document Management and Workflow Applications

> Overview of other supporting KM Technologies

Readers are encouraged to conceptualize different scenarios that suit their respective organizations' technological requirements in order to contextualize the discussions presented through the module.

Needs of Knowledge Workers

- Have a clear understanding of their knowledge base (intellectual assets) for competitive advantage
- Innovate continuously
- Identify and capture strategic knowledge from inside and outside the organization
- Increase collaboration across and beyond the organization
- Leverage existing knowledge and best practices
- Organize and disseminate critical knowledge
- Retain and protect critical knowledge
- Deliver value-added services and products to clients
- Develop metrics that reflect the true value creation activities and results

EC-Council

Requirements of Knowledge workers

To understand how technology can deliver value to the knowledge initiative, a KM practitioner has to first understand the needs of a knowledge worker. Here, we shall briefly discuss the needs of a knowledge worker.

By knowledge workers, we do not confine to just the key roles involved in a knowledge initiative. It encompasses all the users of the KM project. Knowledge workers need to have a clear understanding of their knowledge base (intellectual assets) for competitive advantage. However, knowledge remains a competitive edge only as long as it is exclusive. This brings about the need to innovate continuously. In order to innovate continuously, workers need to identify and capture strategic knowledge from inside and outside the organization. This can be achieved through increased collaboration across and beyond the organization.

Collaboration – formal / informal, personal / impersonal assists in leveraging existing knowledge and best practices for achieving increased efficiency and effectiveness. In order to achieve this, knowledge must first be organized and disseminated so that the workers may apply critical knowledge.

Innovation and use of competitive knowledge raises the issue of retaining and protecting critical knowledge. Technology must address security concerns without hampering effective knowledge sharing. Technology must also enable organizations to deliver value-added services and products to clients, thereby aligning with the basic business drivers – namely market value, customer intimacy and operational efficiency. To this end, workers need to develop metrics that reflect the true value creation activities and results.

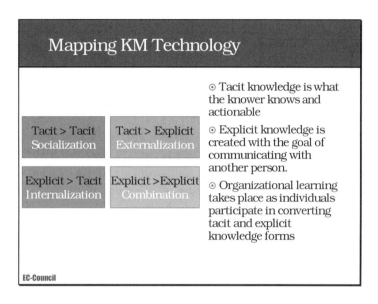

Mapping KM Technology to Transfer Modes

This module introduces knowledge management enabling technology in line with the processes underlying organizational knowledge creation using the Nonaka model discussed in earlier modules.

To revisit the model, we had seen that the essence of this model is to divide the knowledge creation processes into four categories:

> ➢ Socialization (tacit knowledge formation and communication)

> ➢ Externalization (formation of explicit knowledge from tacit knowledge)

> ➢ Combination (use of explicit knowledge)

> ➢ Internalization (formation of new tacit knowledge from explicit knowledge)

The relevance of this approach is that it focuses attention on tacit knowledge (which is featured in three of the four processes) and thus on people and their use of technology.

To summarize our earlier discussions on knowledge types and categories, tacit knowledge is what the knower knows, which is derived from experience and embodies beliefs and values. Tacit knowledge is actionable knowledge, and therefore the most valuable.

Furthermore, tacit knowledge is the most important basis for the generation of new knowledge, that is, according to Nonaka: "the key to knowledge creation lies in the mobilization and conversion of tacit knowledge."

Explicit knowledge is represented by some artifact, such as a document, which has typically been created with the goal of communicating with another person. Both forms of knowledge are important for organizational effectiveness.

These ideas lead us to focus on the processes by which knowledge is transformed between its tacit and explicit forms, as shown in figure above. Organizational learning takes place as individuals participate in these processes, since by doing so knowledge is created, shared, articulated, and made available to others. Creation of new knowledge takes place through the processes of combination and internalization. Thus the knowledge cycle is completed.

Because all the four processes in the Nonaka model aims to foster organizational knowledge creation, technology should be used to support all of them. Although early generations of knowledge management solutions (solutions typically integrate several technologies) focused on explicit knowledge in the form of documents and databases, the upcoming trend is to expand the scope of the solutions in ways possible to integrate technologies that can foster the use of tacit knowledge.

Among these technologies now being applied in some knowledge management solutions are those for:

➢ Online conferences,

➢ Chat,

➢ Collaboration (both synchronous and asynchronous) and

➢ Expertise location.

These technologies are in addition to those for handling documents, such as search and classification, which are already well established yet developing.

Technologically supported collaboration systems, such as groupware, can be effective tools for supporting knowledge dissemination. From a technology standpoint, KM should be seen as:

➢ An opportunity to manage information and content,

➢ To create an environment where knowledge and experience can be easily shared and

➢ To link people with knowledge to those who need it.

Unlike early generation KM, in which technology always seems to provide the answer, the current trend in KM places more focus on human resource and process initiatives supported by technological infrastructures.

The emphasis should be on designing solutions for people and organizations and not make people and organizations adapt to KM technologies. True integration can be considered to be achieved when KM enabling technology is embedded in the natural surrounding and present whenever needed, making interaction with the technology simple and effortless.

Technology Issues

⊙ Use state-of-the art technologies to enable and correlate with knowledge and learning organization
⊙ Implementation of Technology
⊙ Reliability
⊙ Ubiquity and pervasiveness
⊙ Availability—the digital divide
⊙ Security
⊙ Cost
⊙ Bandwidth

EC-Council

Technology issues

The primary technology issues arising in a knowledge management initiative include:

➢ Use of state-of-the art technologies to enable and correlate with knowledge and learning organization. This is especially relevant as collaborative environments keep evolving. For instance, groupware did not support mobile collaborative environments.

➢ Implementation of Technology: The issues in technology can be addressed at the following levels.

  o Interface:

  (a) Human factors

   ▪ Technology learning curves

   ▪ Fear of technological incompetence

  (b) Early adopters

  (c) Pilots and enterprise-wide adoption

➢ Intelligence

  o Knowledge bases

  o Multi-parameter uncertainty

  o Prediction

- o Learning models
- o Autonomous operation
- o Cognitive tuning
- ➢ Reliability
- ➢ Ubiquity and pervasiveness
- ➢ Availability—the digital divide
- ➢ Security
- ➢ Cost
- ➢ Bandwidth

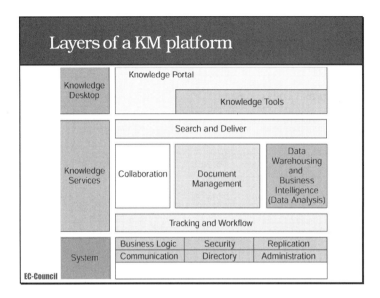

Layers of a KM Platform

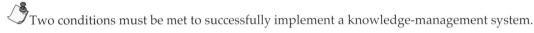Two conditions must be met to successfully implement a knowledge-management system.

> ➤ Knowledge workers must be prepared to work with technology and to document their work.

> ➤ Knowledge-management systems must support an easy way to create, store, and retrieve information from those workers.

The success of a knowledge-management system depends on corporate culture supporting the efforts of its people to produce information that can be used to improve the business. Empowered staff producing high-value content will get more value and benefit from a knowledge-management system than will people in companies that don't support sharing of information and ideas in an open fashion.

This benefit is even greater for those companies that have pricey human resources or that operate in industries that depend on sharing and recycled information. The chances of finding a knowledge-management system are high in the following types of companies:

> ➤ Organizations with huge R&D efforts (such Technology consulting organizations, software-engineering organizations)

> ➤ Organizations with big engineering departments (such as manufacturers)

> ➤ Organizations that rely on documentation (such as those in the pharmaceutical and medical industries)

➤ Accounting and consulting firms

Knowledge-management infrastructures also need to support the capturing of tacit knowledge, the sharing of ideas and documents, and the efficient finding of this information quickly and, more importantly, accurately. This is the foundation of a knowledge-management system that helps to handle information and transfer it into knowledge.

Another characteristic of a system that supports knowledge-management efforts is the existence of a set of common tools used and well known by all users of the system. Tools that provide an entry point to this system either present information or control all interaction with the system. They must be therefore capable of handling all the information that is part of the environment of the knowledge worker. In the best case, only one tool or application should exist for this interface.

Example: The Microsoft KM platform

The Microsoft knowledge-management platform offers a typical, but extended, three-layered architecture that allows the organization to build a flexible, powerful, and scaleable knowledge-management solution.

➤ The Knowledge Desktop layer consists of familiar productivity tools, such as Microsoft Office, and integrates tightly with the Knowledge Services layer.

➤ The Knowledge Services layer provides important knowledge-management services such as collaboration, document management, and search and deliver functionality, with modules for Tracking, Workflow, and Data Analysis.

➤ The System layer is a foundation that includes administration, security, and directories for managing the knowledge-management platform. All services run on the System layer and benefit from the integrated communication services that connect with external solutions, platforms, and partners.

The Microsoft knowledge-management platform relies on the Microsoft BackOffice family of products, which provide the services you need to build the knowledge-management prerequisites (messaging and collaboration and complete intranet) and to extend those prerequisites into knowledge-management solutions by implementing all five knowledge-management enabling modules (Content Management, Communities and Teams, Portals and Search, Data Analysis, and Real-Time Collaboration).

Besides these services, BackOffice provides interfaces for connecting to and integrating with legacy information or knowledge sources, such as RDBMS systems, SNA data sources, or knowledge-management enabling technologies such as Lotus Notes or Lotus Domino. One of the great advantages of BackOffice is the ability to migrate its services from a single server or to multiple servers without experiencing a major change in services or security aspects. This provides a platform that is scalable without the need for changes in the solutions that run on top of BackOffice.

This ability is especially relevant to departmental server solutions where Lotus Notes and Lotus Domino provide a common groupware platform. There, BackOffice extends the departmental groupware functionalities with its integrated and scaleable knowledge-management services. This makes it easy to set up departmental solutions with the Microsoft BackOffice platform, and you can extend or connect them later to enterprise-integrated solutions.

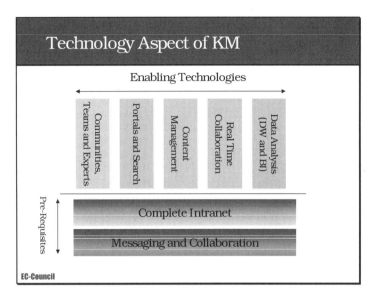

Technology Aspect of KM

For each business problem in an organization, knowledge management evolves through choosing the right technologies depending on the problems that the organization needs to solve. Each organization has its own characteristics based on organizational processes and technologies.

The various modules can be listed as portals and search, content management, real time collaboration, data analysis, expert systems, content intranet and messaging and collaboration.

Two modules are prerequisites. An intranet and a messaging system form the foundation of any knowledge-management system, and they constitute an infrastructure that supports the efficient transport, structure, access, and collaborative management of electronic data. The remaining enabling modules extend that basic infrastructure to a sophisticated knowledge-management system that includes services like content management, variations of information delivery, and data analysis. Automated services such as data tracking and workflow processes are also included as part of the community and team modules.

The implementation of the enabling modules should have a true plug-and-play character. Although some of the modules benefit from the implementation of a previous module, they can be added in any order related to the specific business need that is to be met.

For example, Real-Time Collaboration services, such as video conferencing, can be easily included on top of the prerequisite technologies, but they are enhanced by the metadata services provided in the content management module.

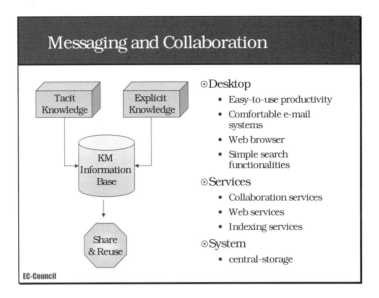

Communications Module

We shall first discuss the essential modules that help facilitate knowledge management.

The entry point to all information and applications in a knowledge-management system can be a groupware, intranet or a portal. If the environment also supports creating content, it's a knowledge-management desktop. Web browsers that can present all kinds of information in a powerful manner are ideal candidates for such desktop functionality.

> Desktop: The desirable characteristics include -

  o Easy-to-use productivity suites integrated in all other desktop services

  o E-mail systems.

    An email client with collaborative features (such as calendaring, task management, and discussion threads) can be integrated with the productivity suite to build a single interface for accessing collaborative information and creating documents.

  o Web browser for browsing and presenting the documents to the user.

    A primary goal of a knowledge-management system is to build a single interface for its users, where as much information as possible is accessible. To achieve that single interface, Web technologies, such as hypertext can be used to present information, as this will give more flexibility when accessing data from the knowledge-management desktop. Web browsers can act as information brokers, while web servers with suitable protocols can be deployed to hide the document store (file system).

- o Simple search functionalities such as integrated file services with the operating system or search services integrated with an application.

➢ Services

- o Collaboration services with a multi-purpose database for capturing the collaborative data. Databases on the collaboration servers can be used to for storing and retrieving information assets. Public folders on these servers can store discussions and collaborative documents.

- o Web services for providing the access layer to documented knowledge. Organizations can adopt web technologies to access information.

- o Indexing services for full-text search of documents. Indexing services can be used to search different document partitions to reflect the scope of the company's information.

➢ System

- o Well-organized central-storage locations such as file, Web servers, and document databases

Introduction to the Intranet

⊙ Intranet is a corporate information network based on Internet technologies, seeking to integrate people, processes and information within the enterprise.

⊙ The enterprise bears the cost of the intranet and manages it centrally, with well defined policies.

⊙ Challenges faced are integration, accessibility, presentation and reliability.

EC-Council

Introducing the Intranet

An intranet is a private computer network based on the communication standards of the Internet. It is smaller version of the Internet that only the members of an organization can see. Intranet business applications use the local-area network (LAN) infrastructure within a company along with Internet Web technology to provide high-performance software solutions.

Such solutions go beyond Web publishing, or Web-based forms, to provide front-office-grade software suitable for the customer service representative (CSR) speaking directly with customers. They have a network user interface (NUI) that resembles a graphical user interface (GUI) but that runs in a Web browser.

The purpose of an intranet is to enable knowledge workers to find the right information to solve problems or drive decisions. A well-organized information network that drives decision-making or provides access to all the relevant data needed to get jobs done supports this basic module of knowledge management. These decisions must be made quickly enough to get or maintain a competitive advantage. A collaborative environment must be extended if it is to meet these requirements.

From an organizational perspective, there must be a role like that of a knowledge librarian, who knows which organizational group or team needs what knowledge is required, where it is located, and how to group and connect information together.

Other roles that can provide useful are the knowledge architect (KA), who is introduced during the transition to a complete intranet.

The role of the KA is to own the technical and political overview of the information infrastructure of the organization. This role negotiates between groups and handles overlapping competencies and border issues so as to optimize the information-gathering process. There can be several knowledge architects who divide the responsibilities for the information services in an organization. The chief knowledge officer (CKO) is responsible for coordinating the KAs.

From an infrastructure perspective, services are needed that support the core characteristics of intranets, such as presenting related information in the form of pointers and links to Web resources, creating and accessing knowledge assets over standard Internet protocols and presenting the right information (groups) to the right people.

The Scale is an important factor in Intranet implementation, but it has no bearing on the logical association of clients that make up an intranet. For example, a workgroup with one web server, a company with several web servers, and a professional organization with ten thousand web servers can each be considered an intranet.

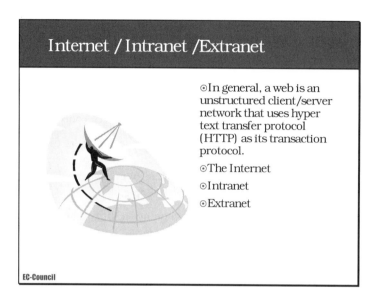

Differentiating Intranet Internet and Extranet

In general, a web is an unstructured client/server network that uses HTTP as its transaction protocol.

> ➤ The World Wide Web comprises all HTTP nodes on the public Internet.

> ➤ An internal web comprises all HTTP nodes on a private network, such as an organization's LAN or WAN. If the organization is a corporation, the internal web is also a corporate web.

> ➤ If a corporate web connects two or more trading partners, it is often referred to as a business-to-business web, or an extranet.

Note that internal webs - also known as intranets - are only logically "internal" to an organization. Physically they can span the globe, as long as access is limited to a defined community of interest.

Internet / Intranet Business Issues

- What is the value to my business in creating an Internet/intranet application?
- How much will it cost?
- How do I guide employees to use it to enhance business productivity?
- How does an intranet compare with traditional networking?
- What kind of organizational infrastructure do I need to support these people?
- Will an intranet parallel my paper system or replace it?
- How are my competitors using these technologies, internally and externally?
- What training will I need to offer users and administrators to use the new Internet/intranet tools?

Courtesy: Sun Microsystems

EC-Council

Intranet Business Issues

It is possible to quantify some benefits such as savings in operating cost, reduction in paperwork. The other intangible benefits of an intranet solution are improved customer service and faster and better access to current and relevant information.

The initial cost of setting up an intranet will include the cost of hardware (web server, network adapter and related hardware), software (server operating system, add-on software, utilities) and labor (setup & maintenance). In the long term, other costs such as server and network upgrades to handle traffic, management tools and manpower, software licenses and upgrade fees, information publishing and archiving costs will arise.

However, expenses can be categorized into three main categories.

> Technology costs: Hardware, software, post-production, and maintenance costs

> Information costs: Subscriptions to external information, marketing, and promotion

> Personnel costs: IT and content provider man-hours for development, and training

An intranet is a technology that is easy to start with and can be a management challenge as it evolves. It is therefore advisable that organizations plan for the growth phases well ahead. Some aspects to be considered are increased traffic and an increasing number of publishers and users. Optimal use of the web and network management tools is recommended to moderate the amount of manual work involved. For instance, new users can be added with the help of online forms that will automatically setup the required accounts.

Presented below is a compendium of issues relating to intranet building and maintenance, which is to be understood before hand:

Training

No technology is leveraged optimally without appropriate training. The publishers will have to be trained in the art of web publishing. It is recommended that training be approached in a two-pronged manner. The core technical intranet development team can be trained to take care of the server management, application development and technical aspects of the intranet. The functional team can handle simpler tasks like publishing documents to html, converting existing data sources like spreadsheets and databases to a format acceptable for the intranet. Both these groups will need different kind of training, therefore the organization needs to identify suitable personnel who will be able to adapt to the new methodology easily.

Outsource

Outsourcing an Intranet is an option, though not generally recommended. The advantages of outsourcing are having faster development cycles, leveraging the expertise and experience of professionals for intranet management and support. However, hand holding support post implementation will be critical to ensure user adoption.

Affect productivity

If done right, an intranet can enhance productivity to a great extent. A lot depends on the type of system the intranet is replacing. If an intranet solution is replacing a traditional paper based information access methodology (ex. printed manuals) the improvement in productivity will be tremendous. On the other hand, if it is introducing a completely new process it may not be possible to measure the productivity in an accurate manner.

Security

The security concerns to be addressed will be similar in nature to that seen on the web except that there is a known user base here. Like the Internet, the intranet will be as secure as its weakest link, which is usually the people managing and using the intranet. If secure infrastructure is used as part of the system such as a secure server, firewall, password protected access and physical security for the server machines, it is highly unlikely for security breaches to occur. Apart from the technical level security check, if the management can implement suitable policies, it check creeping links to unsecured locations, backdoors from the internet to the intranet, proper use of passwords and other security mechanisms provided by the intranet setup.

Timeframe

Unlike most other IT implementations, an intranet can be setup real fast. To start with, an existing network (preferable TCP/IP based) and a machine that can act as the web server is all that is needed. Once a web server package is installed, browsers can be installed on the client machines. Intranets usually grow and improve with time.

Internet / Intranet Technology Issues

- ⊙ Aligning business goals with design specifications
- ⊙ Reusability of existing technology
- ⊙ Content Management Requirements
- ⊙ Legacy application Integration
- ⊙ Intranet Security
- ⊙ Impact on existing infrastructure
- ⊙ Extent of centralized control
- ⊙ Support and maintenance
- ⊙ Operational requirements

EC-Council

Intranet Technology Issues

Common technology issues encountered while developing and deploying an Internet/Intranet application includes:

➢ Aligning business goals with design specifications: It is the business needs that drive the application features and functionalities. Therefore design specifications are drawn in alignment to the business requirements.

➢ Reusability of existing technology: Most organizations will be having IS/It infrastructure, which could have been adopted as organization wide platforms. Much development works might have happened already utilizing those technologies. There fore it is ideal that top the most extent possible the technology available be made to good use while planning for the new initiative instead of junking the existing IT investments.

➢ Content Management Requirements: This is a crucial requirement that need to be carefully studied in the organization's business context and incorporated accordingly.

➢ Legacy application Integration: Most Internet /Intranet applications need to integrate with legacy applications already being used within the organization.

➢ Intranet Security: Security issues with regard to authorizations and access control protocols need to be designed and implemented in accordance with the organization's set procedures.

➢ Impact on existing infrastructure: Any new application development and deployment has to be evaluated with respect to the impact on existing infrastructure.

> ➢ Extent of centralized control: Centralized structure allows for detailed analysis of content usage. It also provides a single picture of user base allows for analysis of knowledge needs across the organization. Extent of centralized/decentralized control need to be decided based on the above mentioned facts.

> ➢ Support and maintenance: This is crucial as support and maintenance is an ongoing process for any internet/intranet application. The efficacy of the application depends on the support and maintenance available.

> ➢ Operational requirements: Operational requirements are the main considerations that drive the design of the application. These need to be well understood as the system features and functionality hinges on these.

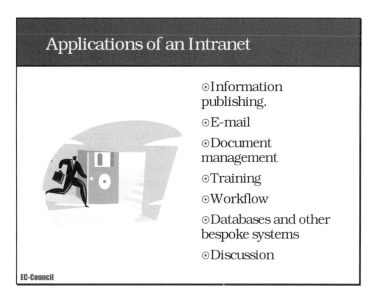

Intranet Components

Intranets play a key role in reducing costs and increasing effectiveness and efficiency of internal information management. Intranet applications serve as productivity, sales, service, and training tools that can be disseminated through the organization at much lower cost than traditional paper, client/server, or mainframe implementations. In addition, intranets enhance the capabilities of traditional applications by extending portions of the application to a wider audience within the organization.

Information publishing: using the intranet to deliver news and other information in the form of directories and web documents.

E-mail: implementing an e-mail system that integrates seamlessly with the intranet, allowing information to be both 'pushed' and 'pulled'.

Document management: using the intranet to allow users to view, print and work collaboratively on office documents (word-processed documents, spreadsheets, presentations, etc.).

Training: using the intranet to deliver training at the desktop.

Workflow: using the intranet to automate administrative processes.

Databases and other bespoke systems: using the intranet as a front-end to organization-specific systems, such as corporate databases.

Discussion: using the intranet as a means for users to discuss and debate issues.

Benefits

⊙ There are three main categories of benefit:

- Direct cost savings: savings in expenditure other than labor - print, paper, telephone, travel costs, etc. - that can be directly attributed to the introduction of the intranet.

- Human Resource savings: savings in the amount of time required to carry out tasks as a result of introducing the intranet.

- Increase in Productivity : increases in output per person attributable to the introduction of the intranet, expressed as a percentage.

EC-Council

Benefits of an Intranet

There are three main categories of benefit:

Direct cost savings: This is the savings in expenditure other than labor. Examples are print, paper, telephone, travel costs, etc. that can be directly attributed to the introduction of the intranet. These can usually be calculated in three steps:

> ➤ The number of incidences of expenditure in the time period

> ➤ The cost of each incidence and

> ➤ The proportion of these that could be eliminated using the intranet.

For example, if the number of formal printed material received per person per year was 1000, the cost in pence per page, including printing and delivery, was 8 cents and the percentage of these pages that could be delivered on-line was 75%, the saving in dollars would be 1000 x (8 / 100) x 75% x the size of the population.

Human resources savings: This is the savings in the amount of time required to carry out tasks as a result of introducing the intranet. These can be expressed in minutes per person per day. To calculate the saving, divide the number of minutes saved by the number of minutes in the day (60 x the number of working hours) and multiply by the size of the population and the average salary.

Increase in productivity: Productivity increases in output per person attributable to the introduction of the intranet, expressed as a percentage. Because personal productivity has such a wide range of implications from job to job and organization to organization, it is probably easier to convert these to simple human resource savings. The actual effect of higher productivity, such as increases in sales, could well be much larger.

Applications and Benefits

Each category of intranet usage has its own associated benefits:

Benefits	Direct cost savings	Human resource savings	Increase in productivity
Information publishing	Print, paper and delivery costs.	Faster access to information; more rapid and easy exchange of information; less duplication of effort and less interruptions	Availability of more accurate and up-to-date information
E-mail	Costs of phone calls, faxes, memos, letters, diskettes and other digital media	Less time spent preparing and checking items to be sent out and less interruptions	Faster access to information
Document management	Print, paper, digital media and delivery costs	Less time for review, editing and revision, less duplication of effort	Faster access to accurate and up-to-date business documents
Training	Savings in travel and accommodation, trainers, rooms and equipment	Less time spent traveling to courses; less time required to reach learning objectives	Immediate access to required knowledge and skills
Workflow	The print, paper and delivery costs	Less time spent per person per form	Faster and more reliable admin processes
Databases/bespoke systems		Less time required to learn and use applications	Information being available that was not previously available

| **Discussion** | Travel and accommodation costs for meetings | Less time spent traveling and in meetings | Faster resolution of issues and concerns |

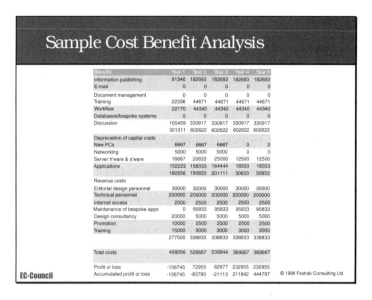

Cost Benefit Analysis Exhibit

This example assumes that information publishing, training, workflow and discussion are implemented, that the write-off period is three years and that year one benefits are 50% of those in subsequent years.

Return on investment

Return on investment is a way of expressing as a percentage the return you have made relative to the amount you have invested:

ROI = (benefits – investment x 100) / investment

Payback period

The payback period is the time it takes to 'break even' on your investment, in other words when the accumulated return on investment figure first exceeds 100%. In the example above, the payback period is 39 months, or three months into the fourth year.

Intranet Technology Requirements

- Uniform Resource Locator (URL) technologies to link related information together into an information Web.

- Directory Services that store information about people's roles and responsibilities in the organization.

- File servers extended with Web servers to access the documents over standard Internet protocols.

- Home pages on the Web servers for each specific business problem, presenting groups of related knowledge assets.

EC-Council

Intranet Technology Requirements

 The technology requirements for developing an Intranet include:

➤ Uniform Resource Locator (URL) technologies to link related information together into an information Web. Use integrated development environments to create, manage, and develop your knowledge-management intranet

➤ Directory Services that store information about people's roles and responsibilities in the organization. Extend the Messaging Directory with information about roles and responsibilities. This will enable workers to search the corporate address book for knowledge contacts.

➤ File servers extended with Web servers to access the documents over standard Internet protocols. Extend the document locations on file servers with standard Internet technologies such as Web services. This tactic will make every knowledge asset stored on these servers accessible from standard Web browsers (through the use of HTTP). It will also streamline the variety of access methods, making it easier for the knowledge workers.

➤ Home pages on the Web servers for each specific business problem, presenting groups of related knowledge assets. Build home pages for related information and information groups. HTML pages should include links to all knowledge sources: not only internal documents but also people and external pages. This will supply your knowledge workers with one-stop access to those related knowledge assets.

The following list of Microsoft technologies that help build a complete intranet is given for illustration purposes.

> ➢ Microsoft FrontPage For building and managing Webs, especially to link the information together and to create Web server home pages.

> ➢ Microsoft Office Web Folders and Server Extensions To enable the storing and accessing of Office documents on Web servers through HTTP/WebDAV.

> ➢ Microsoft Internet Information Server with Active Server Pages (ASP) to access roles and responsibility data in directory services.

> ➢ Microsoft Exchange Server For a global corporate directory service with information about roles and responsibilities.

> ➢ Microsoft Visual Studio For developing easy access to directory data, enabling the finding of people, and including this information within Web server home pages.

User adoption of Intranets can be attacked on many fronts:

> ➢ Design the Intranet as a product, i.e. according to actual work needs, not according to existing content or organization chart

> ➢ Determine who has pain from current state of Intranet and get them to form a focus group.

> ➢ From your focus group, assign ownership to workflows related to new content, so that it gets updated regularly

> ➢ Find ROI talking points for presentations to upper management (less printing, fewer support calls, etc.)

> ➢ Find a C-level champion who will sponsor a release event and will personally challenge managers to develop process efficiencies using the Intranet 6. Join forces with internal brand communicators

Types of Knowledge

This section provides advice on the types of knowledge that could be provided as templates to facilitate user contribution and build the most complete picture around a scenario or topic:

> ➢ Web Link (a value statement and the URL link to the internet page)

> ➢ Document (a value statement and the link to the electronic document file)

> ➢ Quote (literally, quotations and their sources)

> ➢ Idea (an attributable idea the user wishes to post)

> ➢ Note (typically an anecdote, aide memoir or brief commentary)

> ➢ Story (a structured narrative of the challenge, the problems, the process, the solution and the lessons learned)

> ➢ Intelligence (news and other business intelligence, including the source)

> ➢ Discussion (threaded discussions)

> ➢ Publication Reference (Sign-posting the location of physical materials, such as manuals, journals, books, videos, databases etc.)

> ➢ FAQ (the title, question and answer)

> ➢ Contact (to add the rolodex details of customers, suppliers, partners etc. who have specific relevance to the subject-matter of a topic)

> ➢ Opinion (anonymous opinions, encouraging free-flowing debate)

> ➢ Project (designed as objects around which to cluster project specific knowledge)

Corporate Intranets

⊙ Challenges:
- Content is still determined by local contributors, so may not match needs
- Users are further away from contributors, so cannot communicate requirements

⊙ Opportunities:
- Centralised structure allows for detailed analysis of content usage
- Single picture of user base allows for analysis of knowledge needs across the organisation

EC-Council

Challenges and Opportunities of a Corporate Intranet

Intranets pose certain challenges and opportunities that must be factored while undertaking the project.

Challenges

➢ One of the common challenges faced is that of content management in terms of objectivity and quality. Content is still determined by local contributors, so it may not match the needs as envisaged by the organizational knowledge requirements. This means that coordinated efforts need to be orchestrated to procure steady flow of relevant content. New roles and perspectives need to be inculcated to facilitate this.

➢ Users are further away from contributors, so cannot communicate requirements. While an Intranet facilitates collaboration, face-to-face interactivity that is so crucial to any knowledge creation process, as understood by socialization is limited.

Opportunities:

➢ Centralized structure allows for detailed analysis of content usage. This is the greatest opportunity that an Intranet delivers. The organization can get an insight into who uses what and in which context.

> ➤ Similarly, single picture of user base allows for analysis of knowledge needs across the organization. The organization can have one view of its human capital and plan for strategic knowledge needs accordingly.

Communities, Teams , Experts

⊙ Empowers the knowledge worker to get information quickly and proactively

⊙ Technology Requirements
- Directory and membership services
- Forum services
- Self-subscription services
- Workflow services
- Tracking services
- Monitor services
- E-mail services
- Organization-wide databases
- Home pages on Web servers

EC-Council

Communities Teams And Experts

We have seen that the two prerequisite technologies for knowledge management can put all collaboration and document-based knowledge sources together and enable the knowledge worker to browse through informational objects based on knowledge groups. Communities, teams, and experts add to the next level of sharing knowledge and turn it to results.

This technology module focuses on teams and communities. Teams differ from communities in that teams are task driven, and communities are interest driven. Usually a team works closely together (a workgroup) on the same tasks and goals. In many cases, the information produced by a team is closely held within the team until it has reached a level of completeness where it can be shared.

Communities are discussed in detail in elsewhere in the courseware. Communities are mostly driven by interests in the same area and are more loosely coupled. The information shared by a community is closely held at the final release. Communities are especially useful for building knowledge to advanced levels, often by getting successive levels of input from a broad audience.

This enabling module supports knowledge workers' joining communities by subscribing themselves to subject matter sources. The building of communities and teams is characteristic of this module, whether they are driven by the information in the knowledge management system, administered by a knowledge management architect, or service by himself or herself.

Experts form the other major part of this module. The role of an expert is to qualify and filter information. Each expert is related to a limited set of subjects. Those subject matter experts (SMEs) can be defined in two ways. The first is by organizational function (as defined by the knowledge architect). The second is as well-known experts in their team or organization who have assumed the status of an SME for contributing high quality information or for reviewing it. The SME is an important role for anyone working within an intranet related to knowledge management. To maximize the usefulness of the intranet, the information should be filtered (is this really useful information), classified (which type or category of information is this), and grouped together (which information correlates to this). This process is part of the responsibility of the SME.

Communities, teams, and experts also control the process of putting information into the knowledge-management system. Filtering, qualifying, approving, or more complex workflow processes for documents and other electronic data need to be established. In a knowledge-management system, these processes are not strictly based on traditional organizational roles (manager, reviewer, approver, author, and so forth) but more on the SMEs. This can add a great level of flexibility to the knowledge-management system and the automated processes.

Together with the collaborative prerequisite that enables the infrastructure with e-mail services, this component empowers the knowledge worker to get information quickly and proactively from a knowledge-management system right on the knowledge-management desktop. Technology requirements for communities, teams, and experts include the following:

Directory and membership services that support community building. This is achieved by grouping people together into expert teams working on the same set of information or having the same needs and interests in specific information.

> Forum services to create workspaces for communities and teams that contain all related data. Build community forums, and allow flexibility to add forums dynamically on demand. Use moderated forums to allow SMEs to filter and control content.

> Self-subscription services to specific matters of interest for information delivery and subscribing.

> Assign relevant services to assign specific knowledge-management roles to knowledge workers.

> Deploy Workflow services for automating processes based on roles and SMEs.

> Allow tracking services that follow team contacts and team activities.

> Enable active monitoring services that enable SMEs to filter information.

> Use dynamic-distribution lists and automated-subscription services for e-mail.

> Develop E-mail services for automating notification, routing, and simple workflow methods.

> ➤ Implement organization-wide databases that integrate and allow searching for skill data and other HR information to enhance communities and teams.

> ➤ Design home pages on Web servers for each community, team, or expert to speed up the access to knowledge sources.

Expertise Location

📋**Expertise location.** Suppose one's goal is not to find someone with common interests but to get advice from an expert who is willing to share his or her knowledge. Expertise location systems have the goal of suggesting the names of persons who have knowledge in a particular area. In their simplest form, such systems are search engines for individuals, but they are only as good as the evidence that they use to infer expertise.

There are two steps in finding expertise within organizations:

> ➤ Identification phase: Expertise identification is the problem of knowing what information or special skills other individuals have. Expertise identification is a complicated task. The nature of expertise itself, what it is and how it is used, as well as the fact that people grow and change over time, make solving this problem difficult. This is the first problem with which information seekers must deal before they can hope to get information they need. Many people have difficulty articulating how they know who has knowledge about system components, diagnostic methods, business practices, and the like. For many people, "experience" is the primary guide in identifying others with specific expertise. It

stems from performing work and the large gamut of social interaction, both formal and informal, which is part of that work over time.

➢ Selection phase: Expertise selection is appropriately choosing among people with the required expertise. If there are multiple potential experts or people with the requisite expertise, it is necessary to select one (or more) to ask. The drawback with using an explicit profile for selecting expertise is that persons may not be motivated to keep it up to date. Thus it is preferable to gather information automatically, if possible, from existing sources.

The current state of the art is to use:

➢ Explicit profiles

➢ Evidence mined from existing databases

➢ Evidence inferred from association of persons and documents.

For example, the Lotus Discovery Server product contains a facility whereby an individual's expertise is determined using these techniques, while it and the Tacit Knowledge Systems KnowledgeMail product analyze the e-mail a person writes to form a profile of his or her expertise.

Given the properties of on-line discussions, it is reasonable to suppose that a fourth source of evidence could be the content of the questions answered by a person in such a system, with the added advantage that such a person is already willing to be helpful.

Expertise Location Guidelines

- Business Commitment
- Incentives to Collaborate
- Conceptual Query Capability
- Understanding Depth of Experience
- Culture Adaptation
- Automatic Organizational Learning
- Integration into Existing Systems
- Automatic Profile Generation
- Privacy Protection

EC-Council

Guidelines for Deploying an Expert Location System

Business Commitment: The organization must be able to commit to the best practices that will encourage the usage of an expertise location system. The expertise location system must be patronized within the company both before and after deployment. For instance, Dow Chemical created an 11-member executive team with a five-year outlook on knowledge management, including an expertise location component. They attribute some of the $25 million they have saved as a result of their KM initiative to the creation of information stewards for each business group. The role of the information stewards was to educate group members on the value of applying knowledge management technologies to accelerate business strategies.

Incentives to Collaborate: An incentive / reward system to encourage employees to answer requests for collaboration in addition to answering them can go a long way in making expertise location a success. These incentives / reward system may be of the form of increased recognition or capital gains. For instance, the success of Shell Oil's KNIT (knowledge community infrastructure team) has been attributed to an approach towards adoption that treated business units as competing entrepreneurs in the development of their knowledge management strategies. This approach effectively rewarded best practices for their high impact and adoption rates.

Conceptual Query Capability: The expertise system must be able to extract general concepts from a query. It should understand the nature of a user's request within the context of the business environment and extract the relevant concepts of both specific and general queries. For instance, a query that requests expertise on Glaxo Wellcome might be relevant to someone with expertise on Pfizer. However, unless the system can recognize that both Glaxo Wellcome and Pfizer are pharma companies, the match will not be made.

Understanding Depth of Experience: Characterizing employee experience must go beyond keyword associations to incorporate relevant past experience, project roles, peer recognition, etc. The system must be able to customize these criteria for each company. For instance, when RSA needs to assemble a team of developers to test the security of its secure technologies, it is valuable to know their technical experience with cryptography. A solution needs to be customized to take depth of experience into account.

Culture Adaptation: The importance of corporate culture cannot be overemphasized. An expert solution must take into account the specific challenges for knowledge sharing that each company faces. For instance, senior employees in Japanese firms are traditionally more hesitant to disclose personal information to any other party. An expertise location must take these cultural differences into account.

Automatic Organizational Learning: The system must adapt to growing/changing expertise within the company. It should be able to recognize company trends towards specific skill sets and focus results in this direction. For instance, New England Biomedical Research Inc, a biomedical research firm focused on biomedical research, needs to have an expertise locator that must be able to differentiate research projects based on very similar data sources. A system without learning would likely get hung up on commonalties; a system with learning would identify the need to place more emphasis on certain concepts or keywords that are unique to each project.

Integration into Existing Systems: For any expertise location system to be successfully adopted, it needs to effortlessly integrate into existing technologies and data sources that the company might have. This should eliminate the need to duplicate data across multiple content storage locations. A poll by IDC and an internal poll at Hewlett Packard both confirmed that employees prefer to use applications that are well integrated with existing resources. The IDC poll highlighted dissatisfaction with the "fragmentation of information," and the desire for a "single point of access."

Automatic Profile Generation: Popular expertise locator tools try to minimize dependency on an employee's input to his/her profile. Such input requirements drain employee productivity and lead to a underutilization of employees that do not have the time to modify their profiles. For instance, the KM system at the World Bank found that the requirement of profile maintenance was the single barrier to the adoption of the expertise location solution in its initial KM efforts.

Privacy Protection: Privacy is a major concern for most users. For users to be comfortable using a system that catalogues their expertise, they must maintain full control over the privacy of the content stored within their profiles. According to Adriana Vivacqua who prototyped an expertise location system for the MIT Media Laboratories, the system must acknowledge the fact that one computer scientist may not want the others to know what he or she knows about, or may not wish to be bothered about one particular issue. The system must therefore allow scientists to choose which areas of expertise it lets others know about and correct the profile if they think it is incorrect.

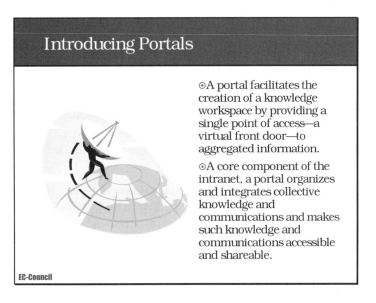

Introducing Portals

⊙A portal facilitates the creation of a knowledge workspace by providing a single point of access—a virtual front door—to aggregated information.

⊙A core component of the intranet, a portal organizes and integrates collective knowledge and communications and makes such knowledge and communications accessible and shareable.

EC-Council

Introducing Portals

One popular component of a knowledge initiative is a knowledge portal. Knowledge portals are single-point-access software systems intended to provide easy and timely access to information and to support communities of knowledge workers who share common goals.

A knowledge portal is a window not into just information, but the connections between the information that transforms it into Knowledge - Thomas Koulopoulos, CEO Delphi Group.

Considered as a core component of the intranet, a portal organizes and integrates collective knowledge and communications and in the process makes such knowledge and communications accessible and shareable.

The evolution of the knowledge portal began with the information portal. They started as applications, typically Web-based, providing a single point of access to distributed on-line information, such as documents resulting from a search, news channels, and links to specialized Web sites. To facilitate access to large accumulations of information, portals quickly evolved to include advanced search capabilities and organizing schemes, such as taxonomies. Here, the emphasis was on information, and these first-generation portals were called information portals. Information portals provide a valuable service on the Internet, by selecting, organizing, describing, and sometimes evaluating, useful sites.

However, with an organization, where different functional and organizational groups and lines of business operate, there may arise different needs for information access and organization.

Vortals are specialized portals in the corporate sector. These are vertical portals since they provide in-depth capabilities that are highly focused on a vertical segment of an organization or field.

Portals support knowledge workers as communities. Knowledge portals provide information to knowledge workers within the company, and they can also quickly supply external suppliers and customers with task-relevant information objects. The goal of such a portal is to build a transparent enterprise, hiding complexity to facilitate knowledge access over the enterprise information stores with legacy applications. Examples of business portal objects can include these team links, incoming mail notification and headers, personal tasks, corporate search and integration of business intelligence data.

Portals also address the creation of catalogs that categorizes related information based on business needs over stores of structured and unstructured enterprise information. This knowledge base allows full-text search against the partitioned data. An extension to the catalogs is the definition of searches against these catalogs by subject matter experts and makes these search definitions available. In order to define the catalogs for an organization, there has to be a very good understanding of the business and its processes.

The case for portals can be based on the following reasons.
> Over time, organizations have accumulated silos of information both internally and externally and accessing relevant information in a timely manner has become a challenge.

> As technology evolved and enabling products mushroomed, having a best of the breed infrastructure did not necessarily mean that they could talk to each other.

> The mode of access also increased and this could have a negative impact on productivity as information was accessed through many different methods, including client software, web browsers, specific applications and individual hard disks.

> Knowledge Management brought about the necessity of sharing knowledge. Individuals found it difficult to easily publish information for enterprise-wide viewing.

> Efficiency was affected, as there existed several different methods for searching and accessing information.

> Non-technical users were highly dependent on the IT department to generate reports or obtain information.

> Difficulty in access levels made several enterprise applications being used lesser.

> Expensive, non-intuitive or even non-existent viewing tools.

> Lack of effective online collaboration tools.

➢ The corporate architecture has several overlapping systems with complex and different user interfaces (many without a browser-based interface).

➢ Expensive and complex (hard coded) integration of different applications, databases and legacy systems.

➢ Security concerns across systems made access and retrieval of information formidable.

➢ There arose a need to have a desktop-centered view of IT applications.

Technology Requirements of Portals

- ⊙ Systems that allow customization
- ⊙ Web browsers with personalization systems
- ⊙ Development suites
- ⊙ Catalog and search services
- ⊙ Notification services
- ⊙ Database replication and transformation services

EC-Council

Technology Requirements of Portals

The technical requirements for a portal are discussed below.

➢ The access layer, is the sub-system that allow customization of the business portal

➢ Next comes the presentation layer - primarily the web browsers with personalization systems that offer the ability to include desktop services such as e-mail, collaboration data, or business-intelligence tools for accessing rich content.

➢ The portal needs to be supplemented with development suites for building and maintaining the business portal pages and sites.

➢ Another essential feature of a portal is catalog and search services that integrate all kinds of information sources and crawl-external resources like partner and suppliers sites or the Internet

➢ Services are required in order to build a virtual single storage location that combines all catalogs for knowledge retrieval and subsequent application.

➢ Notification services keep the users informed about changes by reacting to changes in catalogs and integrate with the e-mail system.

➢ Finally, database replication and transformation services that pull information from different data sources into the search system form the core of a portal technology infrastructure.

Benefits of Portals

- A consistent view of the organization through the use of forms-based authoring of documents, lists, reports, directories, indexes, and pages
- Powerful search and navigational capabilities for homogeneous cross-organizational discovery of relevant content
- Highly structured information categorization and document correlation—essential to the identification and retrieval of relevant search results
- Direct and rapid access to organizational data and knowledge as well as digital media communications through the integration of diverse business applications at the desktop
- Individual, secure, and role-based access to content

EC-Council

Benefits of Portals

There are several benefits to be derived from the portal. While some are quantifiable, many others arise as the intended users use these portals. We have seen that a portal integrates both dynamic and static information and communications from inside and outside an organization through a single user interface. It is the therefore the center of operations for the knowledge workplace, offering search, subscriptions, document management, and digital media services, as well as the integration of business process applications—all made accessible via a highly customizable, flexible user interface.

Portals have transformed the knowledge workplace by leveraging the "pull" of the knowledge worker rather than the "push" of the information technology (IT) department. Some of the core benefits arising out of a portal are:

➤ Rapid and Secure Access to Business Information

People need a consistent place to access needed information, and in a structured way that makes sense. Portals have become the place where such information is aggregated, organized, shared, and discoverable.

➤ Powerful Search

Portals make finding information easier with several features that make searching faster and more efficient by providing a single location to search for information that has been stored in many different places, such as Web sites, file systems, public folders on mail servers, and various databases. Portals improve efficiency by indexing these diverse data and enable searching multiple information sources at one time from one place. Other search capabilities include:

- o Full-text keyword searches—these full-text search options find all documents that match the search terms and return lists of results. "Advanced" search options are often provided; these match search terms with the document's properties, such as author, for more specific and focused results.

- o Browsing by topic—for users who are unfamiliar with where documents are stored, or what keywords to use in full text searching, browsing by categories makes information discovery more successful. It groups like documents and other content, irrespective of form or location. Portals often provide category creation wizards to simplify the time-consuming task of categorizing a large number of documents.

- o Subscriptions—by subscribing to relevant content, users are notified about new or refreshed information on topics that match their interests—a personalized alert service at the desktop.

➤ Security

Security is a fundamental and critical feature for portals, given the wide range of applications and data resources portals expose and the built-in flexibility they offer to the user. Typical portal security measures include the following:

- o Authentication—verifying the identities of the members of a team to allow participation in Web-based collaboration; checking users against an internal employee directory or database

- o Access control—providing users with access to application and knowledge resources appropriate to the workers' roles, departments, and other attributes

- o Auditing—maintaining access logs to track portal users and utilization

➤ Personalization

Portals can be customized for each individual knowledge worker. The flexibility to present information that is especially relevant to each worker, such as project-specific or workgroup-specific information can contribute to the user's sense of control and empowerment. It can also dramatically improve user productivity. Portal personalization can also enrich the predefined roles of a user by facilitating the delivery of more targeted and focused content.

Use of portals Forrester survey 2001 "49 of Global 3,500 – Forrester Research Survey, Fall 2001"

Benefit	Ranking
Benefits information	82%
Company news	78%
Employee Directory	53%
Education & Training	49%
Departmental Info.	37%
Personnel info updates	35%
Company Forms	33%
Financial News	27%
Sales Information	24%
Payroll Adjustments	24%
Industry News	20%
Collaborative tools	16%
Online Help Desk	16%
Travel Booking	14%
Email	12%
Purchase orders	10%

Portals and Document Management

- Version tracking
- Check-in and check-out
- Categories
- Application of descriptive, searchable information or meta data
- Document publishing control
- Automated approval routes
- Online discussions
- Control of document access based on roles

EC-Council

Relating Portals and Document Management

How do the portals assist in document management? A portal supports features such as document locking, versioning, check-in/check-out, and publishing and makes these features accessible to the average user. It delivers simple, document-management features that are integrated with the tools and applications that are used to create and manage documents.

This is especially relevant in the knowledge workspace as large and complex information sources can be difficult to navigate and use because there is little or no organizational structure. File folders, for instance, provide only a hierarchical directory structure as a means of organizing content. There is only one static navigation path to any given document, and users must know the name of the server on which the document is stored, in addition to the directory structure of the folder if they need to access a shared document. Portals offer a number of features that help to streamline document management. These are:

➤ Version tracking—version control records a document's history to help monitor changes and eliminate the possibility of someone overwriting another's modifications.

➤ Check-in and checkout—documents can be reserved by individual users for updating and this capability can prevent others from changing the document until it is "returned" to the workspace.

➤ Categories—content is classified under a set of user-defined categories for better information management and discoverability.

➢ Application of descriptive, searchable information or document profiling provides a way to add searchable information pertaining to a document. By default a document profile includes basic properties such as author and title, but in addition it can incorporate, where available, organizational vocabularies or taxonomies. This meta data can help describe or identify the documents.

➢ Document publishing control—Document routing controls when a document can be published and ready for public viewing, making the distinction between public and private versions of a document an important one.

➢ Automated approval routes—approval routes are an easy way to ensure that a document is effectively reviewed before it is published on the intranet.

➢ Online discussions—Web discussions allow users to conduct online discussions about a document, without modifying it, in true collaborative fashion. When comments are grouped into a single place, document authors can easily streamline them for publication.

➢ Control of document access based on roles—role-based security access identifies a specific set of permissions based on assignation of roles, for example, author, reader, or coordinator.

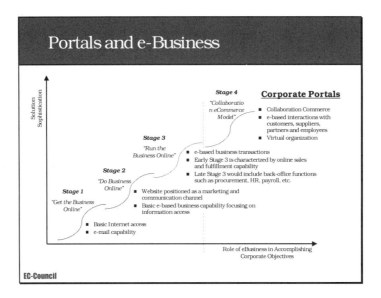

Portals and the e-Business Space

The evolution of portals and their final role in the e-business space are illustrated in the slide given above. Important lessons learnt from portal implementations have been shared by various organizations. Among these are:

➢ It is important to identify the strategic knowledge sources before embarking on the portal initiative

➢ The portal should have organizational alignment and have the support of internal alliances.

➢ A portal initiative should plan for taxonomy development and evolution at the outset itself.

➢ A portal initiative should be able to leverage existing IT infrastructure and applications.

➢ There should be sufficient budget allocated for development and operation

➢ The focus should be on content and applications that are immediately useful and get a lot of use.

➢ Quality of content is more important than quantity of content. Understand that the value of content and connections are time-sensitive.

➢ There should be a clear business case, value proposition and metrics.

➢ The portal team should understand and link internal and external perspectives.

➢ Focus should be on different user groups and on users needs.

➢ Different scenarios for usage should be developed.

➢ The portal should make it easy for employees to distribute content as widely or as narrowly as they decide.

➢ Employees' expertise should be profiled carefully to foster meaningful connections

➢ The portal initiative should be communicated clearly to all stakeholders.

➢ The portal initiative should leverage early adopters and focus on new employees

➢ Modular launches tend to deliver better results, especially when it is based on active participation of employees.

➢ Another pre-requisite is to have the supporting processes and (new) roles clearly defined before the launch.

➢ Garner local support as representatives play an important role.

➢ Change management is crucial to the project success.

➢ Innovative rewards and recognition strategies are critical.

➢ Online communities require careful planning, infrastructure and ongoing support.

➢ Monitor usage, participation and satisfaction levels of multiple stakeholders.

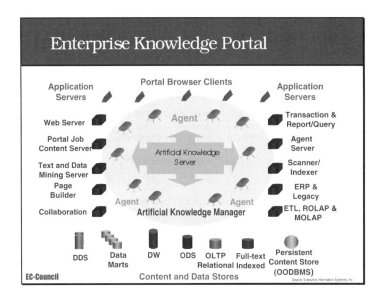

Enterprise Knowledge Portals

An Enterprise Knowledge Portal is an enhanced Enterprise Information Portal (EIP). It is an EIP that is goal directed toward knowledge production, knowledge integration, and knowledge management, and also focuses upon providing, producing and managing information about the validity of the information it supplies. It also provides information about the business and meta-information about the degree to which the user can rely on that information. Moreover, it distinguishes knowledge from mere information, provides a facility for producing knowledge from information by orienting one towards producing and integrating knowledge rather than information. In the architecture shown above, the EKP exhibits a complex environment with high level of decision support technology. This high level of decision support can be related to the complexity seen in multiplicity of systems such as:

> Diversity of data and information stores

> Application servers

> Presence of structured data and unstructured content sources

> Publication and agent capabilities

> Web server and portal capabilities

> Text and data mining capabilities

> Collaborative capabilities

➢ Dynamic integrative capabilities provided by its agents.

IBM defines agents as "Intelligent agents are software entities that carry out some set of operations on behalf of a user or another program with some degree of independence or autonomy, and in so doing, employ some knowledge or representation of the user's goals or desires."

Enterprise portals seek to leverage the collaborative aspects of enterprise content management (ECM) and knowledge management. Summing up, corporate portals are becoming increasingly sophisticated, integrating real-time news, competitive intelligence, business performance reporting, and knowledge sharing. New portal technology will undoubtedly incorporate personalized intelligent agent technology, which searches for information relevant to the individual. Fully customizable to the individual's information needs, intranet portals are today's real-time virtual water cooler and more.

We will summarize the ISYS enterprise portal product ISYS Web for illustration purposes.

➢ Customization - Fully customizable with the flexibility to create the exact interface required for the business need.

➢ Dynamic HTML conversion - Automatically converts documents to HTML promptly as they are served to the browser. All documents remain in their original location and format, reducing overall administrative workload.

➢ Search - ISYS has an accurate search and display capability. There is a very unique set of search methods that fit every need. From simple Boolean search commands to more complex searching.

➢ Navigation - Navigation tools are simple and straightforward. Users can navigate through a document hit-to-hit or document-to-document. View documents in their original format. The original format is maintained during dynamic HTML conversion.

➢ Publishing - Publish large document content in PDF or other publishing document formats.

➢ Outline View - Systems Administrators can limit the delivery to only relevant parts of a document conserving valuable system bandwidth.

➢ Classification - Classify data into separate searchable indexes according to particular business needs.

➢ Access to Information - Gathers content from all information sources into one index. Rules are applied across the enterprise that restricts data that can be searched.

- ➢ Supported information sources

    - o NT and Unix File servers

    - o SQL Databases

    - o Web servers

    - o Domino servers

    - o Microsoft Exchange servers

- ➢ Precision Search Options - ISYS delivers the most precise search options.

    - o Boolean search operators

    - o Natural language search

    - o Concept search

    - o Meta data search

    - o Multiple language options

- ➢ Document Access - Supports existing security rights and privileges.

- ➢ Supports Multiple Servers - Can be deployed on multiple servers and search a mixture of server platforms.

- ➢ Reporting Capability - Administrators can track and log user connection, user requests and security events.

- ➢ Intelligent Notification - Intelligent Agents alert users via e-mail when required information reaches the server

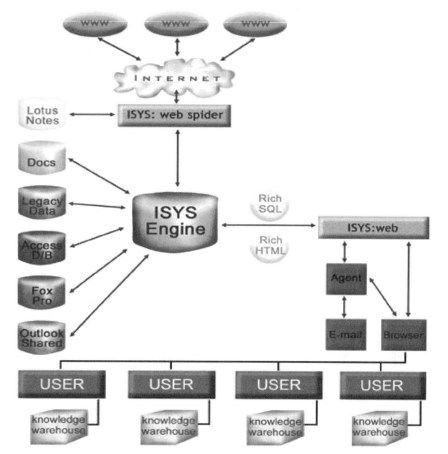

(Exhibit: ISYS EKP Technical Architecture Framework)

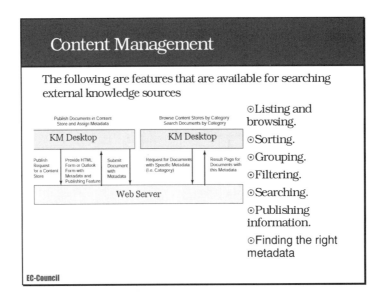

Content Management

We have seen that portals and search component addresses the problem of searching for knowledge in all information sources in the enterprise. This knowledge includes structured and unstructured internal information objects such as Office documents, collaborative data, MIS and ERP systems, and experts, as well as information from outside sources such as partners, suppliers, and competitors.

External sources, and in particular the Internet, represent tremendous potential for gathering knowledge if the criteria for including such information are chosen well. All of the pools of information sources that are part of, and accessible to, the knowledge-management system combine to build the knowledge-management information base.

Content management component handles how knowledge assets get into the knowledge-management information base. To tackle the increased complexity of the knowledge workplace, and to help the knowledge workers to stay focused on solving business challenges, a sophisticated knowledge-management taxonomy needs to be built based on metadata (data that describes other data). Besides, portals also need to publish information in the knowledge base, for example, categories and attributes. The knowledge management information base must therefore be accessible through operations driven by the metadata complex.

The challenge in managing content arises right from the content creation to its publishing. In the publishing process, several things should be considered concerning the knowledge-management taxonomy. Although tagging documents with metadata is important for the quality of content in this stage of document publishing, it can be demanding on the personnel if tagging the metadata is a complex or time-consuming process. The knowledge challenge is to avert building huge submission and posting systems in which users don't get recognized or rewarded, as this will discourage them from providing their knowledge, and therefore fail the purpose of knowledge management.

Technology Requirements

The purpose of a knowledge-management system is to understand how the users of the knowledge-management system interact with the knowledge-management information base. The regular analysis of usage and content to ensure that the knowledge-management system fulfills its purpose and is up to date is essential for the success of the system.

Locating the right metadata is an essential yet challenging process for the knowledge architect. Too much metadata will add high complexity to the system, lowering the overall effectiveness, as it becomes difficult to search, browse, and publish accurately. Too little metadata will lead to rough partitions that bring about fuzzy information results.

The features that are available for searching external knowledge sources are listing and browsing, sorting, grouping, filtering, searching, and publishing information to the knowledge-management information base.

Several of the functionalities required for content management are implemented today in document-management systems. Content that is not valuable to users needs to be identified, and content that has great value can be presented in ranking lists on the knowledge portal or distributed through notification services.

Best Practices

> To increase the usability of the publishing and search functionality of the content management system define each content class and it's associated metadata well.

> Avoid too many content classes, as this will lead to publishing related documents under different content stores, which will result in disjointed result sets. Too few content classes will result in too generalized content, making it difficult to get an exact result set.

> Increased precision in metadata definition makes it easier to find information based on different criteria. This is especially important as an expert might search and browse for the same data using different keywords from those a beginner would use.

> Ensure that, during the publishing process, users can tag the documents according to the defined metadata. For this purpose, define a publishing strategy for documents and integrate it into the knowledge-management system.

> To increase the retention of useful data in the knowledge base, integrate analysis services in the knowledge-management system. Use this data also to personalize the knowledge-management portals.

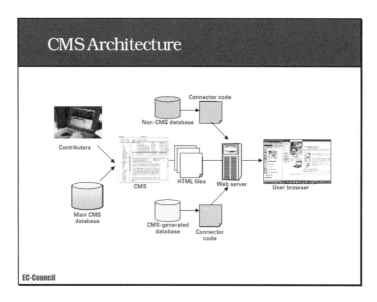

Architecture of a CMS

Content management involves effectively collecting, managing, and making information available in targeted publications. Content, stated as simply as possible, is information put to use. Information is put to use when it is packaged and presented (published) for a specific purpose. More often than not, content is not a single piece of information, but a collection of pieces of information put together to form a cohesive whole. For instance, the Website is just a collection of articles, advertisements, indexes, and pictures – all organized into a coherent presentation.

When content collection takes place, information is either created or acquired. It is then converted to a master format and segmented into discrete chunks called content components. Components are metadata containers for the content that make it easier to organize, store, and retrieve the information.

Each component travels through a content system as a unit. When new content is created it is done one entire component at a time. When content is archived or deleted, it is done by components. When a page is created, it is by pulling together one or more components into a page frame or template.

The content domain is the realm of information that needs to be controlled in order to meet business goals. The content domain is the scope or range of information that is to be captured, managed, and published. The content domain is directly related to the goals of the content management system overall.

Content is managed within a repository that consists of database records and/or files containing content components, plus administrative data (i.e. the system's users). A content management system helps organize and automate collection, management, and publishing processes. A content management system is needed when:

➢ The information at hand that needs to be processed is monumental.

➢ Information is continuously changing and manual processing makes it loose its current relativity.

➢ When there is a need for more than one publication to be created from a single base of content.

➢ When the design of a publication needs to be separated from the content so that as design changes each page of the publication need not be modified afresh.

➢ In order to make content available, the content management system publishes to targeted publications such as Web sites, printable documents, and email newsletters.

There are no universally accepted standards for what content management systems are or do. The majority of content management systems in use today were created to keep pace with the explosive growth of Web sites.

Commercial applications are available that provide content management in a variety of ways. The concepts and offerings around content management will evolve with time and use. It is difficult to clearly state the advantage of any single product, as custom developed versions abound.

Some content management systems store components in files. Most store them in a relational database, and a few store them in object databases that use XML hierarchies rather than relational tables to store the components.

The correct method of dividing content into components is the one that gives the organization using it the greatest advantage within current abilities and resources. This implies that the content must be divided according to well-defined and universally understood rules. The rules can change, however, at any instant, there has to be one set of rules so that at all times the content is organized.

Core Concepts Behind Content Management

➢ Understanding content domain, from which all of the structural decisions flow.

➢ Content components, which allow content processes (collection, management, and publication) to be automated. Components divide information into convenient and manageable chunks. They are a set of discrete objects whose creation, maintenance, and distribution can be automated. They typically share some common attributes, such as format or length.

➢ A framework based on metadata, which unites all the content into a single.

➢ All content management systems should have a concise domain statement. Effective domain statements are no more than a few sentences.

➢ Target publications, which are the end result of any content system. Publishing is simply releasing information that was previously being developed. All publications should have these aspects to them:

- o Author

- o Audience

- o Purpose

- o Publisher

  - ▪ Management staff: responsible for the business of the publication (expenses, revenue, and staffing).

  - ▪ Editorial staff: responsible for acquiring, creating, and formatting content for publication.

  - ▪ Technical staff: responsible for building the system that collects, manages, and publishes the content.

  - ▪ Creative staff: responsible for the look and feel of the publication as well as its appeal and ability to resonate with the target audience.

  - ▪ Architectural staff: responsible for the structural design of the content system and the content itself.

- o Format: This is the way information is encoded. For instance, the publishers might use a product such as Quark® Xpress. Quark has a particular way that it encodes the information entered into it. The publisher works with files that only Quark can decode and manipulate. Additionally, Quark has a set of formatting features (character, paragraph, section, etc.) that can be applied to the information entered that determine how the information will be rendered on the printed page. Only Quark knows how to decode and manipulate these formatting features. The main content management issue with publication formats comes when there is more than one format.

o Structure

As with format, several structures can abound. Issues arise when there is more than one structure. For instance, when there are two publications, three structures are needed – one for each publication and one for the content, since base content should not be constrained by one format or another. In order to produce more than one publication from the same content base, the content base itself must be structured neutrally enough so that the structure of any of the end publications is derivable from the structure of the content base. Extensible Mark-up Language (XML) is becoming and increasingly common way of doing this.

Real Time Collaboration

⊙ Technologies that you should use to implement the real-time collaboration component include the following:

- Chat services with transcript functionality for distance discussion
- Video conferencing for virtual meetings
- Screen-sharing services for sharing the document-creation process, using virtual whiteboards, and sharing applications
- Streaming-media services for recording virtual meetings and video (meeting) on demand services
- Event and meeting databases for organizing the virtual event center

EC-Council

Real Time Collaboration

We had discussed the importance of tacit knowledge and the challenge it presents to KM. Collaboration frameworks show some means of getting the knowledge into a state where an IT system can manage it. This especially focuses on areas where computers can help workers exchange thoughts, documents, and other aids for capturing this tacit knowledge for the knowledge-management information base.

This process of capturing tacit knowledge can begin with the introduction of simple computer-based chat services. Webcasts / conferences / meetings arranged regularly with expert groups over the network to talk about specific topics can be extended with these services, by building automatic transcripts for the chat sessions. Transcripts can be easily enriched with corporate metadata, multimedia and stored in the information base for later search and retrieval.

Webcasts are complex services, which follow a similar concept to video conferencing. The video stream is recorded on video equipment and later transferred to the knowledge-management system. Descriptions and metadata are either merged with this video stream or can be stored in a file or a database.

As ebusiness is transforming the business environment, such virtual meetings are common, and an event database is typically built where upcoming and past meetings are stored together with event titles and descriptions. They are listed or searchable by subject matter, and a hyperlink is provided so that users can join a virtual meeting, even after it has taken place in the first instance.

If the meeting takes place in the future, integration into the e-mail system ensures that this event is marked in the calendar, and, on the event date, a reminder automatically points the participant toward the virtual meeting. After the event or meeting, on-demand services will make that knowledge available by providing the recorded video out of the knowledge information base to the desktop. When integrating this technology into the scenario of automated knowledge-management services, notifications are sent automatically to the appropriate knowledge workers to remind them of an interesting meeting or event. The appropriate URLs can also be listed on the knowledge-management portal. This is real time collaboration.

There can also be real time collaboration over several channels such as the web, PDA, mobile, chat or plain email simultaneously. For instance, an online presentation that consists of slides is sent over the network. The audience receives the video, audio, and slides of the presentation on its desktop. The chat service is integrated as a separate area on the desktop, and it enables the audience to type questions during the meeting into the chat area. These questions are transferred to the presenter or a person controlling the online presentation. On receiving the questions, the presenter can answer them during or at the end of the event. All three sources-the slides as a static document, the chat as a transcript document, and the audio and video as a stream-are linked together and stored in the knowledge-management system.

Real-time collaboration supports sharing the creation process, making it possible for knowledge workers separated by distance to share a single virtual working space and work together to create documents. This includes sharing the creation process using not only a productivity suite but also whiteboard functionality. This kind of technology is also called screen sharing.

One of the areas where real-time collaboration is gaining prominence is e learning. This has been discussed in detail in other modules. Microsoft NetMeeting is a popular collaboration tool.

Groupware, Document Management, Workflow Applications

- ⊙ Groupware encompasses a set of functions designed to help members of a group with tasks of interest to the group as a whole.
- ⊙ Workflow is a group tool in that it requires the participation of a group of people in a company. Workflow applications are designed to know which tasks and procedures to apply to the cases they are designed to process.
- ⊙ The strategic goal of DIM is simple—to reformat the paper form of unstructured data within an organization. This is done by effectively and efficiently inputting, storing, accessing, and using this information on the paper

EC-Council

Groupware Workflow and Document Management

Groupware encompasses a set of functions designed to help members of a group with tasks of interest to the group as a whole. Electronic mail, databases, shared document databases and electronic forums are the components of a groupware solution.

Groupware does more than provide economies of time and space. It also encourages group members to pool their knowledge and experience, resulting in more thorough information processing and better decision making, at a reasonable cost.

Business Process Automation Workflow is a group tool in that it requires the participation of a group of people in a company. But it is geared toward administrative processing of an external event, from the moment it comes to the attention of the company until it's processing is completed.

Workflow applications are designed to know which tasks and procedures to apply to the cases they are designed to process. They break a case down into separate tasks and assign each one to a particular user, or participant, according to the management procedures in effect at the time. The introduction of workflow constitutes a decisive change in the way information technology contributes to business, because the software looks at procedures as a whole, including monitoring of the procedure, assignment of tasks, processing of exceptions and keeping track of time limits, all the while recording data that facilitate the analysis of costs, workloads and quality so vital to an industrial approach to information processing.

Workflow applications are generally linked to electronic document management applications, and they can bring about productivity gains of 20 to 50 per cent in the tasks they automate, and a 30 to 90 per cent reduction in delays.

Workflow is a commonly used term that describes the automation of internal business operations, tasks, and transactions that simplify and streamline current business processes. So, whether you are looking for a solution to handle loan processing, insurance claims, payment processing, or employee performance reviews, Workflow can provide significant and tangible business benefits such as:

 ➢ Improved organizational efficiency

 ➢ Gains in productivity (between 40 and 60 percent)

 ➢ Improved customer service

 ➢ Increased customer retention

 ➢ Enhanced process control and reporting

 ➢ Increased ability to adhere to internal and external regulations

 ➢ Enhanced competitive advantage

A Workflow solution incorporates three basic phases –

 ➢ Mapping - This is the first stage in the adoption of a Workflow solution and involves the crucial task of revealing and recording the entire manual and automatic internal business processes of an organization.

 ➢ Modeling - From there, the organization will begin to develop a model that will help to streamline internal processes whether they are a person-to-person, person-to-application, or application-to-application interaction.

 ➢ Managing - Once the business process model or architecture has been developed, it is ready to be seamlessly integrated across the enterprise. The implementation of a Workflow solution will not only provide significant business benefits as mentioned above, but it will also enable managers to better forecast and manage their projects and personnel, resulting in a more efficient and effective organization.

Document Imaging and Management

The strategic goal of DIM is to reformat the paper form of unstructured data within an organization. Effectively and efficiently inputting, storing, accessing, and using the information that resides on the paper helps achieve this. Taking all important paper documents and converting them into a structured electronic form meet this goal. Once converted, the data within these documents can be stored, retrieved, managed, and otherwise used to make faster and better business decisions.

Benefits from a DIM

> DIM offers a common researchable database and helps in managing the information in a common repository. This is preferred to tracing down the filed copy of the information or reviewing all paper copies looking for references to a topic.

> Ensuring proper handling and release of documents. Documents once brought into a DIM system can be controlled better and used through a common repository.

> Meeting regulatory requirements. Rather than maintaining the voluminous paper records for federal and state regulatory requirements, the pertinent data can now be stored and accessed electronically.

> Reducing liability by ensuring the use of the correct document. With the wrong information disseminated companies are liable. In electronic form, the information is subject to faster revision and better control of these revisions.

> Reducing cost. As noted before, managing paper in its true form is manpower intensive, slow, space intensive, and expensive. It has been noted that DIM systems usually recover payback for the cost for implementation within a year.

A document management system typically makes use of a backend database for storing and managing resources. Resources can be made available to a web browser either by a "publishing" operation, in which the HTML resources are created by the document management system, or by converting the resources to HTML

In some systems the resources are stored in a neutral format within the database. Other systems, such as Inso's Outside In Server enable resources stored in proprietary format, such as Microsoft Word, to be converted to HTML on-the-fly and sent to the client, as described in Inso's briefing document.

With information stored in a neutral back-end database it makes it much easier to change the look-and-feel of a corporate web site. It also makes it easier to manage the web site. For example, hypertext links could be stored separately in the database.

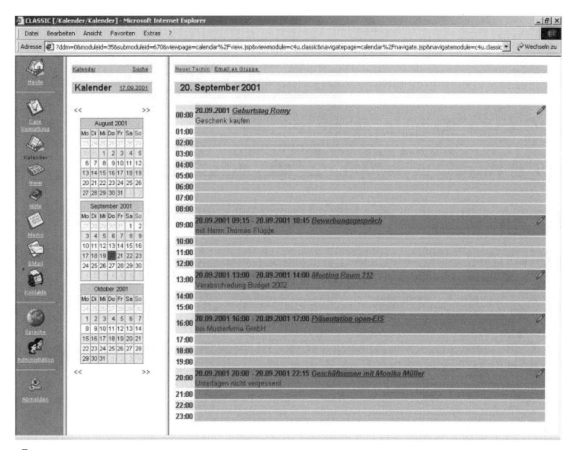

Groupware is technology designed to facilitate the work of groups. This technology may be used to communicate, cooperate, coordinate, solve problems, compete, or negotiate. While traditional technologies like the telephone qualify as groupware, the term is ordinarily used to refer to a specific class of technologies relying on modern computer networks, such as email, newsgroups, videophones, or chat.

Groupware technologies are typically categorized along two primary dimensions:

> Whether users of the groupware are working together at the same time ("real-time" or "synchronous" groupware) or different times ("asynchronous" groupware), and

> Whether users are working together in the same place ("colocated" or "face-to-face") or in different places ("non-colocated" or "distance").

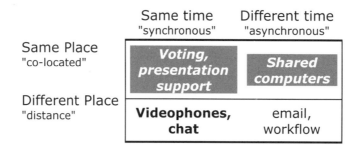

Groupware offers significant advantages over single-user systems. These are some of the most common reasons people want to use groupware:

> To facilitate communication: make it faster, clearer, more persuasive

> To enable communication where it wouldn't otherwise be possible

> To enable telecommuting / cut down on travel costs

> To bring together multiple perspectives and expertise

> To form groups with common interests where it wouldn't be possible to gather a sufficient number of people face-to-face

> To save time and cost in coordinating group work

> To facilitate group problem-solving

> To enable new modes of communication, such as anonymous interchanges or structured interactions

The success of any groupware system rests on the target group's readiness to adopt and use the system. This is in contrast to a single user system, which can be successful even if only the concerned user adopts it.

Groupware has gained broad acceptance and popularity as it can support all four of the facets of knowledge transformation to varying degrees. The objective of discussing groupware in the context of socialization is to focus on two important aspects of organization culture - shared experiences and trust.

Shared experiences are an important basis for the formation and sharing of tacit knowledge. Groupware helps provide a synthetic environment, (often called a virtual space,) within which participants can share certain kinds of experience; for example, they can, listen to presentations, conduct meetings, have discussions, and share documents relevant to the task at hand.

The importance of shared experiences is especially highlighted in the case of a transnational organization, where face-to-face interactions are not always possible. An example of current groupware is Lotus Notes, which facilitates the sharing of documents and discussions and allows various applications for sharing information and conducting asynchronous discussions to be built. Groupware can also be thought to facilitate the combination process, i.e., sharing of explicit knowledge. However, the selection and discussion of the explicit knowledge constitutes a shared experience to some degree.

Certain applications can provide a richer kind of shared experience by supporting real-time on-line meetings—a more recent category of groupware. On-line meetings can include video and text-based conferencing, as well as synchronous communication and chat. Text-based chat is considered to be capable of supporting a group of people in knowledge sharing in a conversational mode. Commercial products of this type include Lotus Sametime and Microsoft NetMeeting. These products integrate both instant messaging and on-line meeting capabilities.

Instant messaging can render an experience akin to that of a personal meeting. It has been found to be less intrusive than interrupting a person with a question but more effective than the telephone in broadcasting a query to a group and leaving it to be answered later. Some of the various groupware applications are discussed below.

Asynchronous Groupware

- ⊙ Email
- ⊙ Workflow systems
- ⊙ Newsgroups and mailing lists
- ⊙ Hypertext
- ⊙ Group calendars
- ⊙ Collaborative writing systems

EC-Council

Asynchronous Groupware

- ➢ **Email** is by far the most common groupware application (besides of course, the traditional telephone). While the basic technology is designed to pass simple messages between two people, even relatively basic email systems today typically include interesting features for forwarding messages, filing messages, creating mailing groups, and attaching files with a message. Other features that have been explored include: automatic sorting and processing of messages, automatic routing, and structured communication (messages requiring certain information).

- ➢ **Newsgroups and mailing lists** are similar in spirit to email systems except that they are intended for messages among large groups of people instead of 1-to-1 communication. In practice the main difference between newsgroups and mailing lists is that newsgroups only show messages to a user when they are explicitly requested (an "on-demand" service), while mailing lists deliver messages as they become available (an "interrupt-driven" interface).

- ➢ **Workflow systems** allow documents to be routed through organizations through a relatively fixed process. A simple example of a workflow application is an expense report in an organization: an employee enters an expense report and submits it, a copy is archived then routed to the employee's manager for approval, the manager receives the document, electronically approves it and sends it on and the expense is registered to the group's account and forwarded to the accounting department for payment. Workflow systems may provide features such as routing, development of forms, and support for differing roles and privileges.

- ➤ **Hypertext** is a system for linking text documents to each other, with the Web being an obvious example. Whenever multiple people author and link documents, the system becomes group work, constantly evolving and responding to others' work. Some hypertext systems include capabilities for seeing who else has visited a certain page or link, or at least seeing how often a link has been followed, thus giving users a basic awareness of what other people are doing in the system -- page counters on the Web are a crude approximation of this function. Another common multi-user feature in hypertext (that is not found on the Web) is allowing any user to create links from any page, so that others can be informed when there are relevant links that the original author was unaware of.

- ➤ **Group calendars** allow scheduling, project management, and coordination among many people, and may provide support for scheduling equipment as well. Typical features detect when schedules conflict or find meeting times that will work for everyone. Group calendars also help to locate people. Typical concerns are privacy (users may feel that certain activities are not public matters), completeness and accuracy (users may feel that the time it takes to enter schedule information is not justified by the benefits of the calendar).

- ➤ **Collaborative writing systems** may provide both real-time support and non-real-time support. Word processors may provide asynchronous support by showing authorship and by allowing users to track changes and make annotations to documents. Authors collaborating on a document may also be given tools to help plan and coordinate the authoring process, such as methods for locking parts of the document or linking separately authored documents. Synchronous support allows authors to see each other's changes as they make them, and usually needs to provide an additional communication channel to the authors as they work (via videophones or chat).

Synchronous Groupware

Commonly used synchronous Groupware
solutions include:

⊙ Shared whiteboards

⊙ Video communications systems

⊙ Chat systems

⊙ Decision support systems

EC-Council

Synchronous or Real-time Groupware

> **Shared whiteboards** allow two or more people to view and draw on a shared drawing surface even from different locations. This can be used, for instance, during a phone call, where each person can jot down notes (e.g. a name, phone number, or map) or to work collaboratively on a visual problem. Most shared whiteboards are designed for informal conversation, but they may also serve structured communications or more sophisticated drawing tasks, such as collaborative graphic design, publishing, or engineering applications. Shared whiteboards can indicate where each person is drawing or pointing by showing telepointers, which are color-coded or labeled to identify each person.

> **Video communications systems** allow two-way or multi-way calling with live video, essentially a telephone system with an additional visual component. Cost and compatibility issues limited early use of video systems to scheduled videoconference meeting rooms. Video is advantageous when visual information is being discussed, but may not provide substantial benefit in most cases where conventional audio telephones are adequate. In addition to supporting conversations, video may also be used in less direct collaborative situations, such as by providing a view of activities at a remote location.

> **Chat systems** permit many people to write messages in real-time in a public space. As each person submits a message, it appears at the bottom of a scrolling screen. Chat groups are usually formed by having listing chat rooms by name, location, number of people, topic of discussion, etc.

Many systems allow for rooms with controlled access or with moderators to lead the discussions, but most of the topics of interest to researchers involve issues related to unmoderated real-time communication including: anonymity, following the stream of conversation, scalability with number of users, and abusive users.

While chat-like systems are possible using non-text media, the text version of chat has the rather interesting aspect of having a direct transcript of the conversation, which not only has long-term value, but allows for backward reference during conversation making it easier for people to drop into a conversation and still pick up on the ongoing discussion.

> **Decision support systems** are designed to facilitate groups in decision-making. They provide tools for brainstorming, critiquing ideas, putting weights and probabilities on events and alternatives, and voting. Such systems enable presumably more rational and even-handed decisions. Primarily designed to facilitate meetings, they encourage equal participation by, for instance, providing anonymity or enforcing turn taking.

However, not all on-line meeting systems have the properties of face-to-face meetings. For example, the videoconferencing system is often judged by its users to be more like a video telephone than like a face-to-face meeting.

Currently, rather than replacing face-to-face meetings, many on-line meetings are found to complement existing collaboration systems and the well-established phone conference and are therefore probably more suited to the exchange of explicit rather than tacit knowledge. On-line meetings extend phone conferences by allowing application screens to be viewed by the participants or by providing a shared whiteboard.

One approach is to integrate on-line meetings with classic groupware-like applications that support document sharing and asynchronous discussion. An example is the IBM-Boeing TeamSpace project, which helps to manage both the artifacts of a project and the processes followed by the team. On-line meetings are recorded as artifacts and can be replayed within TeamSpace, thus allowing even individuals who were not present in the original meeting to share some aspects of the experience. These are being widely adopted on the web as web cast archives.

Some of the limitations of groupware for tacit knowledge formation and sharing have been highlighted by recent work on the closely related issue of the degree of trust established among the participants. But even current groupware products have features that are found to be helpful in this regard. In particular, access control, which is a feature of most commercial products, enables access to the discussions to be restricted to the team members if appropriate, which has been shown to encourage frankness and build trust.

Another approach to tacit knowledge sharing is for a system to find persons with common interests, who are candidates to join a community. Location of other people with similar interests is a function that can be added to personalization systems, the goal of which is to route incoming information to individuals interested in it. There are obvious privacy problems to overcome.

Document Managing and Imaging

In concept, six basic systems comprise a DIM system.

⊙ Input system

⊙ Display system

⊙ Storage system

⊙ Communication and network systems

⊙ Printing and output systems

⊙ DIM controlling software

EC-Council

Document Management and Imaging

We had briefly introduced document-imaging management in earlier pages. Here, we shall discuss the detailed aspects. The requirements to create, store, manipulate, and retrieve document images place unique demands on the system and generally raise the data network traffic The volume and characteristics of data that are dealt with create the need for different storage devices, higher-speed networks, and more accurate displays. These unique characteristics of DIM will be highlighted here.

There are many parts required for a document and imaging system. This is the technology infrastructure and the necessary components needed to assure that the goals of DIM are met. In concept, there are six basic systems that comprise the moving parts of a DIM system. They are as follows:

> Input system - As the transformation of a paper document into an electronic image is begun, there is a need for an input system. The input system, also known as the document capture system, provides for the capture of a paper document for storage and processing within an electronic imaging system. The main moving parts within this system involve scanners, interfaces, and the necessary cabling. On the software side are elements to control the scanner, provide data extraction, and provide for indexing so the images can be properly retrieved. During the document capture process there are many steps to be done.

The first step involves preparing the documents for capture. Not all documents need to be scanned, so the first step would involve selection, movement, labeling, and repair for all documents deemed appropriate to be in the DIM system. Depending on the age and past storage characteristics of the document, the preparation stage can be lengthy. Often retroactive conversion, which involves capture of past records, is necessary for a DIM system to be fully functional. Other times this is done from a current point of time forward. Which conversion method used is a business decision that needs to be made based on corporate goals.

After the documents are readied for capture, they are run through a scanning phase, and, if necessary, as usually is, the images are enhanced (such as edge detection, speckle removal, rotation) to make up for deficiencies and transformation of the paper record. Following this, the data on the paper record (now an electronic image) are extracted via indexing (character representation of the image) or optical character recognition (OCR). This is necessary, since data on the electronic image are inherently not recognizable to the computer database and must be put into a recognizable form. Following indexing, the electronic image is ready for release into the DIM system for later use by office personnel.

➢ Display system - The second system necessary for a DIM installation is the display system. The display system allows people, whether near or far away, to view and access the electronic document images. Components of this system consist of computer monitors, controller boards, and the necessary cabling. Due to the highly complex nature of the visual images, and the extended time periods that personnel are viewing these images, unique characteristics need to be considered.

Typical monitor features that need to be considered, based on the images being viewed, are color versus monochrome, display size, video output, resolution, and glare resistance of the screen. The monitor characteristics need to be matched closely with the controller boards' capabilities in resolution, refresh rate, flip rate, decompression algorithms, and bus support. Closely coupled with the display and controller board is the image viewing software. Often part of the master DIM software, this provides the user with the ability to correct and enhance the image on the screen; annotate the electronic image, as one would annotate a paper document; manipulate the image (pan, zoom, and scroll); and display multiple pages. A typical current system would use a Web interface to provide this control. These elements, if properly selected, provide the speed, resolution, and features that are necessary to work in a document image capacity.

➢ Storage system - The third necessary moving part of a DIM system is the storage system. These devices, drives, media, and interfaces are necessary to manage the storage of imaged data through the life cycle of the document. But the characteristics of DIM put many strains and requirements on a storage system. To store a single page of word processed text may take up 8 KB of data storage, while an image of the same page, uncompressed, will require 1 MB of storage.

It is an order of magnitude different for storage and manipulating these electronic images and therefore whole new storage systems have been created. To select an appropriate storage system three variables need attention—speed of retrieval, cost, and capacity. While RAM storage provides excellent speed, it comes at a very high cost and is therefore limited in capacity. Removable media, such as Zip disks, provide for capacity at an effective cost but trade this for speed of data transfer. The optical drive, with an attached jukebox, provides the optimum cost, speed, and capacity environment for DIM. These optical drives and requisite jukeboxes handle the many disks and allow for the voluminous storage needs of organizations.

➤ Communication and network systems - The fourth necessity for DIM is the communications and networking system. The communication system allows users to be at a distance from the image storage and management devices and allows for the retrieval of data on an entire campus, in the city, or, because of the prevalence of the Web, in the world. A document imaging system puts unusual and additional strains and requirements on networks.

This data flow goes from image creation, to storage devices, down to, upon request, a display screen on a user's workstation. The flow of information is measured in megabytes, and the user will typically demand instant response time. This often requires network segmentation, network monitoring, a fast backbone, and logical placement of the devices so that the enterprise network will not be stressed. Almost always, the current network will require upgrading to support the needs of a document imaging system.

➤ Printing and output systems - The fifth moving part of a DIM system is the printing and output system. This system includes hardware, software, and interfaces required to produce a hard copy, generally on paper, so that it can be accessed independently from the imaging system. Maybe in years to come images will not have to be transferred back into a paper format, but given our current environment, and the lack of a universal electronic medium, it is safe to say that paper will be a common denominator.

In order to provide this feature, printer selection, connection speed, and accelerator boards are issues that need consideration. Other variables to consider include additional memory to form the images onto paper, printer types (laser, ink jet), and the printing format that the DIM package will use (such as PostScript or metacode).

➤ DIM controlling software
The glue that binds these systems together is the document imaging and management software. These software packages contain the storage software, the image viewing software, and the database and will allow the organization to control the workflow of the images throughout the organization. Based on the hardware in the previous five systems, the DIM software integrates the disparate elements into a business application. Software ranges from desktop small-user solutions to enterprise solutions and complex entities.

Other supporting technology

Taxonomies and document classification

Knowledge of a domain can also be encoded as a "knowledge map," or "taxonomy," i.e., a hierarchically organized set of categories. The relationships within the hierarchy can be of different kinds, depending on the application, and a typical taxonomy includes several different kinds of relations.

The value of taxonomy is twofold.

> First, it allows a user to navigate to documents of interest without doing a search (in practice, a combination of the two strategies is often used if it is available).

> Second, a knowledge map allows documents to be put in a context, which helps users to assess their applicability to the task in hand.

The most familiar example of a taxonomy is Yahoo!,62 but there are many examples of specialized taxonomies used at other sites and in company intranet applications.

Taxonomies have proved to be a popular way in which to build a domain model to help users to search and navigate, that each group of users of any size have been known to have their own taxonomy. This popularity is understandable because as on-line tools become central to individuals' work, they naturally want to see the information displayed within a schema that reflects their own priorities and worldview, and that uses the terminology that they use.

Visualizations

Information overload is a trend that motivates the adoption of new technology to assist in the comprehension of explicit knowledge. The large amounts of information available in modern organizations, and the need to integrate information from many sources in order to make better decisions, cause difficulties for knowledge workers and others.

Different visualizations of a large collection of documents have been used with the goal of making subject-based browsing and navigation easier. These methods include text-based category trees, exemplified by the current Yahoo! user interface. Several graphical visualizations have also been described. Themescape uses (among other things) a shaded topographic map as a metaphor to represent the different subject themes (by location), their relatedness (by distance), and the proportional representation of the theme in the collection (by height), whereas VisualNet uses a different map metaphor for showing subject categories. Another approach is represented by the "Cat-a-Cone" system that allows visualization of documents in a large taxonomy or ontology. In this system the model is three-dimensional and is rendered using forced perspective. Search is used to select a subset of the available documents for visualization.

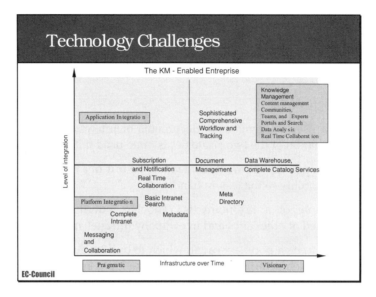

Technology Challenges

Implementing a knowledge-management solution presents many challenges, such as the following:

➢ Complete Integration of Knowledge.

This accounts for how the knowledge is built, located, and related to maximize the utilization of the knowledge management system?

➢ Technical Integration

This explores the infrastructures that are required in the enterprise knowledge-management system.

➢ Central Manageability

This issue addresses what technologies are used for knowledge management in the enterprise and where are the integration points to assemble the system and make it manageable.

Organizations will do well to identify the knowledge-based services that are to be implemented to improve specific business processes and the technology necessary to support these goals. This can be a complex procedure; a strategic matrix of infrastructure requirements measured against the services the knowledge-management system should assist in adjusting the scope of the project appropriately.

One way to tackle the enterprise knowledge-management challenge is to start small by developing intranets or departmental solutions. In this approach, small pilots are built that implement some functionality of the components that enable knowledge management. To keep these pilots manageable, they should be locally controlled and include the information needs of a specific department that's not widely scattered throughout the enterprise.

After the start of the pilots, it is easier to focus on the whole while combining information fragments into an enterprise knowledge-management system. Right from choosing the right technologies, and hiring the vendors that can deliver a sophisticated solution as well as the interfaces and scalability, an organization needs to bind its existing and new information infrastructure and services together.

After the knowledge-management pilots have been deployed, the concepts behind the central junction point for all knowledge-management pieces should be proven. This hub must integrate the pilot systems that were just built. This is the first step in extending the information infrastructure to a centralized, controllable knowledge-management system. An enterprise knowledge-management system builds, on the back end, an equivalent to the knowledge-management portal for the user. As the knowledge-management portal concentrates all information that is valuable to a specific knowledge worker, the central knowledge-management backbone concentrates all information that is valuable to the whole enterprise. After all knowledge-management islands are built and integrated, this backbone will be the entry point for all enterprise-related information. In terms of knowledge management, this central knowledge-management hub, or knowledge-management backbone, is also called a metaserver.

KM Deployment Phases

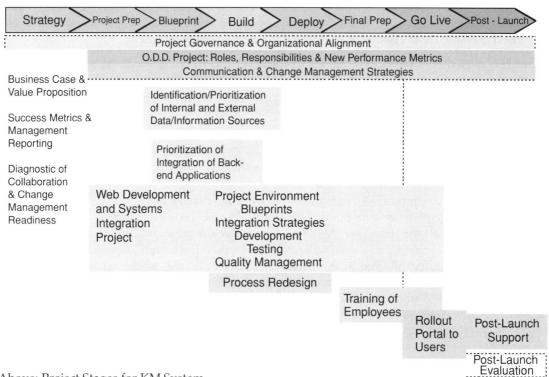

Above: Project Stages for KM System

Top 100 KM companies

(Source: KM World)

80-20	Correlate	Intraspect	Siemens
Accenture	Crystal Decisions	J.D.Edwards	SiteScape
American Productivity & Quality Center	DigitalOwl	Kamoon	Softheon
Applied Semantics	divine	Kana Software	Sopheon
Arbortext	Documentum	Kgain	Stellent
Ariel Performance Group	eGain	Knexa	Stratify
AskMe	eiStream	Knowledge Management Software	Sun Microsystems
Autonomy	Enfish	Knowledge Systems Design	Sybase
Baan	Enigma	LexisNexis	Symtrax
Banter	Entopia	Lotus	Tacit Knowledge Systems
BCI Knowledge Group	Epicentric	META Group	TheBrain Technologies
BEA Systems, Inc.	eRoom Technology	Microsoft	Tower Software
BearingPoint, Inc. (formerly KPMG Consulting)	Factiva	Moreover	Ultimus
Brio Software, Inc	Fatwire	Netegrity	Verity

BroadVision	FileNET	Northern Light Technology	Vignette
Business Objects	Gartner	Open Text Corp.	Xerox
Cadenza	Hewlett-Packard	Oracle	
Captiva	Hummingbird	Ovum	
Cerebyte	Hyperion	PeopleSoft	
Changepoint Corporation	Hyperwave	Plumtree	
Citrix	IBM	Ptech	
ClearForest	IDC	SAP AG	
Cognos	iManage	Selectica	

Summary

- Technology is a critical enabler of KM
- The basic essential modules of a KM system are the Intranet and collaboration modules
- Portals are the single point of entry into a KM system.
- Expert systems allow shortened learning curves and capture of tacit knowledge for reuse.
- Real time collaboration helps in virtual collaboration across various channels.
- Document Mgt. and Content Mgt. Assists in enhancing productivity and timeliness of information availability.

EC-Council

Summary

 Recap

➢ Technology is a critical enabler of KM

➢ The basic essential modules of a KM system are the Intranet and collaboration modules

➢ Portals are the single point of entry into a KM system.

➢ Expert systems allow shortened learning curves and capture of tacit knowledge for reuse.

➢ Real time collaboration helps in virtual collaboration across various channels.

➢ Document Mgt. and Content Mgt. Assists in enhancing productivity and timeliness of information availability.

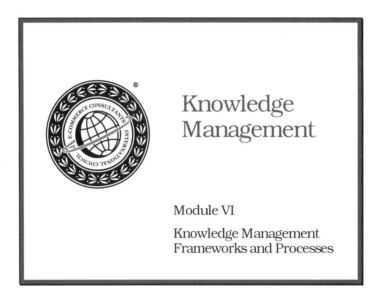

Module VI

Knowledge Management
Frameworks and Processes

Knowledge Management (KM)

Module VI: Knowledge Management Frameworks and Processes

Exam 212-69 Certified e-Business Associate

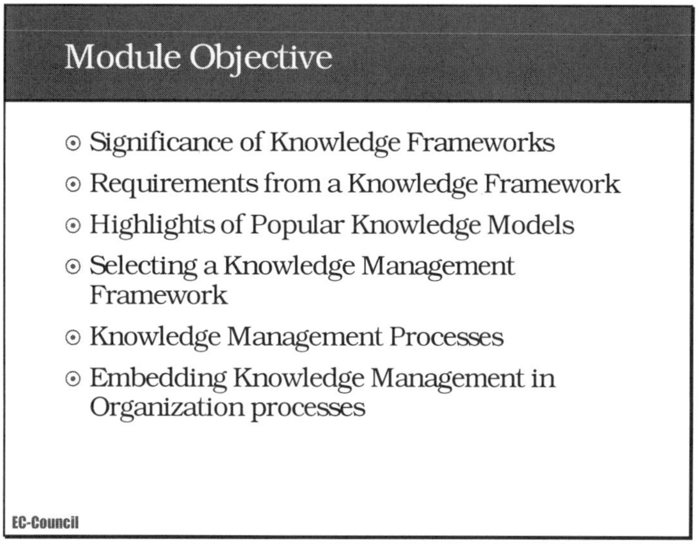

Module Objective

- Significance of Knowledge Frameworks
- Requirements from a Knowledge Framework
- Highlights of Popular Knowledge Models
- Selecting a Knowledge Management Framework
- Knowledge Management Processes
- Embedding Knowledge Management in Organization processes

EC-Council

Objectives

☞ **Module Objectives**

On completion of this module you will be able to:

➢ Understand the significance of knowledge frameworks

➢ Know the requirements from a knowledge framework

➢ Obtain highlights of popular knowledge models

➢ Select a knowledge management framework

➢ Comprehend the knowledge management processes

➢ Understand the embedding knowledge management in the organization processes.

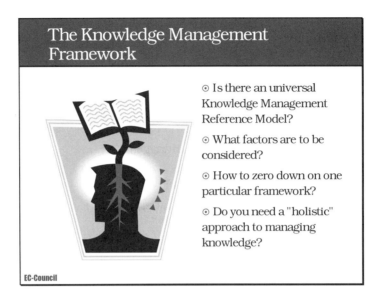

The Knowledge Management Framework

⊙ Is there an universal Knowledge Management Reference Model?

⊙ What factors are to be considered?

⊙ How to zero down on one particular framework?

⊙ Do you need a "holistic" approach to managing knowledge?

EC-Council

Introducing the Knowledge management Framework

Knowledge management involves the creation of value from an organization's intangible assets. Many organizations are developing information systems designed specifically to facilitate the sharing and integration of knowledge.

Two key concerns for knowledge management arise from this approach:

> Firstly, knowledge management encompasses much more than technologies for facilitating knowledge sharing. Practitioners are increasingly beginning to realize that people and the culture of the workplace are also key driving factors that ultimately determine the success or failure of knowledge management initiatives.

> Secondly, emphasis on technology alone projects a narrow view that may inhibit the growth and staying power of knowledge management.

Knowledge management is a young discipline for which a codified, generally accepted framework has not been established. Despite this fact, a diversity of approaches to knowledge management has been implemented across an array of organizations. However, these approaches do not adequately fulfill the knowledge management needs of organizations.

This section looks at the basic concerns that arise while considering a knowledge management framework such as whether there is any universal Knowledge Management Reference Model? What factors are to be considered in developing a framework? How does an organization zero down on one particular framework and if there is a necessity to adopt a "holistic" approach to managing knowledge.

Requirements from a KM Framework

- A knowledge management framework must recognize that knowledge management includes much more than just the knowledge cycle or knowledge management tasks.
  - There is a need for designing multiple feedback loops
  - The framework must allow for multiple activities to occur simultaneously
  - the organizational strategies and goals must be linked to knowledge management initiative
  - Causative factors should be considered while developing a knowledge management framework

EC-Council

Requirements from a KM Framework

Frameworks for knowledge management have been proposed by a number of individuals and organizations. The frameworks can be categorized as either prescriptive, descriptive, or a combination of the two.

Prescriptive frameworks provide direction on the types of knowledge management procedures without providing specific details of how those procedures can/should be accomplished. In essence, they prescribe different ways to engage in knowledge management activities (i.e., suggest a knowledge management methodology).

In contrast, descriptive frameworks characterize or describe knowledge management. These frameworks identify attributes of knowledge management important for their influence on the success or failure of knowledge management initiatives.

Many of the knowledge management frameworks focus only on the knowledge cycle process or tasks. These trace the movement of knowledge through the organization and the tasks required for facilitating such movement. Other critical elements of knowledge management such as integration of knowledge management with the strategic goals of the organization, the people involved in knowledge management activities, the technology infrastructure base involved and the cultural context within which knowledge management is developed are often superficially addressed.

A knowledge management framework must recognize that knowledge management includes much more than just the knowledge cycle or knowledge management tasks. Knowledge management is a continual process of incremental improvement and evolution—not a one-time effort. Therefore, there is a need for designing multiple feedback loops into the knowledge management process and allowing for multiple activities to occur simultaneously during the process.

For any framework to succeed, the organizational strategies and goals must be linked to knowledge management initiative. Causative factors should be considered while developing a knowledge management framework.

This implies that organizations should map their strategy to feasible frameworks and find the best fit to realize their knowledge management objectives. Such a fusion should clearly focus on the knowledge assets of the company, link strategic and operational issues in a consistent manner, and enable leveraging the key knowledge assets at various levels of networking, i.e. between individuals, teams and organizations.

There are tools that facilitate this, though it is imperative to state that these tools are to be considered as facilitators alone and not as a solution by itself. One such tool is m1 tool by Ingenia, whose screen shot is given below.

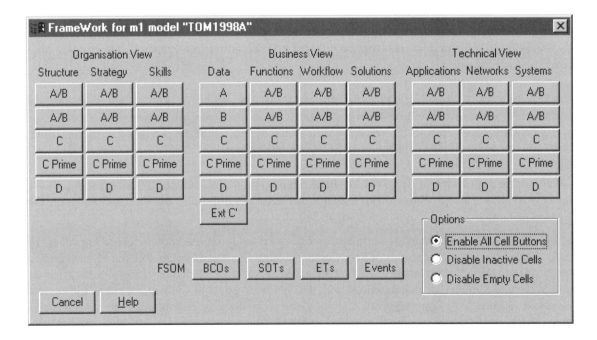

Knowledge Management Framework

- There is no "absolute" framework - All framework have their own objectivity
- Causative factors should be considered while developing a knowledge management framework
- Technology is fundamental to any knowledge management framework
- Organizations should map their strategy to feasible frameworks and find the best fit to realize their KM objectives.

EC-Council

Basics of a knowledge framework

The people, the knowledge people have, share, and need; the culture for knowledge sharing (or lack thereof); organizational business strategies; and the technological infrastructure for knowledge management must all be considered for effective knowledge management initiatives.

We had discussed the importance of system thinking in earlier modules. While approaching a knowledge management framework, it is in the best interest of the organization to adopt a systems thinking approach. By this statement we intend that the organization adopt a framework that takes itself into account in entirety – human, social and corporate capital.

Systems thinking is a conceptual framework for problem solving that considers problems in their entirety. Hence, the organization will be discussed as a whole entity. Problem solving in this way involves pattern finding to enhance understanding of, and responsiveness to, the problem.

Outcomes from systems thinking depend heavily on how a system is defined because systems thinking examine relationships between the various parts of the system. Here, this can be the relationship the organization has established with other organizations or entities. Therefore, boundaries must be set to distinguish what parts of the organization are contained inside the system and what parts are considered as the environment of the organization. The environment of the organization will influence problem solving because it influences the organization, but it is not part of the organization.

Systems thinking is important for knowledge management because it provides an overseeing framework to help ensure that the same general requirements are addressed by knowledge management endeavors across organizations (and with varying methodologies and tools).

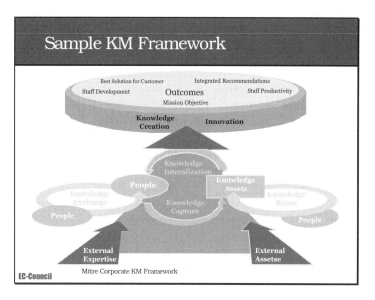

Overview of Popular Frameworks

As there are several frameworks existing, we shall discuss the primary features of some of the popular frameworks here. Some of these have been adopted by consulting organizations, while some consulting organizations have ceased to function as the said entity.

> The Knowledge Research Institute Inc.

(1) Leverage Existing Knowledge, (2) Create New Knowledge, (3) Capture and Store Knowledge, (4) Organize and Transform Knowledge and (5) Deploy Knowledge.

> American Productivity and Quality Center

(1) Identify, (2) Collect, (3) Adapt, (4) Organize, (5) Apply, (6) Share and (7) Create

> PriceWaterhouseCoopers

(1) Find, (2) Filter [for relevance], (3) Format [to problem], (4) Forward [to right people] and (5) Feedback [from users]

> Van der Spek and de Hoog

(1)Conceptualize [including Make an inventory of existing knowledge and Analyze strong and weak points], (2) Reflect [including Decide on required improvements and Make plans to improve process], (3) Act [including Secure knowledge, Combine knowledge, Distribute knowledge and Develop knowledge] and (4) Review [including Compare old and new situation and Evaluate achieved results]

➢ Liebowitz and Beckman

(1) Identify [Determine core competencies, sourcing strategy and knowledge domains], (2) Capture [Formalize existing knowledge], (3) Select [Assess knowledge relevance, value, and accuracy and resolve conflicting knowledge], (4) Store [Represent corporate memory in knowledge repository] (5) Share [Distribute knowledge automatically to users based on interest and work and collaborate on knowledge work through virtual teams], (6) Apply [Retrieve and use knowledge in making decisions, solving problems, automating or supporting work, job aids and training], (7) Create [Discover new knowledge through research, experimenting, and creative thinking] and (8) Sell [Develop and market new knowledge-based products and services]

➢ Holsapple and Joshi

(1) Managerial Influences [including Leadership, Coordination, Control, Measurement], (2) Resource Influences [including Human, Knowledge, Financial, Material], (3) Environmental Influences [including Fashion, Markets, Competitors, Technology, Time, Climate] (4) Activities [including Acquire, Select, Internalize, Use], (5) Learning and Projection as Outcomes.

➢ Kentucky Initiative for Knowledge Management

(1) Acquiring Knowledge [including Extracting, Interpreting and Transferring], (2) Selecting Knowledge [including Locating, Retrieving and Transferring], (3) Internalizing Knowledge [including Assessing, Targeting and Depositing], (4) Using Knowledge, (5) Generating Knowledge [including Monitoring, Evaluating, Producing and Transferring] and (6) Externalizing Knowledge [including Targeting, Producing and Transferring]

➢ Ernst and Young

(1) Knowledge Generation, (2) Knowledge Representation, (3) Knowledge Codification and (4) Knowledge Application

➢ The Delphi Group

(1) Key Concepts and Frameworks for Knowledge Management, (2) How to Use Knowledge Management as a Competitive Tool, (3) The Cultural and Organizational Aspects of Knowledge Management, (4) Best Practices in Knowledge Management, (5) The Technology of Knowledge Management, (6) Market Analysis, (7) Justifying Knowledge Management and (8) Implementing Knowledge Management

➢ Dataware Technologies, Inc

(1) Identify the Business Problem, (2) Prepare for Change, (3) Create the KM Team, (4) Perform the Knowledge Audit and Analysis, (5) Define the Key Features of the Solution, (6) Implement the Building Blocks for KM and (7) Link Knowledge to People

➢ Arthur Andersen Consulting

(1) Evaluate, (2) Define the role of knowledge, (3) Create a knowledge strategy linked to business objectives, (4) Identify processes, cultures and technologies needed for implementation of a knowledge strategy and (5) Implement feedback mechanisms.

Selecting a KM Framework

⊙ Some of the factors to be considered while selecting a
KM framework are:
- Strategy -- the alignment of corporate and KM strategies
- Measurement -- the measures or metrics
- Policy -- the written policy or guidance that is provided by the
organization
- Content -- the subset of the corporate knowledge base
- Process -- the processes used to achieve organization mission
and goals;
- Technology -- the information technology that facilitates
knowledge management
- Culture -- the environment and context in which KM processes
must occur

EC-Council

Selecting a KM Framework

Some of the factors that are to be considered while selecting a knowledge management framework are:

➢ Strategy – The framework should be selected keeping in mind the alignment of corporate and KM strategies

➢ Measurement – The framework should be such that it is possible to measure the knowledge initiatives with suitable measures or metrics

➢ Policy – The framework should be in agreement with the written policy or guidance that is provided by the organization

➢ Content – Both its nature and storage are of importance as it is a subset of the corporate knowledge base. The framework selected should address this aspect.

➢ Process – The framework should be able to encompass the processes used to achieve organization mission and goals.

➢ Technology – It should address the information technology that facilitates knowledge management

➢ Culture – The framework should be amenable to the environment and context in which KM processes must occur

There are two additional dimensions to the KM Process Framework:

> Scope of content: The breadth of knowledge contained within or acted upon by a KM technology or program. Scope of content may address several characteristics of knowledge.

> Depth of functionality: A technology's functional coverage of any of the knowledge activities may be deep or shallow. Depth of a technology is defined as its coverage of four classes of KM functionality: semantic, collaborative, visualization and scale. Scope may range from coverage in one class of functionality (e.g., a tool that learns and updates user profiles) to deep coverage in all four (a fully-integrated KM solution across all knowledge activities).

The KM Process Framework can be used to evaluate a vendor-service offering, a vendor technology, a KM tool, or a KM user program to see which knowledge activities it addresses, which knowledge sub-processes are supported, what scope of content is included, and how deep is the functionality provided in terms of its scope.

There are many examples of enterprises that may choose a knowledge-enabled strategy. Consider the example of British petroleum.

Business objective: Become the #1 in customer service in their industry.

Strategies: Reduce the number of departments that a customer must call for information to only one; enable customers to perform (and develop a preference for) self-service; handle every customer inquiry on the first contact (i.e., the first person reached solves the problem or answers the question); and decrease the number of calls due to problems by 50%.

Actions: Build a knowledge base of the collective expertise of all agents; identify agent experts whose knowledge can be captured, or who can be contacted to assist others; provide access to the knowledge base for all agents; and automate the solicitation and capture of feedback and insight from all agents and users.

KM Strategy

When British Petroleum (BP) constructs an oil production platform, it brings together the combined knowledge of its own experts and an extended community of construction sub-contractors.

BP uses a Notes-based project management system that allows each of the parties to contribute progress reports, to identify bottlenecks, and to quickly resolve hot issues. When an unexpected event occurs, BP uses the roster of employees and contractors to quickly determine who should respond to that event, and puts them together through video-conferencing. This ensures they have minimal problems.

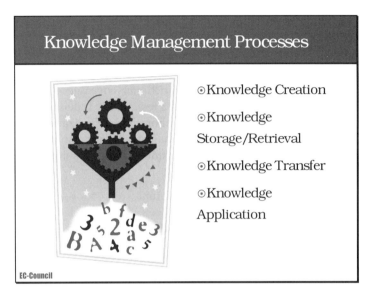

Knowledge Processes

The knowledge management processes can be broadly categorized into knowledge creation, knowledge storage, knowledge distribution and knowledge application. These were proposed by Nonaka.

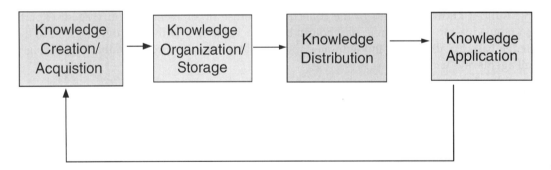

This representation involves a continual interplay between the tacit and explicit dimensions of knowledge and a growing spiral flow as knowledge moves through individual, group, and organizational levels.

Knowledge creation involves:

- ➢ Combining new sources of knowledge
- ➢ Just in time learning
- ➢ Supporting Information Technology
- ➢ Data mining
- ➢ Learning tools

The storage and retrieval of organizational knowledge referred to organizational memory. Organizational memory is defined as " the means and events influence present organizational activities".

Knowledge storage is typically represented by:

- ➢ Knowledge residing in written documentation
- ➢ Structured information stores in electronic databases
- ➢ Codified human knowledge stored in expert systems
- ➢ Documented organizational procedures
- ➢ Processes and tacit knowledge acquired by individuals
- ➢ Networks of individuals

Knowledge distribution occurs through

- ➢ Organizational culture
- ➢ Organizational structure
- ➢ Organization ecology
- ➢ Information archives
    - ➢ Semantic - general, explicit and articulated knowledge

      E.g. organizational archives of annual reports
    - ➢ Episodic - context-specific and situated knowledge

      E.g., specific circumstances of organizational decisions and their outcomes, place, and time

Knowledge Application

- ➢ Basing and relating organizational changes in past experience facilitates implementation of the change

> ➢ Storing and reapplying workable solutions in the form of standards and procedures avoids waste of organizational resources in replicating previous work

> ➢ At the Individual level, it aids decision making while at the organization level, it helps change the status quo

> ➢ Facilitates inter-group knowledge access through

>> o   Supporting Information Technology

>> o   Electronic bulletin boards

>> o   Knowledge repositories

>> o   Databases

This process model forms the basis for the Anderson KM framework.

Knowledge Management Framework

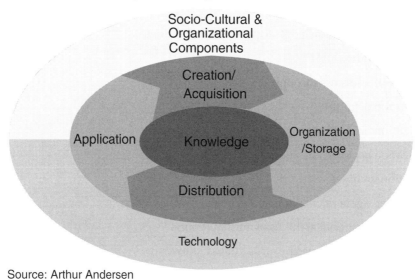

Source: Arthur Andersen

Modes of Knowledge generation

As propounded by Davenport and Prusak knowledge generation happens through:

⊙ Acquisition

⊙ Dedicated Resources

⊙ Fusion

⊙ Adaptation

⊙ Knowledge networking

EC-Council

Modes of Knowledge Generation

Knowledge creation has been widely recognized to be strategically important for organizational learning and innovation. In their book 'Working Knowledge: How Organizations Manage What They Know" by Thomas H. Davenport and Laurence Prusak, knowledge generation has been described as that which is either acquired by an organization or that which is developed within it. Since organizations interact with their environment, they absorb information, turn it into knowledge, and take action based on it in combination with their experiences, values, and internal rules.   All healthy organizations therefore, generate and use knowledge.

Five modes of knowledge generation namely: acquisition, dedicated resources, fusion, adaptation and knowledge networking.

➤ Acquisition

In the corporate setting, the most direct and often most effective way to acquire knowledge is to buy an organization or hire individuals that have it. Companies buy other companies mainly to generate additional revenue; achieve product mix; get access to new markets; or to gain the skills of a senior management team.

Firms acquire other companies specifically for their knowledge. This is most of the times manifested in a company's willingness to pay a premium over the market value of the purchased company because of the value they expect to get from adding that new knowledge to their own knowledge stock.

Example: IBM in 1995 purchased Lotus for $3.5 billion (14 times Lotus's book valuation). IBM believed that the minds who invented Lotus Notes will be valuable in what IBM perceived to be a new world of information-sharing network.

➢ Dedicated Resources

A standard example of a "dedicated resource" in an organization is a research and development department. These groups are established for the specific purpose of coming up with new knowledge/new ways of doing things.

Example: Ernst & Young's Center for Business Innovation, McDonald's Universities

Most R&D department is usually separated from other parts of the organization. This is to give researchers the freedom to explore ideas without the constraints imposed by a preoccupation with deadlines or profits. However, this becomes a disadvantage when technology transfer from R&D to example, production takes place because knowledge creators and users may not be speaking the same language.

To avoid this, managers must ensure that knowledge generated by dedicated resources will be made available throughout the company and that knowledge will be delivered to where it will be useful.

➢ Fusion

This type of knowledge generation, in contrast to dedicated resources, purposely introduces complexity and conflict to create new synergy. It brings together people with different perspectives to work on a problem or project and come up with a joint answer. The premise is that since the group has no familiar solutions in common, they must develop new ideas together or combine their old ideas in new ways.

Five KM principles that can help make fusion work effectively:

o Foster awareness of the value of knowledge sought and a willingness to invest in the process of generating it.

o Identify key knowledge workers who can be effectively brought together in a fusion effort.

o Emphasize the creative potential inherent in the complexity and diversity of ideas (example: seeing differences as positive and not sources of conflict, avoiding simple answers to complex questions)

o Make the need for knowledge generation clear so as to encourage, reward, and direct it toward a common goal.

o Introduce measures and milestones of success. These should reflect the true value of knowledge more completely than a simple balance sheet accounting.

> Adaptation

The ability of a firm to adapt is based on two factors:

- o Having existing internal resources and capabilities that can be utilized in new ways

- o Being open to change or having a high "absorptive capacity"

Therefore, the most important adaptive resources are employees who can easily acquire new knowledge and skills.

> Knowledge Networking

Networks can also act as critical conduits for knowledge. As knowledge generated through networks is informal, knowledge editors or network facilitators are often required to record such generated knowledge.

The common denominator for all these efforts is:

> Adequate time and space devoted to knowledge creation or acquisition

> Management support

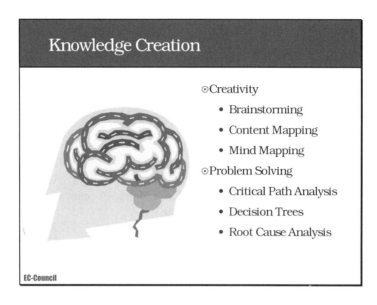

Knowledge Creation

<u>Creativity</u>

One definition of creative thinking is the merging two previously uncombined thoughts, products or processes. Areas within creativity are:

> Brainstorming is a method used to create new ideas by suspending judgment.

> Concept Mapping is a structured process, focused on a topic or construct of interest, involving input from one or more participants, that produces an interpretable pictorial view (concept map) of their ideas and concepts and how these are interrelated.

> Mind Mapping is a graphics-based method of taking notes, brainstorming, and organizing thoughts that helps you relate and arrange random ideas into memorable tree-like diagrams The difference between concept maps and mind maps is that a mind map has only one main concept, while a concept map may have several. This comes down to the point that a mind map can be represented as a tree, while a concept map may need a network representation.

<u>Problem Solving</u>

The difference between Creativity products and Problem Solving products are not as clear-cut as this categorization leads you to believe. For example creativity processes, such as brainstorming and concept maps, can be used to solve problems. Areas within Problem Solving are:

➢ Critical Path Analysis (Project Management) is a method of analyzing a complex project. It helps you to calculate the minimum length of time in which the project can be completed, and which activities should be prioritized to complete by that date.

➢ Decision Trees provide an effective structure in which alternative decisions and the implications of taking those decisions can be displayed and evaluated. They are excellent tools for making financial or number based decisions where a lot of complex information needs to be taken into account.

➢ Root Cause Analysis is a method or series of actions taken to find out why a particular failure or problem exists and correcting those causes. It is similar to what detectives do when a crime occurs.

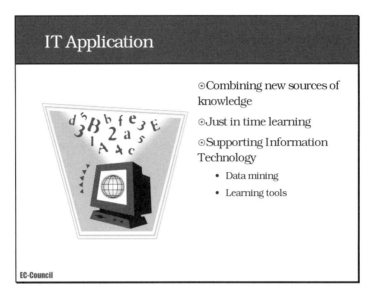

IT Application for Knowledge Creation

Knowledge creation may take a number of forms:

> ➢ Helpdesk systems storing problem solution pairs with search and navigation are some of the premier products.
> ➢ Self-publishing, creating and structuring information for others to access on the Internet or Intranet. HTML editors and XML tools that check for syntax and links are useful.
> ➢ Mind Mapping. Examples of such tools are MindManager, mindmapper, VisiMap.

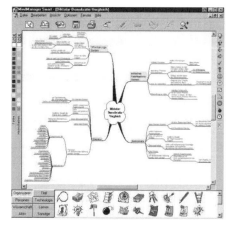

Figure: MindMananger
Screenshot

> Forums. For instance, a linear scrolling interface is considered better design in such tools than a threaded outline such as seen on message boards.

> Simulation. SimCity or similar tools that allow interactive manipulation and show the influences on the system have proved useful.

> Profiling tools. These systems allow participants to create a composite picture and add their unique sources. Intraspect is an example when used to capture competitor profiles.

> Concept mapping and ranking. These assist with surfacing assumptions, help with group alignment and make meaning. Examples are Banxia Decision Explorer, Axon Idea Processor, Quest Map, and Inspiration.

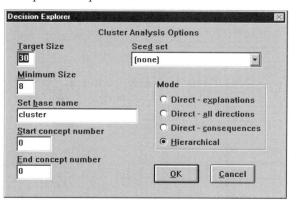

Figure: Banxia Decision
Explorer Screenshot

> Decision Trees. They are excellent tools for making financial or number based decisions where a lot of complex information needs to be taken into account. Examples are Decision Analysis by TreeAge, DATA Interactive, Decision Tree, Analytica, CART, Decision Pro, DPL

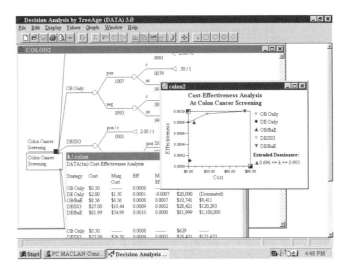

Figure: Data Interactive Screenshot

> ➢ Repertory grids can be used to surface deeper constructs and make personal knowledge explicit.
> ➢ Critical path analysis tool example is Planbee, MinuteMan etc. These are planning tool in which you create a spreadsheet of tasks to complete a project then let the software determine criticality based on dependencies and required start and finish dates.

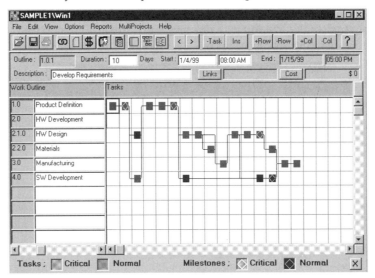

Figure: MinuteMan Screenshot

All these tools need social protocols and trust to deliver and all need additional facilities to index and summarize the content to be really effective.

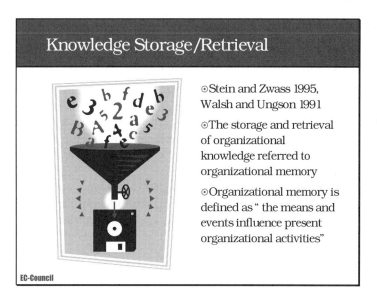

Knowledge Storage / Retrieval

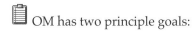 Organizational Memory (OM) is defined by Stein and Zwass (1995, p.89) as "the means by which knowledge from the past is brought to bear on present activities, thus resulting in higher or lower levels of organizational effectiveness." Walsh and Ungson (1991) define OM in its most basic sense as stored information from an organization's history that can be brought to bear on present decisions.

OM has two principle goals:

> ➢ To integrate information across organizational boundaries and

> ➢ To control current activities and thus avoid past mistakes.

Basic functions of OM (Stein and Zwass 1995) are:

> ➢ Perception,

> ➢ Acquisition,

> ➢ Abstraction,

> ➢ Recording,

> ➢ Storage,

> ➢ Retrieval,

> ➢ Interpretation, and

> ➢ Transmission of organizational knowledge.

Walsh and Ungson (1991) propose that organizational memory consists of five retention facilities: individuals, culture, transformations, structures, and ecology.

Stein and Zwass (1995) extend Walsh and Ungson's (1991) definition by proposing that there is an information systems component that serves to augment the interactions between knowledge seekers and human experts. They define an Organizational Memory Information System, OMIS, as a system that functions to provide a means by which knowledge from the past is brought to bear on present activities, thus resulting in increased levels of effectiveness for the organization.

This involves information documentation, organization, storage, retrieval and dissemination. This encompasses the structure of document surrogates, indexing languages, thesauri, natural language systems, catalogs and files, information storage media, retrieval systems, networks and information delivery systems.

Various Forms of Knowledge Storage / Retrieval

- Knowledge residing in written documentation
- Structured information stores in electronic databases
- Codified human knowledge stored in expert systems
- Documented organizational procedures
- Processes and tacit knowledge acquired by individuals
- Networks of individuals
- Organizational culture, structure, ecology information archives

EC-Council

Forms of Knowledge Storage / Retrieval

There are various forms by which knowledge may be stored and /or retrieved. These can include:

➢ Knowledge residing in written documentation. These may be in the form of manuals, policies, reports etc

➢ Structured information stores in electronic databases. These can be databases that are networked or accessed across the enterprise at various levels

➢ Codified human knowledge stored in expert systems. Expert systems take care of detailed knowledge.

➢ Documented organizational procedures. These may be procedure manuals, frameworks, policies etc

➢ Processes and tacit knowledge acquired by individuals. These are information acquired from experience such as best practices database, central knowledge base etc.

➢ Networks of individuals. These can be communities of practice, workgroups, teams etc.

➢ Organizational culture, structure, ecology information archives. Organization culture can also be a component where knowledge is stored and retrieved. These may be in the form of norms, accepted practices, structure, values etc.

What is important is that knowledge is stored and retrieved continuously in one form or the other within organizations and these need not be restricted to information technology tools.

Repositories of Knowledge

- <u>Structured Repositories</u>
  Structured repositories are databases, expert systems and the like. They are characterized by their ease of searchability because they have search aids like indexes, keywords, controlled vocabulary and so forth.
- <u>Unstructured Repositories</u>
  In most organizations these include project reports, sales-call notes and other sources. These are searchable by free text means.
- <u>People as Repositories of Knowledge</u>
  Tacit knowledge resides in the heads of people. The tools to get to this knowledge are phone directories, annotated company directories, company-knowledge yellow pages and other people listings.

EC-Council

Knowledge Repositories

Knowledge repositories can be classified into three based on the nature and structure of their content.

➢ Structured repositories

Structured repositories are databases, expert systems and the like. They are characterized by their ease of searchability because they have search aids like indexes, keywords, controlled vocabulary and so forth.

➢ Unstructured Repositories

In most organizations these include project reports, sales-call notes and other sources. These are searchable by free text means.

The two repositories mentioned above are for explicit knowledge, the knowledge that is out there for all to find, see and use. There's also tacit knowledge.

➢ People as Repositories of Knowledge

Tacit knowledge resides in the minds of people. The tools to get to this knowledge are phone directories, annotated company directories, company-knowledge yellow pages and other people listings.

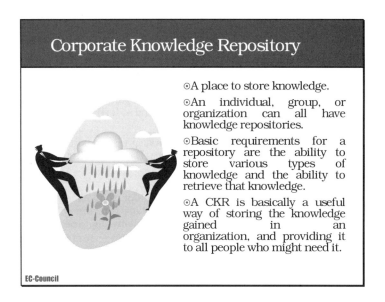

Corporate Knowledge Repository

Organizations have to store knowledge in order to manage them – if at all knowledge can be managed. It is in this context that knowledge repositories gain usefulness. A knowledge repository is a place to store knowledge. An individual, group, or organization can all have knowledge repositories. Basic requirements for a repository are the ability to store various types of knowledge and the ability to retrieve that knowledge. A low-tech knowledge repository could be a set of file folders. A high-tech knowledge repository might be based on a database platform.

A corporate knowledge repository is basically a useful way of storing the knowledge gained in an organization, and providing it to all people who might need it. The idea is behind this is a couple of years old, and builds on the belief, that reality can entirely be mirrored in information systems by using global data models.

Companies like IBM and Digital even developed tools for developing knowledge repositories. However, there are several problems related to the idea, as it requires a standardization of the terminology within the organization (e.g. what is a customer?), and that the information stored tended to become complex. Additionally, there are technical and cognitive problems to be solved as well.

Actually, from the beginning, the entire idea behind creating a knowledge repository was to create global data models, which then could be used for catalogs, also. However, due to several reasons most of these attempts failed, especially in large, diversified organizations.

Less ambitious approaches however survived. For example, Andersen Consulting had a global database containing 'generic processes', that they use in their BPR-projects, and which all employees, could access, in order to use previously gained knowledge. In this case, the intention was not to build a global model, but to support specific purposes. Whenever new knowledge within the domain to be supported is gained, the repository can be updated to include it fur reuse.

 There are two ways of storing corporate knowledge – structured or unstructured.

We have seen that to be a learning organization requires the ability to learn and change the models, frames, the culture that exists based upon experience and thoughtful analysis of that experience. This is where the current concept of dynamic knowledge repositories (DKR) gains prominence.

A dynamic knowledge repository is a knowledge base that encompasses all of the relevant information of a particular project. It includes recorded dialog (i.e. internal knowledge), intelligence collection (i.e. external knowledge), and knowledge product (i.e. a snapshot of an organization's knowledge, with links into recorded dialog and intelligence collection).

The dynamic knowledge repository is the product of concurrent development, integration, and application of knowledge – popularly referred to as the CoDIAK process.

Broadly speaking, any evolving knowledge base falls under the category of a dynamic knowledge repository. For instance, an archived e-mail discussion list is a dynamic knowledge repository. Any Web site where the content is constantly evolving is a dynamic knowledge repository. For that matter, a library of books and magazines is a dynamic knowledge repository. Other examples include archived electronic discussions (e-mail), published papers and source code, weekly summaries of discussions and papers.

Over time, the nature of the dynamic knowledge repositories, as well as its content, evolves.

Within an organization, knowledge can be stored in repositories based on how knowledge is captured and structured. These are highlighted as below.

> Knowledge network model

The individual who has the knowledge transfers expertise through person-to-person contacts. This is basically he tactic-to-tactic mode of knowledge transfer. Here, knowledge management themes discussed under socialization come into play. An individual shares tacit knowledge, (non-formal) technical skills and know-how directly with another. The other individual learns tacit skills through observation, imitation and practice until it becomes a part of his tacit knowledge base.

> Knowledge repository model

Knowledge contribution and use follows a two-step transfer procedure of person-to-repository and repository-to-person. Technology may interface here to cater to the explicit component of the knowledge. This may include databases, knowledge communities etc.

- o Captured knowledge is stored in a knowledge repository, a collection of both internal and external knowledge.

➢ Hybrid Model

As discussed before, knowledge management involves capturing, processing / synthesizing, storing and disseminating knowledge. To effectively do this, many organizations use a hybrid of the network and repository models.

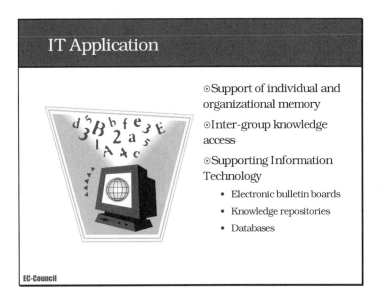

IT Applications for Knowledge Storage / Retrieval

Databases, data mining, search engine, electronic bulletin boards, portals are some of the tools.

> Databases.

> In terms of technology, most current knowledge management activities rely on database and Internet systems. When knowledge is stored explicitly, it is typically in databases either as simple tables (for example, relational databases) or special databases. It is possible to structure part of a knowledge repository as a database.

> Data warehouses

> These are large repositories of important data, can also be used for knowledge management, especially in conjunction with domains such as customer relationship management (CRM) systems.

> Specially Structured Databases.

> Some systems have been developed in Lotus Notes/Domino Server and hence utilize the Notes database structure. These specialized databases are ideal for storing tacit knowledge because of its nature. However, we are seeing a trend towards RDBMS as Notes is being bundled with DB2 database by IBM.

> Electronic Documents.

Others have been developed around electronic document management systems. E.g., DocuShare by Xerox

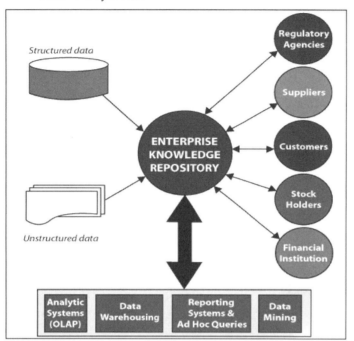

Figure 1: Enterprise Knowledge Repository -Journey from Data to Knowledge

<u>The Enterprise Knowledge Repository and Decision Making in a Learning Organization</u>

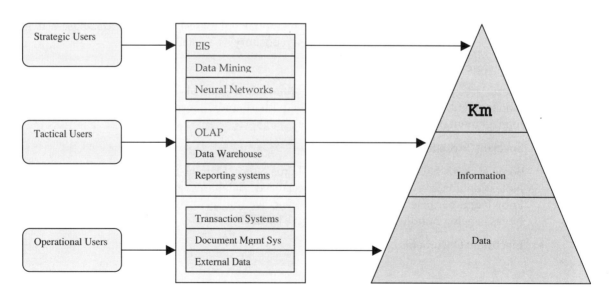

Knowledge Management Copyright © by **EC-Council**

Knowledge Transfer

⊙ Transfer occurs at various levels
- Transfer of Knowledge between individuals
- Transfer of Knowledge from individuals to explicit sources
- Transfer of Knowledge from individuals to groups
- Transfer of Knowledge between groups
- Transfer of Knowledge across groups
- Transfer of Knowledge from the group to the organization.

EC-Council

Knowledge Transfer

Knowledge Transfer tools allow companies to transfer corporate knowledge into a databank or to an employee or group of employees. Transfer can occur at various levels within the organization.

These can be:

➢ Transfer of Knowledge between individuals. This supports learning processes of experts; it involves transfer of both explicit and tacit knowledge. It is achieved primarily through socialization.

➢ Transfer of Knowledge from individuals to explicit sources. This involves transfer of tacit knowledge into explicit sources such as documents, portals, best practices database etc.

➢ Transfer of Knowledge from individuals to groups. This is seen within organization as communities of practice where individual knowledge is shared with a group.

➢ Transfer of Knowledge between groups. When cross-functional teams interact or when different operational units of the organization interact both tacit and explicit knowledge can be shared and transferred.

➢ Transfer of Knowledge across groups. This happens when there are two or more groups interacting on a common framework.

> ➢ Transfer of Knowledge from the group to the organization. This constitutes organization learning and involves transfer of knowledge from various groups to the organization level.

There is however a fundamental difference between technology transfer and knowledge transfer. Technology is technically produced and its transfer is explicit and linear. Knowledge is socially produced, it is both objective and tacit, and its transfer is both explicit and non-linear. Knowledge is generative, productive and reproductive; it cannot be codified and explicated as if it were data. Knowledge transfer has to deal with both the objective and the tacit dimensions of knowledge. The tacit dimension consists of both the experiential and personal knowledge, and its transfer is constrained by the social and cultural contexts in which they are embedded.

The figures below show the transfer between individuals, groups and organization level.

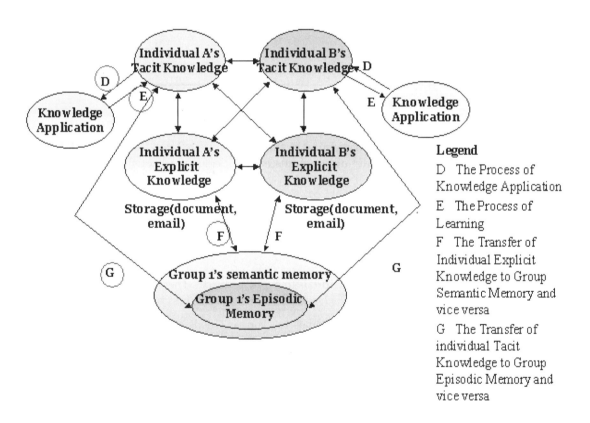

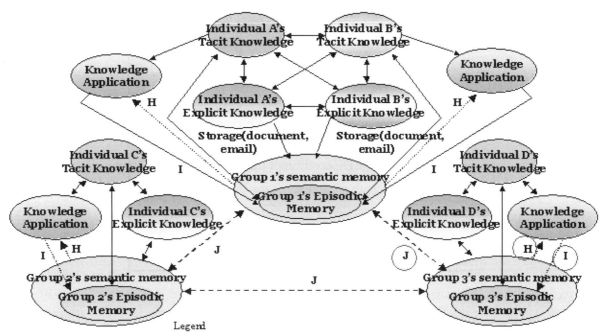

Legend

H An Individual drawing upon group memory and applying the knowledge to a situation.

I The learning derived from an individual in applying knowledge that becomes part of the group's episodic memory.

J The sharing knowledge across group systems, such as the sharing of best practices.

The Five Elements of Knowledge Transfer

⊙ Perceived Value of the Source Unit's Knowledge

⊙ Motivational Disposition of the Source

⊙ Existence and Richness of Transmission Channels

⊙ Motivational Disposition of the Receiving Unit

⊙ The Absorptive Capacity of the Receiving Unit

EC-Council

Five Elements of Knowledge Transfer

 There are five elements need to concern when implemented knowledge sharing. They are:

➤ The value of knowledge source,

➤ Motivational disposition of the knowledge source,

➤ Knowledge transfer channel much be richness and exist,

➤ Motivational disposition of the received knowledge and

➤ Absorptive capacity of the received knowledge.

(Gupta, A. K. & Govindarajan, V., 2000)

The concept of transfer itself is very difficult to capture:

➤ First of all, transfer of knowledge does not imply a full replication of knowledge: "knowledge is transferred as a particular practice following certain rules and procedures that originate in the knowledge sending unit and then undertaken in the recipient unit". (Pedersen, Petersen, Sharma,).

➤ Secondly, knowledge is transferred in organizations whether or not we manage the process at all (Davenport and Prusak, 1998) – this is a part of everyday organizational life. But those firms which leaves knowledge to its own devices put itself in a far from being competitive situation: "at best, this extremely valuable asset remains under leveraged, isolated in pockets of the organization, trapped in individual minds and local venues" (Ruggles, 2000).

Thus, both making knowledge available and managing knowledge transfer are crucial factors for effective organizational learning but to different extent.

The goal of knowledge transfer is to improve an organization's ability to do things, and therefore increase value. Even transmission (sending or presenting knowledge to a potential recipient) and absorption (by that recipient) together (transfer = transmission +absorption) have no useful value if the new knowledge does not lead to some change in behavior, or the development of a new idea that leads to new behavior (Davenport and Prusak, 1998).

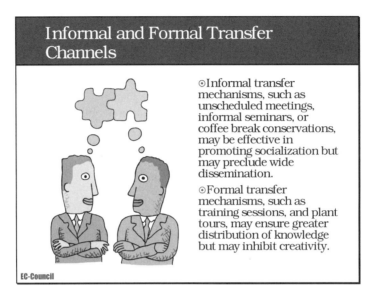

Informal and Formal Channels

There are several transfer networks within an organization. These may be formal, informal, formal or informal in nature.

➤ Informal transfer mechanisms may be effective in promoting socialization but may preclude wide dissemination.

   o Examples include: Unscheduled meetings, informal seminars, or coffee break conservations.

➤ Formal transfer mechanisms may ensure greater distribution of knowledge but may inhibit creativity.

   o Examples include: Training sessions, and plant tours.

➤ Personal channels, may be more effective for distribution highly context specific knowledge.

   o Examples include: Apprenticeships or personnel transfers.

➤ Impersonal channels may be most effective for knowledge that can readily generalized to other context.

   o Examples include: Knowledge repositories.

The effectiveness of these networks will depend on the organization structure and culture and the knowledge-sharing environment fostered within.

IT Applications for Knowledge Transfer

Information technology can support all four forms of knowledge transfer, but has mostly been applied to informal, impersonal means – such as databases, analytical tools, and collaboration tools. Formal impersonal means such as knowledge maps, social network analysis have also been carried out to support knowledge transfer in the organization.

A rich set of next-generation peer networking protocols is the most fundamental building block needed for innovating knowledge transfer. A variety of international standards' bodies have produced a cohesive range of network peer protocol standards, such as BEEP, MIME and SOAP.

Figure: Performance Evaluation Criteria of A Web-Based, Intelligent Agent-Based Framework for KM

KM Activities	Related Theories	Theoretical Propositions	Design Features	Performance Evaluation Criteria
Knowledge Creating	Gestalt Theory (Mayer, 1992)	In Gestalt Theory, problem representation rests at the heart of knowledge creating activity. The theory suggests that tools and techniques should be invented for helping people to represent problems in useful way.	Storyboard-Based Knowledge Creating	Ease of Use of Storyboards; Clarity/Ambiguity of Storyboards; Richness of Storyboards
Knowledge Securing	IPS Model (Newell & Simon, 1972)	The IPS model assumes that human memory consists of two major components: long-term memory and	Content-Based Indexing for Storyboards and	Easy of Storyboard Editing; Effectiveness of Intelligent Access Control

KM Activities	Related Theories	Theoretical Propositions	Design Features	Performance Evaluation Criteria
		short-term memory.	Feedback Messages	
Knowledge Distributing	Information Theory (Shannon, 1948)	Information Theory argues that the ability of individuals to generate and transmit knowledge has the potential to promote interdependency among individuals. It states that mutual awareness is an important issue for supporting collaboration.	Feedback	Timeliness/Responsiveness of Feedback; Negotiation Productivity
Knowledge Retrieving	Cognitive Flexibility Theory (Spiro et al., 1988)	Cognitive Flexibility Theory states that, if users can access various perspectives for solving a problem, they might get a deeper, clearer understanding about the problem. Because of the limited capacity of human memory, too much knowledge makes users experience cognitive overload problems.	Hypermedia-Based Knowledge Presentation	Cognitive Overload; Intuitive/Disorientation of Interface; Flexibility

(Source: An Intelligent Agent-Based Framework for Knowledge Management on The Web: An Exploratory Study of A Virtual Team in Designing A Multimedia System - Seung Ik Baek, Jay Liebowitz, and Srinivas Y. Prasad, Mary J. Granger)

Knowledge Application

⊙ An important aspect of the knowledge-based theory of the firm is that the source of competitive advantage resides in the application of the knowledge rather than in the knowledge itself.

- Directives.

- Organizational Routines

- Self-Contained Task Teams

EC-Council

Knowledge Application

An important aspect of the knowledge-based theory of the firm is that the source of competitive advantage resides in the application of the knowledge rather than in the knowledge itself. Knowledge Application is the key to packaging knowledge to ensure widespread use, converting specialized information into practical tools, and putting new knowledge into practice in the real world.

➢ Directives

This refers to the specific set of rules, standard, procedures and instructions developed through the conversion of specialist's tacit knowledge to explicit and integrated knowledge for efficient communication to non-specialist.

➢ Organizational Routines

This refers to the development of task performance and coordination patterns, interaction protocols, and process specifications that allow individuals to apply and integrate their specialized knowledge without the need to articulate and communicate what they know to others.

➢ Self-Contained Task Teams

These teams are used in situations in which task uncertainty and complexity prevent the specification of directives and organizational routines; teams of individuals with prerequisite knowledge and specialty are formed for problem solving.

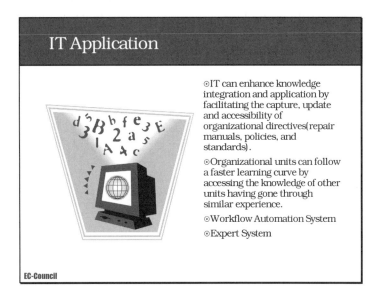

IT Applications for Knowledge Application

Information technology can aid in application of knowledge. It has been reiterated that organizational learning does not take place merely by storing or transferring knowledge. Application of knowledge forms the essence for learning. IT can enhance knowledge integration and application by facilitating the capture, update and accessibility of organizational directives (repair manuals, policies, and standards).

Organizational units can follow a faster learning curve by accessing the knowledge of other units having gone through similar experience. This forms the basis for best practices repository followed at Ford and communities of practice to a certain extent.

Tools that enable knowledge application include workflow automation system, expert systems etc. An example is the Domino Workflow system, which is integral to KM, and helps leverage expertise and information to improve productivity, competence, responsiveness -- and ultimately innovation and competitiveness.

Knowledge of 'how to' process and manipulate data and information is implicit in computer-based systems; knowledge of organizational procedures, for example, is encoded into administrative and office systems that control and facilitate the workings of the organization. Knowledge of policy and precedent can be built into expert and decision support systems to advise decision makers

Expert systems help capture key insights for future application and assists in shortening the learning curve for employees. However, it must be noted that these systems have to be constantly updated and 'refreshed' to ensure that they are reused. The expert system can later form the part of a best practice database with users of the system contributing to its evolution.

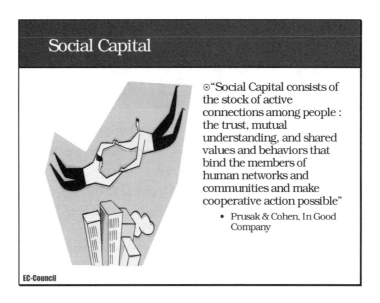

Social Capital

 "Social Capital consists of the stock of active connections among people: the trust, mutual understanding, and shared values and behaviors that bind the members of human networks and communities and make cooperative action possible" - Prusak & Cohen, In Good Company

The central premise of social capital is that social networks have value. Social capital refers to the collective value of all "social networks" [who people know] and the inclinations that arise from these networks to do things for each other ["norms of reciprocity"].

Social capital works through multiple channels:

➢ Information flows (e.g. learning about jobs, learning about candidates running for office, exchanging ideas at college, etc.) depend on social capital

➢ Norms of reciprocity (mutual aid) are dependent on social networks.

  o Bonding networks that connect folks who are similar sustain particularized (in-group) reciprocity.

  o Bridging networks that connect individuals who are diverse sustain generalized reciprocity.

➢ Collective action depends upon social networks although collective action also can foster new networks.

> Social networks that help translate an individual mentality into a team mentality encourage broader identities and solidarity.

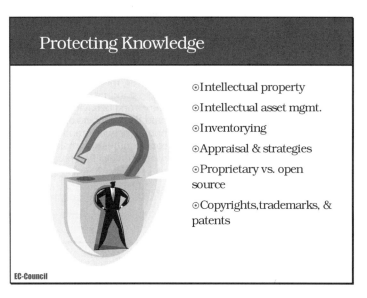

Protecting Knowledge

Intellectual property is a crucial component of a company's assets. Ensuring adequate protection of this property, in the form of patents, trademarks, copyrights and trade secrets is an ongoing task.

As organizations began to realize the value of their knowledge assets, the focus began to shift towards guarding these assets along with the knowledge management process. Most organizations focused initially on patents (example: Dow Chemicals), but extended it out to include other forms of intellectual property, including copyrights, trademarks, and trade secrets. This was because patents are the most concrete of an organization's intangible assets. Moreover, at the initial days of KM patents were beginning to be recognized as having more value. This meant that more time, effort and resources could be spent on them as the return on that investment was going to be much greater.

The next step was to move into non-intellectual property areas such as know-how. Know-how is not legally protected - it is an intellectual asset, not intellectual property. It is central to most organizations, but harder to manage.

We have discussed knowledge inventorying in other modules. Appraisals and strategies are covered under the assessment and strategy modules. Management of the intellectual property portfolio is crucial. It is not a one-time undertaking. Ongoing review of intellectual property assets includes deciding which technology is most valuable, and worth maintaining, and which technology should be discarded.

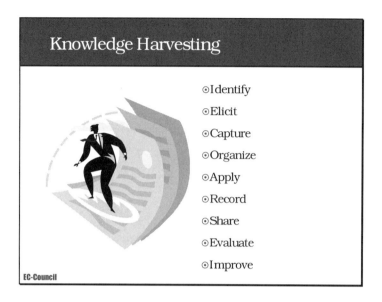

Knowledge Harvesting

Knowledge Harvesting (Charles A. Snyder, Larry T. Wilson) is an integrated set of processes that allow the often hidden (or tacit) insights of top performers to be captured and converted into specific, actionable know-how that can be transferred to others through software. Harvesting can be considered as a subset of the broader, but ill-defined topic of knowledge transfer.

The purpose of Knowledge Harvesting is to capture and express expertise in a form that can be easily accessed and used by others who need the know-how in performance of their tasks. Valuable knowledge about a task or process can be made available to anyone in the organization who needs it on a Just-In-Time basis. Since harvesting can be applied to nearly any kind of human knowledge that is procedurally actionable, the existing expertise or know-how can be captured and formalized into software so that the organization can leverage it and preserve it.

The process of harvesting starts by enabling experts (top-performers) to verbalize their tacit knowledge, thereby making it explicit. Next the steps in the total process consist of capturing, organizing, applying, recording, sharing, evaluating, and improving the know-how

Identify

In any categorization, the first step is to identify the category. In the case of knowledge management, this would involve mapping the organization's key processes and the individuals who possess the best know-how. In this step, the knowledge harvester is ascertaining the origin, nature, or definitive characteristics of the organization's processes. The initiating step involves determining two things, top performing people and their critical activities.

Elicit

Once the experts and activities are identified, an understanding of these activities will be elicited from the experts. Knowledge is gathered from departments such as marketing, research and development, engineering and manufacturing (Davenport, 1996). The activities of the top performers are educed and logically mapped in the knowledge harvesting process. As with expert systems, knowledge engineers realized that the most difficult function of creating an expert system was the process of eliciting information from key performers (experts) about the activities they performed and the rules they used in decision-making. Thus, knowledge management encounters the same problem of uncovering the rules of decision within the activities of key performers. It is not uncommon for the experts to be reluctant to share all of their knowledge because of fear of loss of job security. Companies must make sure that these fears are allayed (Stewart, 1996). Davenport (1996) cautioned that if the company's intentions are not to downsize, then it must ensure employees of their positions within the company, thus, keeping up company morale. It is imperative that the company communicates its intentions to the top performers and provides the culture that encourages sharing of expertise.

Capture

The expertise of the top performers must be preserved to continue the success of the organization. In the elicitation process, a great deal of information will be extracted from top performers and contained therein will be the key decision rules that need to be preserved. The capture phase distills these decision rules from the bulk of information and stores them. Examples of knowledge that might be organized and captured include best practices, patterns, software code, project experiences, and information on tools that have used (Huang, 1998). By seizing and storing the information, the knowledge harvesting process adds value to the future of the corporation. This capturing process makes a permanent copy of the memory of the organization's top performers.

Organize

The knowledge captured from top performers must be arranged in a coherent or systematic form. This procedure of structuring the knowledge into orderly and functional processes allows anyone in the organization to retrieve the necessary information quickly and efficiently. The organization of a corporation's key expertise provides a systematic method of producing the EPSS that allows the organization's knowledge to be carried forward for future use of various applications within the company.

Apply

The purpose of a knowledge management system is to allow all organizational players to apply the same expert knowledge to processes as the top performers. We wish to make the stored knowledge available to everyone as appropriate. The point of a knowledge management system is application by an individual. These individuals may request or seek assistance or advice for performance of a specific task. These applications assist the process of learning by the user.

This learning is aided by context-sensitive assistance embedded in the applications. Support information such as terminology, descriptions, visual aids, and examples should be available on demand. To enhance performance, each individual may be given detailed guidance about information to gather, issues to consider, decisions to make, actions to take, or resources to consult.

Record

Once an application has been created it will require refreshing so that it can evolve with use. This sub-process records the learning that takes place with the user; causing the database of knowledge to be enhanced. This process collects and preserves information on a particular subject. It is the method of preserving the known history of performance, activities, or achievement. This preserved knowledge causes learning in an organizational context. This is a non-trivial process because the application will have to be expertly structured to glean knowledge from the action of the user and ignore everyday data and information. Every element within an application provides a place to record a response. Thus, the application keeps historical records of each learning experience and outcome (Snyder & Wilson, 1998).

The software instantly records all input information generated during the learning/doing process. Process anomalies are recorded, permitting continuous system improvements. The software application can be used by anyone allowing the organization to make effective use of all harvested know-how. The system is user-friendly to enhance motivation to use the system, rather than rely on conventional "cut and try" methodology. Recording means that the application will never forget what has worked in the past and why. Good documentation helps users understand how to handle a similar situation in the future or multiple instances of similar situations can be analyzed as an aggregate (Snyder & Wilson, 1998).

Share

Knowledge that has been captured must be shared or its capture will be irrelevant and the effort and expense wasted. Additionally, sharing will likely lead to the seeking and capturing of other knowledge and uses of previous and new knowledge. This knowledge can be distributed throughout the organization to individuals or groups.

A common knowledge schema is imperative to the distributed architecture and diverse functional characteristics of the devices, equipment, etc. where knowledge is advanced and documented (Snyder & Wilson, 1998). A corporate repository is developed where tangible "intellectual capital" of an organization can be accessed and exchanged. Sharing allows individuals to track activities while significantly increasing efficiency and effectiveness of existing groupware.

Buckman Laboratories is a company that has become well known for its efforts to share knowledge among its more than 1,200 people in over 80 countries (Bowles, 1997: Rifken, 1996). While the idea of sharing knowledge is not new, new learning resources enable the process to be systematized across the organization.

Evaluate

Appraisal will occur during application and sharing. This completes a feedback process. In the elicitation and capture steps some decision rules will be gathered that are of little value or whose application is lost in time. Evaluation should be continuous so that the database can be kept up-to-date, relevant, and as small as possible. Evaluation must be performed in order to determine the effectiveness of the software applications. Repeated use provides the basis for the next process (Snyder & Wilson, 1998)

At the most basic level, learning should be evaluated by assessing the impact on individual performance. Ultimately, the evaluation must be in terms of the contribution to organizational performance.

Improve

The improved sub-process is the continuous betterment of the entire process. By improving the process or the flow of knowledge throughout the organization, the productivity or value to individuals or groups is enhanced. Here we should seek the improvement of both the stored knowledge and its application. An overt process of improvement should cause a greater return on investment. This is because it should foster greater usage and sharing.

KM Process Map

- KM process maps helps identify the information that is really important within the organization
- They also provide insight into how knowledge is both used and produced inside the organization.
- This insight is important "context" that help the knowledge manager make better decisions about the best forms and delivery methods for different types of knowledge.

EC-Council

Knowledge Management Process Map

 Knowledge maps support knowledge management (KM) functions or purposes. A knowledge map can be spatial or two-dimensional, has a beginning and an end, routes and directions, symbols, navigational guides, and legends. The purpose of the knowledge map is to show spatial relationships, and in KM, conceptual relationships. Therefore a KM map can be hierarchical, chronological, or associative - any of which will organize information for ready access, and thus is an integral part of the process of transforming.

Knowledge maps:

➢ Helps define, structure and communicate problem

➢ Helps find and explain influences and levers to desired solution

➢ Fosters creativity through brainstorming solutions to the problem

➢ Help in analyzing risks of solutions by trying to predict outcomes

➢ Help select lowest risk, highest value solution to optimize chances of success, utilizing knowledge acquired through the process.

➢ Helps identify the information that is really important within the organization.

They also provide insight into how knowledge is both used and produced inside the organization. This insight is important "context" that help the knowledge manager make better decisions about the best forms and delivery methods for different types of knowledge.

Embedding Knowledge in Organization Processes

How does an organization go about embedding knowledge in its business process? Outlined below is a suggestive methodology.

➤ Take a particular business process and break it down into its component steps.

➤ Identify the following information about each step in the process:

  o Who typically performs the step, and the required experience/ qualifications

  o What inputs are required for the step?

  o What the desired outputs of the step are

  o What tools/systems are used to perform the step?

  o What dependencies exist, either with other steps within the same process or with an outside processes

➤ Then identify the knowledge that is both used and produced during the execution of the step, and the probable source of that knowledge

Embedding knowledge in organizational routines is made more challenging when the critical knowledge changes rapidly. Both knowledge content and processes must change in relation to each other, a coordination of resources requiring support from a knowledge-sharing culture and collaborative technology. These capabilities remain in a dynamic state constantly, a complex challenge for organizations, individuals, and work practices. In the following pages, we shall illustrate how a particular step in a business process is mapped and embedded.

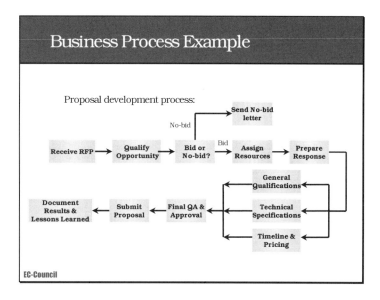

Exhibit. Business process Mapping

For illustration purpose, we shall take a look at the proposal generation process and explore how the organization can embed the knowledge for the particular process.

The first step is to identify the various steps that go into the process from start to finish.

Here we shall detail the technical specification, which is a sub process in the entire cycle.

For the particular step, we shall identify the inputs and outputs of the particular step. This involves finding out who performs the step (Proposal technical manager, Technical SMEs), inputs required (RFP requirements, product specs, prior installation experience (with customer, within industry), competitive offerings, tools / systems required, outputs produced (proposal technical specification & resource estimate) and ascertaining the dependencies such as timeframe and pricing.

Example Contd..Step Outlined: Technical Specifications

⊙ **Knowledge Used:**

- Requirements (source: RFP)
- Product suitability (source: Product specifications, SMEs*)
- Installation parameters (source: Product specifications, SMEs*, Prior installation experience)
- Competitive offerings (source: Prior proposals, SMEs*, new research)
  - *Indicates "tacit" knowledge not yet documented

⊙ **Knowledge Produced:**

- Market demand (source: RFP requirements)
- Market suitability of product (source: Proposal managers* & documents, Competitive analysis, SMEs*)
- Installation parameters (source: Proposal managers* & documents, SMEs*).
- Competitive position (source: Proposal managers* & documents, Competitive analysis, pricing, SMEs*

EC-Council

Exhibit. Embedding Business Process Knowledge

For the step outlines, we shall explore the knowledge applied as well as that generated.

Knowledge Applied include:

> Requirements (source: RFP)

> Product suitability (source: Product specifications, Subject Matter Experts*)

> Installation parameters (source: Product specifications, Subject Matter Experts*, Prior installation experience)

> Competitive offerings (source: Prior proposals, SMEs*, new research)

Knowledge Produced include:

> Market demand (source: RFP requirements)

> Market suitability of product (source: Proposal managers* & documents, Competitive analysis, SMEs*)

> Installation parameters (source: Proposal managers* & documents, SMEs*).

> Competitive position (source: Proposal managers* & documents, Competitive analysis, pricing, SMEs*)

*Indicates "tacit" knowledge not yet documented.

Summary

- ⊙ Knowledge frameworks give a strategic methodology to achieve the knowledge objectives
- ⊙ They must be selected according to the needs of the organization
- ⊙ Knowledge processes include creation, acquisition, storage, retrieval and dissemination
- ⊙ Technology can help organization at each of these knowledge processes
- ⊙ Organizations need to embed knowledge in their processes.

EC-Council

Summary

 Recap

➢ Knowledge frameworks give a strategic methodology to achieve the knowledge objectives

➢ They must be selected according to the needs of the organization

➢ Knowledge processes include creation, acquisition, storage, retrieval and dissemination

➢ Technology can help organization at each of these knowledge processes

➢ Organizations need to embed knowledge in their processes

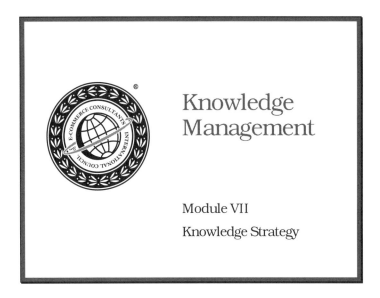

Knowledge Management (KM)

Module VII: Knowledge Strategy

Exam 212-69 Certified e-Business Associate

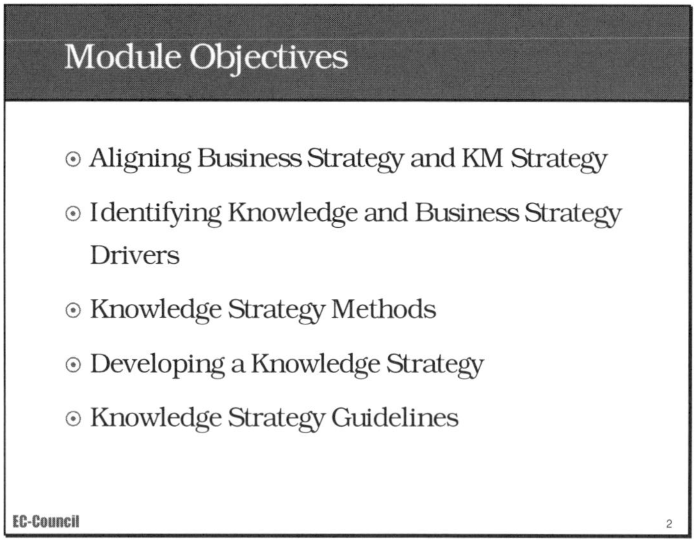

Module Objectives

⊙ Aligning Business Strategy and KM Strategy

⊙ Identifying Knowledge and Business Strategy Drivers

⊙ Knowledge Strategy Methods

⊙ Developing a Knowledge Strategy

⊙ Knowledge Strategy Guidelines

EC-Council

2

Objectives

☞ **Module Objectives**

On completion of this module you will have gained insight into various aspects relating to knowledge strategy. This module engages in discussing the following key areas:

➢ Aligning business strategy and knowledge strategy

➢ Identifying knowledge and business strategy drivers

➢ Understanding knowledge strategy methods

➢ Comprehending essential guidelines to follow while drafting knowledge strategy

Readers are encouraged to identify strategies that exist in their organizations and relate them to the strategies discussed here. Begin by assessing whether your business is knowledge-focused or knowledge enabled, and what business value can derive from knowledge management. Where would KM fit in the overall strategy for business?

'Hence, there is more to knowledge management than just accumulated knowledge. Relevance is critical and the companies that survive from one dominant design generation to the next are those that develop capability as it is required, and before.'

- (W.L. Miller and L. Morris, Fourth Generation R&D, 1998)

3

Research of KM practices in the U.S. it has been found that Knowledge capital is embedded in the enterprise's intangible assets. Gartner Group suggests that Knowledge capital includes intangible assets like brand image (particularly for very influential companies, such as Coca-Cola or Microsoft) as well as intellectual capital. Intellectual capital includes the knowledge of employees; data and information about processes, experts, products, customers and competitors; and intellectual property such as patents or regulatory licenses. For instance, on July 1, 1998 the value of Microsoft's tangible assets was $22.4 billion, but its market value was nearly $260 billion-an I/T ratio of more than 10-to-1.

Therefore we can consider that in today's business environment, knowledge strategy is integral to a successful business strategy. Knowledge strategy designs an organization's future based on using knowledge effectively. Many situations call for this approach, but this is more appealing while facing customer and marketplace uncertainty, increasing product complexity, shifts in competitors and technology, and radical product lifecycles.

It is the role of top management to determine which kinds of knowledge assets are available to them. Still more important, it is the role of top management to consider what kinds of knowledge they are lacking for achieving their strategic objectives. On the basis of the inventory of their knowledge assets, they can form a strategy to create, capture, maintain and utilize the firm's knowledge assets effectively and efficiently.

It is desirable to align organizational knowledge to a defined business strategy. This approach considers knowledge management as processes that optimize creation, sharing, and market leverage of knowledge assets and core capabilities.

Many KM approaches focus on collaborative groupware tools for knowledge sharing and teamwork, and knowledge portals to organize vast amounts of information and filter the right content and access to corporate knowledge.

With the easy entry and investment of new Internet competitors, established firms now face intense pressure to address their own knowledge strategy or face share erosion. Unique knowledge processes (including innovation, design, leveraging research) and brand value (trust, customer loyalty, and identification) are among the only non-replicable assets in a growing number of business sectors.

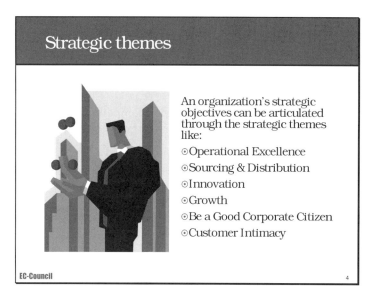

Strategic Themes

An organization's strategic objectives can be articulated through the strategic themes and a strategic theme contains its own set of cause-and-effect relationships. For example, a strategic theme can be growth.

Strategic Themes are the fundaments of the articulated business strategy. Each strategic theme contains its own strategic hypothesis with its own set of cause-and-effect relationships. The multiple indirect linkages required to connect improvements in an organization's intangible assets – the ultimate drivers of knowledge-based strategies – to the tangible customer and financial outcomes of the strategy, will be described in each strategic theme.

If we look at a typical model of business strategy, three broad directions are commonly identified:

> Market growth or value,

> Operational effectiveness, and

> Customer intimacy.

Market growth or overall value through services drives product innovation; Effectiveness drives internal knowledge sharing and management, to leverage use of knowledge to avoid costly reinvention and churn. And customer intimacy drives changes across the organization, requiring innovating for customers, leveraging customer knowledge, and driving revenues through customer retention.

Business Strategy	Corresponding Knowledge Strategy
Product Sales Time to Market Distribution Networks	Product Innovation Intellectual Capital Knowledge Creation
Process Streamlining SCM Accounting and Finance	Process Innovation Knowledge Sharing Developing Learning Culture
Customer Retention Customer Product Needs Revenue Growth Partnering / Alliancing	Product Innovation Customer Knowledge Integration Branding Knowledge

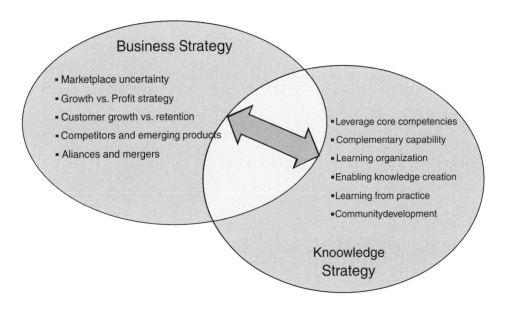

The above figure shows the link between knowledge strategy and business strategy.

Importance of KM Strategy

What should drive a knowledge strategy? It may include the organization mission, the value that the organization offers its members, donors, clients, and constituents. The organization business model (fee-for-service, membership, donations, grant-seeking, etc.)

Knowledge strategies enable companies to enhance their business competencies - whether they are focused on efficient operations, product innovation or customer intimacy. Successful firms are recognizing that they can generate tremendous value for shareholders and customers by strategically managing and acting on knowledge.

Companies having superior knowledge are in a position to coordinate and combine their traditional resources and capabilities in new and distinctive ways, providing more value for their customers than can their competitors.

By having superior intellectual resources, an organization can understand how to exploit and develop their traditional resources better than competitors, even if some or all of those traditional resources are not unique. Therefore, knowledge can be considered the most important strategic resource, and the ability to acquire, integrate, store, share and apply it the most important capability for building and sustaining competitive advantage.

For example, Microsoft has developed unique practices in its forms of software engineering that have been described and copied by competitors. However, other firms cannot replicate the coordination of resources between product lines, staff roles, and deep knowledge of product code, the operating system code, and their internal processes. To the extent that their product lines remain dominant in the marketplace, Microsoft's knowledge-based collective operations establish a powerful beachhead against competition. Both efficient and innovative, their processes keep their product lines advanced and ahead of competitors to a great extent.

One of the valuable things a strategy brings to an organization is clarity. And it can help integrate and focus energy, efforts and resources. As opposed to launching corporate-wide knowledge initiatives without clear business objectives at the outset, the importance of first identifying the business competencies that can be enhanced by knowledge management is emphasized.

Companies develop different knowledge strategies depending on whether they are competing on cost, product innovation or customer intimacy. Another key challenge that knowledge strategists are attempting to address is the need for systems that integrate knowledge, technology and people. Companies must now incorporate people into their knowledge management efforts - enabling access, for instance, to experts.

Firms should place more emphasis on capturing the knowledge and expertise of their employees, and then ensuring it is effectively shared. It is the tacit expertise and experience of individuals that makes a big difference. Many companies are now focused on developing knowledge management strategies and establishing value propositions for these efforts.

Zack (1999) identified core, advanced, and innovative knowledge as the three levels of knowledge development related to building knowledge strategy.

> Core knowledge is commonly shared by all members of an industry, and offers no competitive value. It is the "price to play," such as web-based companies' understanding of Internet technology.

> Advanced knowledge can be differentiated, and therefore provides some competitive advantage. With the same advanced knowledge as competitors, a firm can position and coordinate that knowledge in different ways, creating value for its customers. Advanced and usable user interfaces in web products offer an advantage based on advanced knowledge, but still remains knowledge open to the overall market.

> Innovative knowledge allows a firm to lead its industry by significantly differentiating from its competitors. Firms such as Cisco Systems and Qualcomm developed early core technologies in their product areas, established de facto standards as patented, licensed intellectual property, and created internal processes for building on these standards.

KM Strategy Essentials

⊙ Devise KM strategy before:
- Embarking on KM program
- Designing /changing IT architecture
- Building Knowledge Base
- Acquiring software or tools

⊙ KM Strategy should:
- Address business knowledge needs
- Support key business processes
- Adopt one predominant business focus – i.e. mine data, create new knowledge, use existing knowledge efficiently

EC-Council

6

Essentials Of Knowledge Management Strategy

Knowledge and Strategy addresses the link between knowledge management and business strategy.

Many executives are struggling to articulate the relationship between their organization's intellectual resources and capabilities, and its competitive strategy. They do not have well-developed strategic models that help them to link knowledge-oriented processes, technologies and organizational forms to business strategy, and are unsure of how to translate the goal of making their organizations more intelligent into a strategic course of action. They need a pragmatic, yet theoretically sound model of what I call knowledge strategy.

Organizations should consider the following before embarking on a knowledge management initiative.

- Devise KM strategy before embarking on KM program. It should address designing /changing its IT architecture and building a knowledge base. The organization should also acquire software or tools it needs for the KM program before starting out.

- KM Strategy should address business and knowledge needs, support key business processes and ideally adopt one predominant business focus – i.e. mine data, create new knowledge, use existing knowledge efficiently.

In this module we will discuss four prominent strategies. It is up to individual organizations to decide which strategy or combination of strategies it must adopt keeping in mind its own business needs and strategic objectives.

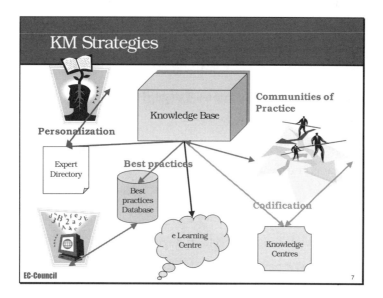

Knowledge Management Strategies

Tierney, (1999) "A company's KM strategy should reflect its competitive strategy." This definition focuses on creating value for customers, turning a profit, and managing people. (HBR)

Zack, (1999) "… the most important context for guiding knowledge management is the firm's strategy. Knowledge is the fundamental basis of competition. Competing successfully on knowledge requires either aligning strategy to what the organization knows, or developing the knowledge and capabilities needed to support a desired strategy."

A CKO must also create strategies for increasing intellectual capital and the organizational capacity to do tasks quicker, cheaper, and a better than the competition and in a manner that meets or exceeds customer's changing expectations

Zack (1999) identified an approach for developing knowledge strategy based on research and practice. His approach offers a comprehensive approach to analyzing strategic gaps in the organization and aligning knowledge management to business strategy.

Zack's model reveals a flow of basic activities, but it does not define techniques for strategic analysis and development. The following figure shows Zack's model as sourced from 'Developing a Knowledge Strategy' published in California Management Review, 1999.

Zack's model "14 Steps"
How do you want to play the game?

What do you need to know?

What do you know?

What's your internal knowledge gap?

What do your competitors know?

What's your external knowledge gap?

What is your learning cycle?

What are your competitors' and industry learning cycles?

What is your learning gap?

What is your internal strategic gap?

What's your external strategic gap?

What's your industry cycle strategic gap?

What's your new current and future strategy?

What's your knowledge strategy?

Generally, the first activity in knowledge strategy is to understand the current business strategy, then affirming or progressing that strategy as the basis for organizational analyses. By using identical processes for current strategy as in knowledge strategy, the organization should be able to distinguish the differences between business goals and knowledge-based strategy. To understand the organization's gaps with internal strategy and with external competitors, an assessment and gap analysis process should be undertaken. The knowledge strategy process used should align business strategy to four dimensions of knowledge resources, organizational practices, strategic resources (technology), and customer relationships.

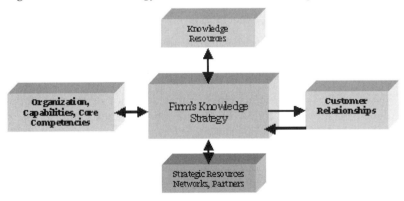

A study performed by the American Productivity and Quality Center in 1996 identified six key strategies for deploying Knowledge Management initiatives. These were:

- Knowledge Management as a Business Strategy –This strategy views knowledge as a key marketplace differentiator, or more specifically, as a product. Companies that pursue this strategy believe that KM is a core competency and critical to the health of the business as a whole. The KM strategy is tightly aligned and integrated with the company's global business strategies.

- Transfer of Knowledge and Best Practices – This strategy is the most widespread, focusing on systematic approaches to knowledge reuse and transfer of best practices. It also focuses on moving knowledge to where it will be used to improve operations or be included in products and services. The strategy aims to design systems and practices to obtain, organize, restructure, warehouse or memorize, reward, repackage for deployment and distribute knowledge.

- Customer-Focused Knowledge – This strategy is focused on capturing knowledge about customers, developing and transferring this knowledge as well as understanding customer's needs and preferences.

- Personal Responsibility for Knowledge - Companies that view this strategy as important believe that individuals should manage their own knowledge environments. For this strategy to succeed critical information and knowledge must be available in easily accessible and reliable knowledge based repositories. Critical success factors for this strategy are identifying content owners and implementing disciplined processes to ensure that the repositories are current and reliable.

- Intellectual Asset Management - This strategy views items such as patents, copyrights, trade secrets and trademarks as information assets. If managed properly, these assets can provide not only short-term returns, but also they can energize the future success of the organization. For obvious reasons, not many organizations are in a position to implement this strategy.

- Innovation and Knowledge Creation – This strategy emphasizes innovation and the creation of new knowledge, through both basic and applied research and development.

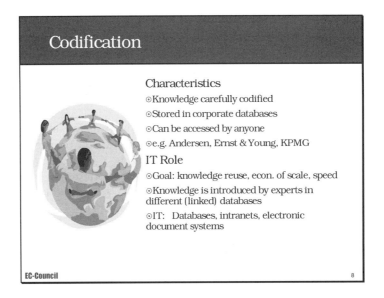

Codification

This strategy emphasizes on codifying explicit resources where business performance depends on effectively mining the data for insight to guide innovation and decision-making.

Codification strategy involves transfer of knowledge from people to document. Knowledge is extracted from the person who developed it, made independent of the person, and reused by the organization. Examples are interview guides, work schedules, benchmark data, market analyses.

Codification strategy as aligned to the corporate advocates reuse economics, heavy IT investment and hiring people who can reuse knowledge and implement.

The IT emphasis is on knowledge centers managed by subject-matter experts in order to provide knowledge required for knowledge workers to perform their job and shorten the learning curve.

The codification strategy is usually seen in companies that sell relatively standardized products that fill common needs, knowledge is carefully codified and stored in databases so that it can be accessed and used--over and over again--by anyone in the organization.

Enablers – retrieval, search, visualization tools such as thematic scaping which presents topographic maps of information resources to reveal concentrations in knowledge areas indicating interest or intensity of activity. (A snapshot of a database.) Another tool is citation tree used for patent intelligence to show patenting activity around own and competition's patents reveals past activity, help predict future trends, and locate potential licensees.

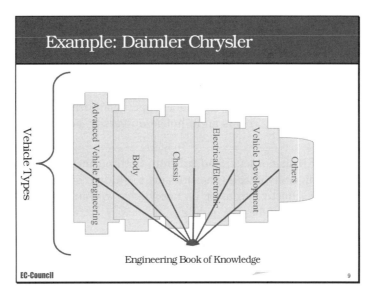

Example: Daimler Chrysler

Codification Example: Daimler Chrysler

Adopting the "knowledge as a product" approach means treating knowledge as an entity rather separate from the people who create and use it. The typical goal is to take documents with explicit knowledge embedded in them — memos, reports, presentations, articles, etc. — and store them in a repository where they can be easily retrieved.

Three commonly found types of projects of the "knowledge as a product" approach are for capturing and re-using:

External knowledge. External knowledge repositories range from information delivery "clipping services" that route articles to executives, to advanced competitive or customer intelligence systems.

> Structured internal knowledge, e.g. embodied in research reports, product-oriented marketing materials, corporate techniques and methods.

> Informal internal knowledge, e.g. discussion databases or "lessons learned" databases.

> Examples of companies that aim at a continual enhancement of their knowledge base — the collection of best practices, methods and reusable work products — include General Motors, Glaxo Wellcome and Daimler Chrysler.

As a Case-in–point, we shall see the Daimler Chrysler knowledge strategy which was built around the codification strategy.

Daimler Chrysler was established in 1997 as a result of the merger between Daimler of Germany and Chrysler of U.S.A. The company fully recognized need to develop synergies and established a policy "one company, one vision". Daimler had a strong German tradition and a Chrysler had been a typical American style of business. They recognized the need to transcend these cultural barriers.

"One Company, one vision" was the proposition that they agreed they needed. Based on this belief, management took action to implement this change in culture. This policy succeeded in a form of the "corporate university". This is an in-house university as well as a virtual university within the company.

Students are comprised of manager level and up from both business units. There are currently over 3000 students. The university enables the students to study the future of the new company. The company focused the effective transfer of knowledge within the theme of post merger integration and on future image of the automobile.

As a result of their activities the time necessary for the development of the new model more than halved. The objectives of the university are (1) management education, (2) leadership development, and (3) continuous study through cooperation with HBS in the U.S.A to strive for assimilation of their knowledge. The Company places importance on not only the virtual situation but also face-to-face issues in the field. They have faith in the cultivation of human capacity and believe that the people are the sprit of the knowledge. They have adopted a codified knowledge strategy and come up with EBOK.

EBOK (Engineering Book of Knowledge): this is the term used by Daimler-Chrysler to describe their repository of knowledge used by design engineers.

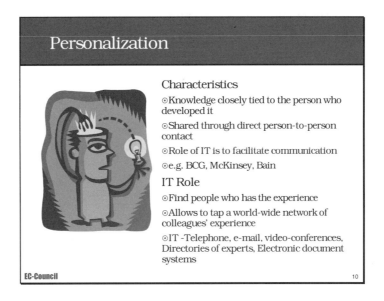

Personalization

Personalization strategy is seen in companies that provide highly customized solutions to unique problems, and knowledge is shared mainly through person-to-person contacts. The chief purpose of technology is to help people communicate.

This strategy places emphasis on externalization and application of tacit knowledge where business performance depends on innovating new solutions to tackle unique problems. The knowledge is closely tied to the person who has created it and remains the primary source. It is shared or disseminated through person-to-person contact.

The role of IT is to help find people who have the needed experience. This allows the organization to tap experiences of personnel globally. The IT emphasis is on collaboration such as expert directories, communication tools like email, video conferencing tools, electronic document systems, intranets, portals etc. Enablers of the strategy include strong knowledge sharing culture, communities of practice creation and related support tools.

Treating "knowledge as a process" usually considers enabling the development and flourishing of communities as a key solution for knowledge leverage. Firms adopting this approach, focus on the creation of communities of interest or practice (self organized groups which 'naturally' communicate with one another because they share common work practices, interests, or aims), to address knowledge generation and sharing. The emphasis in this case is on providing access to knowledge or facilitating its transfer among individuals.

For example, companies like British Petroleum, Skandia, Buckman Laboratories and Matsushita strive to create corporate environments that nurture knowledge communities, in order to facilitate the exchange of ideas and collaboration across the organization.

Comparison of Codification and Personalization

Codification	Competitive Strategy	Personalization
Codification Strategy of knowledge management provides fast and high quality information system.	Company's knowledge Management strategy Reflects its Competitive strategy.	Personalization Strategy of knowledge management provides high levels of strategic solutions
Reuse Economics:	Economic Model	Expert Economics
People-To-Documents	Knowledge Management Strategy	Person-To-Person
Invest heavily in IT	Information Technology	Invest moderately in IT
Hire Graduates train them	Human Resources	Select people after a tough competition
Anderson Consulting Ernst & Young	Examples	McKinsey & Company Bain & Company

EC-Council   11

Comparing Codification and Personalization

The choice of a generic strategy (codification vs. personalization) depends on the answers to these questions:

➢ Are the products standardized or customized?

Professors Morten Hansen and Nitin Nohria of the Harvard Business School, as well as Thomas Tierney, the managing director of Bain, observed that KM needs of knowledge-based service firms (e.g. consulting firms, health care providers, IT services, etc.) fall somewhere between two opposite types:

1. Companies that offer repetitive, similar or modularized services and whose competitive strength lies in delivering such services quickly, cheaply and reliably.

2. Companies that offer one-of-a-kind or custom services and whose competitive strength lies in their high level of expertise, tailor-fitted quality and personalized customer relationship

➢ Is the organization mature or innovative?

When the product or service offered by a company is standardized or mature, then the sales process is focused on well-organized tasks and the product knowledge is relatively rigid – thus more easily codified. In such cases, developing a strategy around the "knowledge as a product" approach seems more suitable. In those cases when the value proposition of the company is based on developing highly customized and/or extremely innovative products or services, adopting a "knowledge as a process" approach that mainly supports the sharing of knowledge, expertise and judgment, seems more appropriate.

The first type of organization creates value by large-scale reuse of knowledge applied to similar recurring types of service. Therefore, it needs to codify and store such knowledge for easy and efficient retrieval, and so has to invest in sophisticated knowledge databases accessible via the company intranet, especially if the company has numerous branches all over the world. Once a project had developed an effective new approach, work processes and templates, these are captured in documents and stored electronically for use in later similar projects.

The second type of organization creates value by high-level expert service tailored to particular clients' needs. Every engagement is unique and every solution requires practically fresh R&D. Successful organizations has high level experts in their niche and, if needed, can outsource other expertise from its strategic partners or network of cooperating firms. Company investment in IT hardware and software is only moderate but hiring of senior professional staff tends to be a crucial and elaborate affair.

➤ Do people rely on tacit or explicit knowledge to solve problems?

Efficient people-to-document (e.g. process documentation, taxonomy) and document-to-people (e.g. tracking, intelligent search engines) processes become crucial for delivering the kind of service found in the first category of companies discussed here.

With regard to the second category, service delivery requires the ability to accurately gauge the particularities of client needs, and to design a responsive solution accordingly. Such services require knowledge with high tacit content, people-to-people transfer of knowledge, effective teamwork among a cross-functional team, innovativeness or improvisation, and excellent people skills.

Professor Hansen calls the approach of the first type, codification strategy and that of the second type, personalization strategy. A company can practice both: the codification strategy in those projects where frequent reuse of knowledge is encountered, and the personalization strategy in other projects where highly tacit and person-centered skills and expertise are important. The need dictates what KM strategy is more appropriate.

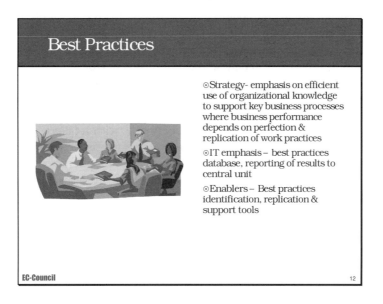

Best Practices

There are six key attributes of knowledge that must be factored into KM practices:

➢ Subjectivity (context and individual background shape the interpretation of knowledge)

More successful companies deal with the challenges of subjectivity by ensuring agreement on general rules and values, cross-functional collaboration in product development and order generation, and increased face-to-face communication. For instance, Danish hearing aid manufacturer Oticon ensures that team membership is constantly shifting, as experts shuttle between teams.

➢ Transferability (knowledge can be extracted and transferred to other contexts)

Internal and external benchmarking, market research, external alliances, and competitor analysis can facilitate transferability of knowledge. Lateral thinking is needed to bring knowledge into entirely new contexts and even from entirely new industries. Japanese auto component company Aisin AW draws lessons actively from the consumer electronics industry giant Akihibara in Tokyo. A European engine company actively participates in a variety of public research projects where it partners with universities and even competitors.

➢ Embeddedness (knowledge is often in a static and buried form that makes it difficult to extract or reformulate)

Best-practice KM techniques for dealing with embedded knowledge include knowledge databases, corporate yellow pages, job rotation, teamwork with suppliers, and co-location of product development staff. Finnish metal group Outokumpu has a solid IT infrastructure to make it easier to find knowledge among its staff. Apprenticeships and collocation with suppliers can help in the automotive sector.

➢ Self-reinforcement (the value of knowledge increases and not decreases when shared)

Self-reinforcement knowledge networking practices for jump-starting the knowledge value chain include online training, formal networks with retailers, joint problem solving, alignment with partner IT systems, and easy access for service data. Amazon links book purchases with past customer book preferences; an international conglomerate gets all its employees to write year-end reports containing their successes and outlook for the next year. SAP opened SAP University in 1999; it offers blended e-learning courses, and employees can set up their own sites and present a skill set.

➢ Perishability (knowledge can become outdated)

Coping with perishability of knowledge involves continuous training related to standards and design rules, development optimization, FAQs, and clear division of responsibilities. Intel speeds chip development via a "Copy EXACTLY!" initiative to avoid overdoing customization and ensure that best practices can be precisely replicated across its global chip plants; chip-turnaround time has been cut from 7 years to 2 years. It is important to balance standards with creativity, of course.

➢ Spontaneity (knowledge can develop unpredictably in a process)

As for spontaneity in knowledge creation, it is certainly difficult to "create creativity," but quite possible to ensure that the frequency of valuable knowledge generation can be increased via creativity techniques, Internet access for all staff, ideas contests, and greater freedom in individual aspirations. 3M, Sony and Nokia are particularly good at unleashing new ideas via a "search, collide, decide and try" process. Ford lets its employees "log on and tune in" via the Net -- all its employees get free Internet access at home. Fuji Xerox has a creative Knowledge Dynamics Initiative with projects like a Virtual Hollywood.

Best practices strategy emphasizes on efficient use of organizational knowledge to support key business processes where business performance depends on perfection and replication of work practices. The IT emphasis is on best practices database, reporting of results to central unit and the enablers are best practices identification, replication and support tools.

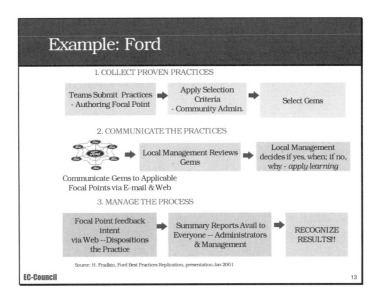

Best Practices Example: Ford

In 2001, Fortune 500 ranked Ford #5. Its 2001 Global Revenues was $162 Billion and 2001 Global Unit Vehicle Sales were 7 million, with an employee base of 354,000 Employees. There are many Knowledge Sharing Processes at Ford. These include Enterprise Portals, Document Repository, GIS, e-Books and Best Practice Replication (BPR).

We will focus on the best practice replication strategy practiced in Ford. The strategy allows Write, Search, and Read access to Ford Employees, with valid ID and who have received proper training. The detailed BPR Process is considered confidential information. Incidentally it is a 62-step process that has been pruned to a 40-step process for licensing purposes. It is a robust business process for the collection and approval of high value practices that can be shared and implemented throughout the enterprise. It is an ideal application for building people relationships by sharing valuable knowledge – fosters team learning, and technology is used to enable nimble and intuitive communication of knowledge.

The genesis of BPR can be traced as follows. In Jun '95, informal process of faxing practices amongst vehicle operations was introduced. In Jun '96, Ford launched BPR formally across vehicle operations – 53 plants globally. In Feb '00 a derivative of process for Health and Safety for communicating concerns and incidents was developed and BPR version 2.0 was launched. In Dec '00 a derivative of the process for was developed for environmental application. The next development was in Feb '01 when the process was adapted for replicating key findings of 6-Sigma projects.

From Aug '96 till present, ford has launched 53 Communities of Practice. This includes Product Development, Ford Land, HR, Quality, Service, Finance, MP&L, Ford Production System, Recruiting, Plant IT, Paint, Final Area, Body, Machining, Facilities Engineering, and Engine Design. The BPR captures only proven, high value practices and it is possible to quantify value-add to the business as well as manage the process. Ford has since licensed its BPR with Business Partners providing the people and the content, while the IT group provides the enabling tool.

An overview of the procedure is as given below.

a. Draft Practice: Focal Point enters all the content of Proven Practices into BPR.

b. Review Draft Practice: Gatekeeper reviews Draft Practices for content completeness and clarity. Collaborates with Subject Matter Experts.

c. Approved Practice: Gatekeeper approves only High-Value Proven Practices.

d. Automatic email notification of Approved Practices to all the Community Focal Points at each Location.

e. Practices reviewed by team members at each location to determine applicability.

f. Adopt/Adapt/ Not Adopt Decision: Each location Leadership decides priorities of applicable practices. "Copy with Pride"

g. Feedback: At each location, Focal Point provides feedback to the System - adoption decision and value of the adoption.

h. Reports: Location Summary Report, Community Summary Report, etc., available to any Ford Employee.

i. Recognition of both the Best Practice Creator as well as the Replicator – Placards.

Ford has had more than 10,000 replications yearly and the 2,800+ active high value practices have resulted in $1.5+ Billion of identified value and $1 Billion of actual value added to the company.

Ford has als53 Communities of Practice launched with 2,115 Focal Points. The health and safety and environmental derivates of the process proactively distribute incidents and corrective actions. Patents have been applied for the software and process derivatives and the process licensed to Shell Oil, Nabisco, and Kraft Foods.

Ford advocates the following best practice strategies:

1. Culture of knowledge sharing must exist, 2. System must have automatic feedback, 3. Hi-Tech works only if there is Hi-Touch, 4. Provide peer-recognition of people who share knowledge, 5: The system must be available to the grass-roots level, 6: Senior Leadership sponsorship is necessary, but not sufficient, 7: System must be able to capture the value of the practice, 8: If you

build it they will not come. Push the knowledge to users, 9: Establish a process for filtering out trivial, low-value practices, 10: Tell stories, with sufficient details.

KM Strategy – Communities of Practice

- ⊙ "Communities of practice demonstrate a shift from authority of position to authority of knowledge" - Charles Savage
- ⊙ Relationship between practice and knowledge
- ⊙ Local innovation
- ⊙ Reciprocity – keeping knowledge effective
  - Peripheral participation
  - Losing favor with firms; taking away valuable training instrument
- ⊙ Role of technology – should support diffusion of know what and development of know how

Communities of Practice

Communities of practice (CoP) have been discussed in detail in a previous module in the courseware. To recap, communities of practice demonstrate a shift from authority of position to authority of knowledge. They nurture a relationship between practice and knowledge. It encourages local innovation. The role of technology should be to support diffusion and development of knowledge. In this module, we will trace how the concept of CoP evolved at Xerox.

An anthropologist from the Xerox Palo Alto Research Center (PARC), a member of the work-practices team, traveled with a group of tech reps to observe how they actually did their jobs -- not how they described what they did, or what their managers assumed they did. That research challenged the way Xerox thought about the nature of work, the role of the individual, and the relationship between the individual and the company. It was the first shot in a revolution.

Here's what the anthropologist saw: Tech reps often made it a point to spend time not with customers but with each other. They'd gather in common areas, like the local parts warehouse, hang around the coffee pot, and swap stories from the field.

The anthropologist saw the exact opposite. The time at the warehouse was anything but dead. The tech reps weren't slacking off; they were doing some of their most valuable work. Field service, it turns out, is no job for lone wolves. It's a social activity. Like most work, it involves a community of professionals. The tech reps weren't just repairing machines; they were also co-producing insights about how to repair machines better.

These technicians were knowledge workers in the truest sense. And it was through conversations at the warehouse -- conversations that weren't a step in any formal "business process" or a box in any official "org chart" -- that knowledge transfer happened.

So Xerox turned conventional wisdom on its head. Rather than eliminate the informal conversations in pursuit of corporate efficiency, Xerox decided to expand them in the name of learning and innovation. Using the Denver area as a pilot project, PARC distributed two-way radio headsets to the tech reps. The radio frequency over which the tech reps communicated became a "knowledge channel" through which they asked each other questions, identified problems, and shared new solutions as they devised them.

But the headsets had limitations. For one thing, no one captured the knowledge the tech reps created. The field staff might communicate in real time to diagnose an unfamiliar problem and generate a solution, but the insights often evaporated once they finished the job.

In France, working with Rank Xerox, PARC recently unveiled Eureka, an electronic "knowledge refinery" that organizes and categorizes a database of tips generated by the field staff. Technically, Eureka is a relational database of hypertext documents. In practice, it's an electronic version of war stories told around the coffee pot -- with the added benefits of an institutional memory, expert validation, and a search engine.

Eureka operates as a free-flowing knowledge democracy, much like the natural, informal collaborations among tech reps. It relies on voluntary information exchanges. Any tech rep, regardless of rank, can submit a tip, but they are neither required to nor are they explicitly rewarded. In Eureka, the coin of the realm is social capital: the incentive to be a good colleague, to contribute and receive knowledge as a member of the community.

In developing Eureka, PARC sent a researcher to travel with field technicians. When problems with copiers arose, the researcher asked to see the manuals the tech reps consulted. Early on, before they got comfortable with the PARC representative, the tech reps would pull out the "official" company manual -- clean, pristine, and neatly organized. Over time, though, they started showing the researcher their "real" manual. It was the standard book -- but highlighted, dog-eared, filled with scribbles in the margins and annotated with notes and reminders.

Each tech rep was keeping two sets of books: the formal and the informal, the official and the improvised. Thus CoP evolved at Xerox as a social process built around informed participation: people need information to do their work, but it is only through working that they get the information they need.

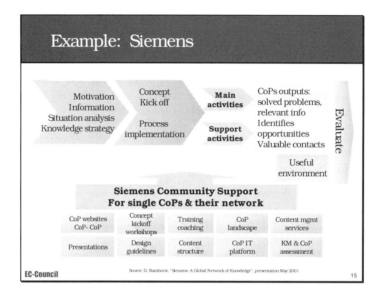

Communities of Practice Example: Siemens

Siemens introduced the Knowledge Strategy Process (KSP) in 2001 as a method for business owners and teams to determine strategy and action plans, in consultation with Dutch KM company CIBIT in Utrecht. This is basically an iterative strategy of identifying clusters of competency and knowledge, and mapping codification status across time, based on current and projected market dynamics.

Transforming from a product seller to a solutions provider, Siemens Information and Communication Networks (ICN) devised a business development KM practice called ShareNet in 1999 to help share project knowledge across technologies and markets in different stages of maturity. Sales staff now finds themselves playing the role of strategy-management consultants who have to be able to interpret trends and design new opportunities together with the customer.

Knowledge areas covered include financing, planning, engineering and operation. This helps sales staff devises customized telecom solutions using existing service packages, business plans and profitability paths. ShareNet helps tap and share local innovation in different parts of the world via project debriefings, manuals, codified databases, structured questionnaires, chat rooms and hot lines. Technically based on OpenText's LiveLink, it is used by 7,000 sales and marketing staff.

Its success is due to leadership support (from the ShareNet Committee which includes local and global representatives), organizational support (global editor, regional contributors, training bootcamps), motivation system (via ShareNet "shares" for contributions which can be exchanged for equipment or conference fees), organizational culture (promoting sharing via messages like "Unlike in school, copying is not only allowed -- it is required"), and quantifiable benefits (eg. cost saving by re-use of tenders, increased revenues by competing faster, and alignment with customer needs by spotting worldwide trends).

Another innovative KM practice comes from Siemens ICN VD (German sales unit), called Knowledge Networking Service. The objective of knowledge networking at ICN VD is to "create a living network of knowledge amongst all employees." Key requisites for this are a mix of high tech and high touch networking, encouraging voluntary participation, and creating a mix of interdisciplinary backgrounds.

An editorial team helps manage a "Knowledge & More" personal account statement for employees. Employees receive points for submitting business tips used by call centres and other service staff; these points can be tallied and converted into prizes. All staff are trained on how to use the KM Intranet, via an "Intranet Driving License." They are also sensitized to use it regularly.

Siemens Industrial Services, with 22,000 people in over 70 countries, uses a knowledge-sharing tool called Know-How Exchange to connect experts, employees and their diverse project experiences. Areas of expertise here include engineering layouts, project structures, plant building and contract negotiation for automotive and textile plants.

Employees were encouraged to take part in this Exchange and develop a sense of personal responsibility for their participation, so as to create a win-win situation for all. The Exchange has a growing number of entries of references, tools, products, customers, industry sectors and technologies. Know-how Transfer has been integrated into standard business processes such that at any point an employee can learn from others' experiences.

KM also extends successfully to Siemens' subsidiaries, such as semiconductor unit Infineon Technologies, established in 1999. With production sites in five countries, it initiated the Knowledge Exchange Networking (KECnetworking) to serve the competitive semiconductor segment where knowledge has a relatively short "half-life."

Knowledge is shared internally and with IBM, Toshiba, Motorola, NEC, Nokia and Sony. The primary aim for such cooperation and network formation are sharing of risk and development costs, and reducing time to market. The KM initiative uses Communities of Practice (including NetMeeting and face-to-face get-togethers) to interconnect experts across restructured divisions and different locations swiftly integrate new employees and reduce redundancies at different sites.

A search interface called "Knowledge Spider" has been developed, searching across people, teams, events and activities. The KM initiative is actively promoted via in-house magazines and public relations campaigns, and hopes to win the key European Quality Award.

KM capacity building at Siemens is promoted by yet another initiative, the Knowledge Community Support (KCS) project, founded in 1999 with support from units like Corporate Technology, Siemens Business Services and Siemens Qualification and Training. It promotes the use of knowledge communities within Siemens, via coaching, hotlines, resources, newsletters and its own Web site. It maintains an employee portal and a directory of all knowledge communities in the company. KCS expects that in future, community management will be as common as project management.

Courses on KM ("Knowledge Master") are also offered as a joint partnership between Siemens Qualification and Training (SQT) and University of Munich, blending live case studies with academic trainers and business tutors. The Knowledge Web learning portal includes abstracts of relevant literature and a Web board for discussion.

Siemens' Management Learning Programs, founded in 1997, has different offerings for managers, executives and leaders as well.

Siemens also blends KM and e-learning at its Siemens Learning Valley (SLV) initiative, founded in 2001 in Belgium and Luxembourg (branded as "Where Knowledge Shapes (Y)our Future"). Online courses can be taken via HorizonLive. A newsletter called SLV Gazette spreads awareness about this program and the associated Knowledge and Learning Index (KLIX).

BRIDGING KNOWLEDGE ISLANDS

Another unit at the global giant is Siemens Business Services, focusing on IT services, systems integration, consulting and outsourcing. It has over 33,500 employees in more than 80 countries. As the group's first exclusively services business, it faced challenges in areas like uniting over 40 separate "knowledge islands" with different KM architectures. It created a unified KM framework called knowledgemotion.

Motivation principles used were intrinsic (as in assignments) and extrinsic (via gifts). Incentives were also used negatively -- poor adopters of KM were denied senior positions. Communities of practice are nurtured by knowledge brokers, who facilitate the addition of "knowledge asset candidates" and trade assets on the knowledge market such as checklists, case studies, templates, architectures, business frameworks and practice guides.

The Knowledge Maturity Level of the organization and KM RoI are tracked along with the lifecycle of knowledge assets. Other KM focus areas here include knowledge maps, subject matter experts, project debriefings, knowledge portals and translation of knowledge asset summaries into English for use globally.

The KM practice at Siemens Medical Solutions, KnowledgeSharing@MED, involves Practice Area Leaders, high-impact initiatives, balanced scorecard, the KnowledgeSquare know-how database, expert pages, and mobile solutions for sales representatives to access key information on handheld devices.

Another area at Siemens where KM has helped is via Business Communities for mergers and acquisitions, called MAKE (M&A Knowledge Exchange), applied during M&A activity with Mobisphere, Fujitsu Siemens, Siemens Nixdorf and Robert Bosch. Target knowledge areas include integration, knowledge "packaging," new templates, ensuring employee buy-in and project debriefing.

Yet another area of KM focus at Siemens is the use of e-business methodology. It formed the Centre for e-Excellence in May 2000 to analyze business transformation via the Internet. A quarter of the sales of Siemens itself is expected to be eventually transacted via the Internet -- 50 per cent or more of its consumer products. Knowledge communities have therefore been formed around key areas like supply chain management, e-readiness and IT infrastructure.

Challenges faced by Siemens on the KM front include balancing energies, resources and rewards for local versus global KM initiatives on a daily basis, managing the knowledge-sharing tension between different business units, and nourishing KM during hard economic times.

"Only a maximum of 50 to 100 people can be helped to network daily. Knowledge networking for thousands at a time will not work," the authors advise. "Only when we have made up our minds that sharing knowledge is important, not only for efficiency's sake, but also to increase the essential humanization of the business and social environments in which we work, will we be prepared for the tasks confronting us."

"When established procedures are not conducive to the sharing of knowledge, the company must be ready to restructure itself into an organization more amenable to knowledge sharing. Over time, the intrinsic benefits of sharing knowledge should become apparent and the system then becomes self-perpetuating, thereby rendering incentive systems obsolete," they add.

More details on Siemens can be read in 'Knowledge Management Case Book: Siemens Best Practices' edited by Thomas Davenport and Gilbert Probst; 2002 John Wiley/Publicus Corporate Publishing

Examples of Strategy

Company	What did they do?	Knowledge Management Approach		
		Personalization?	Quantitative?	Qualitative?
NASA SEL	Set up a separate organization which collected and distributed experience.	Yes	Yes	
Daimler Chrysler	Created three experience factories in three different company departments.	Yes	Yes	Yes
Telenor Telecom Software	Made an expert system based on own empirical data for effort estimation and risk management, and modified roles.	Yes	Yes	Yes
Ericsson Software Technology	Set up new organizational roles to increase oral communication of experience.	Yes		Yes
Australian Telecom Company	Collected existing explicit information regarding software development and made it searchable.			Yes
ICL High Performance Systems	Introduced an Intranet-based system with an "engineering knowledge database"			Yes
ICL Finland	Made an Intranet-based system with three structural layers.	Yes		Yes
sd&m	Set up a knowledge management group and Intranet system.	Yes		Yes

Courtesy: Torgeir Dingsøyr, DCIS, NTNU

EC-Council   16

Exhibit. Strategies

The exhibit shows examples of strategy followed by organizations with a focus on personalization and codification, listing the qualitative and quantitative nature as well.

Company	What did they do?	Knowledge Management Approach		
		Personalization?	Quantitative?	Qualitative?
NASA SEL	Set up a separate organization which collected and distributed experience.	Yes	Yes	
Daimler Chrysler	Created three experience factories in three different company departments.	Yes	Yes	Yes
Telenor Telecom Software	Made an expert system based on own empirical data for effort estimation and risk management, and modified roles.	Yes	Yes	Yes
Ericsson Software Technology	Set up new organizational roles to increase oral communication of experience.	Yes		Yes
Australian Telecom Company	Collected existing explicit information regarding software development and made it searchable.			Yes
ICL High Performance Systems	Introduced an Intranet-based system with an "engineering knowledge database"			Yes
ICL Finland	Made an Intranet-based system with three structural layers.	Yes		Yes
sd&m	Set up a knowledge management group and Intranet system.	Yes		Yes

Benefits Reported

Company	What was the effect?	Reported benefit		
		Developer satisfaction?	Lower cost?	Higher quality?
NASA SEL	Reduced number of defects, reduced software production costs, increased use.		Yes	Yes
Daimler Chrysler	The case gives no information on the effect for the company.			
Telenor Telecom Software	The company indicates that estimation accuracy has improved, and focus on risk management has increased.		Yes	
Ericsson Software Technology	The company claims that the initiative was "more valuable" than a database and measurement-approach.			
Australian Telecom Company	Good acceptance of product amongst users.	Yes		
ICL High Performance Systems	A perception that it has facilitated a "new mode of working"	Yes		
ICL Finland	Saved time, because it is easier to find documents. Easier to learn new project members about project work.	Yes	Yes	
sd&m	Previous problems due to rapid growth have diminished.	Yes		

Courtesy: Torgeir Dingsøyr, DCIS, NTNU

EC-Council

17

Exhibit. Benefits

The exhibit shows the benefits accrued by the organizations with a focus on satisfaction, quality and cost issues addressed.

Company	What was the effect?	Reported benefit		
		Developer satisfaction?	Lower cost?	Higher quality?
NASA SEL	Reduced number of defects, reduced software production costs, increased use.		Yes	Yes
Daimler Chrysler	The case gives no information on the effect for the company.			
Telenor Telecom Software	The company indicates that estimation accuracy has improved, and focus on risk management has increased.		Yes	
Ericsson Software Technology	The company claims that the initiative was "more valuable" than a database and measurement-approach.			
Australian Telecom Company	Good acceptance of product amongst users.	Yes		
ICL High Performance Systems	A perception that it has facilitated a "new mode of working"	Yes		
ICL Finland	Saved time, because it is easier to find documents. Easier to learn new project members about project work.	Yes	Yes	
sd&m	Previous problems due to rapid growth have diminished.	Yes		

Guidelines

- ⊙ Knowledge-based strategies begin with business strategy
- ⊙ Knowledge-based strategies need to be linked to traditional measures of performance
- ⊙ Executing a knowledge-based strategy means nurturing people with knowledge.
- ⊙ Organizations leverage knowledge through networks of people who collaborate.
- ⊙ People networks leverage knowledge through organizational "pull"

EC-Council

18

Guidelines for Knowledge Strategy Formulation

Knowledge Strategy guidelines:

➤ Knowledge-based strategies begin with business strategy. The intellectual capital and its ramifications are meaningless without the corporates' objectives of serving customers and outperforming the competition. Corporate learning, information technology, or knowledge databases are all means to achieve excellence in business and therefore business strategy should dictate knowledge strategies.

➤ Knowledge-based strategies should be linked to traditional measures of performance. Intangible assets, such as knowledge, are difficult to account using traditional financial measures, but knowledge needs to be connected to measurable improvements in performance --including improvements on the top line and bottom line. Failing to do so will pronounce the death of the knowledge management initiative.

Knowledge can have a clear impact on measures such as sales, costs, cycle time, productivity, and profitability. These links need to be delineated and projected. Various instances of success should be tracked to the superior use of knowledge.

➤ Executing a knowledge-based strategy is about nurturing people with knowledge and not just warehousing knowledge. It is the knowledgeable people around who can create lasting competitive advantages for organizations. Organizations have designed and maintained elaborate systems to capture and share their "explicit knowledge" which shows up in manuals, databases, employee handbooks etc. This kind of knowledge alone does not make a winning proposition. Organizations should also address the capture and utilization of "tacit knowledge". Unless backed by a conducive cultural atmosphere that supports learning, cooperation, and openness tacit knowledge can never be put to work in an organizational context. Therefore it is imperative that the strategy has solid foundations in nurturing the people with knowledge.

➤ Organizations leverage knowledge through networks of people who collaborate and not through complex networks of technology that interconnect and make collaboration possible. Enabling technologies like groupware and the generation of collaboration tools are not really center to organizational knowledge management. It is not the high-budget, tech-spending that makes things work but the people who are willing to collaborate, share and develop new knowledge. The networking is about people and technology only help providing a platform for people who want to connect. Once the system of internet worked people who collaborate in virtual proximity starts working the combination of people and technology produces networks of people who transform themselves informal groups whose collective knowledge leads to accomplishment of specific tasks.

➤ People networks leverage knowledge through organizational "pull" rather than centralized information "push." It is the worker's need for help in solving business problems that drives knowledge development and sharing. We can see that the demand for knowledge is what makes the driving force and not the information pushed by organizations so that people may use the information made available to them. Learning is up to each individual -- it's not something that management can require. The essence of successful knowledge-based strategies is a company's capacity to raise the aspirations of each employee.

Summary

- ⊙ Knowledge strategy must be in alignment with the corporate strategy
- ⊙ Knowledge strategies include codification, personalization, best practices and CoP
- ⊙ Organizations should decide on a strategy or a combination depending on their needs.
- ⊙ Identification of business and knowledge drivers are crucial to selecting a KM Strategy
- ⊙ The two main approaches to knowledge are as a 'product' and as a 'process'

EC-Council   19

Summary

Recap

- ➢ Knowledge strategy must be in alignment with the corporate strategy.

- ➢ Knowledge strategies include codification, personalization, best practices and CoP.

- ➢ Organizations should decide on a strategy or a combination depending on their needs.

- ➢ Identification of business and knowledge drivers are crucial to selecting a KM Strategy.

- ➢ The two main approaches to knowledge are as a 'product' and as a 'process'.

Knowledge Management (KM)

Module VIII: Knowledge Management Assessment and Planning

Exam 212-69 Certified e-Business Associate

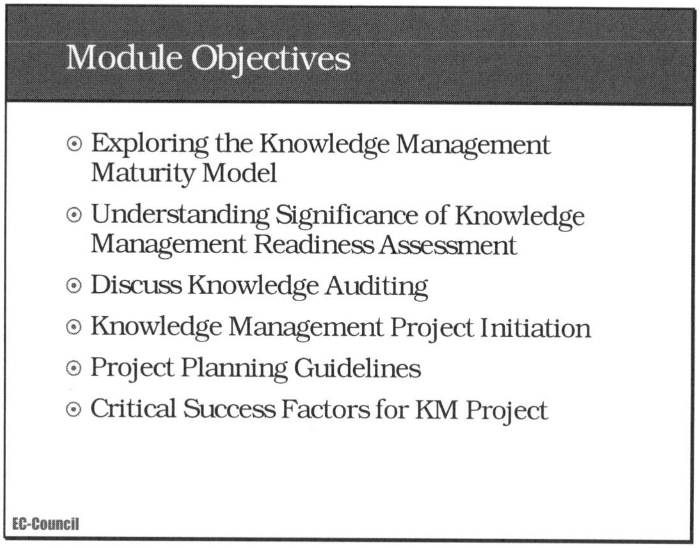

Module Objectives

⊙ Exploring the Knowledge Management Maturity Model

⊙ Understanding Significance of Knowledge Management Readiness Assessment

⊙ Discuss Knowledge Auditing

⊙ Knowledge Management Project Initiation

⊙ Project Planning Guidelines

⊙ Critical Success Factors for KM Project

EC-Council

Objectives

🖙 **Module Objectives**

On completion of this module you will be familiar with different aspects that deals with planning and assessment for a KM initiative. This module engages in discussing the following key areas:

➢ Knowledge management maturity models

➢ The significance of knowledge management readiness assessment

➢ Assess the readiness of an organization to undertake a knowledge management initiative

➢ Knowledge Auditing

➢ Have an overview into KM project initiation

➢ KM Project Planning Guidelines

➢ Understand the CSF for KM Project

This module is intended to be a precursor to developing a Knowledge Management Strategy.

Readers are encouraged to conceptualize their organizations in the various context discussed through the module.

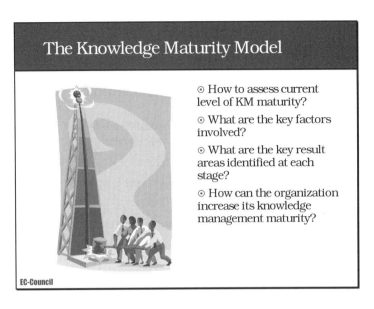

The Knowledge Maturity Model

⊙ How to assess current level of KM maturity?

⊙ What are the key factors involved?

⊙ What are the key result areas identified at each stage?

⊙ How can the organization increase its knowledge management maturity?

EC-Council

The Knowledge Management Maturity Model

How does an organization know where it stands with regard to its ongoing knowledge initiatives? Similarly, how does an organization evaluate a previous knowledge management effort? Even when it comes to an organization embarking on a formal knowledge initiative, how does it identify what aspects of its strategic goals are already being met without any explicit evidence.

Several years of examining knowledge management as a discipline have shown that its employment in real life is hampered by a number of barriers. A number of these barriers have been tackled but a systematic assessment of the status of knowledge management in an organization has been missing.

This is where the knowledge management maturity model comes gains prominence. The models discussed are loosely modeled on the capability maturity model and bears similar assessment levels. There are increased efforts going on for reaching a popularly accepted framework. This section will look at two models – the one proposed by Infosys and another by Siemens.

While these models try to encompass the entire organization into its assessment, it is up to individual organizations to select a maturity model based on its suitability and applicability. The Infosys model has been proposed by V. P. Kochikar, Principal Knowledge Manager of Infosys Technologies Limited and the Siemens model has been developed in-house and applied within the organization.

The Knowledge Management Maturity Model (KMMM) yields objective information describing the status of an organizational unit in terms of knowledge management.

Focus Model: KMM (Infosys)

⊙ A staged framework for leveraging knowledge - proposed by V. P. Kochikar

⊙ An assessment tool for an organization's current level of KM maturity

⊙ A mechanism to focus, and help prioritise, efforts to raise the level of KM maturity

⊙ Each level has a set of prerequisites the organization is required to meet

⊙ A given maturity level implies a certain level of organizational capability

EC-Council

Need For Maturity Model

There is widespread recognition among knowledge-intensive organizations of the need to leverage their knowledge assets effectively. This is however tempered by the realization that the path to achieving this involves significant change in terms of process, mindset and culture within the organization. It is unlikely that this change can be achieved in one giant leap, and a staged framework is thus desirable.

Before getting on to details of the KMM model, a few key assumptions that went into the development of the model are presented here.

> Each level has a set of prerequisites the organization is required to meet (which also has cost implications).

> A given maturity level implies a certain level of organizational capability (from level 4 onwards, quantitatively) subject to the prerequisites being met.

> Each maturity level clearly maps on to the company's business goals (i.e., the meaning of each level in business terms is clear)

The KMM assessment methodology is closely modeled on that of the Software Engineering Institute's (SEI) Capability Maturity Model (CMM). It revolves around the key result areas (KRA), and consists of the following steps:

1. Initially, a questionnaire is administered to selected practice representatives and knowledge management group (KMG) members. This questionnaire is designed to gauge the level of knowledge life-cycle activities in the organization. There are 2-3 questions pertaining to each KRA.

2. The assessment team is set up and trained in the KMM model as well as the assessment methodology.

3. The team then carries out an onsite investigation to gauge the level of KMM compliance. The investigation will consist of studying project deliverables, the knowledge technology infrastructure, knowledge life-cycle processes, as well as interviews with line personnel, senior management and KMG members.

4. The assessment team derives a KM maturity profile based on an analysis of the compliance with each KRA, and presents its results to an audience consisting of line personnel, senior management, and KMG members. The audience is first given an opportunity to respond in a draft findings presentation. Improvement areas are discussed.

5. In case the assessment focuses on KMM levels 3 or above, the KMG shall be subjected to an audit to ensure compliance of their quality processes with CMM level 4 or above.

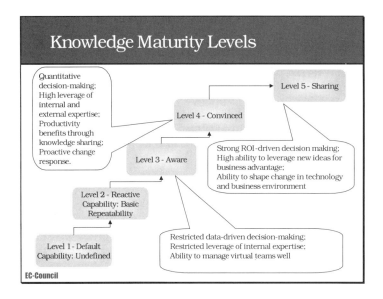

Knowledge Management Maturity Levels

Level 1: Default "Knowledge, we've got plenty of – what we need is to work hard"

<u>Description and Behavioral Characterization</u>: At the default level, the organization displays the following characteristics:

- ➢ Absence of awareness of the need to manage knowledge
- ➢ Conviction in anything other than survival-level tasks low
- ➢ Belief in formal training being the sole mechanism for learning; all learning is reactive
- ➢ Organization's knowledge is fragmented in isolated pockets, and stays in people's heads.

The four dimensional attributes can be described thus:

- ➢ Knowledge Acquisition / Updation

   Formal training (largely "push"); Unstructured on-the-job learning

- ➢ Knowledge Sharing / Dissemination

   Synchronous mechanisms only - Informal discussions, word of mouth;

- ➢ Knowledge Reuse

   Accidental

- ➢ Virtual Teamwork

Non-existent

Level 2: Reactive - "We need to leverage all our knowledge, but we're too busy to do that"

<u>Description and Behavioral Characterization:</u> The organization displays the following characteristics:

➢ The organization shares knowledge purely on need basis; only routine and procedural knowledge shared.

The four-dimensional attributes at this level have the following characteristics:

➢ Knowledge Acquisition / Updation

Formal training ("push" and reactive "pull"); Self-driven learning; Mentored on-the-job learning

Research confined to the 'research group'.

➢ Knowledge Sharing / Dissemination

Sharing sessions within isolated pockets. Systems are relied upon for indispensable tasks only.

➢ Knowledge Reuse

Sporadic; still motivated largely by personal drive

➢ Virtual Teamwork

Happens with watertight partitioning and significant physical travel.

Level 3: Aware - "At least we've made a beginning in managing our knowledge"

<u>Description and Behavioral Characterization:</u> The organization displays the following characteristics:

➢ Content in knowledge systems is fit for use for all functions; the knowledge really meets need.

➢ A basic knowledge infrastructure has been established.

➢ Data collection on utilization started, and data collection towards creation of capability baseline has begun.

➢ The beginnings of an integrated approach to managing the knowledge life cycle are visible.

➢ Enterprise-wide knowledge propagation systems are in existence, although awareness and maintenance are moderate.

> ➤ Internal expertise is leveraged in technologically complex and unfamiliar areas, or where it is imperative.

> ➤ The organization collects and understands metrics for KM; KM activities begin to be translated into productivity gains.

> ➤ Ability to respond to environmental change moderately high.

> ➤ Managers recognize their role in, and actively encourage, knowledge-sharing activities.

> ➤ The organization is able to see a link between KM processes and results.

The four dimensional attributes can be described thus:

> ➤ Knowledge Acquisition / Updation

> Formal training ("push" and proactive "pull"); Training available remotely (only in static mode). On-the job learning is structured. Fledgling research and environment scanning efforts; knowledge gained through these is disseminated throughout the organization

> ➤ Knowledge Sharing / Dissemination

> Occasional organization-wide sharing sessions; an incipient 'knowledge market'

> ➤ Knowledge Reuse

> Some reuse in customer-fronting activities; significant evangelization still needed. Process assets begin to be used.

> ➤ Virtual Teamwork

> Virtual teamwork happens, but coordination overheads still present

Level 4: Convinced - "We've reached where we are by managing our knowledge well, and we intend to keep it that way"

<u>Description and Behavioral Characterization</u>: The organization displays the following characteristics:

This stage is the take-off stage, where the KM movement has reached a level of momentum sufficient to make it self-sustaining. An enterprise-wide knowledge-sharing system in place – quality, currency and utility of information is high; usage is high. Knowledge processes have been scaled up across the organization. Organizational boundaries breakdown as knowledge barriers do. Quantification of benefits of knowledge sharing and reuse is at project level – business impact clearly recognized. Projects leverage organization-wide processes; set goals, estimate, monitor based on norms; processes are stable. Feedback loops are qualitatively better and tighter. Ability to sense and respond proactively to environmental changes

> ➤ Knowledge Acquisition / Updation

Formal training is advocated (proactive "push" and "pull").

Internal and external sources of expertise well used in learning.

Research and environment scanning well established.

➢ Knowledge Sharing / Dissemination

Regular organization-wide sharing sessions are adopted.

Significant asynchronous sharing is seen through systems usage.

Mature 'knowledge market' exists.

➢ Knowledge Reuse

Large-scale reuse in customer-fronting activities; some reuse in other areas too.

➢ Virtual Teamwork

"True" virtual teamwork

Level 5: Sharing - "We're sharing knowledge across the organization, and are proud of it"

Description and Behavioral Characterization: The organization displays the following characteristics:

Culture of sharing has institutionalized; sharing becomes second nature to all. Organizational boundaries are rendered irrelevant. Knowledge ROI is integral to decision-making. Continuous tweaking of the knowledge processes for improvement happens. The organization develops an ability to shape environmental change; organization becomes a knowledge leader.

➢ Knowledge Acquisition / Updation

Formal training (continuously evolving). Organization is a net "giver" of learning.

➢ Knowledge Sharing / Dissemination

Knowledge flows frictionless, with no spatial or temporal decay.

➢ Knowledge Reuse

Large-scale, conviction-driven reuse of knowledge is seen.

➢ Virtual Teamwork

Cohesive team including customer

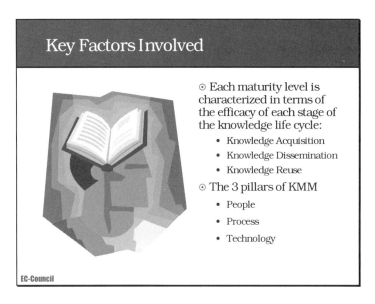

Key Factors Involved

📋 The knowledge life cycle is conceived as consisting of the following stages, and each maturity level is characterized in terms of the efficacy of each of these stages:

➤ Knowledge Acquisition / Updation – this is the stage where the knowledge is first generated / absorbed by any organizational unit (the term organizational unit here denotes an individual, project team, department, task force, or any aggregation of one or more of these).

➤ Knowledge Sharing / Dissemination - Sharing implies packaging the knowledge / expertise in a form fit for use, and delivering it to the point of use, at the time of use. Sharing may be synchronous – direct person-to-person, or asynchronous – through capture, storage and subsequent delivery.

➤ Knowledge Reuse – this represents the stage where the knowledge / expertise shared is actually put to use for performing a task.

📋 A fourth dimension is also included – Virtual Teamwork - to consider the ability to support working across geographical distances with people who have perhaps never met each other to be a guide of the organization's culture and mechanisms for knowledge-sharing in general.

KM is considered as being represented by three pillars/prongs – People, Process and Technology. Each maturity level can thus be characterized by certain observable capabilities along each of these three prongs, with successive levels exhibiting higher capabilities. Accordingly, at each level, there is a defined set of Key Result Areas (KRAs).

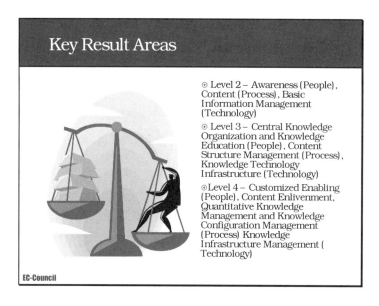

Key Result Areas

Each KRA is specific to one of People, Process or Technology, and the KRAs at a given maturity level collectively serve to represent the organization's observable KM capability at that level.

There are 15 KRAs in all. Level 1 does not have any KRAs, as it is the default level; level 5 KRAs are not classified as people, process or technology-related.

Level 2 Key Result Areas

Content Capture (Process)

Knowledge indispensable for performing routine tasks is documented. Multiple databases of 'knowledge' exist (usually in disparate formats, making access and consolidation difficult).

Content compilation is done reasonably well; however, creation is still ad-hoc primarily due to scalability issues. 'Process assets', or databases of past work deliverables are available. Content management responsibility is dispersed through the organization.

Knowledge Awareness (People)

Awareness of knowledge as a resource that must be managed explicitly (however, the "somebody-else-should-do-it" syndrome prevails!). Awareness of what knowledge (internal or external) is appropriate for sharing internally or externally e.g. IPR issues. Senior management recognizes need for formal knowledge management. A Knowledge 'database administrator' role exists.

Basic Information Management (Technology)

Rudimentary knowledge-recording systems in existence – data formats are diverse, data is fragmented, data integrity is low, and data obsolescence is high. Tools for managing knowledge lifecycle activities used disparately.

Level 3 KRA

Content Structure Management (Process)

The organization has developed the ability to structure, categorize and access content. An integrated logical content architecture exists. Knowledge is structured – a taxonomy of knowledge topics exists. The knowledge content is augmented with pointers to people.

A content management process, which includes the creation, editing, streamlining, publishing, certification and maintenance of content, has been defined. Standard ways of creating content have been defined, in the form of templates and processes. The content management process is owned by a central knowledge organization.

Knowledge Technology Infrastructure (Technology)

The organization has established a basic knowledge infrastructure. Single-point access to knowledge is available across the organization (the knowledge itself is not integrated – only access is available), usually by means of an intranet portal. The portal provides a view into content, as well as to experts across the organization. Enterprise-wide knowledge-propagation systems in existence – awareness and maintenance are moderate. Environments supporting virtual teamwork are available; usage is patchy, primarily due to lack of integration with regular working environment, bandwidth issues or mindset issues.

Central Knowledge Organization (People)

A dedicated KM group (KMG) exists at the organization level for infrastructure management and content management. This group's processes and roles are well defined. The group's progress is planned, monitored and tracked as per quality processes not below CMM level 4.

Knowledge Education (People)

Training in KM processes for KM group; formal training program for contributors, users, facilitators, champions, etc. with feedback.

Level 4 KRA

Content Enlivenment (Process)

The organization's KM effort has reached a level of maturity where content can be said to be truly 'enlivened' with expertise. Experts across the organization are committed to respond to requests.

There is a high level of synchronization between knowledge entering repositories and its being used (more of what goes out comes in, and conversely), thus ensuring that content grows in areas where the demand for it is greatest.

Customized Enabling (People)

Training (all modes) is available at time and point of need.

Knowledge Infrastructure Management (Technology)

Enterprise-wide knowledge-sharing systems, which have been in place for some time, see usage taking off. Quality, currency and utility of knowledge in the systems are high. The physical technology and content architectures for knowledge sharing are seamless. An integrated working environment exists, that supports virtual teamwork.

Knowledge Configuration Management (Process)

An organization-wide process has been defined for integrating and managing the knowledge content configuration – logical as well as physical. All content is managed according to this defined process.

Quantitative Knowledge Management (Process)

Knowledge sharing is measured quantitatively to reduce variance across the organization. The benefits of knowledge sharing and reuse at the individual project / function level are quantified, and the business impact of sharing and reuse are clearly recognized.

Capability baselines are created and used. Significant asynchronous sharing happens through systems usage. The content management process uses quantitative data. Knowledge creation, sharing, reuse levels are quantified.

A few examples of knowledge metrics:

> ➢ The percentage of content used within different time frames;
>
> ➢ The time lag between entry and use of content
>
> ➢ Quality ratings for the content in terms of universally recognized 'currency' units

Similar metrics exist to measure the performance of the infrastructure, the response quality of experts, and the "expertise" component of content.

Level 5 KRA

Please note that level 5 KRAs are not classified as people, process or technology-related.

Expertise Integration

The organization provides a commitment that content and (human) expertise will be available as an integral package. Thus, the user is guaranteed that appropriate expertise is available to help understand content and tailor it to specific need. This is the highest level of maturity of the sharing process, as true sharing requires a judicious mix of synchronous and asynchronous mechanisms, to achieve significant gains with optimal utilization of experts' time.

Knowledge Leverage

The organization has the ability to measure the contribution of knowledge to competence. The availability of knowledge inputs needed by individuals to perform tasks is guaranteed in quantitative terms. Knowledge processes are continuously tweaked: the organization uses performance measures to improve content management and technology infrastructure. Baselines improve continuously. Knowledge ROI becomes integral to decision-making.

Innovation Management

Organization has the ability to assimilate, use and innovate based on ideas both external and internal. Processes exist for leveraging new ideas for business advantage. Knowledge base considerations are explicitly used in taking on a new customer / project.

Siemens AG KMMM

Siemens AG Knowledge Management Maturity Model (KMMM) is a methodology to develop Knowledge Management goal oriented, systematically and holistically. It consists of two models, a development model and an analysis model.

The development model defines five maturity levels and provides information how to make the next reasonable step in Knowledge Management Development. The analysis model helps to take account of all-important aspects of Knowledge Management and reveals which topics should be developed in future. As a third component an auditing process is defined which structures planning, data collection by interviews and workshops, and feedback sessions.

Development Model

The development model defines five maturity levels and provides information how to make the next reasonable step in Knowledge Management development. The maturity levels were inspired by the levels of CMM from the Software Engineering Institute at Carnegie Mellon University and have been thematically worked out for Knowledge Management matters.

Level 1: Initial - KM activities are non systematic and ad-hoc. No language for describing organizational phenomenons from a knowledge point of view.

Level 2: Repeated - Pilot projects and single activities labeled as "KM"

Level 3: Defined - Standardized processes make creation, sharing and usage of knowledge efficient.

Level 4: Managed - Creation, sharing and usage of Knowledge is organizationally integrated and improved (Measurement!)

Level 5: Optimizing - KM is developed continuously and self organized

Analysis Model

The analysis model helps to take account of all-important aspects of Knowledge Management and reveals which topics should be developed in future. These 64 topics are arranged in eight key areas, which are partly based on the enablers of the EFQM Model for Business Excellence and have also been extended or differentiated to represent KM specific aspects. The next level of detail after key areas is called 'topics'. At the moment there are 64 topics defined, between 7 and 9 in each key area. The representation of the key areas in an octagon is designed to express conceptual relationships between the key areas through the "spatial" arrangement. Adjacent key areas / sectors are "close" to each other in terms of content, while opposite sectors represent antitheses of the corresponding key distinction

Generally KMMM leads to understanding and appreciation of a gradual and integral development of Knowledge Management. It delivers the important qualitative and quantitative information to navigate this journey. Quantitative results include a maturity profile of the organization showing the maturity level for each key area. Qualitative results comprise information about the organization's daily KM practice as well as ideas and action proposals for improvement.

KMMM Assessment Process

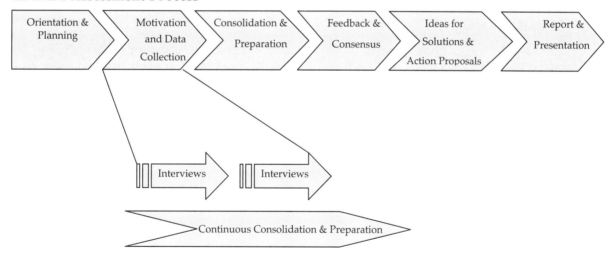

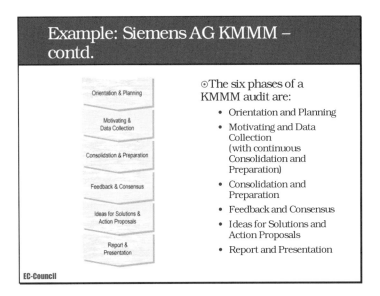

Example: Siemens AG KMMM – contd.

⊙ The six phases of a KMMM audit are:

- Orientation and Planning
- Motivating and Data Collection (with continuous Consolidation and Preparation)
- Consolidation and Preparation
- Feedback and Consensus
- Ideas for Solutions and Action Proposals
- Report and Presentation

KMMM Auditing

In KMMM an **auditing process** is defined which structures planning, data collection by interviews and workshops, and feedback sessions. The combination of different methods (e.g. interviews with groups and specific individuals, inclusion of different roles in the organization) is designed to minimize the bias from subjective representations. The six phases of a KMMM audit are:

➢ Orientation and Planning

➢ Motivating and Data Collection (with continuous Consolidation and Preparation)

➢ Consolidation and Preparation

➢ Feedback and Consensus

➢ Ideas for Solutions and Action Proposals

➢ Report and Presentation

For the quality of the results it is very useful to work with *pairs* of consultants. Only in discussions between two *experienced* KM consultants can the observations be critically analyzed before the topics are assessed. Because of the broad and holistic understanding of KM required in this procedure, the demands made on these consultants are high.

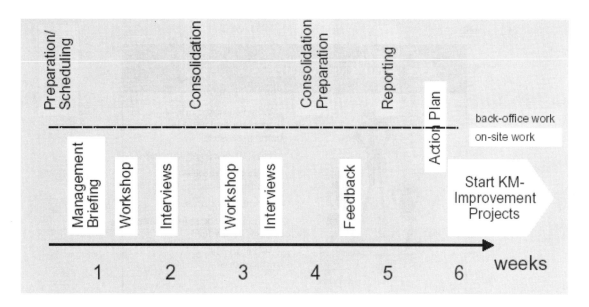

KMMM Assessment Process (Source: Siemens KMMM)

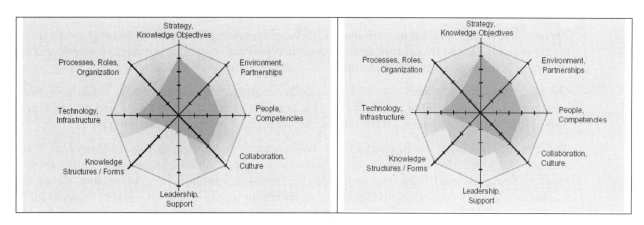

Example of Quantitative Results and Goals (Source: Siemens KMMM)

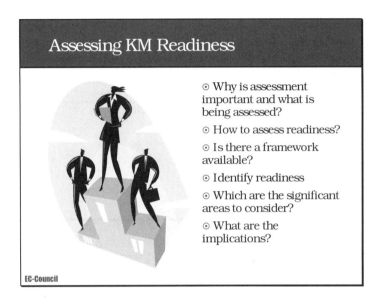

KM Readiness Assessment

For any knowledge management initiative to be successful, organizations have to undergo a strategic change in the way it functions. This section will discuss the importance of assessing the readiness of the organization to undertake a knowledge management program.

Once an organization adopts a suitable knowledge management framework, it needs to assess whether it has the capability to achieve it. This not only helps in conducting a gap analysis but also prepares the organization for the requirement analysis of the project-planning phase.

The common concerns that organizations have regarding assessment are addressed in this section. These include common concerns such as the importance of knowledge management, what is being assessed, how can readiness be assessed, whether there exists any standard framework to assist organizations its effort, which are the significant areas to be considered and what the implications are for the organization.

When an organization is starting small – such as a team within the organization contemplating on assessing knowledge management readiness, irrespective of whether the organization as a whole is in a favorable disposition, assessment can help the team in building a business case for knowledge management, apart from identifying supporting resources existent with the organization.

Why is assessment gaining increasing prominence? It has been difficult to characterize knowledge management as a highly successful endeavor. This has been compounded by the fact that best practices can sometimes be just anecdotal. It was also noted that some large consulting houses that had joined the KM bandwagon have since backed away from knowledge management practices.

Importance of Assessing KM Readiness

- To assess the capability of the organization to meet the basis requirements for undertaking a KM initiative
- To identify key elements that can potentially hinder progress, or undermine the success of a KM undertaking.
- To identify those critical components available to the organization that can serve as a source of strength in supporting a successful implementation.
- To identify what prerequisites are not in place for the KM initiative to succeed.
- To assist the organization in focusing on the essential building blocks for managing knowledge assets

EC-Council

Importance of Assessing KM Readiness

Why is it important to undertake an assessment exercise? The primary reasons are discussed below.

A readiness assessment helps the organization to assess its capability to meet the basic requirements in order to undertake a knowledge management initiative. This is especially important if a framework has been identified and the organization needs to allocate its resources appropriately to ensure the success of the project.

Another reason to undertake a readiness assessment is to identify key elements that can potentially hinder progress, or undermine the success of a KM undertaking. Identifying these elements can help the organization take specific action points to address these concerns and sort out the stumbling blocks.

The readiness assessment can also help the organization to identify those critical components available to the organization that can serve as a source of strength in supporting a successful implementation. Often organizations embark on Km programs without realizing the reuse or extended potential of the resources it has in hand.

Every knowledge management strategy will have a set of prerequisites in order to meet its objectives. A readiness assessment can help organizations to identify what prerequisites are not in place for the KM initiative to succeed.

The readiness assessment can also serve in assisting the organization in focusing on the essential building blocks for managing its knowledge assets. This can help gain a fresh insight into the knowledge assets with the organization.

How to assess organizational readiness for KM?

- There is no "one" complete assessment procedure.
- Adoption of an assessment framework should be based on the goals of the organization
- Assessments are usually in the form of questionnaires and ideally should have user participation
- To derive value, the results of the assessment and the consequent changes made should be reflected in the KM roadmap

EC-Council

How to assess organizational readiness

There is no "one" complete assessment procedure. Therefore organizations have to decide which framework to adopt based on the metrics of the framework that closely align with the corporate strategy.

Adoption of an assessment framework should be based on the goals of the organization. Assessments can take several forms including interviews, software, workshops, group discussion, meetings or even the popular format – questionnaire. Assessments are usually in the form of questionnaires and ideally should have user participation. The organization may decide to have one person (such as a senior executive) to complete the assessment or choose to have several people complete the assessment independently, and then convene to compare (and even combine) scores.

The assessment may also be administrated as a group. Typically, the group setting is ideal for administering the assessment as this may serve as the impetus to discuss relevant knowledge capture issues. Whatever, the mode, participation of users who can accurately assess organizational readiness is critical for extracting value from an assessment.

To derive value, the results of the assessment and the consequent changes made should be reflected in the KM roadmap. The assessment exercise is designed to reveal flaws in a number of important areas in the organization. If there are many areas in which improvement is needed, beginning the assessment process may seem daunting, and having flaws revealed can be uncomfortable. However, it should be perceived as a head start as the organization can take focused action to address these flaws before the KM initiative than realize it after much time and resources have been spent in vain.

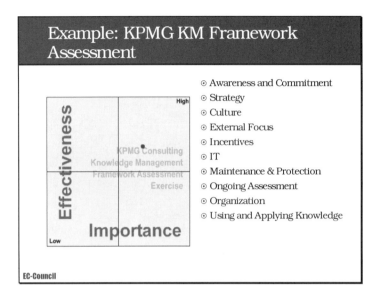

KM Framework Readiness Example: KPMG

1) Awareness and Commitment: Shows whether the staff understands the concept of knowledge management and whether senior management is committed to its use.

2) Strategy: Whether the organization has committed to a programme of knowledge management improvement and how it is managed to ensure business benefit.

3) Culture: Shows whether the behaviors within an organization enable effective knowledge management.

4) External Focus: Demonstrates whether an organization is attempting to look beyond its own boundaries in order to maximize its business opportunities.

5) Incentives: Whether the organization properly rewards those that support its efforts towards knowledge management.

6) IT: Indicates whether the IT in place is sufficient and used effectively enough to support knowledge management.

7) Maintenance & Protection: How well the organization protects and maintains its information and knowledge assets.

8) Ongoing Assessment: Whether the organization measures the impact knowledge management and particularly the management of intellectual assets has on the organization. (5 questions)

9) Organization: The degree to which the organizational structure supports knowledge management.

10) Using and Applying Knowledge: Whether the business actually uses and exploits the knowledge inherent in the company in an effective manner.

Assessment statements in these areas of strategic importance are weighed under two parameters: importance and effectiveness.

   a) **Importance:** How *important* the statement is to your overall organization's success in its current business situation.

   b) **Effectiveness:** How well you consider your organization is *performing* in this area.

Importance (within current Business Environment)

4	3	2	1
Critical to the success of the organisation's overall business strategy	Important contribution to the organisation's overall business strategy	Benefit expected to one part of the organisation	Not important

Effectiveness

4	3	2	1
Fully and effectively implemented and regularly reviewed for improvement	Not effective yet, but improvements or other actions being implemented	In place but not fully effective and no plans to improve	Has not been addressed

The score is attributed according to the level selected under the two parameters.

> ## Implications
>
> ⊙ Organization identifies the 'gap' between its current status and the desirable one
> ⊙ Organization is in a position to develop focused plan of action to maximize returns from the KM initiative
> ⊙ Organization can examine knowledge flows to understand the interactions and dependencies
> ⊙ Organization gets a fresh insight into its people, processes and technology assets
>
> EC-Council

Implications

The implications that an assessment renders to an organization are discussed below.

➢ Organization identifies the 'gap' between its current status and the desirable one.

The readiness assessment is a practical and inexpensive process used to assess the knowledge management capability of an organization. The flexibility of using the readiness assessment lies within its ability to be tailored to any organizations specific knowledge needs. These may be team composition, scope of process coverage, scope of organizational coverage and scope of documentation review to name a few.

➢ Organization is in a position to develop focused plan of action to maximize returns from the KM initiative. The organization has the opportunity to strengthen its weak areas before embarking on the initiative and thus can ensure better results and returns.

➢ Organization can examine knowledge flows to understand the interactions and dependencies. An assessment gives a fresh perspective regarding the different knowledge flows, networks – both formal and informal that exists within the organization. This can be leveraged to ensure successful adoption and implementation of the knowledge initiative.

➢ Organization gets a fresh insight into its people, processes and technology assets. Irrespective of an internal assessment, a readiness assessment with a framework enables organizations to realize existing resources and revalue them from a knowledge perspective.

Enhancing Organizational Knowledge Maturity

The path to KM *nirvana* is long and arduous. The staged KMM model we have defined is designed to facilitate this organizational change. The model acts as a tool to help the reader

> To conceptually understand a framework which their organization can use to assess its current level of KM maturity;

> To focus and prioritize efforts to raise the level of their organization's KM maturity.

> To map KM maturity to organizational capability (from level 4 onwards, quantitatively).

In the agile organization knowledge management is first about learning, second about application, third about purpose. Increasing an organization's knowledge management maturity involves addressing these three issues holistically. When an organization needs to learn quicker it must shorten the time of acquisition and diffusion of knowledge.

Collaborative learning supported by a purposeful infrastructure and culture puts more diversity of thought into closer knowledge exchange and development proximity, and creates an architecture from which intelligence at the higher organizational level emerges. In the end, though an organization may well manage knowledge, it will never control it

Ways to realize the need for betterment is often reflected by:

- ➤ Identifying key performance indicators and metrics derived from them.

- ➤ Valuing intellectual assets on a regular basis.

- ➤ Adopting a suitable audit methodology such as the balanced scorecard approach.

- ➤ Measuring impact on business processes and ultimately the bottom line.

Knowledge Auditing

- ⊙ Knowledge Auditing is a review of the knowledge required by a company, department or group in order to carry out its objectives effectively.
- ⊙ It identifies owners, users, uses and key attributes of core knowledge assets.
- ⊙ It is often carried out along with a Knowledge Management Assessment.
- ⊙ It involves a needs analysis, information analysis, competencies and communication audits, and a review of interactions and knowledge flow.

EC-Council

Knowledge Auditing

The knowledge audit is an important phase or step of a knowledge management initiative, and is used to provide a sound analysis into the company or organization's knowledge 'health'. The audit is a fact-finding, analysis, interpretation, and reporting activity, which includes a study of the company's information and knowledge policies, its knowledge structure and knowledge flow.

The knowledge audit serves to help the audited unit to determine if it 'knows what it knows' and 'knows what it doesn't know' about its existing knowledge state. It will also help it to unearth what it should know to better leverage knowledge for business and competitive advantage. This enlightenment sets the agenda for the knowledge management initiative, programme, and implementation.

A complete knowledge audit will evaluate the company's knowledge environment, its knowledge ecosystem, its knowledge utilization and sharing: in essence the knowledge enhancing social and behavioral culture of the people within the company. It offers a detailed examination, review, assessment and evaluation of a company's knowledge abilities, its existing knowledge assets and resources, and of its knowledge management activities.

A knowledge audit will help the audited company to determine what knowledge is being managed and how well it is being managed. The audit helps to make the knowledge in the company visible and actionable.

At the most detailed level, the knowledge audit investigates and evaluates the company's information systems, its processes and its knowledge enabling technology. It will examine how well current processes support knowledge capture, dissemination, use and sharing. Ultimately, the knowledge audit will reveal the company's knowledge management strengths, weaknesses, opportunities and threats and risks. There is an array of knowledge auditing methods and tools such as knowledge inventory, knowledge mapping, knowledge-flow and gap analysis that makes the audits effective.

Need for Knowledge Audit

⊙ Improve customer (member) service
- Faster responses & more accurate information
- Closer understanding of needs (member retention)

⊙ Improve Internal efficiency
- Lower costs & improved quality through less rework
- Accelerate effective decision making

⊙ Ease employee attrition headaches
- Faster integration of new employees
- Protect against in-house knowledge loss

⊙ Stimulate innovative thinking
- Delivers stronger value proposition to members

EC-Council

Need for Auditing Knowledge

 The business case for conducting a knowledge audit include some of the following:

➢ Improve customer (member) service

   o Faster responses & more accurate information. It details 'what knowledge exists in the company and where it exists', which is crucial in determining better customer service and helps deliver more value to the customer.

   o Closer understanding of needs (member retention)

➢ Improve Internal efficiency

   o Lower costs & improved quality through less rework. It helps to identify and uncover dormant and potential knowledge resources; in particular people based knowledge, so that this knowledge can be productively used. It enables the mapping of internal and external knowledge flow and formal and informal communications networks. This facilitates the identification of inefficiencies reflected in duplication of efforts, knowledge gaps and knowledge-bottlenecks

   o Accelerate effective decision-making. It provides scientific evidence to determine if corporate knowledge value potential is being maximized

➢ Ease employee attrition headaches

- o Faster integration of new employees. It allows for the measuring and assessing of the relative value of the knowledge entities as perceived by the initiators and users, i.e. the employees and offers valuable measurement and assessment of the effectiveness of corporate knowledge capabilities and competency outside of the company, in particular customers, partners and even competitors

- o Protect against in-house knowledge loss

➢ Stimulate innovative thinking

- o Delivers stronger value proposition to members. It offers a formalized and evidence based accounting of knowledge that exists or is embedded in the company, and how that knowledge moves through the company. It allows hidden knowledge to become highly visible, knowledge assets to become more tangible, and therefore more measurable and accountable.

Among other benefits that a knowledge audit can bring about are as follows:

➢ It helps the organization to identify and chart the knowledge that is required to support its goals and the individual tasks and activities

➢ It can gauge how efficiently and effectively the organization captures and use knowledge held by the company's external interests, such as customers and partners

➢ It facilitates more efficient and effective KM initiatives and programmes

➢ It produces independent and objective, evidence-based knowledge-value indicators, which can then be used to plan, implement and further measure the KM project's success in achieving its defined goals

Knowledge Sources

- ⊙ Known (at least by some) information repositories
  - Documents, databases, applications, etc.
  - Org chart, project teams, focus groups, directory listings, etc.
- ⊙ Subject Matter Experts (SME)
  - The "go to" people
- ⊙ Sharing practices
  - Formal & informal events that generate reusable knowledge nuggets
    - Project reviews, status meetings, etc.
- ⊙ Knowledge flows/processes
  - Work processes that generate knowledge

EC-Council

Sources of Knowledge for Audit

It is essential to identify knowledge sources while conducting a knowledge audit. These may be in the form of known information repositories such as documents, databases, applications etc

Sources of knowledge can also be identified from tools such as organization chart, organization structures such as project teams, focus groups and directory listings.

Another source of knowledge are the subject matter experts who people go to when they need crucial information to complete their tasks.

Sharing prior work and experiences using technology to archive written work in repositories is another knowledge source. Apart from creating opportunities to capture tacit knowledge - this may require collaborative environments to help share that experience that is so hard to capture. This may be a formal or informal event that can help in knowledge generation.

Knowledge flows and processes can be mapped. Mapping the expertise of an organization is valuable for several reasons. Easy access to a map of expertise of the organization can connect people when they need guidance resulting in quicker response rates, reduction of re-invention of the wheel, increased employee satisfaction and more. Maps can be used then to pull people in to assist on current projects or for offering training to employees who have existing good basic skills to equip them with additional skills the organization will need for future projects. Considerations include: skills, expertise, experience, and location.

Knowledge Audit Methods

- ⊙ Methods
  - Information repository (inventory)
  - Ethnographic (observation)
  - Interviewing (group or individual)
  - Survey (hardcopy, e-mail, online)
- ⊙ A combination of one or more of the above
- ⊙ Selecting the Audit Method

EC-Council

Knowledge Audit Methods

 There are several audit methods. Among them are:

➢ Information repository (inventory) - The output of Knowledge Inventory will deliver the following benefits:

     o   Identification of core knowledge assets and flows - who creates, who uses

     o   Identification of gaps in information and knowledge needed to manage the business effectively

     o   Areas of information policy and ownership that need improving

     o   Opportunities to reduce information handling costs

     o   Opportunities to improve coordination and access to commonly needed information

     o   A clearer understanding of the contribution of knowledge to business results.

➢ Ethnographic (observation) – This method explores the following aspects.

     o   Methods of allocating wealth, status, and power

     o   Norms of acceptable social behavior and the means of regulating it

- o Protocols for making decisions, communicating, working together, and other group activities

- o Means of identifying, creating, retaining, and passing on the collective knowledge of the group

- o Relationships for interacting with each other and the outside world, and for passing on their legacy to the future

- o Artifacts in which they have embedded their perceptions of the world around them and themselves, including their history, customs, knowledge, and skill, whether in books, pottery, paintings, financial reports, marketing brochures, or electronic documents

➢ Interviewing (group or individual) – The focus is on people and their intellectual assets. It examines the information the personnel of the organization produces and charts the flow of this information to the decision makers and those who need the information to perform their jobs. The audit will examine and interview staff and focuses on what is currently happening, what staff members would like to improve, and guidance toward improvements.

➢ Survey (hardcopy, e-mail, online) – This is a popular method of knowledge audit and involves questionnaires or checklists. The purpose of the checklist is to stimulate the thinking process and uncover the common linkages, overlaps, and gaps to the various sources of information within the organization.

A combination of one or more of the above may be adopted by the organization. The figure below shows how a methodology may be selected.

```
            ┌─────────────────────────┐
            │     Define Goals of the  │
            │     Knowledge Audit      │
            └─────────────────────────┘
                         │
Beginning the            ▼
Knowledge          ┌─────────────────────────┐
Audit              │ Identify Financial and Other │
                   │      Constraints         │
                   └─────────────────────────┘
                              │
                              ▼
Selecting the      ┌─────────────────────────┐      ┌──────────────────┐
"Against" Measure  │ Determine the "Ideal State" │◄──│ Assign Desirably  │
                   └─────────────────────────┘      │  High Values     │
                              │                      └──────────────────┘
                              ▼
                   ┌─────────────────────────┐
Selecting the      │   Select Audit Method    │
Audit Method       └─────────────────────────┘
                              │                      ┌──────────────────┐
                              ▼                  ◄═══│   Use the KM      │
                   ┌─────────────────────────┐      │ assessment tool  │
                   │ Select Aspects of the Audit │   └──────────────────┘
                   └─────────────────────────┘
                              │
                              ▼
                   ┌─────────────────────────┐
Performing the     │       Perform Audit      │
Knowledge Audit    └─────────────────────────┘
                              │
                              ▼
                   ┌─────────────────────────┐      ┌──────────────────┐
                   │ Document Knowledge Assets │───►│   Knowledge      │
                   └─────────────────────────┘      │    Assets        │
                                                    └──────────────────┘
```

Source: Amrit Tiwana,
The KM Toolkit

Basic Audit Methodology

- ⊙ Identification of major processes & the information required to complete them
  - What knowledge is needed to do their jobs?
- ⊙ Determining explicit (documented) knowledge assets and tacit (undocumented).
  - Where are staff getting it from?
  - Location, purpose, format, etc.
- ⊙ Determine knowledge gaps
  - What is being asked by members and not delivered immediately?
  - Are there unknown barriers hindering sharing knowledge or best practices?

EC-Council

Basic Audit Methodology

Steve Goodfellow, president of Access KM outlines the basic audit methodology as comprising of the following steps.

- ➢ Identification of major processes and the information required to undertake them.

  - o This involves ascertaining what knowledge the people involved need, to do their jobs.

- ➢ Determining explicit (documented) knowledge assets and tacit (undocumented).

  - o This involves asking questions such as where the staff sources their information.

  - o It also seeks to map the location, purpose, and format of the information at hand.

- ➢ Determine knowledge gaps

  - o What is being asked by members and not delivered immediately?

  - o Are there unknown barriers hindering sharing knowledge or best practices?

Common Audit Tools

- ⊙ Organization chart
- ⊙ Employee directory
- ⊙ Identify cross functional teams
  - Quality, process improvement, etc.
- ⊙ Existing workflow maps
- ⊙ Pertinent IT documentation
  - Directory structures, shared drives, intranet site(s), known applications, strategic projects/direction, etc.

EC-Council

Challenges For Auditing Knowledge

Knowledge audits are very challenging because it is a multi- disciplinary field of study that includes several critical areas, each of which requires substantial knowledge and experience to perform, including at a minimum:

- ➢ IT organization and systems,
- ➢ Organizational dynamics/culture,
- ➢ Human resources,
- ➢ Library & IS,
- ➢ Training /education /learning,
- ➢ Communications,
- ➢ Intellectual property/law,
- ➢ Business & competitive intelligence.

Knowledge audits should start with the existing organizational chart / structure so that the audit can be tailored to the organization. Similarly employee directory can give an overview of who's who and where in the organization. This is useful when it comes to mapping knowledge flows.

As knowledge audits are multi-disciplinary, the audit needs to identify cross-functional teams and identify business processes in strategic areas such as quality control, process improvement etc.

Apart from the employee directory, any existing workflow maps can give an insight into the people, process and technology (optional) involved. In addition, there are certain issues that need to be acknowledged. People are not pre-disposed to revealing their information gathering and communication chains. The more impersonal the process of information gathering, the less that will be revealed.

Fortunately, most current technologies being marketed as knowledge management are either file systems, document management systems or tools to search them. Most experts, even those who may be missing other opportunities, know that this is where you find knowledge and that it moves over networks. These tools are important; as one cannot implement knowledge management systems without considering both content and flow within the organization. Herein lies the value of a knowledge audit.

Sample Audit Outline

- ⊙ Identify potential areas of focus for an audit
- ⊙ What are the key processes involved in this area/department
- ⊙ Have management identify key individuals to be included prior to conducting the audit
- ⊙ Identify known explicit information sources
- ⊙ What type of information, not contained in the above sources, do members ask for?

EC-Council

Sample Audit outline

> Potential areas of focus for an audit - Examples are:

  o Improve quality and speed of call center responses to member questions

  o Streamline efforts of annual conference production

  o Enhance quality of educational programs to members

> What are the key processes involved in this area/department:

  List not only main processes (e.g. responding to member inquiries), but also sub processes (e.g. responding to phone call, responding to e-mail, responding via mail, responding via meetings, conferences, etc.)

> Have management identify key individuals to be included prior to conducting audit.

> Identify known explicit information sources. Examples can be:

  o Explicit information sources (detailing information formats and location)

    ▪ Policies -Hardcopy and MS Word -Shelf, local PC

    ▪ Member database -Central organization database -Dept server

    ▪ Conference info -Dept. database, people heads -Dept server

➢ What type of information, not contained in the above sources, do members ask for? Example: Where does the member go to find this information? Subject Matter Experts.

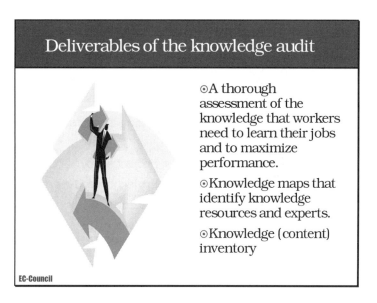

Deliverables of a Knowledge Audit

The deliverables of a knowledge audit may include the following.

➢ A thorough assessment of the knowledge that workers need, in order to learn their jobs and to maximize performance. This may be in the form of a report.

➢ Knowledge maps that identify knowledge resources and experts. This is dealt in detail in the section on knowledge mapping.

➢ Knowledge (content) inventory. This can be in the form of a core process / knowledge chart; supplier / user matrix; a knowledge map or tree; an initial set of information standards; a sample set of inventory records; a detailed report, including charts, diagrams and tables of knowledge assets.

➢ Map showing steps from inquiry to service completion. This can also contain knowledge flows mapped during the process of inquiry.

➢ Accessible directory of existing applications and their purpose. This gives the organization an estimate of its existing resources and a means to assess the gap to the desirable state.

➢ Organization of documents that assist in developing or modifying taxonomy structure

> Framework for developing a Subject Matter Expert system, taxonomy, etc. Subject Matter Experts are those in your organization who demonstrate the highest level of expertise in performing a specialized job, task or skill.

Knowledge Management Project Initiation

Knowledge management projects are often characterized by lagging time schedules and delivery of value that is tangible to the organization. To ensure that the motivation persists till the successful completion of the project, organizations would do good to pay attention to planning their project properly.

The foundation steps are environment assessment and developing the project charter.

Environment assessment can be done through a readiness assessment as discussed earlier in this module. The organization can use any of the audit methods as well to ascertain the knowledge health of the organization.

Developing a project charter involves defining a project scope, outlining the project objectives, identifying the authority for the success of the project as well as management checkpoints.

The project organization also needs to be determined – such as who the steering group team members would be and who would constitute the project team. In essence, once an organization knows what it is trying to achieve and recognize the scope of activity, it can easily allocate resources and personnel strategically.

Experience has shown that important efforts succeed only when taken out of routine corporate operations and given special management attention and emphasis. Detailed project planning can go a long way in ensuring the success of the project.

The figure below shows the project initiation process pictorially.

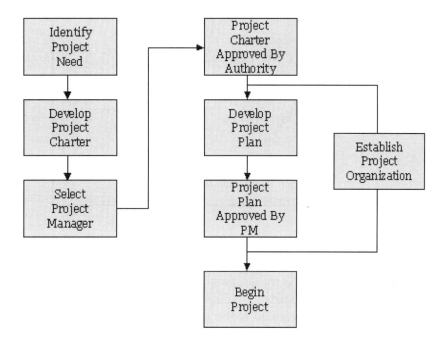

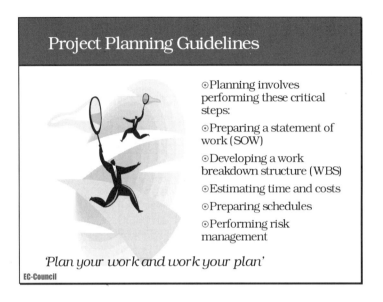

Project Planning Guidelines

⊙Planning involves performing these critical steps:

⊙Preparing a statement of work (SOW)

⊙Developing a work breakdown structure (WBS)

⊙Estimating time and costs

⊙Preparing schedules

⊙Performing risk management

'Plan your work and work your plan'

EC-Council

Project Planning Guidelines

A KM project is implementing knowledge management disciplines, tools, and techniques to build a system that will achieve specific goals and objectives. The challenge, of course, is to collect, organize, and distribute knowledge to achieve goals and objectives that are often as vague as the definition of KM. This can lead to scope creep and overlooking customer wants and, ultimately, wreaks havoc on cost, quality, or schedule performance.

Planning involves performing these critical steps:

> Preparing a statement of work (SOW)- Also called a SOW, this document is a contract between the project manager building the KM system and its recipient, or customer. From a KM perspective, the customer is often within the user community and the project team comes primarily from the IT organization. Considering the vagueness that surrounds KM, a SOW makes good sense and can preclude a host of misunderstandings surrounding the functionality of a KM system and responsibilities for performing specific tasks. A well-written, definitive SOW provides a meaningful basis for planning a KM project.

> Developing a work breakdown structure (WBS) - The work breakdown structure is a top-down, general-to-specific hierarchical listing of components of a KM system and their respective tasks to complete. An effective WBS reaches a level of detail that enables development of a meaningful schedule, makes valuable assessments of progress, and

ensures completeness of the tasks. A heuristic is that the lowest level of tasks in a WBS cannot exceed 80 hours to complete, or the equivalent of two weeks of work for a full-time equivalent.

➤ Estimating time and costs - The real value of a definitive WBS is its use in estimating the time and costs for a KM project. It provides the level of granularity that allows for "rollups" to different levels of tracking and monitoring. The estimating for time should involve the application of the three-point estimate. This approach can reduce the dramatic influences of extreme optimism and pessimism that often accompany estimates. Hence, the three-point estimate reduces the tendency to exaggerate. The best approaches for applying this estimating approach is having the individuals who perform the tasks do the estimating. The people assigned, however, are often not available, so the project manager must make the initial estimates.

➤ Preparing schedules - The combination of the SOW, WBS, and estimates provides the basis for developing a meaningful, integrated schedule for the KM project. The SOW provides the mandatory dates; the WBS provides the listing of the tasks to perform; and the estimates provide the length of time to perform each task. The schedule is first developed by identifying the dependencies, or logical sequence, among the tasks and then applying the flow times for each one. The eventual result is the calculation of four dates for each task.

➤ Performing risk management - Because KM projects face many variables, risk management is absolutely essential. Like all projects, some risks have a higher probability of occurrence and a greater level of impact than others. The project manager who performs a risk management can increase the likelihood of project success by identifying the necessary measures that need to be established to respond to certain risks affecting cost, schedule, and quality. Here are some risks that many KM projects can face and that can impact cost, schedule, and quality:

  o Failure to obtain management buy-in

  o Failure to tie the KM system into the overall strategic direction of the company

  o Inability to get employees to share knowledge

  o Lack of detailed requirements

  o Lack of integration among development tools

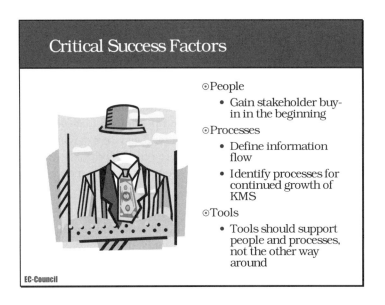

Critical Success Factors

 Knowledge management solutions and strategies encompass:

> People aspects: training, development, recruitment, motivation, retention, organization, job design, cultural change and encouraging thinking and participation.

> Process aspects: process innovation, re-engineering; both for radical and continuous improvement.

> Technology aspects: information and decision support systems, knowledge-based systems and data mining systems.

Various kinds of knowledge management initiatives or projects are possible, including:

> Organization-wide strategic reviews leading to a full   implementation strategy.

> Task, process, function or team-specific analysis and design projects.

> Projects that address individual aspects in isolation: such as the people, process or technology aspects.

However, the essence of any knowledge management initiative is that it should cater to the three critical success factors – namely people, process and technology – either in whole or individually.

From a project management perspective, ensuring stakeholder support is the people factor, identifying information flows and critical business processes address the process factor and finally technology should be seen as one that supports people and processes and not the other way around.

Summary

- ⊙ KMMM helps organization know where they stand with respect to knowledge maturity
- ⊙ Knowledge audit assists in ascertaining the knowledge health of the organization
- ⊙ Knowledge readiness assessment guides the organization in allocating resources prior to a knowledge initiative.
- ⊙ Planning at a detailed level can add to the successful completion of the KM project.
- ⊙ Schedules, WBS and cost estimation are important aspects of planning

EC-Council

Summary

 Recap

- ➢ KMMM helps organization know where they stand with respect to knowledge maturity
- ➢ Knowledge audit assists in ascertaining the knowledge health of the organization
- ➢ Knowledge readiness assessment guides the organization in allocating resources prior to a knowledge initiative.
- ➢ Planning at a detailed level can add to the successful completion of the KM project.
- ➢ Schedules, WBS and cost estimation are important aspects of planning

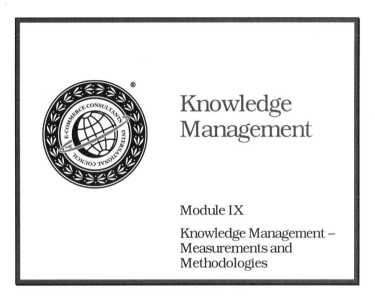

Knowledge Management (KM)

Module IX: Knowledge Management Measurements and Methodologies

Exam 212-69 Certified e-Business Associate

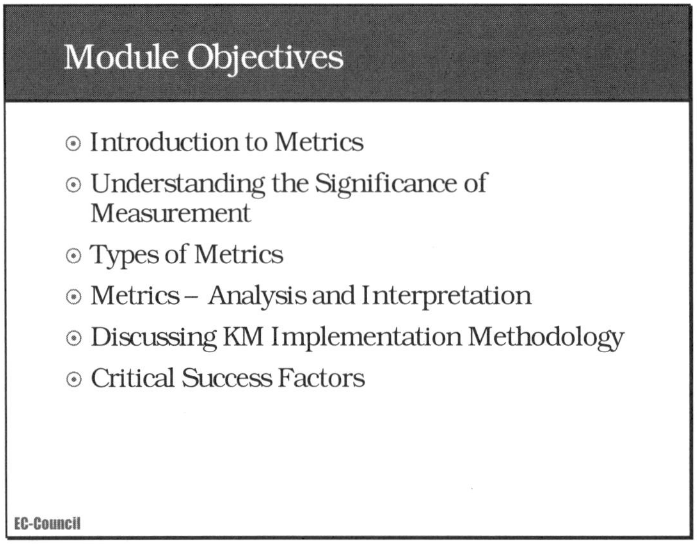

Module Objectives

⊙ Introduction to Metrics

⊙ Understanding the Significance of
Measurement

⊙ Types of Metrics

⊙ Metrics – Analysis and Interpretation

⊙ Discussing KM Implementation Methodology

⊙ Critical Success Factors

EC-Council

Objectives

☞ **Module Objectives**

On completion of this module, you will have gained insight into KM measurements and methodologies. This module engages in discussing the following key areas:

> Introduction to Metrics

> An understanding the Significance of Measurement in the context of knowledge management.

> Types of Metrics

> Analysis and Interpretation of Metrics

> Discussing KM Implementation Methodology

> Critical Success Factors for KM project implementation

Basics

- A measure is defined as a formula that describes a key performance indicator (KPI)
- A metric is the numeric value assigned to the measure
- For example, a measure might be "customer service time" and the metric might be " 1 working day
- Best Practices
  - Select limited number of KPIs and communicate them clearly to stakeholders.
  - Balance use of both leading and lagging KPIs
  - Include at least one KPI related to cost, to quality, and to cycle time in each set of KPIs

EC-Council

Basics Of Measurement And Metrics

Measure – To ascertain or appraise by comparing to a standard [1]. A standard or unit of measurement; the extent, dimensions, capacity, etc., of anything, especially as determined by a standard; an act or process of measuring [2]; A result of measurement [3].

In the present context, a measure is defined as a formula that describes a key performance indicator (KPI). However, without a trend to follow or an expected value to compare against, a measure gives little or no information. It does not provide enough information to make meaningful decisions. Here lies the importance of metrics.

Metric - A quantitative measure of the degree to which a system, component, or process possesses a given attribute [1]. A calculated or composite indicator based upon two or more measures [2]. A quantified measure of the degree to which a system, component, or process possesses a given attribute [3].

In the present context, a metric is used to refer the numeric value assigned to the measure. A metric is a comparison of two or more measures.

For example, a measure might be "customer service time" and the metric might be "1 working day

There are different approaches to measuring performance. For instance as per the methodology advocated by APQC, rules for using measures are to:

➤ Select only five to eight measures and clearly communicate them to all stakeholders. Incorporate both leading measures that drive performance and lagging measures that are (example: outcome or results oriented).

➤ Use measures to track progress against goals or targets, not to create competition among teams, business units, or individuals.

➤ Include at least one measure related to cost, to quality, and to cycle time in each set of measures.

➤ Communicate results in a direct, clear, and succinct manner (e.g. a scoreboard, dashboard, or one-page sheet that clearly communicates the measures and performance relative to established targets).

A related term to measure and metric is indicator.

Indicator - A device or variable that can be set to a prescribed state based on the results of a process or the occurrence of a specified condition. For example, a flag or semaphore [2]. A metric that provides insight into software development processes and software process improvement activities concerning goal attainment [3].

Significance of KM Measurement

- To fortify and supplement the business case for implementation
- To provide feedback and thereby help guide and tune the implementation process
- To assess the approach to a target or goal
- To measure, post-implementation, the value of the initial investment decision and the lessons learned
- To develop benchmarks for future comparisons
- To aid learning from the effort and developing best practices

EC-Council

Significance of KM Measurement

Measurement and reporting on the status and progress of knowledge assets is essential to ensure that senior management understands and appreciates the significance of KM's contribution to the top line and bottom line results.

The most important of assets in the organization are its people, their knowledge, and all the forms of intellectual capital that the organization possesses. That is what makes the organization operate.

Knowledge management pays attention to three factors in this alignment:

- It introduces measurement of knowledge,

- It brings wider recognition of knowledge in the organization, and

- It raises new factors that are worthy of measurement attention, such as networking and team activities.

Metrics are particularly important to KM because a Return On Investment (ROI) for KM often takes significant time to appear. Putting a KM program in effect will impact other business processes as the organization learns to use and leverage the new KM capabilities. This cultural infusion to KM can take long time as high as 18 to 36 months in some cases. According to Gartner Group, "in no case should a KM program (at the enterprise level) be expected to show ROI in less than 12 months."

Potential users of these metrics include:

> ➢ Strategic decision makers,

> ➢ Special project decision makers,

> ➢ Funding and approval stakeholders,

> ➢ Government agencies involved in approval or regulation, or

> ➢ Customers.

In knowledge management measurement, the aim is to select and/or formulate those concepts useful in measuring and influencing knowledge management performance. Some concepts will prove useful because they directly relate to core notions about the goals of knowledge management, and in that sense, have normative significance as performance criteria. For example, providing for the growth of knowledge is one of the goals of knowledge management.

> ## Types of Metrics
>
> ⊙ There are three broad categories of KM metrics
> - Outcome metrics (enterprise or overall value) concern the overall organization and measure large scale characteristics such as increased productivity or revenue for the enterprise.
> - Output metrics (project or task) measure project level characteristics such as the effectiveness of Lessons Learned information to capturing new business.
> - System metrics (technology tool) monitor the usefulness and responsiveness of the supporting technology tools.
>
> ⊙ Metrics describe what you can do, <u>not</u> what you must do or even what you should do.
>
> EC-Council

Types of Metrics

KM initiatives need to continually measure their progress in achieving their objectives to ensure success. KM, and all organizational initiatives, cannot guarantee that plans and strategies will succeed given the complex and dynamic nature of modern organizations. Well-designed performance measures yield direct indications of the efficiency and effectiveness of people, processes, and programs, which help managers to understand and adapt their organizations. Therefore, metrics provide a valuable means for focusing attention on desired behaviors and results.

There is no one "right" set of measures for KM initiatives and most KM initiatives will require a combination of measurement types and classes to effectively communicate with the key stakeholders. The measures must reflect the overall mission and strategy of the organization.

However, they may be broadly classified into three categories as detailed below:

> ➤ <u>Outcome Measures</u>, which determine the impact of the KM project on the organization, help determine if the knowledge base and knowledge transfer processes are working to create a more effective organization. Outcome measures are often the hardest measures to evaluate, particularly because of the intangible nature of knowledge assets. Some of the best examples of outcome measures are in the private sector. For example, energy giant Royal Dutch/Shell Group reports that ideas exchanged in their community of practice for engineers saved the company $200 million in 2000 alone.

➢ <u>Output Measures</u>, which measure direct process output for users, give a picture of the extent to which personnel are drawn to and actually using the knowledge system.

➢ <u>System Measures</u>, which relate the performance of the supporting information technologies to the KM initiative. They give an indirect indication of knowledge sharing and reuse, but can highlight which assets are the most popular and any usability problems that might exist and be limiting participation. For example, the web page statistics are a system measure.

Metrics must accommodate different views of decision makers in the organization (senior executives, middle management, and others). Knowledge management helps balance strategy to include perspective of customer, internal processes, and innovation.

In essence outcome metrics concern the overall organization and measure large-scale characteristics such as increased productivity or revenue for the enterprise. System metrics monitor the usefulness and responsiveness of the supporting technology tools. Output metrics measure project level characteristics such as the effectiveness of lessons learned information to capturing new business.

What needs to be noted is that metrics are not necessarily transferable across organizations. An organization needs to work towards identifying metrics that suits its strategic goals. Metrics have to be developed in collaboration with all decision-makers in order to develop useful metrics and also to leverage existing organizational metrics. There are many KM metrics available and organizations must prune them down to identify critical success factors.

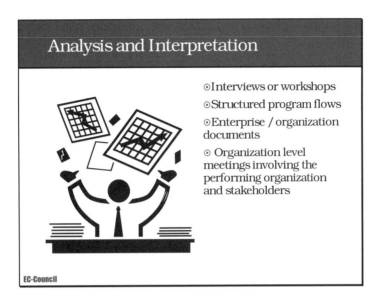

Analysis and Interpretation

Once the measures have been collected, they should be analyzed within the framework chosen. The frameworks are discussed in the following pages. This will ensure that the measures are linked to the objectives of the initiative and associated with the strategic goals of the organization. To be noted in particular is whether the measures give a direct or indirect indication of effects so that the team and stakeholders don't misapprehend or foster unrealistic expectations of performance.

 To facilitate analysis and interpretations, organizations can chose any of the following means.

> Interviews or workshops: Stakeholders can be interviewed individually or through a group setting in a facilitated workshop to draw out opinions and generate group consensus. The preeminent choice depends on the people, organizational culture, the information needed, and people's availability. In each case, it is important to structure the sessions proactively. Facilitation of any session is advocated to urge managers to talk about the type of decisions they commonly make and what decision-making information would be useful by asking "what if" questions.

> Structured program flows: Tracing the flow from the program competency to the uses of these competencies by direct users through to the end user benefits is another way to identify the information desired from performance measures. This technique of tracking the flow is particularly useful for programs for which it is difficult to directly identify or calculate measures for the ultimate end user benefits.

> ➤ <u>Agency/organization documents</u>: Documents from the performing agency and stakeholder organizations can contain useful information regarding an organization's goals, priorities, measures, problems, and business operations.

> ➤ <u>Meetings involving the performing organization and stakeholders</u>: Many organizations have steering committees comprised of representative internal and external stakeholders. Observing the interchange at meetings can yield the priorities and issues that the stakeholders feel are important.

Analysis is one of the most critical steps in the measurement process. Examples can be: Are they using the knowledge? Are people sharing meaningful knowledge openly? Have people participated during the pilot and then stopped? Were any anecdotes showing that people became more efficient or solved a problem faster because of the knowledge?

The search for an answer will yield valuable insights and ideas on how to improve the KM project. It is imperative to collect and prioritize new ideas and revisit the original plans and assumptions to see if they need to be changed. It is normal that several will need to be modified in an iterative fashion. This is a good time to assemble the KM project team and build a consensus on what should be changed, how to change it, and when to introduce the changes. The measures should be updated accordingly along in alignment with the framework to make sure they are tightly coupled to the modified KM plans.

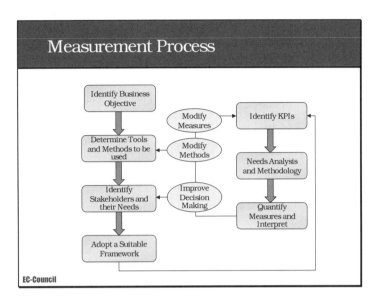

The Measurement Process

The first step in the measurement process is to identify the business objective. Along with this, the metrics team also needs to identify who will use the measures. This can be a KM project champion, officers and managers, participants, approval authority, internal customers and other stakeholders.

One valuable technique is to brainstorm a list of all possible users for the measures and then review the list to remove duplicates and add any positions or organizations not included previously.

However, this should not turn into a huge list, as it is not possible to generate metrics that appeal to all and give a detailed view at the same time. A key part of defining the business objective and KM methods (pre-requisite to the metrics process) is to focus the KM initiative on specific organizational needs. These activities should have identified the primary stakeholders, and this list can help consolidate the final list into stakeholders who are substantially connected to the initiative.

The next step is to determine the tools and methods to be used for the measurement purpose. These may be questionnaires, resources of quantitative nature or informal interviews. The latter involves identifying the stake holder's needs and concerns and the decisions they will make to identify the information that they need from the measures. This is the third step in the process. They may want to determine how valuable the knowledge assets are to the organization in practice, how effective the KM system is in enabling knowledge sharing and reuse, or both. Thus, measures have to be tailored to each need.

Based on the needs identified, a suitable framework may be adopted to facilitate measurement.

A framework helps ensure that the metrics are aligned to the project objectives and the organization's strategic goals. A conceptual framework is needed for the performance measurement and management system. Every organization needs a clear and cohesive performance measurement framework that is understood by all levels of the organization and that supports objectives and the collection of results.

The benefit of a framework is to convey the measures in a contextual and relevant manner than merely listing them. A framework can show how actions contribute to overall goals, the mechanisms by which actions produce benefits, the rationale for conducting the KM project, and, in some cases, provide an analytical tool for making investment trade-offs.

There are several ways to construct a framework using organization schemes such as a balanced set of measures, benchmarking, target setting, matrices, hierarchies, flow diagrams, and even management systems. The best choice for the KM initiative depends on which one, or ones, relate to the needs identified and can be easily gauged and understood. This can include costs, benefits, relationships, and impacts of the KM processes and measures to each other, and to business objectives.

Some of the frameworks are discussed below.

Online workgroup's process through the exchange of knowledge: The measures used to monitor the performance of this virtual meeting directly relate to the meeting's effect on the participants, but do not indicate the success or failure of the virtual meeting in achieving the business objectives of the KM initiative. For this analysis, the desired impacts at the end of the process are delineated and specific measures defined to monitor them.

Matrix: A matrix measure is good for showing the rationale for prioritizing and selecting among a group of KM projects, and is often used in portfolio management. Matrices are effective for condensing many interdependent factors into a readable format. For example, one matrix can show the relationship among KM activities, points of contact, expected results, measures used, actual results, stakeholders, and resource costs.

Causal Diagrams: Causal loop diagrams represent the structure of a system by showing the relationships between its key parts. This helps in understanding the underlying structures that drive behavior and provides a visual representation with which to communicate that understanding.

The diagram generally consists of one or more closed loops that represent cause and effect relationships between variables. In a causal loop diagram, a link is an arrow between two variables that represents a relationship. There are two types of links, "same" and "opposite". "Same" links are indicated by an "s," and represent that a change in the first variable results in a change in the same direction in the second variable. "Opposite" links are indicated by an "o," and represent that a change in the first variable results in a change in the opposite direction in the second variable.

<u>Balanced Scorecard</u>: This provides a view of business performance by combining financial measures, which tell the results of actions already taken, with operational measures of customer satisfaction, internal processes, and the enterprise's innovation and improvement activities – the drivers of future performance.

The most important characteristic to consider when choosing or defining a KM performance measure is whether the metric tells if knowledge is being shared and used. For example, a metric for a Best Practices database might be the number of times the database has been accessed. A large number of accesses suggest that people are reading the document, but this does not definitively indicate if it was useful to anyone or if it improved operational efficiency or quality. A better metric would be to track database usage and ask a sampling of the users if and how the information helped them. In addition, the measures used should be tied to the maturity of the KM initiative, which has a lifecycle where it progresses through a series of phases

The American Productivity and Quality Center produced a study based on a consortium of companies on *Measurement for Knowledge Management**. This study identifies and discusses how the need for metrics differs through the stages.

In the pre-planning phase, an Integrated Product Team can use its complementary mix of expertise to do process and risk analysis, develop strategies, and project results.

The goals of the start-up phase are to generate interest and support for KM, which creates a higher value on measures that convince people KM is worthwhile, such as anecdotes, comparisons to other organizations, and levels of funding and participation.

The pilot project phase concentrates on developing evidence of success and Lessons Learned that can be transferred to other initiatives. In this phase, more definitive measures are needed, such as changes in business costs (e.g. reduced support and resources), cultural changes (e.g. increased sharing among groups), and the currency and usage of collected knowledge bases.

For the growth and expansion stage, KM is being institutionalized across the corporation, and therefore measures that reflect enterprise-wide benefits are needed. These include KM proficiency gauged against Best Practices, formal KM elements in performance evaluations, and sophisticated capital valuation calculations.

(Source: "Measurement for Knowledge Management," Released February 2001, APQC.)

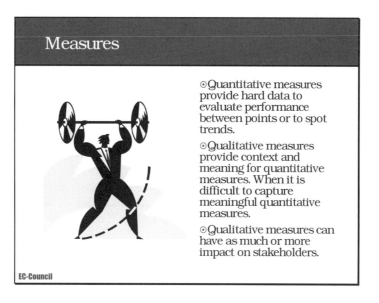

Qualitative and Quantitative Measures

Measurements for KM initiatives can be quantitative or qualitative and, in general, a measurement program should include both types of measures.

> Quantitative measures provide hard data to evaluate performance between points (such as last month to this month), or to spot trends.

> Qualitative measures provide context and meaning for quantitative measures. When it is difficult to capture meaningful quantitative measures (such as the value to the individual for being a member of a community of practice), qualitative measures (such as a story from a member about how the community helped him solve a critical problem) can have as much or more impact on stakeholders.

A closely related concept to the need for qualitative measures is the notion of tangible and intangible benefits. A tangible benefit is concrete and can have a direct measurement of its value. In contrast, an intangible benefit cannot be definitively described by a quantitative value. For example, the value of a machine can be computed from its production rate compared to its operating costs while the value of a company's brand image to its profitability cannot be easily computed. As we will discuss in a later section, quantitative measures can provide an indirect although uncertain indication of intangible value.

It is difficult to account for the know-how or tacit knowledge in a person's mind, or in the collective minds of the organization. In addition, unlike physical assets, which are depleted when they are used, intellectual assets actually grow when they are used. In many respects, intellectual assets have no value until they are re-used or applied in new situations. Several techniques have been developed to assess the value of intangibles to an organization.

Examples of a few other well-known measurement techniques are summarized below.

> Intangible Assets Monitor: Developed by Karl Sveiby in 1997, this model defines three types of intangible assets that account for the book-to-market discrepancy in the value of many companies: individual competence, internal structure, and external structure. Sveiby believes that people are the only true agents in business and that all assets and structures, whether tangible or intangible, are a result of human actions. The organization needs to have a very good understanding of its corporate goals and objectives in order to apply the Intangible Assets Monitor since the indicators are specifically chosen to have the maximum impact (good or bad) on those goals.

> Skandia Navigator: The Skandia Navigator, developed by Leif Edvinsson at Skandia Assurance and Financial Services in Sweden, combines the theory on which the Intangible Assets Monitor is based with the Balanced Scorecard approach. In 1994, Skandia published the results of this framework as the first supplement to their annual report, using the term intellectual assets instead of intangible assets for the first time. The Skandia Navigator defines two components of intellectual capital: Human Capital plus Structural Capital.

> Intellectual Capital Index: Developed by Johan and Goran Roos, this approach emphasizes the flows of intellectual capital as well as the stocks. The Roos index provides a framework for measures in two general categories: Human Capital (competence, attitude, intellectual agility, knowledge capital, and skill capital) and Structural Capital (external relationships, internal organization, renewal and development, strategic processes, flow of products and services).

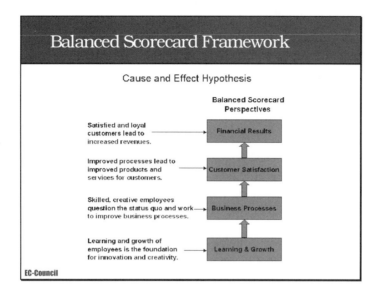

Balanced Scorecard

A balanced scorecard aligns measures with strategies in order to track progress, reinforce accountability, and prioritize improvement opportunities. A traditional balanced scorecard integrates four related perspectives is shown above. In their book 'The Balanced Scorecard', Kaplan and Norton set forth a hypothesis about the chain of cause and effect that leads to strategic success. This cause-and-effect hypothesis is fundamental to understanding the metrics that the balanced scorecard prescribes.

These perspectives as propounded by the balance score card institute is listed as under:

> **Customer perspective**: How do customers see us?   General mission statements need to be made concrete - with specific measures of what matters to customers, namely time, quality, performance/service, and cost. Improved customer satisfaction leads to loyal customers and increased market share, which directly affect the bottom line -- whether that line equals profit, ROI (return on investment) or ROCE (return on capital employed) in the private sector, or NOR (net operating result) or IOH (overhead) in the public sector.

> **Internal perspective**: What must we excel at?   To achieve goals on cycle time, quality, performance and cost, managers must devise measures that are influenced by subordinates' actions. Since much of the action takes place at the division and workstation levels, managers need to decompose overall cycle time, quality, product, and cost measures to local levels. That way, the measures link top management's judgment

about key internal processes and competencies to the actions taken by individuals that affect overall command objectives.

➢ **Learning and Innovation perspective**: Can we continue to improve and create value? An organization's ability to innovate, improve, and learn ties directly to that organization's value. That is, only through the ability to adapt to evolving new missions, create more value for customers, and improve operating efficiencies can a command maximize use of existing mission capabilities while meeting the personal and developmental needs of its service.

➢ **Financial perspective**: How do we look to stakeholders? Ideally, organizations should specify how improvements in quality of life, cycle time, mission readiness, training opportunities, equipment and new mission directives leads to improved near-term readiness, increased retention, progress in modernization and re-capitalization programs, reduced manning requirements, increased personal or training time, faster skills acquisition, or to reduced operating expenses. The challenge is to learn how to make such an explicit linkage between operations and finance. Financial performance measures indicate whether the organization's strategy, implementation, and execution are contributing to bottom line improvement. (Typical financial goals have to do with profitability, growth and stakeholder value.) The Navy's financial goals are to apply its Total Obligation Authority (TOA) to meet two general objectives: first, to provide appropriately sized, positioned, and mobile forces to shape the international environment, and second, to maintain war fighting superiority through modernization.

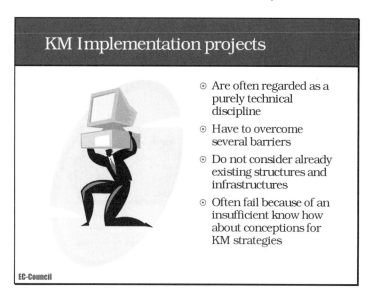

Need for Implementation Methodology

Knowledge management projects are often considered to be laborious for reasons such as:

➤ Being regarded as a purely technical discipline

➤ Need to overcome several barriers within the organization itself

➤ Do not consider already existing structures and infrastructures

➤ And often fail because of an insufficient know how about conceptions for KM strategies

The need for a methodological approach arises in this context. A Methodological Basis helps in:

➤ Supporting companies to assess their current KM maturity level

➤ Giving them recommendations in order to reach a higher level

➤ Improving their organizational and technological infrastructure

➤ Pointing out to them next generation KM technologies and their successful implementation

In the following pages we shall see how a KM implementation methodology works and understand the need for such an approach to a KM initiative.

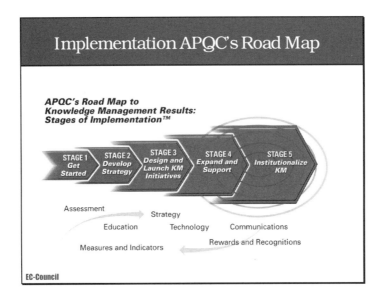

APQC KM Road Map

In this module we will detail one implementation methodology. APQC's methodology has been chosen for its widespread popularity and success stories. Further information on the same can be obtained from APQC. The following has been extracted from their popular publication 'Showcasing Successful Knowledge Management Implementation', published 2000 / 183 pgs. ISBN 1-928593-41-0

Stage 1: Get Started

Learning where the organization lies is the first important task along its path to knowledge management success. APQC implementation roadmap is detailed below.

If one or more of the following statements is true, the organization is likely ready to embark on Stage 1 of the journey.

> ➤ Knowledge management has emerged as a topic of interest in the organization.

> ➤ At least a few employees have explored the benefits of KM for the organization.

> ➤ Someone has had a personal stake in developing interest in KM.

> ➤ You or other members of the organization have learned about KM through participation in consortia or conferences.

> ➤ The organization has created a high-level rationale or vision for pursuing KM.

KEY ACTIVITIES FOR STAGE 1

1. Make the concepts of KM real for others in your organization. Create a clear, tangible picture of the benefits of KM as they relate to goals in your organization. Use simple definitions and simple language to explore real problems, opportunities, and the potential value that KM addresses.

2. Identify others to support the development of KM. To find advocates of knowledge management, look around the organization for current activities that might already be related to KM. Look for smaller communities or groups that are currently sharing knowledge, and make connections with these people. Recruiting well-respected, influential people is always a good idea.

Next, consider which of the following phrases gets attention: Cost cutting? Improved efficiency? Pressure from competitors? Streamlined information access? Simplified processes? As an agent of change, find the greatest motivating value factor in the organization to influence others to support KM initiatives.

3. Look for windows of opportunity to introduce the benefits of KM. Find where KM will be most valued by talking to people involved with strategic initiatives, internal consulting groups, or people inside the company with whom you've developed personal relationships. Then answer the following questions. What are their objectives? What issues are being addressed? How can KM help the organization meet those objectives and deal with those issues?

4. Capitalize on the Internet and enlist the IT department to provide tools and a balanced view of KM.
Make connections with IT leaders to find out what KM possibilities are available with existing technology. Find out what capabilities realistic upgrades might provide. Remember that the IT department can truly be a catalyst for emerging KM support technologies.

ROADBLOCKS TO SUCCESS

 > Ignoring corporate culture and history not addressing issues that might hinder KM

 > Attempting to sell an enterprise wide approach without building evidence first

 > Asking for a large budget before creating a compelling value proposition

Stage 2: Develop Strategy

If one or more of the following statements is true, the organization is ready to proceed to the next stage.

> ➤ The organization has established a KM exploratory group or steering committee for KM.

> ➤ An executive sponsor in the organization supports further exploration of KM.

> ➤ The organization is looking for successful, internal grassroots efforts already under way.

> ➤ The IT organization is interested in actively supporting KM initiatives.

> ➤ The organization has stories of how knowledge sharing has helped the organization in the past.

> ➤ The organization has identified pilots that allow you to demonstrate how KM will benefit the organization.

> ➤ The organization has secured ownership, funding, and buy-in for pilots.

The overall objective of Stage 2 is to formulate a KM strategy that fits the business model. From there, business opportunities are identified and initialized as pilot initiatives. A task force takes charge of these activities on behalf of the organization.

KEY ACTIVITIES FOR STAGE 2

At Stage 2, the organization has reached an important turning point. Perhaps a personal vision of capturing, sharing, and using information and knowledge has become an organizational exploration of business potential. With the support of an executive sponsor, the organization can now explore specifically how KM will work for the business. The key activities of Stage 2, and some helpful hints, are summarized for the organization here.

1. Form a KM task force: Base this cross-functional team on the core group that has already formed around KM. The team members will identify opportunities for pilots and set the standards for methods to be used across all initiatives.

2. Select pilots or identify current initiatives that could work as pilots. APQC recommends three pilots. The organization can select new strategic pilots or adopt current grassroots efforts already under way. Address issues that are important to the business, and design the pilots to show demonstrable, relevant results. Select pilot sponsors with the resources to help the initiative along.

3. Find the resources to support the pilot. The most important resources are skilled staff members who can facilitate the initiative and who are authorized by management to focus their time on it. Other resources include IT applications that might need to be created or modified. They may be extensive or the organization may have them already.

Stage 3: Design and Launch KM Initiatives

The organization has already come a long way. The organization has formed a task force, identified and designed a pilot, and located resources. Now the organization is approaching Stage 3, that point of launching successful pilots and gathering results.

If one or more of the following statements is true, the organization is at the midway point of the journey.

> ➤ The organization has designed a pilot and implementation strategies.

> ➤ The organization has launched communities of practice, an interactive KM Intranet site, or some other pilot initiative.

> ➤ The organization have enlisted and trained pilot facilitators and leaders.

> ➤ The organization have established pilot measures and indicators and developed a system for tracking and reporting results.

> ➤ The organization has created strategies for learning from the KM initiatives.

> ➤ The organization has mapped out strategies for expanding the pilot initiatives across the organization.

Stage 3 can be a rewarding time of new organizational growth and vitality. The overall objectives of Stage 3 are to conduct successful pilots, provide evidence of KM's business value, and capture lessons learned.

KEY ACTIVITIES FOR STAGE 3

At stage 3, the benefits of capturing, sharing, and using information and knowledge have begun to take definite form. This is the time to harness the momentum from the first two stages and focus on details, such as a formal budget. Leadership now needs to see the potential for measurable gains and ROI from successful pilots.

1. Fund the pilots. Assign a KM oversight group, such as a steering committee or cross-unit task force, to reallocate organizational resources, such as money and time, for KM initiatives. Every best-practice partner, including the World Bank, Chevron, HP Consulting, Xerox, and Siemens, reported having a KM task force to provide supervision and support for the reallocation of organizational resources.

2. Develop methodologies that can be replicated. Avoid building knowledge collections without an active community to contribute to the effort. Combine knowledge providers and knowledge users in a seamless community of practitioners. Allow these active communities to form voluntarily from natural groupings that span boundaries; encourage participation with face-to-face networking and community-driven Web sites. Establish a process for screening; filtering, and validating shared knowledge from the sites before presenting it as organizational

knowledge.

3. Capture lessons learned. The oversight group must discuss lessons learned at regular meetings and provide a common space for sharing the results. To complete this most crucial last step, answer questions such as "What made the pilots most successful?" and "Are the results worth investing in for expansion?"

LOOKING AHEAD

After the company assesses the pilots, KM will continue along one of three paths, KM efforts will be expanded to new initiatives, existing initiatives will be improved, or the status quo will be maintained, in which case employees will likely revert to prior behavior.

Stage 4: Expand and Support

By now, the organization has gained quite a bit of expertise. The organization has launched pilots, gathered results, captured some important lessons, and decided to continue the KM journey. Stage 4 involves expanding KM initiatives throughout the organization, which necessitates rapid and highly visible growth.

If one or more of the following statements is true, the organization is steadily nearing the final stage of the journey.

> ➢ Other departments in the organization are expressing a demand for KM, based on pilot results.

> ➢ The organization has begun to market KM throughout the organization.

> ➢ The organization has made the entire organization aware of KM.

> ➢ The organization has an expansion strategy in place for the KM initiatives.

> ➢ The organization has identified the resources necessary for expanding the KM efforts.

The overall objectives of Stage 4 are to develop and market an expansion strategy and to effectively manage KM growth. Being given the green light to expand adds the pressure of meeting formal business evaluations and ROI justification.

KEY ACTIVITIES FOR STAGE 4

Getting through this highly visible stage requires meeting ROI demands and carefully managing KM growth. The good news is that KM is at this point well on its way to being considered a necessary organizational competency.

1. Develop an expansion strategy. The organization can choose to apply the pilot selection criteria for programs in other departments or develop an all-at-once strategy to universally implement KM. Regardless of the approach, provide the appropriate resources, such as a group of core facilitators, CoP leaders, a corporate KM group, or a chief knowledge officer. Make sure the necessary technology is in place and that appropriate user support is available. Deal with cultural challenges. Deal with language issues; software exists that can automatically translate shared information in global CoPs. The organization can deal with the "silo" mentality, for example, by obtaining active support from senior leadership.

2. Communicate and market the strategy. Publicize KM initiatives throughout the organization. Some options include incorporating KM training into new-hire orientation; training managers and quality coordinators; holding an open house, knowledge fair, or regular meetings; or advertising on the intranet or through brochures and pamphlets.

3. Manage growth. Control the confusion from the explosion of KM initiatives that normally happens at this stage. A consistent online policy can keep KM resources organized, consistent, and easily accessible. World Bank, for example, has a technology group that spends about 50 percent of its time on technology issues related to KM and managing information on the internal and external Web.

STAGE 4 SUCCESS DETERMINANTS

> Appoint a central cross-functional KM group to create an expansion strategy, identify required resources, and alleviate confusion from rapid growth.

> Resources to successfully support widespread KM initiatives must be conscripted or developed from other units.

> Communicate the KM strategy using vigorous marketing.

LOOKING AHEAD

To progress to Stage 5, several best-practice advanced firms assessed their KM efforts and addressed weaknesses in their KM strategy. Chevron used an internal corporate KM group; World Bank engaged an outside team of KM practitioners; and Xerox embedded KM evaluation into its Xerox Management Model assessment process.

Stage 5: Institutionalize Knowledge Management

Stage 5 is a destination, a new beginning, and a journey of its own. To fulfill the potential of this stage, the company must redefine its strategies, its organizational structure, and its performance assessments.

If one or more of the following statements is true, the organization is beginning to integrate KM throughout the organization. KM is on its way to becoming how the organization do business.

> ➤ KM is directly linked to the business model.

> ➤ KM initiatives are widely deployed throughout the organization.

> ➤ All the managers and employees are trained to use the KM technologies.

> ➤ The organization methodically assesses the KM strategy, identify gaps, and outline methods to close the gaps.

> ➤ The organization has a formal support structure in place to maintain KM.

> ➤ The organization has rewards programs in alignment with the KM strategy.

> ➤ Sharing knowledge is now the norm in the organization.

Stage 5 places the organization among a few select companies who have reached this stage of institutionalized KM.

KEY ACTIVITIES FOR STAGE 5

At Stage 5, the organization is beginning to understand that KM is a business strategy not just a database and needs to be an integral part of the business model. KM at this point becomes a necessary organizational competency with unlimited potential to benefit every unit of the organization.

1. Embed KM in the business model. This step is necessary to obtain CEO and senior executive support. The organization can accomplish this step by including KM in the mission statement, management model, or assessment process. Expect financial pressure to increase at this stage, and early barriers, such as functional silos, to disappear.

2. Realign the organization's structure and budget. Reorganize budget and departmental responsibilities to accommodate the wide deployment of KM as a business strategy. World Bank, for example, shifted KM leadership to operations from the chief information officer, as KM evolved from a database to an all-encompassing strategy. The budget increased from $13 million to $57 million in two years and included a formal consolidation of budgets from activities that had been contributing to KM. The organization will find at this stage that organizational structure will, to some extent, naturally evolve to better fit this new way of working.

3. Monitor the health of KM. Take the pulse of KM initiatives regularly. The organization can employ an external evaluation panel, conduct internal maturity evaluations, or include KM feedback on employee surveys.

4. Align performance evaluation and rewards with KM strategy. Since performance appraisals are the basis for promotion and pay, including KM standards with reviews sends a dramatic message about its role. Institute recognition awards programs for people who exemplify the ideals of the KM strategy.

5. Balance an organizational KM framework with local control. Link company wide business goals to KM activities to provide necessary consistency. At the same time, allow individual groups to develop KM resources that meet their specific needs. Allow business needs to drive the KM policy.

6. Continue the journey. As the organization becomes a true knowledge-sharing enterprise, demand for knowledge processes will continue to increase, as will savings of time and money. Maintain senior leadership support to help the organization keep pace with demand.

LOOKING AHEAD

Critical success factors for continuing the KM journey include maintaining committed and involved leadership, forming a motivating and consistent vision, developing an evolutionary process (not a "big bang" approach), starting initiatives when and where people are ready, identifying role models, and communicating constantly and effectively about initiatives and business needs.

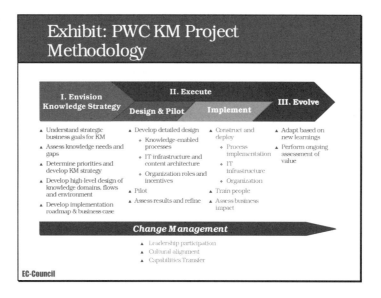

Exhibit. PWC KM Project Methodology

PricewaterhouseCoopers offers a "global, structured and applied Knowledge Management Strategy". The methodology helps organizations to identify and collect:

> ➢ The explicit knowledge kept in various databases - relational or otherwise,

> ➢ The tacit knowledge present at the heart of the various know-how of the company.

All this aims at organizing, structuring, sharing the knowledge in order to analyze, apply, develop and put it at the employees' disposal afterwards.

Building a structure that encourages the growing and sharing of knowledge focuses on four main aspects:

> ➢ Content

> ➢ People

> ➢ Processes

> ➢ Systems and technologies.

The success of the implementation of such a strategy is dependent on the players' commitment and direction. Throughout the project and then during rollout, they will come to follow the evolution of the benefits brought by the Knowledge Management strategy. This is made possible by indicators put in place throughout the project, which provide trends and measures.

This strategy is based upon a method in four main consecutive steps and one transversal step. Any of these steps can be repeated in order to broaden the application field of Knowledge Management:

- ➢ "Envision": define and / or validate scope and milestones of Knowledge Management project, involve main players in the project.

- ➢ "Design / Pilot": design new processes; assess roles and technical choices, implement pilot project.

- ➢ "Implement": complete project implementation.

- ➢ "Evolve": essential phase which:

    - o Ensures continuity of Knowledge Management by capabilities transfer

    - o Assesses project results and plans possible new development.

- ➢ "Change Management": throughout these four phases, several actions to accompany change are carried out. They are key to the success of Knowledge Management. They include the implementation of new roles and responsibilities, the creation of focus groups and the transfer of capabilities.

PricewaterhouseCoopers believes that each step should be carried out with tools, methods and techniques - applicable or not according to your company's situation and objectives. Each of these steps - independent from one another, yet complementary - is structured by an inflow, an implementation and a deliverable.

A successful implementation of Knowledge Management in any company means its increased value and competitive advantage. However, a successful implementation is necessarily multidimensional and goes well beyond its mere technical execution. Tools by themselves will not solve human problems. People remain the key success factor of the organization and are consequently the efficient and motivated players in knowledge managing and sharing.

Example: Methodology adopted by British Petroleum

- ⊙ Phase 1 - Customize Pilot Process and Create Stakeholder Alignment
- ⊙ Phase 2 - Capture Key Learning and Good Practices
- ⊙ Phase 3 - Establish and Leverage Communities of Practice
- ⊙ Phase 4 - Adapt and Apply Best Practices in Pilot Operations
- ⊙ Phase 5 - Train and Coach Internal KM Practitioners
- ⊙ Phase 6 - Monitor, Review and Optimize Pilot Learning and Impact

EC-Council

Example of a Methodology: British Petroleum

The following is the methodology adopted by British Petroleum and SAIC.

> Phase 0 - Identify and Select Pilot Projects

The purpose of this phase is to create awareness of the possibilities of KM-based performance improvement among business leaders and stakeholders, identify potential pilots, and then assess and select a pilot for delivery. A set of standard KM project selection criteria is customized for the business and used to rank pilots based on their potential knowledge-based business benefits, local business leader advocacy, transferability of learning and results, and overall project feasibility.

> Phase 1 - Customize Pilot Process and Create Stakeholder Alignment

The focus of this phase is to engage key pilot stakeholders, including the local leadership team, staff and other contributors to customize the KM methodology to fit the specific business improvement needs of the pilot. Local business buy-in is created and a plan is developed and agreed that fits both the operational tempo and needs of the business participants.

> Phase 2 - Capture Key Learning and Good Practices

The focus of this phase is to elicit and harvest operational know-how to fill the knowledge gaps needed to meet the pilot performance improvement targets. The majority of knowledge generation and capture will be performed through a series of individual interviews and the facilitation of on-the-job team learning processes before, during, and after major work activities.

➢ Phase 3 - Establish and Leverage Communities of Practice

The focus of this phase is to engage and enable relevant practitioners inside and outside the local pilot business area to share and transfer know-how and good practices to the work teams involved in the pilot. At least one Community of Practice (CoP) will be established for subject area practitioners contributing knowledge to the Pilot.

➢ Phase 4 - Adapt and Apply Best Practices in Pilot Operations

The focus of this phase is to enable and ensure the know-how gained from the pilot work teams, CoP interactions, and other sources are applied on the job to improve existing processes and deliver the agreed performance targets.

➢ Phase 5 - Train and Coach Internal KM Practitioners

The focus of this phase is to transfer and embed KM competencies and techniques in staff participating in the delivery of the pilot effort. Using a phased approach, the lead responsibility for delivery of KM practices is purposefully shifted from the KM consultant to local KM staff over the duration of the pilot.

➢ Phase 6 - Monitor, Review and Optimize Pilot Learning and Impact

The focus of this phase is to manage efficient tracking and completion of the pilot deliverables. Results will be documented in a report and presentation that includes a review of the benefits achieved versus planned, recommendations for KM strategy and broader implementation based on KM pilot learning and practices.

(Source: Science Applications International Corporation)

Critical Success Factors

⊙ Vision and leadership - KM strategic plan

⊙ Organizational and communication training

⊙ Business performance measurements

⊙ KM mission interface and alignment

⊙ KM architectures and infrastructure

⊙ KM integration and resourcing

⊙ Governance - policies and procedures

Source: KMWorld

EC-Council

Critical Success Factors

Implementing a KM system can be complex and dynamic, irrespective of the amount of planning that goes behind the development of the idea. There will be resistance to change to the newly envisioned target organization following the implementation of the KM initiative. Personal and group interests can deflect the commitment needed to successfully implement such a system.

In order to successfully implement a KM initiative, it is essential that the following critical success factors be considered with all seriousness:

> **Vision and leadership**: KM initiative must follow a clear strategic plan. A clearly defined, inspirational vision statement for the value of what the KM system is intended to accomplish within the enterprise is needed to keep the initiative in-focus all along. A well-designed KM strategy and an implementation methodology tailored to the enterprise and its constituents are definitely a factor that can determine success.

It is essential that throughout the planning, building and implementing phases of a KM project, strategic planning sessions with the enterprise's leadership, mission area leaders and cross-functional representations as well as customer focus groups are formally facilitated.

> **Organizational and communication training**: Every organization has its own business process flows, procedures. KM implementation strategy must look into these individualistic needs and cater to the organizations specific requirements. Since the KM

implementation is going to bring about changes within the organization's current processes and procedures it is necessary that communication within the organization is adept and aiding cultural aspects of the change to be brought. Effective training plans in order to aid receptiveness to the new initiative are key to the success of the initiative.

It is necessary that an enterprise wide knowledge sharing culture be rolled out through training and change management techniques.

➢ **Business performance measurements**: Business drivers based on client demands, even if the enterprise itself does not recognize that, must absolutely lead a KM system. Leadership must define the business vision by demonstrating how a KM system can improve business processes and transform the enterprise. It is essential that the benefits of KM be realistically measured. Business performance needs to be measured in terms of both tangible (cost, schedule, performance) and intangible.

➢ **KM mission interface and alignment**: KM initiative needs coordinated activities within an enterprise in order to ensure that it is possible to achieve the overall business vision of a KM system without compromising current service levels and existing business. Here in it is imperative that the KM system needs to be well aligned to the existing enterprise's culture, mission, goals and business strategies.

➢ **KM architectures and infrastructure**: KM tools and the required infrastructure are essential and central to a successful KM system. KM technology tools are the enablers of a KM system. The KM system tools to be deployed must fit in to the organization's existing IS/IT infrastructure and compliant to the enterprise architecture. This will lead to eliminating unwanted IS/IT costs and will serve as the best value solution for the enterprise.

➢ **KM integration and resourcing**: KM system integration is to be planned and resourced properly to ensure a successful KM implementation and maintenance. A systems approach taking into account, planning, design, development and managing throughout KM system life cycle is key to KM technology implementation.

➢ **Governance**: It is essential that proper systems and procedures be developed for KM system governance. KM executive steering groups can handle the task of disseminating KM policies, procedures and best practices. These policies and procedures need to be continuously improved to cater to KM system overall usage and adoption.

Summary

- Metrics is a numerical representation of a measure
- Metrics help in quantifying key performance indicators
- There are three kinds of metrics – output, outcome and system metrics
- A balanced scorecard aligns measures with strategies in order to track progress
- Adopting a methodological basis helps organizations have clearer communications and support in assessing KM maturity.

EC-Council

Summary

 Recap

- ➢ Metrics is a numerical representation of a measure

- ➢ Metrics help in quantifying key performance indicators

- ➢ There are three kinds of metrics – output, outcome and system metrics

- ➢ A balanced scorecard aligns measures with strategies in order to track progress

- ➢ Adopting a methodological basis helps organizations have clearer communications and support in assessing KM maturity.

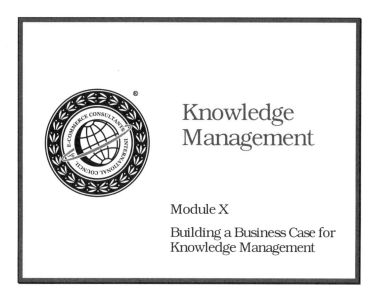

Knowledge Management (KM)

Module X: Building a Business Case for Knowledge Management

Exam 212-69 Certified e-Business Associate

```
┌─────────────────────────────────────────────────┐
│  Module Objectives                              │
├─────────────────────────────────────────────────┤
│                                                 │
│   ⊙ Introducing the Business Case               │
│                                                 │
│   ⊙ Presenting the Value Proposition            │
│                                                 │
│   ⊙ Measuring the Return on Investment          │
│                                                 │
│   ⊙ Developing a Business Case                  │
│                                                 │
│                                                 │
│                                                 │
│  EC-Council                                  2  │
└─────────────────────────────────────────────────┘
```

Objectives

☞ Module Objectives

On completion of this module you will be able to:

➢ Introduce the business case concept within in your team

➢ Present the value proposition to the stakeholders

➢ Measure the return on investment

➢ Develop a convincing business case

Developing a comprehensive business case is essential to communicate to the senior management and the stakeholders, the importance of the knowledge initiative and obtain sponsorship that is critical to the success of the project. A comprehensive business case involves a process that goes beyond financial estimates to the core business issues concerning the processes and practices, which are the fundamental reasons why organizations should invest in knowledge management.

Nevertheless, a business case has financial indicators as an integral part. Because of their inability to capture certain issues, financial figures alone are not sufficient for a full business justification of an investment. At the same time it is important to understand that the estimates, financial and other, which are used for investment evaluation are always opinions about the future and are thus not as accurate as is suggested or thought.

The Business Case

⊙ A Business Case is a tool to support planning and decision-making.

⊙ Business Cases are generally designed to answer the question: What are the likely financial and other business consequences if we take a particular course of action?

⊙ A good Business Case shows expected cash flow consequences of a decision and also includes the methods and rationale that were used for quantifying both costs and benefits.

3

Definition of Business Case

A business case is a tool to support planning and decision-making. They are generally designed to answer the question " What are the likely outcomes – financial and business consequences if a particular course of action is adopted."

A good business case describes expected cash flow consequences of a decision and also includes the methods and rationale that were used for quantifying both costs and benefits.

A business case is a model of what the organization expects to be able to achieve when it uses resources – not restricted to technology alone - to support improvements in its process and practices. It is a sophisticated model, which is produced to facilitate decision making in the IT management process (Akkermans 1995; Proctor 1995; Corbitt 1995) and to help in this respect with what-if questions (Karlin 1982).

The technology based business case model is produced at distinctly different levels.

➢ A high-level or macro model is produced when general concepts are employed in the case. The purpose of the macro model is to present a conceptual picture which will contextualize the problem or opportunity at a high level as well as provide a suggested solution. Example: To state that knowledge management can benefit the organization with enhanced decision-making capability is a macro level benefit conceptualization.

➢ An intermediate or meso level model will add a little more detail. This will express the dimensions of the problem and also a proposed solution. However, this will still be expressed primarily in generalities. Continuing with the same example, adding a detail such as enhanced decision making capability due to faster access to information is a meso level conceptualization.

> A detailed or micro level model attempts to be closer to the reality and thus to use more specific or life-like representations or values. In other words, metric and / or measures that are quantifiable play a significant role in these models.

The primary purpose of the micro model is to understand the detailed impact of the proposed solution or course of action. However, all models are by their nature simplifications of the reality that they represent (Zelm et al 1995). In our earlier example, quantifying the opportunity cost (in monetary estimates) that might occur if decision-making is delayed due to lack of timely information forms a micro level model.

In fact sometimes the simpler the model the more meaningfully it may be used. Complex models may actually cloud the central nature of the issues being studied and thus reduce the explanatory power and consequently the value of the model.

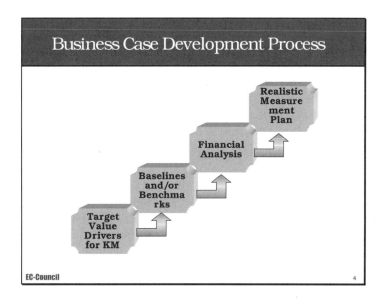

The Business Development Process

We have seen that a business case is a justification for pursuing a course of action in an organizational context to meet stated organizational objectives or goals. A business case frequently involves considering the value of an investment in terms of its potential benefits and the resources required to set it up and to maintain it, i.e. its on-going costs.

One of the major impediments in producing a business case is the fact that the benefits of an investment are often a function of the values of the organization and the executives who are making the investment decisions. Thus a business case will inevitably or inherently have a significant degree of subjectivity associated with it.

There are four basic steps in developing a business case for knowledge management. These are:

> Targeting value drivers for KM

> Establishing Baselines / Benchmarks

> Doing a Financial Analysis

> Carrying our a realistic measurement plan

A well-made business case or investment proposal consists of certain standard components such as:

> Objective and Benefits

A well-defined business case should have a clearly expressed business objective and set of benefits. These set the terms of reference for clarity in the communications with the stakeholders and the management. Often these are high-level business benefits that need to be comprehensively expressed as a set of opportunities the organization can take advantage of, or problems that need to be resolved.

It may also include a list of specific and detailed benefits, their relevant metrics, measuring methods and responsibility points represented by particular stakeholders, as well as a justification that the proposed plan will produce an acceptable organizational return. This involves the quantification of the contribution made by the benefits, which requires associating financial numbers (IRR / ROI) or benefit values with benefits wherever possible.

> List of stakeholders and beneficiaries of the investment.

Stakeholder sponsorship and management endorsement are critical success factors. So they must be identified prior to the making of the business case. Their needs and pain points must be identified and target KM value drivers must be presented accordingly in the business case. These should be highlighted and expressed in such a way that appropriate stakeholders can control them, and that it can be ascertained if these outcomes have actually been realized.

> A statement of how the proposed IT expenditure will support the corporate strategy.

To be of value to an organization the business case should be expressed in terms of identifiable or quantifiable objectives and actions. Thus it should start with the large picture of what will be achieved by the initiative.

> An evaluation of the appropriateness of the technology and operational plan.

Next, an evaluation of the appropriateness of the technology should be addressed in the form of baselines or benchmarks to correlate with the operational plan. A detailed drill-down exercise is needed to establish the precise outcomes.

> An evaluation of the risks associated with the investment.

Change does not come without associated risks and this must be clearly outlined in the business case so that realistic expectations are maintained. Thus the business case is a cornerstone of the process of ensuring value-for-money by the proposed investments.

A comprehensively produced business case is as much a plan as a justification. It is worth noting that a business case can only be formally produced after a considerable amount of initial work with stakeholders and process analysts has already been done. Thus the business case is not the first step in the process of introducing a new information system.

A good business case is the foundation for establishing goals, buying-in management and staff, being funded, staying on track and measuring to achieve results and project success. The purpose of writing business cases is to provide management with a comprehensive evaluation of a significant issue for their decision, including:

> What needs to be done and why

> When it needs to be done and how

> Who is going to do the work

> How much will it cost, and

> The alternatives and risks.

Why a business case is crucial for KM initiative?

In a study by Lotus Development Corporation to read the pulse of the marketplace in the emerging field of KM and to reach conclusions on best methods for deployment in corporations, C level executives ranked the barriers to KM deployment as shown in the table below.

Not surprisingly, the top two barriers have to do with the lack of a compelling business case and executive understanding and support. The champions of KM within a company must use hard facts, not faith, to secure the resources for KM investment. Financial Analysis and a realistic measurement plan help overcome these barriers to KM deployment.

	1	2	3	4	5	Mean*
Lack of a compelling business case with clearly understood benefits	0	1	1	4	11	4.47
Lack of executive understanding and support for Knowledge Management initiatives	0	1	3	4	8	4.19
Management attention is diverted to other initiatives	0	0	3	7	6	4.19
Cultural resistance to sharing knowledge	0	1	4	7	5	3.94
Lack of work processes that embed Knowledge Management efforts into routine activities	1	1	2	7	5	3.88
Lack of motivational incentives to encourage knowledge sharing in the organization	1	2	2	5	5	3.75

* Responses were on 5-point scale: 1-None, 2-Little, 3-Some, 4-Great, 5-Very Great

Matters for consideration include full identification of implementation and life cycle costs, project sponsorship and ownership, human and organizational costs, intangible and tangible benefits, risk management and the time scale of likely benefits. It is critical that the business case shows that a project is aligned with identified business and organizational needs.

There is no one format to cover all these matters. Business cases will vary according to the maturity of the technology under consideration, the available finances and choice of systems, industry sector pressures, organizational business strategy and direction and the management and decision making culture.

Appropriate criteria for comparative assessment of KM business cases are difficult. The area is relatively new and not yet fully understood. The cost/benefit relationship spans both intangible and tangible matters. Business cases based on financial criteria can be biased towards the short-term quick pay off and may overlook other areas where KM can contribute to business value. In this broader perspective, value is regarded as the sum of the return for the resources deployed, the business impact (including organizational readiness and risk management) and the technology impact.

Adding value needs to be considered not just as a dollar return, but also as a performance return. Increasing value may result from improved performance towards the organization's mission, innovation, reduced cost, increased quality or speed, improved flexibility, or increased staff and customer satisfaction. Benefits come not from the technology, but from the new products and services or the enhanced business processes made available from innovative application of Knowledge management initiative.

An indicative outline of a KM related business case typically includes the following elements:

> A definition and analysis of a business need, threat, opportunity, or problem

> The proposed solution expressed in terms that decision-makers can understand

> A discussion of alternative solutions considered and why they were rejected

> Life cycle cost estimates and estimated budget requirements. This is the total estimated cost for the KM program over the time period involved, including direct and indirect initial costs plus any periodic or continuing costs for operation and maintenance.

> A cost-benefit analysis

> Return on investment (ROI) analysis. A business case is more than a projection of ROI calculations for the project. In fact Return on Investment calculation is only one part of the business case.

➤ An investment risk analysis (including, technical, organizational, and financial risks). Risk analysis is used to identify and assess factors that may jeopardize the success of the project or achievement of desirable goals. This helps define preventive measures to reduce the probability of these factors from occurring and identifying countermeasures to successfully deal with these constraints when they develop.

➤ Proposed project time frames and delivery schedules.

Target Value Drivers For KM

We shall explore some of the target value drivers for KM here. While the most significant barriers to KM reside within the organization, the single most significant driver of KM, competition, comes from without. Competition includes securing a competitive advantage and increasing productivity, and is also seen as a reaction to peer pressure.

Some of the target value drivers (opportunity) are:

> Process and Product Quality – This appeals to firms experimenting with, researching and sharing best practices to increase quality of products, and serve and enhance performance. The KM strategy followed is usually the spread of best practices. Examples are Chevron and Texas Instruments.

> Knowledge-Based Products – This is about generating additional knowledge value in the value chain to deliver higher value, "intelligent" products, and establish uniqueness through a variety of knowledge-based enhancements. Examples are: Arthur Anderson and FEDEX

> Customer Intimacy – Firms that are interested in cultivating an intimate knowledge of customers for the purpose of providing world class service, or to customize and target marketing of products and services by increasing the breadth and depth of customer interactions are appealed by this. Examples are: AMEX and PointCast.

> Innovation – Organizations that seek to expand knowledge required to rapidly generate, produce and market new and innovative products and services are attracted to this value

driver, as it decreases their time to market. Examples are: Hewlett Packard and Microsoft.

> Intellectual Property - These enterprises find that increasing and managing a portfolio of codified and/or patented knowledge that contributes to their financial value. Example: Dow, Monsanto.

In order to delineate the KM value drivers that appeal most to the organization, it is imperative that key role players need to ask themselves in order to list their target value drivers.

This may be in the form of questions such as:

> What is the most important information you need to act on business goals?

> How often do you need it? Where do you get it?

> How do you learn about the competition? Where do you get the information?

> What must you know about your customers to serve them better? Where are your gaps in customer information?

> What corporate information systems do you rely on the most? Why?

Knowledge audit discussed in earlier chapters may be revisited to get more insight.

Before starting on the business case, the project team must have reached a consensus on the framework to be adopted.

A framework helps ensure that the metrics are aligned to the project objectives and the organization's strategic goals. Indeed, this is one of the key findings of the National Performance Review study of Best Practices in Performance Measurements in high-performing organizations, as shown by the following conclusion:

"A conceptual framework is needed for the performance measurement and management system. Every organization needs a clear and cohesive performance measurement framework that is understood by all levels of the organization and that supports objectives and the collection of results."

A framework is a more useful way to convey the measures than merely listing them. A framework can show how actions contribute to overall goals, the mechanisms by which actions produce benefits, the rationale for conducting the KM project, and, in some cases, provide an analytical tool for making investment trade-offs.

There are several ways to construct a framework using organization schemes such as a balanced set of measures, benchmarking, target setting, matrices, hierarchies, flow diagrams, and even management systems. The best choice for the initiative depends on which one, or ones, make it easy for the team to gauge and understand the costs, benefits, relationships, and impacts of the KM processes and measures to each other, and to your business objectives.

Frameworks have been discussed in the preceding modules.

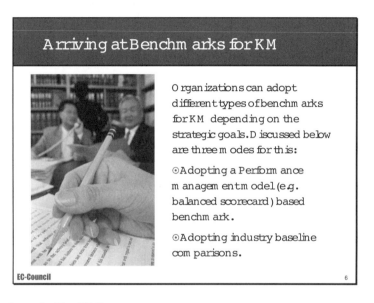

Arriving At Benchmarks For KM

Organizations can adopt different types of benchmarks for KM depending on their strategic goals to be met.

> Adopting a Performance management model (e.g. balanced scorecard) based benchmark.

The goal behind benchmarking is to identify "Best in Class" business processes, which, when implemented, will lead organizations to achieve those strategies (e.g. customer perspective). These initiatives will include conducting benchmarking studies of important knowledge management processes (For e.g. business processes aligned to foster better customer relations) Benchmarking allows organizations to gain a better understanding of the performance and enablers of "best in class" knowledge management process.

> Adopting industry baseline comparisons.

For this purpose, organizations can use industry or "like business" comparisons as baseline. Examples are Average/norm and Best practices. Additionally, organizations can determine performance improvement goals for each measure. These may be quantified, not quantified, tangible or intangible.

Benchmarks for the KM project can be developed using any of the modes stated above. The presentation of these measures in the Business case would add to its credibility. Apart from this, these could later be used as target performance measures to evaluate the KM project success.

Organizations should then set priorities for their Knowledge objectives. This can be short term, medium term and long term basis. This is illustrated in the figure presented below.

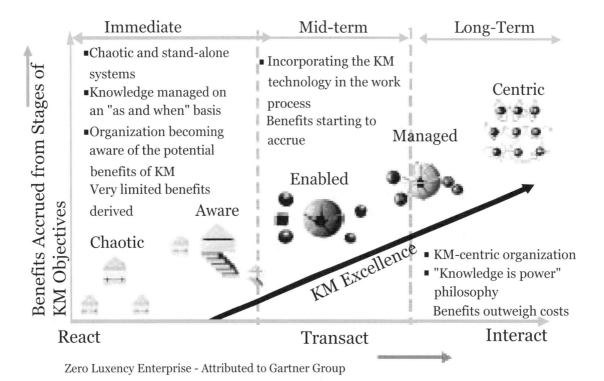

Zero Luxency Enterprise - Attributed to Gartner Group

In essence, to prioritize the KM objectives, organizations must:

> Take a "snapshot" of the current business state

> Develop concrete, measurable goals to improve the current business state

> Develop a set of metrics to measure the outcomes

> Obtain commitment from business leaders to achieve the project goals

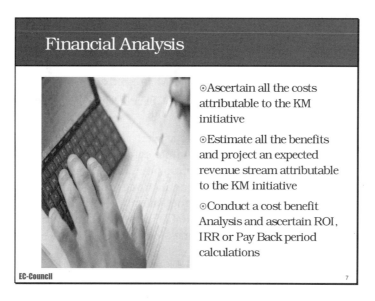

Financial Analysis

⊙ Ascertain all the costs attributable to the KM initiative

⊙ Estimate all the benefits and project an expected revenue stream attributable to the KM initiative

⊙ Conduct a cost benefit Analysis and ascertain ROI, IRR or Pay Back period calculations

EC-Council 7

Basics of Financial Analysis

In conducting financial analysis, some of the steps followed include:

➢ Costs

    o   Identify KM Technology / Infrastructure needs

For this purpose, identify existing technology and reuse or build upon what is present within the organization. Next, organizations must develop a cost profile for each project at hand. The infrastructure needs identified must be validated with key clients and preferred scenarios identified.

    o   Forecast Total Project Cost and Determine Cost of Migration / Transition Plan for KM

This exercise will give the organization an estimate of the capital investment required, migration cost from current system to the proposed system and an overview of the stages involved in the transition plan. This is a critical aspect, as unless costs are quantified, it cannot be matched with the benefits forecasted. The costs of a KM initiative can be calculated, although in some cases certain expenses must be estimated. Where the project is based on in-house development of KM systems, combined with manual document collection and profiling, expense calculations must total hardware acquisition, software development and the ongoing cost of content managers to organize research archives.

There are various sources of cost estimates. These include obtaining quotations from the different contributors to the project. These could include suppliers, contractors, consultants, outsourcers, etc.

➤ Benefits

Identifying and quantifying benefits from a KM project can be a challenging task. This is especially true as organizations may assign varying priorities to the business value that can be derived from these benefits.

Enterprises may use a mixture of quantitative as well as qualitative benefits to evaluate a KM initiative. Tangible benefits from KM can be quite compelling to project in the business case, and are often done so at the cost of overlooking the intangible benefits. Demonstrable bottom-line and top-line benefits make up a strong business case, but addressing the additional benefits here can turn the KM proposition into a persuasive one. Therefore, it is crucial to address both the tangible (quantifiable) as well as intangible (qualitative) benefits when we talk of business benefits in the business case.

➤ Cost Benefit Analysis

One of the most popular methods of quantifying benefits is the estimation of Return on Investment (ROI)

Estimation of ROI for KM systems is particularly difficult for three reasons:

o A sizable proportion of KM benefits are intangible and therefore hard to convert to financial figures. For instance, being able to have intimate insight into the customer behavior is an intangible benefit that a KM solution can bring about. The challenge here is to assign a financial value to this intangible benefit.

   Examples of such benefits:

   ▪ Faster and informed decision making abilities

   ▪ Competitive intelligence as a result of knowledge sharing

o There is a difference in the way of functioning once the KM system is operational. This means that before and after comparison metrics is difficult. For instance, increased efficiency resulting from a portal implementation can result in both cost and timesavings. This can lead to increased productivity as the organization has more resources to allocate to other business challenges. The organization's approach to assessing productivity evolves as business processes evolve and as a result, new metrics emerge within the organization to measure a metric (such as increased productivity) previously non-existent. Therefore, the metric used to assess a particular benefit (such as increase in productivity from Intranet implementation) may itself be out of context once the project goes live. It is therefore difficult to establish a baseline to compare both pre and post implementation results.

o   There are too many other independent variables

Usually, results of the cost benefit analysis are projected in terms of ROI, Internal rate of return (IRR) or the projects payback period.

Measurement Plan

For effective measurement, benefits must be estimated. It is quite challenging to produce detailed financial estimates of the anticipated benefits. However some attempt needs to be made in this respect. The key to producing competent financial estimates is to understand how the business process and practices which will be affected by the IT investment will actually change the way costs are incurred or revenue is generated or assets are used. If this is achieved, then useable figures may be estimated.

Projects whose merits cannot be measured and projected to estimate the returns on the capital invested seldom find management sponsorship. It is here that a convincing business case can make all the difference.

The business case is particularly important to a KM initiative because:

➤ It is crucial for securing the essential funds for the project.

➤ It is important to gain senior management appreciation and support, without which, internalization of the KM program (which will effect changes in the organization's culture, processes and business practices) is a daunting task.

KM provides two major benefits to an organization:

➢ Improving the organization's performance through increased effectiveness, productivity, quality, and innovation.

➢ Increasing the financial value of the organization by treating people's knowledge as an asset similar to traditional assets like inventory and capital facilities. Each of these benefits has distinct qualities that can be measured, such as the effectiveness of sharing and the intrinsic value of knowledge assets.

Measurements for KM initiatives can be quantitative or qualitative and, in general, a measurement program should include both types of measures.

Quantitative measures provide hard data to evaluate performance between points (such as last month to this month) or to spot trends. Qualitative measures provide context and meaning for quantitative measures. When it is difficult to capture meaningful quantitative measures (such as the value to the individual for being a member of a community of practice), qualitative measures (such as a story from a member about how the community helped him solve a critical problem) can have as much or more impact on stakeholders.

A closely related concept to the need for qualitative measures is the notion of tangible and intangible benefits. A tangible benefit is concrete and can have a direct measurement of its value. In contrast, an intangible benefit cannot be definitively described by a quantitative value. For example, the value of a machine can be computed from its production rate compared to its operating costs while the value of a company's brand image to its profitability cannot be easily computed. Quantitative measures can provide an indirect although uncertain indication of intangible value.

o It is difficult to account for the know-how or tacit knowledge in a person's head, or in the collective heads of the organization. In addition, unlike physical assets, which are depleted when they are used, intellectual assets actually grow when they are used. In many respects, intellectual assets have no value until they are re-used or applied in new situations, demonstrating a new economic law of increasing returns.

A measurement plan for the knowledge management project should take the following factors into consideration.

➢ Strive for Appropriate Level of Precision

➢ Perform Quantitative and Qualitative Analysis

➢ Measure Participation and Business Impact

➢ Update priorities and commitments from stakeholders. The next slide shows various phases of KM, so that priorities for each phase may be identified.

   o Set goals those are measurable and tied to the Strategic "Do Wells"

   o Set goals those are outcome or action oriented

- Leverage information to increase new product sales

- Provide real time information to reduce order-processing time

- Improve customer service ratings by providing real time historical service knowledge to CSRs

Example of a Balanced Scorecard

	Objectives	CSF's	Metrics
Financial	Demonstrate clear value with respect to the business strategy	Tangible, quantifiable examples of reductions in cycle time and improvements in discoveries	•Metrics derived from 'serious anecdotes': –# of anecdotes –$ Value of anecdotes –Cycle time improvements
Participant	Gain frequent and sustained adoption of KnowledgeMail	•High vol. of needs that can't be met through existing channels •Critical mass of expertise •High quality of responses (timing, usefulness) vs. alt. search methods •Low impact on workload	# Searches per user/week •% of participants that are active •Avg # of public terms/user •% Searches with experts •Avg expert response time •Usefulness rating •% of users who say 'don't take- it-away' at the end of the pilot
Operations	Provide reliable, easy-to-use technology that can easily be incorporated into work processes	•Training of all participants •Effective help resources •Persistent, clear communications •Active, sustained mgt support •Incorporation of sharing into	•Usability/friendliness rating •# of Help Desk calls/week

Capabilities & Culture	Ensure proper participant training and pilot execution	performance evaluations	• % of participants trained • % Pilot milestones met

Issues to avoid while deciding on metrics

- o   Using too many metrics

- o   Delayed and risky reward ties

- o   Choosing metrics that are hard to control

- o   Choosing metrics that are hard to focus on

- o   Choosing metrics that measure the hard results and neglect the "soft stuff"

- o   Choosing metrics that are too rear-view oriented

- o   Measuring the wrong things

To summarize, feedback, funding, follow-on, and focus provide guidance concerning why we must measure. These words lead to answers to such questions as: Are we on the right track? Are we doing something wrong or measuring the wrong thing? How does return on this investment compare to other infrastructure investments? Are we focused on the right thing? What behaviors or results are the most important to us? Should we focus on qualitative or quantitative measures? Measurement programs should be viewed as tools to provide feedback, as the organization becomes more knowledge centric.

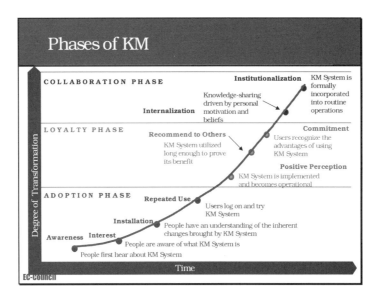

Phases of a KM Project

The above figure shows the different phases of the KM program. This is discussed here, as it will help the readers in visualizing what aspects of KM phases need to be addressed as part of the whole picture. This can help while presenting the business case, in alignment with the stakeholders needs. They can be listed as:

- Adoption Phase
    - Awareness - People first hear about KM System
    - Interest - People are aware of what KM System is
    - Installation - People have an understanding of the inherent changes brought by KM System
    - Repeated uses - Users log on and try KM System
- Loyalty Phase
    - Positive Perception - KM System is implemented and becomes operational
    - Recommended to others - KM System utilized long enough to prove its benefit
    - Commitment - Users recognize the advantages of using KM System
- Collaboration Phase
    - Internalization - Knowledge-sharing driven by personal motivation and beliefs

o   Institutionalization - KM System is formally incorporated into routine operations

The following graph illustrates Different Measures for Different Stages of the Life cycle of the project.

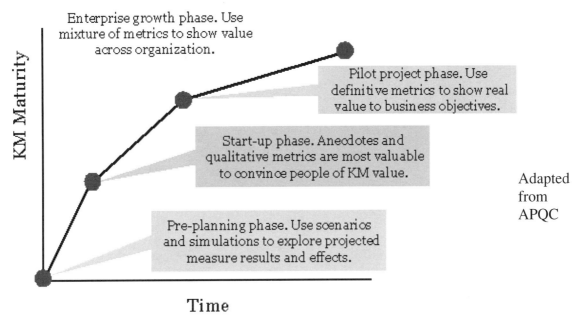

Enterprise growth phase. Use mixture of metrics to show value across organization.

Pilot project phase. Use definitive metrics to show real value to business objectives.

Start-up phase. Anecdotes and qualitative metrics are most valuable to convince people of KM value.

Pre-planning phase. Use scenarios and simulations to explore projected measure results and effects.

Adapted from APQC

A KM initiative also has a lifecycle where it matures from an early start-up phase to a pilot project phase and then to growth and expansion phase.

The American Productivity and Quality Center produced a study based on a consortium of companies on *Measurement for Knowledge Management*. This study identifies and discusses how the need for metrics differs through the stages. The goals of the early phase are to generate interest and support for KM, which creates a higher value on measures that convince people KM is worthwhile, such as anecdotes, comparisons to other organizations, and levels of funding and participation.

The pilot project phase concentrates on developing evidence of success and Lessons Learned that can be transferred to other initiatives. Thus, more definitive measures are needed, such as changes in business costs (e.g. reduced support and resources), cultural changes (e.g. increased sharing among groups), and the currency and usage of collected knowledge bases.

For the final stage, KM is being institutionalized across the corporation, and therefore measures that reflect enterprise wide benefits are needed. These include KM proficiency gauged against

Best Practices, formal KM elements in performance evaluations, and sophisticated capital valuation calculations.

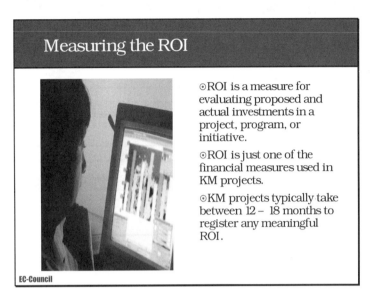

ROI

The estimation of ROI is given special mention here, as most often, this aspect is widely projected by software vendors. The calculations involved in arriving at their respective ROI differ. The organization needs to arrive at its own estimation methods, projecting the benefits to be realized. The scope of discussion here is to emphasize the importance of backing each benefit or measurement with reliable and contextual facts pertaining to the organization in order to convince the stakeholders.

ROI is a measure for evaluating proposed and actual investments in a project, program, or initiative. ROI provides a quantitative method of demonstrating the value of a project by comparing the costs associated with current business practices, with the cost associated with the new practice. For example, reduction in operating costs or in time spent performing a task can be calculated as cost savings.

Performance measures for KM build on the experience in accounting and management for other types of intangible initiatives such as learning and training. Metrics are particularly important to KM because a ROI for KM often takes significant time to appear. Putting a KM program into effect will impact other business processes as the organization learns to use and leverage the new KM capabilities. Many of the organizational changes will be intangible characteristics cannot easily be quantified. This can take 18 to 36 months in some cases. According to the Gartner Group, "in no case should a KM program (at the enterprise level) be expected to show ROI in less than 12 months."

Summary	
Project:	**Microsoft SharePoint**
Annual Return On Investment (ROI)	**409%**
Payback Period (Years)	**0.25**
Net Present Value (NPV)	**332,358**
Average Yearly Cost of Ownership	**212,667**

Annual Benefits	Initial	Year 1	Year 2	Year 3
Direct	0	434,500	442,900	451,468
Indirect	0	70,000	70,000	70,000
Total Benefits Per Period	0	504,500	512,900	521,468

Depreciation Schedule	Initial	Year 1	Year 2	Year 3
Software	0	0	0	0
Hardware	0	0	0	0
Total Per Period	0	0	0	0

Expensed Costs	Initial	Year 1	Year 2	Year 3
Software	60,000	112,000	112,000	112,000
Hardware	0	4,000	4,000	4,000
Consulting	20,000	0	0	0
Personnel	0	70,000	70,000	70,000
Training	0	0	0	0
Other	0	0	0	0
Total Per Period	80,000	186,000	186,000	186,000

Financial Analysis	Results	Year 1	Year 2	Year 3
Net cash flow before taxes		318,500	326,900	335,468
Net cash flow after taxes		159,250	163,450	167,734
Annual ROI - direct and indirect benefits		398%	403%	**409%**
Annual ROI - direct benefits only		311%	316%	321%
Net Present Value (NPV)		98,478	222,070	**332,358**
Payback (Years)	0.25			
Average Cost of Ownership (TCO/Years		266,000	226,000	212,667
3-Year Cumulative ROI	931%			
3-Year IRR	397%			

Basic Financial Assumptions	
All Government Taxes	50%
Discount Rate	15%

(Exhibit: ROI calculation for Microsoft SharePoint Portal)

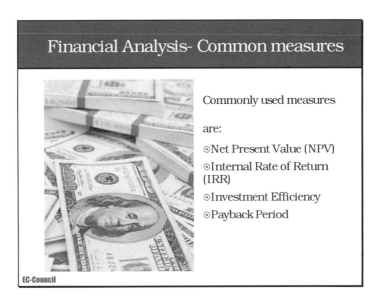

Financial Analysis- Common measures

Commonly used measures are:

- Net Present Value (NPV)
- Internal Rate of Return (IRR)
- Investment Efficiency
- Payback Period

EC-Council

Other Financial Analysis Methods

➢ Net Present Value (NPV) - Amount of money whose compound interest, if invested at a constant interest rate, would produce a cash flow of equivalent value to the project cash flow.

➢ Internal Rate of Return (IRR) - The interest rate received (and paid) for a series of positive and negative cash flows. It is the discount rate at which the Present Worth of the cash flow stream is equal to zero.

➢ Investment Efficiency - Attempts to place the Present Worth of a project into the context of the size of the initial investment.

➢ Payback - Refers to the amount of time that must pass before the cumulative cash flow of the project becomes positive.

		measure	PW	IRR	NPV	PVR	Payback	ROM
Projected Benefits								
Tangible								
Shared								
Intangible								
Projected Costs								
Tangible								

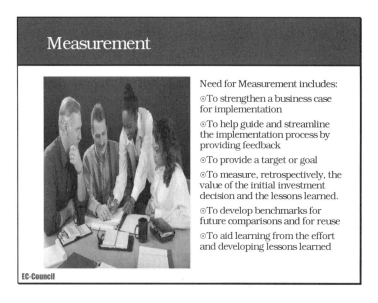

Role Of Measurement In Business Case

The reasons behind measurement can be enumerated as:

- ➢ To strengthen a business case for implementation
- ➢ To help guide and streamline the implementation process by providing feedback
- ➢ To provide a target or goal
- ➢ To measure, retrospectively, the value of the initial investment decision and the lessons learned.
- ➢ To develop benchmarks for future comparisons and for reuse
- ➢ To aid learning from the effort and developing lessons learned

We have seen that there are both tangible and intangible benefits. For instance, some of the benefits can be listed as:

- ➢ Increase productivity by minimizing "reinventing the wheel"
- ➢ Leverage scale and expertise across the firm, amidst rapid growth or downsizing
- ➢ Improve the ability to attract, retain, and develop people
- ➢ Improve management of risk
- ➢ Increase client satisfaction

➢ Improve quality and speed of technical decisions about product development

➢ Reduce product/business development cycles

➢ Enhance learning opportunities

➢ Identify new ways to create value for employees, the enterprise, and shareholders

Common measures: These measures can be used for all KM initiatives:

Outcome
- Time, money, or personnel time saved as a result of implementing initiative
- Percentage of successful programs compared to those before KM implementation

Output
- Usefulness survey where users evaluate how useful the initiative has been in helping them accomplish their objectives
- Usage anecdotes where users describe (in quantitative terms) how the initiative has contributed to business objectives

System
- *Latency (response times)*
- *Number of downloads*
- *Number of site accesses*
- *Dwell time per page or section*
- *Usability survey*
- *Frequency of use*
- *Navigation path analysis*
- *Number of help desk calls*
- *Number of users*
- *Frequency of use*
- *Percentage of total employees using system*

KM Initiative	**Key System Measures**		**Key Outcome Measures**
Best Practice Directory	• Number of downloads • Dwell time • Usability survey • Number of users • Total number of contributions • Contribution rate over time	• Usefulness survey • Anecdotes • User ratings of contribution value	• Time, money, personnel time saved by implementing best practice • Number of groups certified in the use of the best practice • Rate of change in operating costs
Lessons Learned Database	• Number of downloads • Dwell time • Usability survey • Number of users • Total number of contributions • Contribution rate over time	• Time to solve problem • Usefulness survey • Anecdotes • User ratings of contribution value	• Time, money, personnel time saved by applying lessons learned from others • Rate of change in operating costs
Communities of Practice or Special Interest Groups	• Number of contributions • Frequency of update • Number of members • Ratio of the number of members to the number of contributors (conversion rate)		• Savings and/or improvement in organizational quality and efficiency • Captured organizational memory • Attrition rate of community members versus non-member cohort

Expert or Expertise Directory	• Number of site accesses • Frequency of use • Number of contributions • Contribution/update rate over time • Navigation path analysis • Number of help desk calls	• Time to solve problem • Number of problems solved • Time to find expert	• Savings and/or improvement in organizational quality and efficiency • Time, money, or personnel time saved by leveraging expert's knowledge or expertise knowledge base
Portal	• Searching precision and recall • Dwell time • Latency • Usability survey	• Common awareness within teams • Time spent "gathering information" • Time spent "analyzing" information	• Time, money, or personnel time saved as a result of portal use • Reduced training time or learning curve as a result of single access to multiple information sources • Customer satisfaction (based on value of self service or improved ability for employees to respond to customer needs
Lead Tracking System	• Number of contributions • Frequency of update • Number of users • Frequency of use • Navigation path analysis	• Number of successful leads • Number of new customers and value from these customers • Value of new work from existing customers • Proposal response times • Proposal "win" rates • Percentage of business developers who report finding value in the use of the system	• Revenue and overhead costs • Customer demographics • Cost and time to produce proposals • Alignment of programs with strategic plans

Collaborative Systems	• Latency during collaborative design process • Number of users • Number of patents/trademarks produced • Number of articles published plus number of conference presentations per employee	• Number of projects collaborated on • Time lost due to program delays • Number of new products developed • Value of sales from products created in the last 3-5 years (a measure of innovation) • Average learning curve/employee • Proposal response times • Proposal "win" rates	• Reduced cost of product development, acquisition, and/or maintenance • Reduction in the number of program delays • Faster response to proposals • Reduced learning curve for new employees
Yellow Pages	• Number of users • Frequency of use • Latency • Searching precision and recall	• Time to find people • Time to solve problem	• Time, money, or personnel time saved as a result of yellow pages use • Savings and/or improvement in organizational quality and efficiency
e-Learning Systems	• Latency • Number of users • Number of courses taken/user	• Training costs	• Savings and/or improvement in organizational quality and efficiency • Improved employee satisfaction • Reduced cost of training • Reduced learning curve for new employees

(Above: Summary of Key Performance Measures / Indicators (KPIs) Source: DONCIO Publication)

Summary

- A business is critical in gaining executive sponsorship and management endorsement
- Financial Analysis as represented by ROI, IRR, NPV quantify business returns
- Measurement is critical to rationalization of the business case
- Stakeholders and a suitable knowledge framework should be identified before starting the business case
- Measurement should collaborate with various phases of KM project cycle.

EC-Council

Summary

 Recap

➢ A business is critical in gaining executive sponsorship and management endorsement

➢ Financial Analysis as represented by ROI, IRR, NPV quantify business returns

➢ Measurement is critical to rationalization of the business case

➢ Stakeholders and a suitable knowledge framework should be identified before starting the business case

➢ Measurement should collaborate with various phases of KM project cycle.

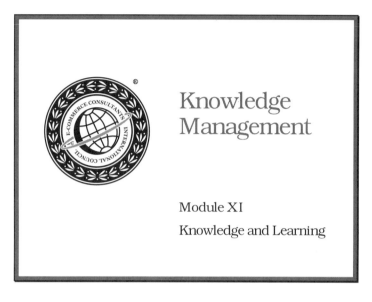

Knowledge
Management

Module XI

Knowledge and Learning

Knowledge Management (KM)

Module XI: Multiple Choice Questions

Exam 212-69 Certified e-Business Associate

Multiple Choice Questions

Module 1

1. The knowledge management solutions and strategies encompass which of the following critical elements:
   a. People, Processes and Technology.
   b. Practices and Technology
   c. Policies, People and Practices
   d. People, Practices and Place

2. Which of the following is a stated objective of any knowledge management initiative?

   a. Manage knowledge workers
   b. Manage knowledge as an asset
   c. Store knowledge
   d. Use Knowledge

3. Intellectual Capital in the context of knowledge management

   a. Includes human capital, and social capital, but excludes customer capital, and organizational capital
   b. Includes human capital, and social capital, and organizational capital but excludes customer capital
   c. Includes human capital, social capital, organizational capital and customer capital
   d. Includes human capital, and social capital, and customer capital but excludes organizational capital

4. The individual and collective capabilities of the employees of the organization, including their knowledge, skills, abilities, competencies, education, and experience form:

   a. Human Capital
   b. Social capital
   c. Organizational Capital
   d. Customer Capital

5. The informal networks, relationships, trust, and shared understanding between individuals in organizations amount to:

   a. Human Capital
   b. Social capital
   c. Organizational Capital
   d. Customer Capital

6. Property, patents, copyrights, business processes, systems, codified policies and procedures, etc. are examples of:

    a. Human Capital
    b. Social capital
    c. Structural/Enterprise Capital
    d. Customer Capital

7. A structured attempt to describe all the parts of a field or subject by way of representing the subject with classifications including all terms related to the subject, the meaning of terms, and their interrelationships is called:

    a. Taxonomy
    b. Anatomy
    c. Ontology
    d. Anthology

8. Classification schemes, which attempt to describe all the parts of a field or subject; generally as a tree structure, but not showing interrelationships.

    a. Taxonomy
    b. Anatomy
    c. Ontology
    d. Anthology

9. Early KM initiatives (pre-1995) focused on:

    a. The appropriate structuring and flow of information to decision makers
    b. Customer satisfaction and service standards that were considered important to the firm
    c. Achieving effective Performance and is people-centric
    d. The improvement of competitiveness and functional effectiveness

10. The current state of knowledge management is oriented towards:

    a. The appropriate structuring and flow of information to decision makers
    b. Customer satisfaction and service standards that were considered important to the firm
    c. Achieving effective Performance and is people-centric
    d. The improvement of processes via re engineering

Module 2

1. Knowledge Management initiatives based themselves on the premise of:

   a. Continual learning, which organizational process for creating new knowledge to meet persistent change.

   b. Continual learning, which is an individual process for creating new knowledge to meet persistent change

   c. Continual learning, which is both an individual and organizational process for creating new knowledge to meet persistent change

   d. Individual learning process for creating new knowledge to meet persistent change

2. Data are:

   a. Statements about reality or about other data.

   b. Statements about reality or about other data placed in a context.

   c. Statements about reality or about other data and subjective in nature

   d. Statements about reality or about other data organized to certain preferences

3. Data become information:

   a. When they are organized according to certain preferences.

   b. When they are placed in a context

   c. When they are organized according to certain preferences and placed in a context, which defines their meaning and relevance

   d. When they are processed to gather more data

4. Data are:

   a. Purely *objective* – they do not depend on their user.

   b. *Objective-subjective*, in the sense that it is described in an objective way (texts, pictures, etc.) but its meaning is subjective, depending on its user.

   c. Purely *subjective* – each person experiences something in a different way.

   d. *Subjective-objective*, in the sense that it is a purely personal characteristic, but everybody may examine its outcome.

5. Information is:

   a. Purely *objective* – they do not depend on their user.

   b. *Objective-subjective*, in the sense that it is described in an objective way (texts, pictures, etc.) but its meaning is subjective, depending on its user.

   c. Purely *subjective* – each person experiences something in a different way.

d. *Subjective-objective*, in the sense that it is a purely personal characteristic, but everybody may examine its outcome.

6. Knowledge is

a. Purely *objective* – they do not depend on their user.
b. *Objective-subjective*, in the sense that it is described in an objective way (texts, pictures, etc.) but its meaning is subjective, depending on its user.
c. Purely *subjective* – each person experiences something in a different way.
d. *Subjective-objective*, in the sense that it is a purely personal characteristic, but everybody may examine its outcome.

7. Competency is:

a. Purely *objective* – they do not depend on their user.
b. *Objective-subjective*, in the sense that it is described in an objective way (texts, pictures, etc.) but its meaning is subjective, depending on its user.
c. Purely *subjective* – each person experiences something in a different way.
d. *Subjective-objective*, in the sense that it is a purely personal characteristic, but everybody may examine its outcome.

8. Tacit knowledge is represented by:

a. Policies, procedures, instructions, standards and results, readily communicated, often through written documentation.
b. Individual or group experience and expertise, is implicit and mostly documented.
c. Individual or group experience and expertise, is implicit and rarely documented.
d. Policies, procedures, instructions, standards and results, communicated, though not documented.

9. Explicit knowledge is represented by:

a. Policies, procedures, instructions, standards and results, readily communicated, often through written documentation.
b. Individual or group experience and expertise, is implicit and mostly documented.
c. Individual or group experience and expertise, is implicit and rarely documented.
d. Policies, procedures, instructions, standards and results, communicated, though not documented.

10. Tacit-to-Tacit knowledge transfer happens by way of which of the following knowledge creation mode?

a. Externalization
b. Socialization
c. Combination
d. Internalization

Module 3

1. External organizational learning is:

   a. Learning concepts external to the organization
   b. Fostered through individual learning
   c. "Inter-organizational learning", which involves learning from outside - other organizations.
   d. "Intra-organizational learning", which involves learning from other locations or departments of the organization.

2. Personal Mastery is:

   a. A discipline of aspiration that involves formulating a coherent picture of the results people most desire to gain as individuals (their personal vision), alongside a realistic assessment of the current state of their lives today (their current reality).
   b. A discipline of reflection and inquiry skills that is focused around developing awareness of the attitudes and perceptions that influence thought and interaction. By continually reflecting upon, talking about, and reconsidering these internal pictures of the world, people can gain more capability in governing their actions and decisions
   c. A collective discipline that establishes a focus on mutual purpose. People learn to nourish a sense of commitment in a group or organization by developing shared images of the future they seek to create, and the principles and guiding practices by which they hope to get there.
   d. A discipline of group interaction. Through techniques like dialogue and skillful discussion, teams transform their collective thinking, learning to mobilize their energies and actions to achieve common goals, and drawing forth an intelligence and ability greater than the sum of individual members' talents.

3. Mental Models is:

   a. A discipline of aspiration that involves formulating a coherent picture of the results people most desire to gain as individuals (their personal vision), alongside a realistic assessment of the current state of their lives today (their current reality).
   b. A discipline of reflection and inquiry skills that is focused around developing awareness of the attitudes and perceptions that influence thought and interaction. By continually reflecting upon, talking about, and reconsidering these internal pictures of the world, people can gain more capability in governing their actions and decisions
   c. A collective discipline that establishes a focus on mutual purpose. People learn to nourish a sense of commitment in a group or organization by developing shared images of the future they seek to create, and the principles and guiding practices by which they hope to get there.
   d. A discipline, people learn to better understand interdependency and change, and thereby to deal more effectively with the forces that shape the consequences of our actions.

4. Shared Vision is:

   a. A discipline of reflection and inquiry skills that is focused around developing awareness of the attitudes and perceptions that influence thought and interaction. By continually reflecting upon, talking about, and reconsidering these internal pictures of the world, people can gain more capability in governing their actions and decisions
   b. A collective discipline that establishes a focus on mutual purpose. People learn to nourish a sense of commitment in a group or organization by developing shared images of the future they seek to create, and the principles and guiding practices by which they hope to get there.
   c. A discipline of group interaction. Through techniques like dialogue and skillful discussion, teams transform their collective thinking, learning to mobilize their energies and actions to achieve common goals, and drawing forth an intelligence and ability greater than the sum of individual members' talents.
   d. A discipline, people learn to better understand interdependency and change, and thereby to deal more effectively with the forces that shape the consequences of our actions.

5. Team Learning is:

   a. A discipline of aspiration that involves formulating a coherent picture of the results people most desire to gain as individuals (their personal vision), alongside a realistic assessment of the current state of their lives today (their current reality).
   b. A collective discipline that establishes a focus on mutual purpose. People learn to nourish a sense of commitment in a group or organization by developing shared images of the future they seek to create, and the principles and guiding practices by which they hope to get there.
   c. A discipline of group interaction. Through techniques like dialogue and skillful discussion, teams transform their collective thinking, learning to mobilize their energies and actions to achieve common goals, and drawing forth an intelligence and ability greater than the sum of individual members' talents.
   d. A discipline, people learn to better understand interdependency and change, and thereby to deal more effectively with the forces that shape the consequences of our actions.

6. Systems Thinking is:

   a. A discipline of aspiration that involves formulating a coherent picture of the results people most desire to gain as individuals (their personal vision), alongside a realistic assessment of the current state of their lives today (their current reality).
   b. A discipline of reflection and inquiry skills that is focused around developing awareness of the attitudes and perceptions that influence thought and interaction. By continually reflecting upon, talking about, and reconsidering these internal pictures of the world, people can gain more capability in governing their actions and decisions

c. A discipline of group interaction. Through techniques like dialogue and skillful discussion, teams transform their collective thinking, learning to mobilize their energies and actions to achieve common goals, and drawing forth an intelligence and ability greater than the sum of individual members' talents.

d. A discipline, people learn to better understand interdependency and change, and thereby to deal more effectively with the forces that shape the consequences of our actions.

7. The primary difference between individual and organizational learning is that:

a. Organizational learning involves an additional phase, dissemination
b. Individual learning involves an additional phase, dissemination
c. Organizational learning involves knowledge creation
d. Organizational learning does not involve knowledge dissemination

8. Human capital can be traced to:

a. Training, incentives and education at the infrastructure level.
b. Integrated product teams at the infrastructure level, enabling connectivity at the information technology level, which in turn fosters relationships at the information management level.
c. Physical assets at the infrastructure level that facilitates the use of hardware and software at the information technology level.
d. Informational assets that facilitates organizational functioning

9. Social capital can be traced back to:

a. Training, incentives and education at the infrastructure level.
b. Integrated product teams at the infrastructure level, enabling connectivity at the information technology level, which in turn fosters relationships at the information management level.
c. Physical assets at the infrastructure level that facilitates the use of hardware and software at the information technology level.
d. Informational assets that facilitates organizational functioning

10. Corporate capital can be traced back to:

a. Training, incentives and education at the infrastructure level.
b. Integrated product teams at the infrastructure level, enabling connectivity at the information technology level, which in turn fosters relationships at the information management level.
c. Physical assets at the infrastructure level that facilitates the use of hardware and software at the information technology level.
d. Informational assets that facilitates organizational functioning

Module 4

1. Transactive Memory (TM) systems are:

    a. Transactional memory systems that store knowledge
    b. Knowledge repositories that provide individuals with access to more knowledge than any one individual could possibly possess alone.
    c. Knowledge retrieval systems that provide organizational knowledge access.
    d. Knowledge repositories that store transactional information.

2. Expertise recognition, retrieval coordination, directory updating, information allocation are processes that constitute:

    a. Operative Memory Systems
    b. Transactive Memory systems
    c. Knowledge repositories
    d. Transactional Memory systems

3. In the context of learning organizations, organizational cultures that exhibit 'high sociability and low solidarity' is termed to have a:

    a. Networked culture
    b. Mercenary culture
    c. Fragmented culture
    d. Communal culture

4. In the context of learning organizations, organizational cultures that exhibit 'low sociability and high solidarity' is termed to have a:

    a. Networked culture
    b. Mercenary culture
    c. Fragmented culture
    d. Communal culture

5. In the context of learning organizations, organizational cultures that exhibit 'low sociability and low solidarity' is termed to have a:

    a. Networked culture
    b. Mercenary culture
    c. Fragmented culture
    d. Communal culture

6. In the context of learning organizations, organizational cultures that exhibit 'high sociability and high solidarity' is termed to have a:

    a. Networked culture
    b. Mercenary culture
    c. Fragmented culture
    d. Communal culture

7. Knowledge storage, Dissemination and Knowledge retrieval are the issues dealt by which aspect of Knowledge management

    a. Technology
    b. Culture
    c. People
    d. Places

8. Attributes such as risk tolerance, degree of hierarchy, reward structure, collaboration, values, and innovation vs. adaptation are measured prior to a KM initiative using:

    a. Culture audit
    b. Technology audit
    c. Knowledge audit
    d. Systems audit

9. This person is in charge of assembling all the knowledge components to make something worthwhile. Helps knowledge creators realize their dreams. In KM jargon, he is a:

    a. Knowledge packager
    b. Knowledge visualizer
    c. Knowledge activist
    d. Knowledge seeker

10. A person committed to a cause and will marshal the knowledge needed to support the case. Can also be a knowledge maverick, often questioning the status quo and raising doubts in others about the efficacy of their hard-won knowledge. Initiates change. In KM jargon, he is a:

    a. Knowledge packager
    b. Knowledge visualizer
    c. Knowledge activist
    d. Knowledge seeker

Module 5

1. A private computer network based on the communication standards of the Internet, that only the members of an organization could see is popularly known as:

   a. LAN
   b. WAN
   c. Intranet
   d. Extranet

2. Systems with the goal of suggesting names of persons who have knowledge in a particular area is termed as:

   a. Decision ware
   b. Expertise location systems
   c. People search systems
   d. Search engines

3. A _____ organizes and integrates collective knowledge and communications and in the process makes such knowledge and communications accessible and shareable.

   a. Search Engine
   b. Decision ware
   c. Portal
   d. Internet

4. Understanding content domain, Content components, A metadata based framework, etc are core concepts behind:

   a. Document content management
   b. Knowledge Management
   c. Content management
   d. Information Content Management

5. A commonly used term that describes the automation of internal business operations, tasks, and transactions that simplify and streamline current business processes:

   a. Workflow systems
   b. Video communications systems
   c. Collaborative writing systems
   d. Chat systems

6. The strategic goal of DIM is to:

   a. Reformat the unstructured data within an organization.
   b. Reformat the paper form of unstructured data within an organization.
   c. Reformat the structured data within an organization.
   d. Reformat the unstructured knowledge within an organization.

7. The class of technology designed to facilitate the work of groups which may be used to communicate, cooperate, coordinate, solve problems, compete, or negotiate is popularly called:

   a. Shareware
   b. Netware
   c. Groupware
   d. Know ware

8. Groupware technologies where in the users are working together at the same time is termed:

   a. Synchronous groupware
   b. Workflow systems
   c. Adaptive synchronous groupware
   d. Asynchronous groupware

9. Which of the following is an example of Asynchronous Groupware:

   a. Shared whiteboards
   b. Video communications systems
   c. Chat systems
   d. Workflow systems

10. Which of the following is an example of Synchronous Groupware

   a. Group calendars
   b. Hypertext
   c. Chat systems
   d. Collaborative writing systems

Module 6

1. _____ frameworks provide direction on the types of knowledge management procedures without providing specific details of how those procedures can/should be accomplished.

   a. Prescriptive
   b. Distinctive
   c. Descriptive
   d. Restrictive

2. _____ frameworks characterize knowledge management and identify attributes of knowledge management important for their influence on the success or failure of knowledge management initiatives.

   a. Prescriptive
   b. Distinctive
   c. Descriptive
   d. Restrictive

3. Depth of a KM technology is usually defined as its coverage of four classes of KM functionality. These classes are:

   a. Semantic, collaborative, visualization and scale.
   b. Semantic, distributive, visualization and scale
   c. Semantic, distributive, analytical and scale
   d. Semantic, distributive, analytical and collaborative

4. The storage and retrieval of organizational knowledge, which is also defined as " the means and events that influence present organizational activities" is referred to as:

   a. Knowledge Management
   b. Organizational memory
   c. Information management
   d. Decision support

5. To integrate information across organizational boundaries and to control current activities and thus avoid past mistakes are the principal goals of :

   a. Knowledge Management
   b. Organizational memory
   c. Information management
   d. Decision support

6. Databases, expert systems and the likes that are characterized by their ease of search ability due to availability of search aids like indexes, keywords, controlled vocabulary and so forth in the KM parlance form:

   a. Structured repositories
   b. Semi Structured repositories
   c. Knowledge bases
   d. Unstructured repositories

7. In most organizations knowledge resides in the form of project reports, sales-call notes and other sources. In KM parlance, these are referred to as:

   a. Structured repositories
   b. Semi Structured repositories
   c. Knowledge bases
   d. Unstructured repositories

8. The individual who has the knowledge transfers expertise through person-to-person contacts. This is basically he tactic-to-tactic mode of knowledge transfer. The model that propounds this concept is:

   a. Knowledge repository model
   b. Knowledge network model
   c. Structured repository model
   d. Unstructured repository model

9. The model that propounds that knowledge contribution and use follows a two-step transfer procedure of person-to-repository and repository-to-person is the:

   a. Knowledge repository model
   b. Knowledge network model
   c. Structured repository model
   d. Unstructured repository model

10. The purpose of _____ is to capture and express expertise in a form that can be easily accessed and used by others who need the know-how in performance of their tasks.

    a. Knowledge transfer
    b. Knowledge management
    c. Knowledge Harvesting
    d. Knowledge acquisition

Module 7

1. Knowledge that is commonly shared by all members of an industry, and offers no competitive value as per Zack's work relating to building knowledge strategy is:

   a. Core Knowledge
   b. Advanced Knowledge
   c. Innovative knowledge
   d. Out-dated knowledge

2. Knowledge that can be differentiated by the members of an industry, and offers competitive value, as per Zack's work relating to building knowledge strategy is:

   a. Core Knowledge
   b. Advanced Knowledge
   c. Innovative knowledge
   d. Out-dated knowledge

3. Knowledge that allows a firm to lead its industry by significantly differentiating from its competitors, as per Zack's work relating to building knowledge strategy is:

   a. Core Knowledge
   b. Advanced Knowledge
   c. Innovative knowledge
   d. Out-dated knowledge

4. Knowledge Transfer strategy involving transfer of knowledge from people to documents termed as:

   a. Personalization
   b. Codification
   c. Documentation
   d. Content management

5. _____ strategy is seen in companies that provide highly customized solutions to unique problems, and knowledge is shared mainly through person-to-person contacts

   a. Personalization
   b. Codification
   c. Documentation
   d. Content management

6. Knowledge is often in a static and buried form that makes it difficult to extract or reformulate This key attribute which needs to be factored into KM practices is referred to as:

   a. Subjectivity
   b. Transferability
   c. Embedded ness
   d. Perish ability

7. The value of knowledge increases and not decreases when shared. This key attribute which needs to be factored into KM practices is referred to as:

   a. Subjectivity
   b. Transferability
   c. Embedded ness
   d. Self-reinforcement

8. Knowledge can be extracted and transferred to other contexts. This key attribute which needs to be factored into KM practices is referred to as:

   a. Subjectivity
   b. Transferability
   c. Embedded ness
   d. Self-reinforcement

9. Knowledge can develop unpredictably in a process. This key attribute which needs to be factored into KM practices is referred to as:

   a. Subjectivity
   b. Transferability
   c. Spontaneity
   d. Self-reinforcement

10. Context and individual background shape the interpretation of knowledge. This key attribute which needs to be factored into KM practices is referred to as:

    a. Subjectivity
    b. Transferability
    c. Spontaneity
    d. Self-reinforcement

Module 8

1. In the knowledge life cycle the stage where the knowledge is first generated / absorbed by any organizational unit is:

   a. Knowledge Use
   b. Knowledge Reuse
   c. Knowledge Sharing / Dissemination
   d. Knowledge Acquisition / Updation

2. In the knowledge life cycle the stage where the knowledge is packaged in a form fit for use, and delivered to the point of use, at the time of Knowledge Use is referred as:

   a. Knowledge Use
   b. Knowledge Reuse
   c. Knowledge Sharing / Dissemination
   d. Knowledge Acquisition / Updation

3. In the knowledge life cycle the stage where the knowledge / expertise shared is actually put to use for performing a task is termed as:

   a. Knowledge Use
   b. Knowledge Reuse
   c. Knowledge Sharing / Dissemination
   d. Knowledge Acquisition / Updation

4. A readiness assessment helps the organization to:

   a. Evaluate the resource requirements in order to undertake a knowledge management initiative.
   b. Assess its capability to meet the basic requirements in order to undertake a knowledge management initiative.
   c. Evaluate the time requirements for a knowledge management initiative.
   d. List the knowledge requirements in order to undertake a knowledge management initiative.

5. The company's knowledge environment, its knowledge utilization and sharing, the knowledge enhancing social and behavioral culture of the people within the company etc are evaluated by:

   a. Information Systems audit
   b. Culture audit
   c. Knowledge audit
   d. Technology audit

6. The KMM assessment methodology talks about how many key result areas (KRA)?

   a. 15
   b. 14
   c. 10
   d. 12

7. Culture of sharing has institutionalized; sharing becomes second nature to all. Organizational boundaries are rendered irrelevant. Knowledge ROI is integral to decision-making. Continuous tweaking of the knowledge processes for improvement happens. The organization develops an ability to shape environmental change; organization becomes a knowledge leader. This represents which level of knowledge maturity as per KMM?

   a. Level 2
   b. Level 3
   c. Level 4
   d. Level 5

8. As per Siemens AG KMMM, 'KM is developed continuously and self organized' stage correspond to which level?

   a. Level 2: Repeated
   b. Level 3: Defined
   c. Level 4: Managed
   d. Level 5: Optimizing

9. Identification of core knowledge assets and flows – (who creates, who uses); Identification of gaps in information and knowledge needed to manage the business effectively; Areas of information policy and ownership that need improvement; Opportunities to reduce information handling costs; Opportunities to improve coordination and access to commonly needed information; Clearer understanding of the contribution of knowledge to business results.- These are benefits of which audit method?

   a. Information repository (inventory)
   b. Ethnographic (observation)
   c. Group Interviews
   d. Individual Interviews

10. Methods of allocating wealth, status, and power; Norms of acceptable social behavior and the means of regulating it; Protocols for making decisions, communicating, working together, and other group activities; Means of identifying, creating, retaining, and passing on the collective knowledge of the group; Relationships for interacting with each other and the outside world, and for passing on their legacy to the future etc. These are benefits of which audit method?

a. Information repository (inventory)
b. Ethnographic (observation)
c. Group Interviews
d. Individual Interviews

Module 9

1. In the context of knowledge management, a measure is defined as:

    a. A Unit of measure
    b. A formula that describes a key performance indicator (KPI).
    c. A comparison of performance
    d. A metric

2. In the context of knowledge management, a metric is used to refer:

    a. The numeric value assigned to the measure
    b. A comparison of performance
    c. A formula that describes a key performance indicator (KPI).
    d. A Unit of measure

3. While measuring the efficacy of KM program it is ideal to:

    a. Select only two to three measures
    b. Select as many measures as possible
    c. Select least number of measures
    d. Select only five to eight measures

4. Measures, which determine the impact of the KM project on the organization is generally referred to as:

    a. Outcome Measures
    b. Output Measures
    c. System Measures
    d. Efficiency Measures

5. Measures, which measure direct process output for users, give a picture of the extent to which personnel are drawn to and actually using the knowledge system is referred to as:

    a. Outcome Measures
    b. Output Measures
    c. System Measures
    d. Efficiency Measures

6. Measures, which relate the performance of the supporting KM technologies that are an indirect indication of knowledge sharing and reuse, is referred to as:

   a. Outcome Measures
   b. Output Measures
   c. System Measures
   d. Efficiency Measures

7. Measurements for KM initiatives can be:

   a. Quantitative
   b. Qualitative
   c. Quantitative or qualitative
   d. Descriptive

8. KM measures that provide hard data to evaluate performance between points (such as last month to this month), or to spot trends are usually:

   a. Quantitative
   b. Qualitative
   c. Quantitative or qualitative
   d. Descriptive

9. _____ measures provide context and meaning for quantitative measures, when it is difficult to capture meaningful quantitative measures (such as the value to the individual for being a member of a community of practice).

   a. Quantitative
   b. Qualitative
   c. Quantitative or qualitative
   d. Descriptive

10. Which of the following is not ranked as critical to the success of a KM project

    a. Vision and leadership
    b. Organizational and communication training
    c. Business performance measurements
    d. Personnel with similar experience

Module 10

1. A KM business case must essentially demonstrate:

   a. The functionality of the KM solutions available
   b. The KM initiative's alignment with the organization's strategies
   c. The competency of the project team
   d. The effectiveness of the technology solution

2. To present a conceptual picture which will contextualize the problem or opportunity at a high level as well as provide a suggested solution is the purpose of a:

   a. Macro model business case
   b. Meso model business case
   c. Micro level model business case
   d. Contextual model business case

3. To understand the detailed impact of the proposed solution or course of action is the purpose of a:

   a. Macro model business case
   b. Meso model business case
   c. Micro level model business case
   d. Contextual model business case

4. One of the reasons why ROI calculations for KM are particularly difficult is:

   a. A sizeable amount of benefits are intangible in nature
   b. Costs are not easy to estimate
   c. Cots are often fluctuating too much
   d. Lack of financial analysis skill sets

5. Business Case also provides with a framework to:

   a. Schedule project tasks
   b. Allocate accountability for delivering benefits from the investment
   c. Allocate resources for project implementation
   d. Cost KM projects

6. Success of CRM strategies are best measured at:

   a. Departmental level
   b. Enterprise level

   c.   Business Unit level
   d.   Territory level

7.   Metrics are particularly important to KM because:

   a.   Measurement of costs of current operations as a basis for comparison
   b.   ROI for KM often takes significant time to appear
   c.   KM measurements are easy to achieve
   d.   Enterprise level benefits estimation is easy

8.   Number of downloads, Dwell time, Usability survey, Number of users, Total number of contributions, Contribution rate over time etc are examples of what measures of a KM best practice initiative?

   a.   Out put measures
   b.   Outcome measures
   c.   System Measures
   d.   Usage Measures

9.   Usefulness surveys, Anecdotes, User ratings of contribution value etc. are examples of what measures of a KM best practice initiative?

   a.   Out put measures
   b.   Outcome measures
   c.   System Measures
   d.   Usage Measures

10.   Time, money, personnel time saved by implementing best practice, Number of groups certified in the use of the best practice, Rate of change in operating costs etc. are examples of what measures of a KM best practice initiative?

   a.   Out put measures
   b.   Outcome measures
   c.   System Measures
   d.   Usage Measures

<u>Keys to Multiple Choice Questions</u>

Module 1

1. a   2. b   3. c   4. a   5. b   6.c   7.c   8.a   9.a   10.c

Module 2

1.c   2.a   3.c   4.a   5.b   6.c   7.d   8.c   9.a   10.b

Module 3

1.c   2.a   3.b   4.b   5.c   6.d   7.a   8.a   9.b   10.c

Module 4

1.b   2.b   3.a   4.b   5.c   6.d   7.a   8.a   9.a   10.c

Module 5

1.c   2.b   3.c   4.c   5.a   6.b   7.c   8.a   9.d   10.c

Module 6

1.a   2.c   3.a   4.b   5.b   6.a   7.d   8.b   9.a   10.c

Module 7

1.a   2.b   3.c   4.b   5.a   6.c   7.d   8.b   9.c   10.a

Module 8

1.d   2.c   3.b   4.b   5.c   6.a   7.d   8.d   9.a   10.b

Module 9

1.b   2.a   3.d   4.a   5.b   6.c   7.c   8.a   9.b   10.d

Module 10

1.b   2.a   3.c   4.a   5.b   6.b   7.b   8.c   9.a   10.b